D1590029

Banda

Banda

Philip Short

Routledge & Kegan Paul
London and Boston

First published in 1974
by Routledge and Kegan Paul Ltd
Broadway House, 68–74 Carter Lane,
London EC4V 5EL and
9 Park Street,
Boston, Mass. 02108, USA
Set in Monotype Times New Roman
Printed in Great Britain by
Cox & Wyman Ltd, London, Fakenham and Reading
© Philip Short, 1974

ISBN 0 7100 7631 2

Library of Congress Catalog Card No. 73-76089

Contents

Introduction

At noon on New Year's Day, 1964, a procession moved off from the headquarters of the Malawi Congress Party in Limbe, twin township of Nyasaland's principal trading centre, Blantyre. At its head was a coffin, borne by six pallbearers, and a huge wooden placard, surmounted by a cross, proclaiming:

FEDERATION CORPSE
Born 1953   Died 1963
here lies condemned
the relics of Welenskey's Federation*

As the jostling, shouting throng progressed through the town, its ranks swelled until, when it reached journey's end in a field by a community hall in the African suburb of Soche, it numbered about 3,000. A forest of banners advised, proclaimed and pleaded – 'Roy, go back to boxing',† 'Ngwazi has dissolved stupid federation', and 'Satan, burn this evil spirit to ashes'.[1] Small boys in ragged breeches ran amongst the crowd, bright with the dresses of the Party's Women's League. Men in tattered shirts and much-mended shorts rubbed shoulders with others in dark suits with furled umbrellas, businessmen and civil servants. Babies lurched on their mothers' backs as the women danced, kicking up the dust, and red-shirted members of the Party's Youth League tried vainly to keep order.

At about two o'clock the people parted to let through a vermilion Ford convertible, preceded and followed by a convoy of Land Rovers. In it sat a small, compact figure, immaculate despite the heat in a three-piece woollen suit, heavy featured in middle age, with slightly greying hair – the Messiah, the conqueror – Ngwazi‡ Dr Hastings Kamuzu Banda.

*The name of the Federal Prime Minister, Sir Roy Welensky, was misspelt.

† Welensky was at one time a professional boxer.

‡ A chiNyanja praise-word used to describe a man of exceptional achievements.

2 Banda

As Banda walked towards the rostrum where he was to speak, the crowd gave the rhythmic, pounding African slow handclap of welcome. The women ululated and danced around him to the accompaniment of drumming. There was hysteria in the air. When finally Banda spoke, removing the dark glasses he habitually wore and gesturing fiercely with a fly-whisk, to recount for the hundredth time the story of Nyasaland's struggle for independence, it was with jubilation mixed with sorrow for the lives that struggle had cost. 'Now at last,' he declared, 'the Federation is dissolved, dissolved, dissolved.'[2]

As he left, the coffin was doused with petrol and set on fire. To the flames were added the placards which had accompanied the cortège, and Federal signboards torn down earlier that day by Party militants. One read, 'Federal Government: Lady Armitage Infant School', commemorating the wife of the former Governor of Nyasaland who, four years earlier, had jailed Banda and more than a thousand of his followers.

If there was rejoicing in Nyasaland and Northern Rhodesia, the mood in Southern Rhodesia was more sombre. Banda had welcomed the end of the Federal era with a short broadcast at midnight on New Year's Eve in which he said simply, 'We are without Welensky'.[3] But in Salisbury the chief architect and last Prime Minister of the Federation has spoken of his 'utter contempt' for the British Government which had brought about its demise.[4] In the same city the Southern Rhodesian Prime Minister, Winston Field, assured his supporters ominously that, 'We will not in any circumstances whatever give in to the cry for a lowering of standards and a hand-over of authority to people who are not fitted yet to wield that authority.'[5]

The long, glass-topped table at which Welensky had presided over meetings of the Federal cabinet was packed up and transported to, of all places, Nyasaland, for the use of Banda's Government. The ashes from the funeral pyre were driven to the Shire river, thence to be washed down to the Zambezi and out to sea. The Central African Federation, in which for ten years Nyasaland and the two Rhodesias had been yoked in unwilling partnership, was truly dead.

Banda, more than anyone else, was responsible for the break-up of the Federation. It was his greatest political achievement. The possibility of closer association between the three Central African territories brought about his entry into active politics, and for twenty-five years dominated his political life. Throughout this time all his political energies were directed first to the prevention of federation, and then, when that had failed, to its destruction. At grass-roots level it has been from this basis that Banda's power has derived among the rural masses of independent Malawi and, in the realm of international affairs, his stature as one of Africa's most extraordinary statesmen.

Yet the breaking of the Federation was a means to an end, not an end in itself. Banda's overriding pre-occupation through the greater part of his life was with the advancement of the people of his country. First as an intending medical missionary, later as a cooperative farmer and a philanthropist, and finally as a politician, he sought to promote the welfare of Nyasas. The six years of nationalist struggle during which he carved a new nation out of Nyasaland were the culmination of a much longer struggle, and a task for which in turn the long years he had spent abroad had helped to prepare him. Banda has been in a much more real sense than most African leaders the 'Father and Founder' of the nation he now rules with absolute and disciplinarian authority. Indeed, to many he is Malawi.

The break-up of the Federation created not only Malawi but also, soon afterwards, Zambia, formerly the Protectorate of Northern Rhodesia. In the course of a few months, the dividing line between the white-ruled South and the black North became sharply defined at the Zambezi, and the way was clear for Southern Rhodesia's fateful U.D.I. on 11 November 1965. Thus was black Africa presented with the bitterest and most intractable of its problems of that decade; Britain with its worst African crisis since Suez; and Afrikaner politicians in the white redoubt of South Africa with a major obstacle to the 'outward-looking' policy then slowly gathering momentum in the last months of Verwoerd's premiership.

For Banda, Rhodesia brought disillusionment with black Africa and political isolation. He retreated from the militancy of the anti-Federal campaign and, with a mixture of pragmatism,

common sense and airy idealism, launched himself on a course
whose object was that same racial dividing line between North
and South which the break-up of the Federation had helped to
buttress. The result has been an experiment unique in African
politics, one of the few sincere attempts to find a peaceful solution to the problems of apartheid and the oppression of black
men by white in Southern Africa.

The trend of Banda's ideas in the latter half of the 1960s, and
the reversal of the orthodox African nationalist policies which
he had pursued so successfully in breaking the Federation, have
brought him obloquy from other African statesmen. Those who
five or even fifteen years earlier lionized him and looked on him
as their mentor now dismiss him as at best a sell-out and at
worst a traitor to his country.

Which is Banda – black saint or white stooge? Is he, as the
British Conservative M.P., Sir Godfrey Nicholson, described
him, 'possibly the most remarkable living African'?[6] Or is he,
as a Ghanaian doctor put it who knew him as a general practitioner in Kumasi, 'the greatest rogue that ever went unhung'?
Or is he, in the words of President Nyerere's ruling party newspaper, the *Nationalist*, 'a rotting cancer'?[7] The real Banda is
both saint and stooge,* a tortuous, tortured figure whose
character has become a study in contradiction and paradox. To
discover why one must look first at the early years of his life and
the solitary odyssey which preceded his rise to power.

* In its usual English connotation.

Chapter 1
The Child of Two Worlds

Banda was born in February 1898* in a small village† a few miles east of the tiny trading centre of Kasungu, in what was then British Central Africa. The territory, known formerly as trans-Zambezia, had been proclaimed a protectorate only seven years before. In 1896 the Chewa chief, Mwase, whose headquarters were at Kasungu, was pacified by British troops,[1] and the following year the first primary schools were set up in his area by a party of teachers from the Livingstonia mission of the Church of Scotland.[2] It was a time of transition. In Britain, the reign of Queen Victoria was drawing to an end and the Edwardian era was about to begin. In Africa, the ways of the Arab slavers were being replaced by the no less foreign ways of the Christian West.

In this world of conflict between old and new, known and unknown, the first child of Mphonongo, a member of the Banda‡ clan, and his wife Akupinganyama, a Phiri, began his

*Banda's birthdate is the subject of much controversy. The date given above is that claimed by his uncle, the Rev. Hanock Msokera Phiri (R. I. Rotberg, *The Rise of Nationalism in Central Africa*, O.U.P., 1965, p. 187 n, and Phiri, interview with the author, Kasungu, 15 March 1969), and by two other old men who remembered Banda as a child, Mr Msulira and Mr D. Chipeta, both of Kasungu (manuscript interviews dated 31/2/68 [*sic*], privately held). All three recalled that the 1898 Angoni rising at Fort Jameson (now Chipata), sixty miles south-west of Kasungu, occurred at about the time of Banda's birth. The official birthdate now given by the Malawi Government, 1906, is clearly inaccurate. Banda himself has admitted to 1902 being 'more or less correct' (Rotberg, op. cit., p. 186 n). While in many ways this last date fits well with the known facts of Banda's early life, it is not entirely satisfactory. Banda's rejection of the 1898 birthdate, moreover, is not convincing, for he rejects with it *in toto* Phiri's testimony (Rotberg, op. cit., p. 187 n), and substantial parts of this can be independently verified.

† This is probably the village now known as Chiwengo (Msulira, op. cit., and *Sunday Mail*, 5 June 1960).

‡ The name Banda is said to be derived either from the word *banda* (a small hut), or from *ku-wanda* (to beat down grass) because the Bandas are reputed always to take the lead on the march. (A. G. O. Hodgson, 'Notes on

life.[3] He was named Kamuzu, meaning 'a little root', to commemorate the ending of his mother's barrenness by a potion
prepared from root-herbs by a *sing'anga* (medicine man).[4]
Mphonongo and his wife were unexceptional people[5] who, like
all their tribe, lived by subsistence farming. Like other Chewa,
too, they were pagans, and by Chewa custom a child could not
become a full member of the community until its first initiation,
about a month after it was born.* Only then could it be removed
from the *chikuta*, the secluded hut where its mother was confined, and taken to its parents' house – a small, round hut of
wattle and daub with a thatched roof and a grass door.

At the age of about four, following normal Chewa practice,
Banda was considered too old to remain under the parental roof
and went to live with his maternal grandparents.† With his
grandfather, Chayamba, and his grandmother, Chiyendawaka,
he learnt the rudiments of farming, being given, so he has
recalled, a small plot of land to cultivate with a child's hoe.[6] In
the evenings the old people recounted the folk tales of the tribe,
part history and part parable, in which was stored its accumulated wisdom. Among the Chewa this was the first part of any
young person's education. When the child grew a little older the
process was extended further: small huts known variously as
masanje, mafuthwa or *manyengwa* were built on the outskirts of
the village or in a dry river-bed, and there for a few days he was
encouraged with other small boys and girls of his age to play at
being an adult – being married, cooking, brewing beer, dying
and being buried – in short, performing all the duties of adult
life.[7]

---

the Achewa and Angoni of the Dowa District of the Nyasaland Protectorate', *Journal of the Royal African Society*, vol. 63.)

 * When this took place, the child was handed over a fire from mother to
father and back. The couple then had intercourse while the mother held the
child in her arms. By this act the sexual taboo surrounding the birth was
lifted. (J. P. Bruwer, 'The Composition of a Chewa Village (Mudzi)',
African Studies, Johannesburg, December 1949.)

 † It was felt that by this age a child was *wochenjele* (aware) in a way which
would inhibit its parents' sex life. Its departure from the parental hut
traditionally came soon after weaning, but nowadays children are often
weaned at a much earlier age. (Bruwer, op. cit.)

It was perhaps during his stay with Chayamba that two events occurred which made a profound impression on the young Banda. The first was when he witnessed an operation being performed on a man who had been shot in the back with an arrow. The man was held on the ground, face downwards, below a young tree, while a string was tied from the arrow to a bent, springy branch. When the branch was released it flew upwards, pulling out the arrow. Only after this had been done could the wound be treated with herb medicines.[8] The second was the death of a woman in childbirth, an event which was popularly held to indicate that she had committed adultery.[9] It may be too fanciful to see in these occurrences the beginnings of Banda's ambition to become a doctor, but certainly they fixed themselves in his mind sufficiently deeply for him to recall them many years later.

Until now Banda had had little contact with white men or the white man's way of life. But in 1905, at the age of seven, he went to his first European-style school.[10] It seems likely that he was encouraged to do so by his uncle, Hanock Phiri, for his parents opposed the idea: Banda has recalled that they disliked the Scots clergy who had charge of education in the district, being particularly incensed at their vigorous condemnation of beer-drinking.[11] Phiri, who was to have a considerable influence over the young Banda's life, was clearly, even in his youth, a remarkable man. Born in 1884, he enrolled at the age of thirteen in one of the first schools to be opened in Kasungu and six years later went to study at the Overtoun Institute at Livingstonia, which was then and for many years after the foremost educational institution in Central Africa. While there he was baptized into the Christian faith by Livingstonia's founder, Dr Robert Laws.[12]

The year 1905 was in other ways an important one for Banda. He left Chayamba's house to live in the *mphala*, the communal hut where the unmarried youth lived, both boys and girls.[13] Shortly afterwards his sister was born,[14] and at about the same time his parents separated and his mother remarried.* Banda

* Msulira, op. cit.; see also *Sunday Mail*, 5 June 1960, and *Hansard*, Zomba, 27 May 1964, pp. 34–5. Little is known of the nature of this break-

went to live in his father's village,* and it was from there that he walked each day to the Mtunthama Primary School, established that year by missionaries from Chilanga,[15] a few miles west of Kasungu.

At Mtunthama Banda came under the tutelage of the Rev. Lameck Manda, one of the first African converts to Christianity in the territory. He was an apt pupil, but even so the winning of an education was in those days a painfully slow process. Manda's tiny school was, as Banda later recalled, only a 'bush school', where the learning of the alphabet represented the summit of academic achievement.[16] Nonetheless, Mtunthama brought him into contact with the missionaries and their alien, yet strangely attractive ideas. Banda became a catechumen and was baptized into the Church of Scotland by Dr George Prentice, the pastor of the Kasungu district.† He took as his Christian name the surname of another missionary he admired, John Hastings.[17]

Banda's espousal of Christianity and his taking of a western forename in no way implied any rejection of his African heritage, and at the age of about twelve or thirteen‡ he underwent the

———————————

up or of its effect on Banda. It may well not have been great, for in the matrilineal Chewa society the family unit holds a much less important place than in a patrilineal society. The father/mother/children relationship which characterizes the latter is replaced in the former by more complex but no less binding ties through which all the male members of a family on the mother's side (*nkhoswe*) are responsible for all the female members of the family on that side (*mbumba*). Similarly a woman's eldest brother is responsible for her children, not her husband.

*It would have been more normal for Banda to have lived with his mother's people after a separation of this kind. Why he did not do so is not clear.

†Unattributable interview. The Durban *Sunday Tribune* (28 July 1963) reported that Banda was baptized by a missionary of the Dutch Reformed Church, the Rev. D. C. B. Vlok, but this is highly unlikely for the Kasungu district came under the D.R.C. only for one brief period between 1900 and 1901 (R. J. Macdonald, *A History of African Education*, Ph.D. thesis, microfilm, Edinburgh University, 1969).

‡i.e. the age of puberty.

vinyau initiation rite, the most important event in the life of a Chewa boy.*

The ceremony traditionally begins at dawn, when the head of the intending initiate is shaved and he is given food to sustain him through the day. The boy then leaves his parents' hut, where his mother† remains behind, and is led to an open space in the bush accompanied by two friends, a little older than himself, who have already become *vinyau*. There he is blindfolded and stripped naked, and warned on pain of death not to reveal anything of what he will see. When the blindfold is removed he finds himself surrounded by *vinyau* executing a strange, whirling dance. They wear black wooden masks, gashed with red paint. From time to time the figures brush against him, filling him with terror. These, he is told, are the spirits of his ancestors.

Then his trials begin. The *chiwinda*, or leader of the ritual, comes, in Kambalame's words, 'with cruel eyes to put him through certain things'. These may take many forms: he may be tied over the fork of a tree with his head and feet hanging downwards, or suspended head downwards above a lighted fire (being swung around so that he is not actually burned). Sometimes the *vinyau* will bind him and put warrior ants on his body; or they may roll him in grass where gum and the itching *mucuna* bean have been strewn. All the while he is reminded of his past misdemeanours, which the *chiwinda* and his associates will have

---

* Banda's initiation into *vinyau* has never been directly confirmed, but evidence of it is to be found in Hansard (Zomba, 15 July 1963, pp. 869–70); and in *Our African Way of Life* (H. K. Banda and T. Cullen Young, eds., Lutterworth Press, 1946). Banda was sufficiently well versed in *vinyau* to be able to write that a description of it contained in the title essay of the book, the work of a young writer named Kambalame, 'reflects the younger generation's slackening hold upon the old things. Its chronological sequences are not always wholly correct. . . .' (p. 25). He would hardly have been in a position to make such a comment were he not himself an initiate; nor otherwise would he have written, as he did later in the same passage, that no uninitiated Chewa man had full status as an adult. Despite its apparent errors of detail, the description of *vinyau* given in *Our African Way of Life* is probably as close as one can come to the ceremony Banda underwent, and it is from this that the account which follows is principally drawn. (See also Hodgson, op. cit., p. 136.)

† In Banda's case presumably his step-mother.

discovered beforehand to determine how severely he should be treated.

The ceremony was witnessed by the men of the village (including the boy's male relatives other than his father, who was not allowed to be present), and it was perhaps this aspect of the initiation as a public spectacle, coupled with its ritual cruelty, which led the early missionaries to regard it as a kind of fertility orgy. Had they known that their young protégé in Kasungu was participating in *vinyau* they would certainly have expelled him from the Church. Banda himself later wrote of *vinyau* as 'a kind of masonic brotherhood. . . . It has its special vocabulary and phraseology, and is rigidly restricted to initiates only. But it also has another side, like carnival in the Mediterranean, with an appearance of licence, an appearance of temporary relaxation of customary law.' While it was the carnival which caught the attention of the Scots pastors, it was the brotherhood of *vinyau* which was more important, for whereas the former was transient, the latter remained with a Chewa all his life, binding him to his tribe.

Initiation marked the last stage in a young Chewa's traditional education. The separation of the boy and his mother reflected the recognition that they were unalike, and modesty must be put between them. The blindfolding before the ritual symbolized the coming of troubles which would not be foreseen, like disease and death. The cruelty signified the trials and tribulations which would be encountered in the world of adulthood. After the ritual as such was over the youth would go to live, sometimes for as long as two months, in a small hut built for him by a stream or in a thicket. There he would be given instruction by an older initiate – 'one, as it were, a doctor', as Kambalame puts it. Its object was to make him 'a man of knowledge and wisdom' and it apparently consisted of a code for right living embodying the precepts of Chewa morality.

At about the time of his initiation Banda left the little school at Mtunthama and began attending the Chilanga Full Primary School, where Hanock Phiri was now teaching.[18] Phiri had completed standard seven, the highest then available at Livingstonia, in 1910, and moved to Chilanga about a year later.[19]

There he taught his young nephew reading, writing and grammar, arithmetic, history and geography. History fascinated Banda. He and Phiri talked at length of the traditions of the Chewa, about which the latter was extraordinarily knowledgeable (he was later to become one of the custodians of its oral history), and it is probably from this time that Banda's enduring interest in the pre-colonial history of Central Africa derives.[20] They talked, too, about the moves then afoot among Nyasa* teachers to form an inter-denominational territory-wide association, and other ideas for the advancement of Africans being discussed by Phiri's friends at Livingstonia.[21] Their grievances were the same grievances which would infuse African protest in Nyasaland for the next forty years: the lack of educational facilities; instances of discrimination (although at this time these were few and far between, if only because the Protectorate's non-African population was so small); and the fear of being dispossessed of their land.[22]

In 1912, in response to the enactment of the District Administration Ordinance, which stated that an assembly of gazetted principal village headmen would be regarded as the only authentic spokesman for each district – thus denying educated Africans any voice, however small, in the processes of government – these discussions culminated in the establishment of the North Nyasa Native Association at Karonga.[23] It was the first secular vehicle Nyasas had created for the expression of their protests,†

---

*The British Central African Protectorate was renamed Nyasaland in 1907.

†The outbreak of the First World War, and the Government's clampdown on African religio-political activities which followed the Chilembwe rising in January 1915, brought a temporary halt to these developments, and it was not until 1919 that the N.N.N.A. resumed meeting. It was subsequently taken as a model for other native associations formed elsewhere in Nyasaland. The Chilembwe rising was *the* event in the early political history of colonial Nyasaland, and its story has been told fully elsewhere (see for instance G. Shepperson and T. Price, *Independent African*, Edinburgh University Press, Edinburgh, 1958). But while its leader is now hailed as Malawi's first martyr, and the forerunner of modern nationalism, it appears that at the time Banda was little affected by the rising (ibid., p. 508, and E. S. Munger, *President Kamuzu Banda of Malawi*, American Universities' Field Staff, Hanover, N.H., October 1969, p. 5).

and for young Hastings Kamuzu Banda at Kasungu, his first indirect contact with another abiding preoccupation in his life, politics.

By 1913 Banda had completed standard two[24] and was between times working as a pupil teacher at his old school at Mtunthama under the Rev. Lameck Manda, for which he was paid fourpence a month.[25] Phiri left Chilanga to teach at another village school, but Banda continued his studies there for standard three, which he passed in 1914. He was now ready to go on to Livingstonia, as Phiri had done before him. But then tragedy struck.

Years later Banda described what happened thus:*

In the year 1915 an examination was due for the Teachers in one of the Districts under the Livingstonia Mission in Northern Nyasaland of the then United Free Church of Scotland. Selection of men to go to the training centre for the course leading to full certification was the purpose of the examination and there presented himself a very youthful pupil-teacher, small also in stature. He was not more than thirteen years old, but from the age of about ten he had passed all the tests open to him. At the other end of the scale, as it were, was a European who happened to be available for the conduct of the examination, though not attached to the District and therefore not intimate with the teacher personnel. The number of examinees was large, the examination hall – actually the Station Church – was small, but the unlucky small pupil-teacher found himself in a distant seat, too far from the blackboard easily to see the questions thereon written. At one point he stood up in order to see more clearly over the shoulder of the man in front of him. The European misconstrued the action and debarred the boy from further participation in the examination.[26]

* The ages Banda gave in this account are based on a birthdate of 1902, and are hence out of line with those given elsewhere in this book. Taking 1898 as his true birthdate, he would have been sixteen, not thirteen, at the time of the examination and he would have 'passed all the tests open to him' from the age of about thirteen, not ten (this would coincide roughly with his entry into Chilanga). The year of the examination, given in this extract as 1915, should, according to both Phiri and Msulira (op. cit.), be 1914. Banda, however, has indicated that he was still in Nyasaland at the time of the Chilembwe rising (Shepperson and Price, op. cit., p. 508, and Munger, op. cit., p. 5).

A lesser man might have decided there and then that the winning of an education was not for him, but on Banda the incident had quite an opposite effect. It was for such an eventuality as this that his *vinyau* instruction had been designed to prepare him. The experience instilled in him the determination to make good. A few days later he left Kasungu secretly, heading, as he hoped, for the other great institution of learning in that part of Africa, the Church of Scotland's Lovedale College in South Africa.[27] The route he took, passing between Mchinji and Lilongwe and crossing the Zambezi near Tete,[28] was well established, for Nyasas had for some years been travelling south to find work in the farms and mines of Southern Rhodesia and South Africa. But even for a grown man the 400-mile journey through the bush between Kasungu and the nearest Southern Rhodesian township, Shamva, was reckoned to be 'thirty days' footing', and many of those who set out were murdered by bandits in Portuguese East Africa.[29] For a sensitive sixteen-year-old, travelling alone, it must have been a daunting experience.

Chapter 2

In Pursuit of an Education

By the time Banda reached Hartley, his meagre savings, the fruits, presumably, of his pupil teaching at Mtunthama, were exhausted. So too, perhaps, was his energy. At any rate, he took a job as a sweeper at the local hospital, remaining there for two years.[1] With his first wages he wrote home to his mother in Kasungu: it was the first news his family had had of him since his abrupt disappearance several months earlier. He discovered later they had thought he had been eaten by lions.[2]

While at Hartley, Banda's incipient interest in medicine* was reinforced and made concrete by the appalling conditions in which African patients at the hospital were treated. He resolved to make his way to Scotland and there qualify as a doctor,† an ambition which was to sustain him for the next twenty-five years. But it was a difficult time. Banda was paid a pittance, and in those first decades of this century Southern Rhodesia boasted a crude racialism far worse than anything which at that time obtained in its richer and more sophisticated sister-country, South Africa.

By 1916 Banda had saved nearly enough to contemplate travelling on to Johannesburg. In August, however, just as his plans were nearing fruition, an old friend arrived in Hartley from Kasungu: it was Hanock Phiri. Phiri had spent the three years since leaving Chilanga in teaching at village schools in the Kasungu and Mchinji districts. Now, tiring of this occupation, he had decided to make his way south in the hope of obtaining

---

*There is one further shred of evidence that Banda showed leanings towards medicine while still at Kasungu. According to Hanock Phiri (quoted in Rotberg, *Rise of Nationalism*, p. 187 n), Banda was taught the rudiments of first aid by Dr Prentice. Prentice later recalled Banda as a young man who had helped out at the mission but remembered his name incorrectly as James Banda.

†In that first letter to his mother Banda is said to have written that he would not return home until he had become a physician.

there the higher education which was not available to him in Nyasaland.[3] He and his nephew joined forces and in January 1917, a few weeks before Banda's nineteenth birthday, set out together for the Union.[4]

At this time it was not easy for Nyasas to enter South Africa, for the Union government, faced with a massive influx of foreign workers, had clamped down on the movement of labour from outside its borders. By Phiri's account, it was Banda who discovered that the way round this difficulty was to take work on contract. So they travelled to Mafeking,* the entry point into South Africa for the railway through Bechuanaland, and there signed on for twelve months with the Maronjeni colliery in Dundee, Natal. Phiri worked underground as a native mine captain and Banda on the surface as a 'pumping boy' (pumping water). But the conditions were bad and after three months Phiri decided, so he has recalled, that 'we must desert'. On one of their days off they slipped away, heading now for Johannesburg.[5]

At Charlestown, a small railside settlement on the boundary between Natal and the Transvaal, they met in a canteen an elderly Scots eccentric named MacArthur, who claimed to have been a classmate of David Livingstone in Blantyre, Scotland. Hearing Banda and Phiri speaking with Scots accents, he inquired where they were from, and on learning that the two young men were from Nyasaland and that they could read the Bible, offered them a place to sleep at his house.[6] When Phiri told him of their purpose in coming to South Africa MacArthur suggested they work their passages to America, where they could seek the help of one of the Negro churches. To this end he promised to speak to a friend who worked on a passenger ship voyaging between Durban and New York. But the war was at its height and the next day they learnt, so Phiri recollected, that 'all the British ships are drowned by the Germans'.[7]

---

* Banda has always maintained that he walked the entire distance to South Africa. He once wrote: 'I walked to Johannesburg – a distance of 1,000 miles – but not in a single stretch; I walked and walked and walked' (*Africa Today*, New York, June 1960). It seems certain, however, that the part of the journey between Hartley and Mafeking was made by train. According to Phiri their prospective employers then arranged for them to be transported from Mafeking to Dundee (Phiri, interview).

On hearing of this disaster, MacArthur told them there was nothing more he could do but pray. Afterwards he reported: 'God has answered my prayer. . . . God said one of you will finish his higher education and help his country. And one of you, also, his work will be successful in the country. That's what God has answered. . . . God will open the way for you. . . .'[8] Besides furnishing them with this spiritual consolation, MacArthur paid their train fares to Johannesburg.[9] There Banda and Phiri found work in the Witwatersrand Deep mine at Boksburg. The latter remained only a year before leaving for the Rhodesias, but Banda stayed on, first as a machine oiler and later as a miner.[10] Although conditions were harder below ground, the pay was better than the ten shillings a month he had been earning on the surface.

To the country boy from Kasungu, the rough and tumble of Johannesburg came as a violent shock. In the shanty towns where most Africans lived (if they were not housed in mine compounds, as Banda was), he was launched into a brawling, sprawling world. He rubbed shoulders with murderers[11] and priests, whores and housewives, tearaways and schoolmasters, many of them, like himself, migrants from outside South Africa's borders. Johannesburg was an ugly, pioneering town. For Banda, then twenty, it was a shattering revelation of urban African society. A shy, slight figure, deeply imbued with the puritanism of the Scots missionaries of his boyhood at Kasungu, he seems as much as possible to have held aloof from those around him.* His withdrawal into himself, which apparently stemmed from this time, was to last with few interruptions throughout his life.

Very little is known about Banda's life in the mines, but one story which he did recount is worth repeating here. It concerned a time when the group of men with whom Banda was working was in the charge of a brawny Afrikaner ganger. He was one of those men who, as Banda once described them, 'can't say a word without cursing', and he relied heavily on the sjambok as

---

*Commenting on Banda's shyness, the Rev. Mother Emily Modikoane, who knew him in South Africa, said he was 'always one-sided, I mean not mixing with others much' (interview with the author, Inyanga, Southern Rhodesia, 20 August 1969).

an instrument of persuasion. Banda was by this time fascinated by medicine and read all he could about it, and he was convinced that one of his fellow workers had tuberculosis. One day the ganger set about this man, who was plainly unable to take the punishment being meted out. Banda leapt on the ganger's back. He stumbled, and they both fell to the ground. But as they were being taken to the compound office for the incident to be reported to the mine police, the ganger ordered the driver to turn back. He would be a laughing stock, he said, if it became known that he had been downed by 'a little runt of a Kaffir' like Banda. After this, said Banda, although conditions were still bad, the ganger treated them less harshly.[12]

Outside the mines, life for a young African in Johannesburg could have been worse. Although a wide gap, part racial and part economic, separated Africans and Europeans, the crude racialism which Banda had found omnipresent in Southern Rhodesia had yet to become a South African institution. As he later recalled:

> When I was working . . . [at the] Witwatersrand Deep mine, I could go into any of the shops in town and try on shoes next to white people without anybody objecting. I could not do that in Rhodesia. In Rhodesia I had to get off the pavement when white people passed.*

Apartheid had not yet spread its tentacles through South African society and the politics of the day was that of Smuts and Hertzog. The conflict of ideas and personalities between these two men fired Banda's imagination and revived in him the interest in politics which had first become apparent during his boyhood at Kasungu. He followed avidly through the columns of the Johannesburg *Star* and the *Rand Daily Mail* their campaigning for the election of 1924, and studied in the same way the other great political question of the time – whether Southern Rhodesia should join the Union or continue on its own as a self-governing colony.[13] 'It was here [on the Rand] that I learnt my politics,' Banda afterwards recollected.[14]

---

* *Star*, 2 December 1958. The reference is to a visit Banda made in 1923 to Bulawayo. (See Munger, *Kamuzu Banda of Malawi*, p. 2, and *Rhodesia Herald*, 2 December 1958.)

Johannesburg also brought Banda into contact with African politicians. He became friendly with Clements Kadalie,* a fellow Nyasa and former classmate of Hanock Phiri, who in 1919 founded the Industrial and Commercial Workers Union, the first African trade union in South Africa.[15] It was probably through Kadalie that Banda made his first acquaintance with Garveyism and perhaps through him too that he may have heard the legend of the 'Black man from the North' who would one day come to liberate the Africans of South Africa from their white oppressors.[16] Another key figure whom Banda is said to have met at about the same time was A. B. Xuma, afterwards President of the African National Congress of South Africa.†

Garveyism‡ was then the principal external influence on politically-minded Africans throughout Southern and Central Africa, and many looked to the American Negro movement as their inspiration.§ Banda again encountered Garveyism in 1921, when he attended a multiracial meeting in Johannesburg addressed by one of the great speakers of the day, Dr J. E. Kwegyir Aggrey, the famous American-educated Ghanaian who was then visiting the Union as a member of the Phelps Stokes educational commission. Dr C. T. Loram described the scene in a letter to Dr Jesse Jones:

Aggrey was great. He screamed, he yelled, he argued, he almost wept. It was fine to see the effect on the people. . . . Aggrey's 'you'll

---

* Many years later, when Banda was making a name for himself by his opposition in London to the imposition of federation, Kadalie claimed him as his nephew (Munger, op. cit., p. 12).

† Hanock Phiri (op. cit.) and the Rev. Mother Modikoane (op. cit.) both said that Banda knew Xuma in Johannesburg. According to some other accounts, however (see for instance Munger, op. cit., pp. 7–8), the two men did not meet until some years later when Banda was in America.

‡ The philosophy of Marcus Aurelius Garvey, the colourful Jamaican who in 1920 founded the Universal Negro Improvement Association in America with the slogan 'Africa for the Africans'.

§ In Nyasaland, Garvey's newspaper, the *Negro World*, was banned and a number of Africans, including Isaac MacDonald Lawrence, later a prominent figure in the Nyasaland African Congress, were prosecuted for having it in their possession (Shepperson and Price, *Independent African*, p. 494).

catch more flies with molasses than vinegar' failed to move . . . a running fire of black criticism Aggrey would not let me check. 'All right my black brothers, you just wait until after this meeting, I've got something to tell you about Marcus Garvey that I don't want these white folk to hear.'[17]

After the meeting Aggrey spoke of the corruption then rampant in Garvey's movement. But Banda was impressed not so much by what Aggrey said as by the way in which he said it. Aggrey rekindled in the young Nyasa the ambition, implanted four years earlier by MacArthur, to travel to America.

Banda had not lost sight of his original objective in coming to South Africa – the furtherance of his education – and had meanwhile enrolled at a night school operated by the Methodist mission in Albert Street, Johannesburg, where he completed standard eight.[18] But the school proved less important for its academic facilities than for its environment, because on the opposite side of the street stood another mission, run by the African Methodist Episcopal Church. Banda was attracted to this Ethiopian, black separatist church for the same reasons as he had been attracted to Garveyism.[19] Both stressed the right of black men to run their own affairs, and both sought to raise their status in their own eyes and in the eyes of the non-black world. Banda became a member of the A.M.E. Church in 1922 and wrote to Phiri, telling him that he had found the calling which Phiri had been seeking and had been unable to find and enclosing £4 for his train fare.[20] His uncle joined him and, towards the end of 1923, was ordained an African Methodist minister.[21]

In November of that year, at the A.M.E.'s annual conference in Bloemfontein, Phiri and Banda met Bishop W. T. Vernon of the American parent church and presented him with a ceremonial fly-whisk, 'a good tail with [an] ivory handle'.[22] The Bishop was evidently impressed by the pair.* Phiri was a qualified teacher and a Church member of proven zeal, while Banda, then twenty-five years old, had for some time been teaching at A.M.E. Sunday schools.[23] It was decided that Phiri should return to Nyasaland to start an A.M.E. mission, and (perhaps

* And perhaps also by the fly-whisk (see p. 23).

at Phiri's prompting) that Banda should go to America to complete his education.[24] The one condition was that he should pay his own steamship fare to New York.*

At the next A.M.E. conference, in 1924, the Church's Presiding Elders (who now included Phiri) formally confirmed Bishop Vernon's offer to underwrite the young Nyasa's education.[25] In the interim, Banda – who was now employed as a ticket clerk in the mine compound manager's office, a post he had obtained through his fluency in English and African vernacular languages[26] – had saved £50. Phiri had raised a further £45 by selling an organ intended for the A.M.E.'s new mission in Nyasaland,† and together these sums were sufficient to buy a concession ticket. After attending an A.M.E. school at Bethel for a few months,[27] Banda took ship in July 1925 for the United States, where he arrived, so it is said, 'with few friends and £2 in his pocket'.[28]

Banda's first years in America were spent at the A.M.E.'s Wilberforce Institute near Xenia, Ohio, where he studied agriculture, civics, Latin and Spanish in addition to the normal high-school subjects, and apparently participated in the activities of the debating society. Despite poor health, due to the change in climate, Banda did well, and with three other students, including an African, was allowed to take his final examinations after three years instead of the normal four.[29] But when he emerged, complete with diploma, the A.M.E.'s financial support came to an end.[30]

The solution to this problem was provided by Aggrey, whom Banda had re-encountered at Wilberforce. Aggrey arranged for him to address groups of wealthy white people interested in hearing about Africa at first hand 'from a real African'.[31] For

---

*Only now did Banda finally renounce the idea of going to Lovedale, where he was on the verge of attempting to gain admittance (Banda, Face to Face with John Freeman (television interview), B.B.C. transcript, 22 April 1960).

† Phiri (op. cit.) was very clear about the details of this transaction. By his account the funds so raised, together with the money Banda had saved, amounted to about £90. Banda, however, has stated that all the money required for his boat fare (by his version about £50) was saved by himself.

the next four years the fees from these lectures, supplemented by earnings from vacation jobs, were Banda's principal means of support,* and it was through one such appearance that he came to enter university. After speaking at the Kiwanis Club in Marion, Indiana, Banda fell into conversation with a Dr Herald, who suggested that he enrol at his own *alma mater*, the University of Indiana at Bloomington.[32] Herald evidently helped him to obtain a place, and perhaps also gave him some financial assistance, for early in 1928 Banda commenced a pre-medical course there.†

Banda remained at Indiana for two years, completing four semesters and attending a summer-school session. He may also have taken vacation courses in agriculture, a subject which, with his Chewa farming background, was beginning to interest him.‡ His teachers later recalled him as a quiet, serious student, who always sat in the front row during lectures so as not to miss a word the lecturer said. Mrs W. N. Culmer, over whose garage Banda lived for some months, remembered that he was 'very smart' but that he 'didn't have a great deal of personality'. It was not that he was unfriendly, she added, 'he just had nothing to say'.[33] Banda's 'smartness' and his lack of self-confidence were interlinked, the one being his way of covering up the other. Like many shy people, he was preoccupied with his image.

The same picture has emerged of the intense young student, totally committed to his studies, at the University of Chicago, to which Banda transferred early in 1930 to take a degree in History and Political Science.[34] Banda's explanation for this move throws a useful light on his thinking about the purpose of

* *Observer*, 8 March 1959, and unattributable interview. Banda has recalled spending two years working six hours a day as a farm labourer in addition to his school work. On another occasion he took employment as a janitor to support himself. (*Nyasaland Times*, 23 March 1963, and Banda, Speech marking Youth Week celebrations, Zomba, 31 March 1968.)

† Rotberg, op. cit., p. 187. Clyde Sanger (*Central African Emergency*, Heinemann, 1960, p. 186) says that after leaving Wilberforce Banda enrolled at a southern university but disliked it so much that he left within a week. This is possibly a mistaken reference to Indiana.

‡ Cf. *Hansard*, Zomba, 2 February 1968, p. 373. Banda also studied Greek while at Indiana (ibid., 28 October 1964, p. 267).

education. He felt, he said later, that a purely medical education was too narrow: he had no desire to become one of those doctors who 'know everything about medicine and nothing about anything else'.[35] Phiri and Banda had talked at length about this subject in South Africa and had concluded, by Phiri's account, that Nyasaland needed teachers, because 'when we will have our own schools, we ... [shall] help our country'; doctors, 'to understand about the diseases'; and lawyers, 'to protect ourselves when we are in danger'.[36] In America Banda refined these ideas. He rejected the Tuskegee principle, and with it the conclusions of the Phelps Stokes Commission in which Aggrey had played such a prominent part. While it was true, he argued, that Africa needed technicians, craftsmen and artisans, this was not its first priority. What was needed first was to make available a broadly based education in the liberal arts, for without this Africans would always remain subjugated.[37]

Besides these theoretical considerations, material factors also influenced Banda's decision. While at Indiana, he met a Professor of Linguistics at Chicago who was researching into Bantu languages.* There were at this time very few southern African students in America, and on the strength of his knowledge of chiChewa† Banda was offered a place at the university. Having decided to take advantage of the opportunity thus opened, it was only natural that Banda should study history and politics, the two great loves of his life besides medicine.

At Chicago Banda seems to have lived a more normal, less ascetic life than had been the case hitherto. Early on he found lodgings with a Mrs Corrine Saunders, a Negro woman who, as he later recalled, treated him like a son.[38] His courses absorbed him and he clearly enjoyed cooperating in the research pro-

*This was perhaps the Dr Edward Sapir, subsequently of Yale, referred to by Mark Hanna Watkins in his 'A Grammar of Chichewa: A Bantu Language of British Central Africa', University of Chicago dissertation, published by the Linguistic Society of America as a supplement to its journal, *Language*, No. 24, April–June 1937 (Kraus Reprint Corporation edition, New York, 1966, p. 7). See also Sanger, op. cit., p. 187.

†chiChewa, the language of Banda's tribe, is a dialect of chiNyanja, the language normally spoken in central and southern Malawi. There are differences in pronunciation and in a number of word meanings.

gramme into chiChewa,* himself growing fascinated by the subject with its close links with Chewa history. It was an interest
which was to reappear at intervals over the next forty years.

One development, however, cast a shadow over these years:
Banda's deteriorating relationship with the A.M.E., with which,
despite its no longer supporting him, he had remained in close
touch. On his entry forms for Indiana, for instance, he had listed
Bishop Vernon as his guardian,[39] and some of the fees from his
speaking engagements and from Church meetings which he
addressed as a lay preacher he donated to the Nyasaland Foundation, set up by the Bishop and his wife to finance the Rev.
Phiri's evangelizing in Kasungu. Banda had heard tales of corruption in the A.M.E. since his arrival in America, but had
disbelieved them out of his faith in Bishop Vernon. In May 1932,
however, the Church's General Conference suspended the
Bishop for misusing Church funds: it was alleged (but apparently never proven) that he had also embezzled monies given to
the foundation.

Much discouraged, Banda wrote an unhappy letter to Phiri
in which he explained what had happened. He was 'really disappointed with it', he declared. All the money he raised was
siphoned off by the American clergy, with the result that missionaries in the field got nothing. He was seriously considering
resigning from the A.M.E., he added, if his uncle would grant
him permission to do so. Phiri apparently obliged, for shortly
afterwards Banda cut his last links with the Church. He continued, however, to send his uncle money for missionary work,
and their correspondence is pathetically full of references to the
latter's debts and Banda's inability to pay them.[40]

Banda's letters to Phiri during the years he spent in America
illustrate vividly the extent to which Banda was imbued with
Chewa social precepts, with their stress on courtesy and respect
for elders. At a time when Hastings K. Banda, as he styled
himself, was in his middle and late thirties, and his uncle was

*According to Watkins (op. cit., p. 7), Banda was 'a very excellent
informant', who continued to give information in 'spare moments' between
the time of his departure from Chicago and the publication of the dissertation.

only fourteen years older, he commenced his communications 'Dear Sir', and ended them 'Respectfully yours'. Only after the Second World War, when Banda was a fully qualified doctor, did he begin to use a less formal mode of address.[41]

A recurrent theme throughout these letters was Banda's desire to return to Nyasaland to serve its people. Late in 1932 he told Phiri he would be prepared to enter Government service instead of working, as he would have preferred, as a medical missionary, if thereby he would be better able to further the cause of Nyasa advancement. 'My whole aim,' he wrote, 'is to help my country.'[42] Seven years later he returned to this theme: 'All along my aim has been to obtain a liberal and professional education and to return to Nyasaland in the service of my people.'[43]

Banda graduated as a Bachelor of Philosophy on 22 December 1931,[44] and afterwards took a short postgraduate course in chemistry.[45] He planned, so he wrote to Phiri, to go on to Edinburgh and there complete his doctoral studies, either at the University or at the School of Medicine of the Royal College of Physicians and Surgeons.[46] But that long-standing ambition was not yet to be fulfilled, and instead he enrolled as a student at the Meharry Medical College, in Nashville, Tennessee, a leading Negro institution through which had passed some years previously another Nyasa student, Dr Daniel Malekebu, later head of the Providence Industrial Mission at Chiradzulu which John Chilembwe had made famous.[47]

Meharry brought Banda face to face with a degree of racialism he had not encountered before in America. Bloomington and Chicago had had their segregated hotels and restaurants, and in a host of small ways black Americans had been made to know that they were second-class citizens. Even at Xenia there had been racialism, but of a different kind: it was there that Banda first became conscious of shades of colour, and he later commented scathingly that the darker-skinned girls were almost never invited out. This impression was reinforced when, some years later, he was friendly with a family at Kokomo, Indiana, who kept a flat in Chicago to which only the lighter-skinned members, who could pass for white, would go.[48] But all these things were pinpricks compared with the naked racialism of Tennessee, where the Ku Klux Klan held sway and nigger-baiting was a favourite pastime. It was the same kind of difference as existed in the 1910s between South Africa and Southern Rhodesia.

One experience stood out above all others during Banda's years at Meharry. He witnessed a lynching.* The brute savagery with which the white mob literally tore to pieces a black man remained fixed in his mind all his life.

One further factor played a part in Banda's attitude to racial problems. In 1932 he had written to Phiri that white as well as black Americans had shown him much kindness.[49] But while this was true, the greater part of the help he received, particularly after his departure from Wilberforce, came from white people.† White members of clubs like the Kiwanis not only gave generously to the young African who addressed them, but also assisted him in more direct and personal ways. Dr Herald helped him enter Indiana; Mrs Douglas Smith, wife of the inventor of Pepsodent and a leading philanthropist of the day, at whose home in Winnetka Banda often stayed during vacations,[50] and an unnamed member of the Eastman Kodak family assisted him financially at Chicago;[51] and another friend from his Marion days, Dr Walter B. Stephenson, President of the Delta Electric Company, contributed jointly with Mrs Smith to the costs of his training at Meharry.[52]

It is not hard to see how in these circumstances Banda developed the extraordinary deep-seated and sincere non-racial beliefs which were later to underlie his policies as a political leader. On the one hand he had witnessed and endured crude racialism at its worst, in Southern Rhodesia and Tennessee; and on the other he had been the beneficiary of charity given not by his own race but by another. Such experiences taught Banda the truth of Aggrey's dictum, that in order to produce harmony you have to play on the white keys as well as the black.[53]

---

* Munger, op. cit., p. 7, and unattributable interview. Some sources place this incident during Banda's stay at Chicago, but this seems unlikely.

† It was perhaps this which led Phiri to remark, many years later, that the Negroes had 'neglected' Banda (Phiri, op. cit.).

Banda's interest in politics grew stronger in America, but he had still not reached the point of personal involvement. Although he now came directly under the influence of Garveyism – and of Dr W. E. B. DuBois, who, while disagreeing with Garvey on tactics, likewise sought to develop Negroes' sense of historical tradition and racial pride – he seems to have had few personal dealings either with the Garveyites[54] or with DuBois's National Association for the Advancement of Coloured People.

As in South Africa, it was apparently white politics which interested Banda most, particularly at Chicago when the subject formed part of his degree course and he studied closely the campaign which brought Roosevelt to the Presidency in 1932. Banda admired Roosevelt, and wholeheartedly supported the New Deal programme of socialistic reform begun during the months between the election and Roosevelt's inauguration in 1933. But even without the New Deal, Banda responded favourably to the American way of life with its emphasis on individual freedom and enterprise. As he said, many years later:

If in America some people are very rich and others are very poor, it is just that the former have initiative, and work hard too. There are others who are unfortunate and through no fault of their own are poor, but not . . . miserably poor. . . . There is always a chance in America of the poor boy of today becoming the millionaire of tomorrow. Always a hope.[55]

It might seem a curious judgement for a man to make who had lived through the Depression, seen at first hand the poverty it engendered, and discovered from the receiving end the inequality of white Americans and black. It was evidently a judgement made on the basis of Banda's own success, and not on the failures of others.

Banda spent nearly five years at Meharry, working at his studies with single-minded devotion. He told Phiri towards the end of his stay there that he had been so busy with his work that he had had 'scarcely time to do anything outside [it]',[56] and it was perhaps during this time that he acquired the convulsive nervous twitch which ever since has contorted his face when he is nervous or on edge. In May 1937 he was awarded a

Doctorate of Medicine,[57] graduating with an overall percentage of 82·24.*

Banda now needed but one more qualification before he could return to Nyasaland: the British licentiates which would enable him to practise in the Protectorate, where his American degree was not recognized. A few months after leaving Meharry he boarded a ship bound for Scotland, there to embark on the last phase of his extended academic career.

*This included final year grades of 99·45 in surgery, 90 in obstetrics and medical jurisprudence, 89 in orthopaedics, 88·5 in applied anatomy and 88 in pathology and preventive medicine. He was least proficient in tuberculosis. (Rotberg, op. cit., p. 188.)

Chapter 3
General Practice

Banda's three years' stay in Scotland played a crucial part in determining the course, not only of his medical career, but also of the development of his political interests. It saw, on the one hand, the abrupt ending of his long-held and deeply rooted ambition to return to Nyasaland as a medical missionary; and on the other, the focusing of his political attention firmly on to Nyasaland. And, more important than either of these, it saw Banda for the first time taking an active, as against a passive, interest in politics, and seeking through his own efforts to influence the course of events in his homeland. The completion of his medical qualifications – the original reason for his travelling to Scotland – turned out to be the least important aspect of the years he spent there.

During his stay in America Banda had communicated regularly with Hanock Phiri and others of his immediate family, but he had had scant contact with the African political figures emerging in Nyasaland: his only known correspondence was with the Livingstone Native Welfare Association, two of whose founding members, J. E. C. Mattako and Sam K. K. Mwase, were Nyasas from Kasungu.[1] Nor had he been able to follow at all closely the wider political developments taking place in Central Africa.* It was not until his arrival in Edinburgh, where early in 1938 he enrolled at the School of Medicine of the Royal College of Physicians and Surgeons,[2] that he began to study in detail events in his homeland. In this he was encouraged by meetings with Scots missionaries who had worked at Livingstonia and other mission stations in the country, many of whom had become involved in the aspirations of the people in their charge.[3]

* But see *Hansard*, Zomba, 10 December 1963, p. 947, and Banda, Face to Face with John Freeman (television interview), B.B.C. transcript, 22 April 1960. Banda had, however, watched the progress of South Africa's attempts to develop an independent foreign policy (*Hansard*, Zomba, 30 October 1964, p. 257).

Banda's arrival in Edinburgh coincided with a climax in a phase of Central African politics about which the missionaries, and many others both in Britain and in Africa, felt strongly. This was the closer association of Nyasaland and Northern Rhodesia with Southern Rhodesia.[4]

The advantages of some form of association between the three territories had been discussed ever since white settlement began in the area in the 1890s, but it was not until 1915, when Cecil Rhodes's British South Africa Company proposed the amalgamation of Northern and Southern Rhodesia, that a serious attempt was made to give the idea substance. At that stage, however, neither the Northern Rhodesian settlers, some of whom wanted a merger with Nyasaland, nor the Southern Rhodesians, who regarded the northern territories as backward and unproductive, were in favour of the plan. In 1923 this position began to change. In that year Southern Rhodesia became a self-governing colony, and the Duke of Devonshire affirmed (albeit in the context of East Africa) the paramountcy of African interests in any conflict with those of immigrant races. Soon afterwards Northern Rhodesia was transformed into a protectorate, and the 4,000-odd Northern Rhodesian settlers began to realize that it might not be their destiny to develop on the Southern Rhodesian pattern. More than a little uncertain of Imperial intentions and fearful of African domination and the progressive erosion of 'the white man's way of life', the Northern Rhodesians looked South for their security. This time the Southern Rhodesians responded with alacrity, for Northern Rhodesia had in the meantime established the presence of vast reserves of copper ore. In the grouping they envisaged, Nyasaland was to be reluctantly included, mainly to placate the tobacco farmers in eastern Northern Rhodesia who still favoured a union with the neighbouring protectorate.

The Hilton Young Commission, sent out from London in 1928 to investigate the possibilities of closer association in Central and East Africa, dampened these aspirations. It approached the problem from the standpoint of paramountcy and was by and large unimpressed by the amalgamationist arguments of the Northern and Southern Rhodesians (the

Nyasaland settlers were 'divided and uncertain', but did not favour association with Southern Rhodesia). The majority of the commissioners concluded that since there were 'so many reasons' for eventually linking Nyasaland and at least a part of Northern Rhodesia with the three East African territories, they could not recommend 'the forging of any fetters which might bind them [the protectorates] permanently to the South'.[5]

In 1930 the debate was abruptly revived by the promulgation of the *Memorandum on Native Policy in East Africa* by the new Labour Colonial Secretary, Lord Passfield, reasserting unequivocally the paramountcy of African interests and making clear that it would apply in Central Africa no less than in East Africa.[6] This provoked an outburst of anguished indignation from the unofficial members of the Northern Rhodesian Legislative Council, who declared that such a policy was 'contrary to natural law' and demanded an immediate conference in London. Their request was refused, as were many others subsequent to it, but the incident had lent the amalgamationists' cause sufficient momentum to sustain it in the face of almost any adversity. In 1933 the Northern Rhodesian unofficials voted overwhelmingly in favour of amalgamation in the Legislative Council. Two years later a Greater Rhodesian League was formed by a vociferous minority of settlers in Nyasaland, to work for the territory's absorption into Southern Rhodesia. In 1936 Southern Rhodesian and Northern Rhodesian settlers meeting at Victoria Falls resolved that amalgamation under Southern Rhodesia's constitution was 'in the best interests of all the inhabitants of both colonies'. Toughened by the intransigence of successive colonial secretaries, and spurred on by the spectre conjured up by the Hilton Young Commission of an African-dominated grouping on Southern Rhodesia's borders, the movement in favour of closer association went from strength to strength.

The Southern Rhodesian Prime Minister, Godfrey Huggins, then intimated that if closer association proved impossible his country might have no choice but to strengthen its ties with South Africa. This was a prospect well calculated to alarm the Colonial Office and the protectorate governors, and Huggins played on their fears with great skill. When, shortly afterwards, the Northern Rhodesian settlers began to exert pressure for internal constitutional reform, the British Government took refuge in the appointment of another commission, chaired by Viscount Bledisloe. It was charged with inquiring 'whether any ... closer cooperation or association between Southern Rhodesia, Northern Rhodesia and Nyasaland is desirable and feasible, with due regard to the interests of all the inhabitants, irrespective of race ... and to the special responsibility of Our Government ... for the interests of the Native inhabitants.'[7]

In September 1938, as the Bledisloe Commission was returning to England after a three months' tour of Nyasaland and the Rhodesias, Banda wrote to the Anti-Slavery and Aborigines Society in London to ask if it could arrange for the commission to see him. He explained that he represented 'no tribe or native organization', but that he thought he deserved a hearing 'as one of the only two natives in Nyasaland with an education of University rank'. The letter concluded, in sharp contrast to the diffident manner in which Banda phrased his request, with a lengthy description of his academic qualifications.[8]

Banda's evidence to the commission, submitted as a written memorandum a few weeks later,[9] was destroyed together with other Colonial Office papers during the blitz of 1940. In retrospection, therefore, it is the fact of his having given evidence which is primarily important, rather than what he may have written. It is possible, however, to cast some light on Banda's attitudes at the time the memorandum was prepared.

Since leaving Chicago, Banda had viewed political issues from the standpoint of historical determinism. In 1935, in one of the very few political exercises he undertook while at Meharry, he had written a long paper denouncing the Italian invasion of Abyssinia. The invasion was to be condemned, Banda had argued, mainly because it was retrogressive. Colonial governments in general stood for progress and Italy had betrayed this principle.[10] In the particular case of Nyasaland, Banda held this to be axiomatic. As he wrote in a letter to Phiri, 'our Government is for us and is trying to help us.'[11] It is highly probable, in view of Banda's personal experience of the 'retrogressive' attitudes prevalent in Southern Rhodesia and South Africa, that he also argued on these lines to the Bledisloe Commission.

South Africa was at this time much in Banda's thoughts following a chance meeting, shortly before he left New York for Scotland, with (now Doctor) A. B. Xuma.[12] Hence it is possible – particularly in the light of the stand Huggins had taken – that he may also have discussed in the memorandum South Africa's role in Central African affairs. Certainly Banda appreciated, decades before anyone else had even thought about it, the nature of the South African threat to Africans in British-ruled territories. As he described it to friends, the real problem would come in the distant future, when the British dependencies attained self-government. Then South Africa would seek in self-protection to extend her influence northwards by 'buying off' the African leaders in power.[13] It was to prove a prophetic insight.

Whatever Banda may or may not have written in his evidence to the Bledisloe Commission, the one certain fact is that he vigorously opposed any closer association between the protectorates and Southern Rhodesia. In this he was not alone. During their stay in Central Africa, the commissioners had encountered among Africans in the protectorates an unvarying rejection of any scheme which would bind their countries more closely to the South. Chiefs, leaders of the native associations, clerks, mineworkers and peasant farmers were united in their opposition.[14] And equally strong objections were voiced by the Scots missionaries, who in Nyasaland at that time amounted to a third of the European population.

Despite this unanimity, the Commission's report, published in March 1939, did not reject outright the possibility of amalgamation. Instead it produced a laboured and all-embracing compromise. The commissioners predicted that the three territories would probably become 'more closely interdependent in all their activities', and 'identity of interests' would 'lead them sooner or later to political unity'. 'If this view should commend itself also to Your Majesty's Government in the United Kingdom,' the report continued, 'we recommend that it should take an early opportunity of stating its acceptance of the principle.'

The commissioners had however been sufficiently impressed by African objections to add: 'It is the fear that the balance [of interests] is not fairly held between the two races in Southern Rhodesia that alone prevents a recommendation being made for immediate amalgamation; the avowed policy of segregation, under the name of "Parallel Development", and the institution of the colour bar stand in the way.' Thus the 'principle of amalgamation' was to be accepted, but its implementation was to be indefinitely delayed. Out of this confusion came only two practicable suggestions, both designed as interim measures: the amalgamation of Nyasaland and Northern Rhodesia, about which nothing was ever done, and the setting-up of an inter-territorial council as an advisory body to coordinate government services.[15]

By leaving the door thus ajar, the Bledisloe commissioners paved the way for the developments of the 1940s which culminated in the creation of the Central African Federation. Nonetheless, it was ironically appropriate that the cause of the amalgamationists, whose motivation derived from their essentially racialistic desire to perpetuate their way of life, should have met its principal obstacle in their own racial policies.

While the Rhodesian settlers protested this new defeat, Banda's missionary contacts in Edinburgh proved fruitful in new directions. This time the matter was not ostensibly political. The Nyasaland Government had agreed to send Chief Mwase* to England for six months to help in an analysis of chiNyanja being undertaken by the London University School of Oriental and African Languages.[16] The Rev. T. Cullen Young, who had served at Livingstonia for many years, recommended that Banda be appointed the chief's adviser for the duration of his stay. 'He ... is not only acquainted with London,' Young informed the government, 'but is a very sound fellow of good judgement and character.'[17] At the time Young did not appreciate the full justice of this comment, for it was not until some years later that Banda revealed his identity with the small boy

---

*This was the successor to the Chief Mwase who had reigned when Banda was a boy. The old chief had died three years earlier. (Banda to Phiri, 14 February 1937, privately held.)

whom, twenty-five years before, Young had expelled from the examination hall in Kasungu.[18]

Mwase's arrival in Britain in the autumn of 1939 gave Banda his first chance in fifteen years to discuss at length with a fellow countryman the political developments taking place in Nyasaland. From the young chief he learnt of the growth of the native associations, which now operated in almost every district of the country; of developments in African education; of the problems caused by labour emigration; and of Nyasas' reaction to the threat of closer association. Together they pondered their country's destiny and that of their race. Mwase was especially impressed by the lack of racial tension in Britain, and the ease with which both he and Banda were accepted into British society. He wrote home that before his arrival he had not quite believed Banda's descriptions of Britain, but he could now see that 'Dr Banda was quite right'.[19]

This pleasant and fruitful interlude was brought to an end by the commencement in September of hostilities between Britain and Germany. In Central Africa, as in Britain itself, all energies were directed to the defeat of the Axis and issues like closer association were hastily swept aside. After Mwase's return to Nyasaland a few months later, Banda again lost touch with events at home.[20] But his political interest had now been aroused, and the break proved temporary.

The influence of the missionaries and other returned Scots expatriates continued throughout Banda's stay in Edinburgh, affecting his personality no less than it affected him politically. With Cullen Young, the Rev. Matthew Faulds from Karonga, the brothers John and Frederick Moir* – who had travelled to trans-Zambezia in the 1870s to found the African Lakes Corporation – and with the family of his former missionary in Kasungu, Dr George Prentice, Banda could discuss the old days and debate the shape of the new. He came to feel less detached from Nyasaland, and hence more secure, and with

*When the brothers died, Frederick in November 1939 and John four months later, Banda wrote a lengthy tribute to them in a Presbyterian magazine (*Other Lands*, Edinburgh, July 1940, pp. 144–5).

some of these men formed the first deep friendships he had made since leaving Kasungu.

Even in this company, however, Banda was reluctant to discuss his own past. He seemed to feel that it was more romantic if it remained shrouded in mystery, and on the rare occasions when he agreed to recount shyly some anecdote of his wanderings, it was always to portray himself in a heroic light.* There was in this an element of gilding the lily, for Banda's story was remarkable enough without further embellishment. But it was a consistent trait, which manifested itself equally in Banda's unwillingness to admit to his true age, and the stress he frequently laid on his 'youthfulness'.† Occasionally this characteristic would reveal itself as overt vanity. A friend has recalled how he would 'purr like a cat' when his achievements were praised.[21] But usually it showed itself in more complex ways, in which there was often an element of self-deception, contrasting with the rectitude of his character in other respects.

Banda was now in his early forties, 'still absurdly youthful looking',[22] as he put it, and possessed of sufficient eccentricities to intrigue his Scots friends. His puritanism, for instance, outstripped even theirs. As a teetotaller, he had been scandalized to discover, on docking at Glasgow from America, that a Presbyterian city could boast so many public houses.[23] Other normal social practices also shocked him. It amazed him that in Edinburgh, 'the very home and Mecca of the Church of Scotland',‡ contemporary morality permitted married men to hold other men's wives for the purpose of ballroom dancing. When he recalled how the Scots missionaries had denounced the Chewa dances of his boyhood as 'savage, primitive [and] sinful',§ his

---

* For example, the tale of his encounter with the Afrikaner miner on p. 16.
† See the text quoted on p. 12.
‡ Banda, Speech marking Republic anniversary celebrations, 6 July 1968, Malawi Information Department transcript. Banda began using the term 'Mecca' to describe Edinburgh during the time he lived there.
§ ibid. Years later, as a politician, Banda transformed this experience into the theme of a set speech, usually addressed to members of the League of Malawi Women. In it he contrasted the propriety of African traditional dances, where men and women danced separately, with what he had found in America and Europe. It invariably ended: 'If God is going to burn anyone

incredulity was complete. To Banda, this aspect of western morality was repugnant in a way which was as deeply rooted as it was utterly genuine, and he became excitable and argumentative when discussing it.[24]

The strictness of Banda's moral outlook was partly the legacy of his mission schooling and partly, perhaps, the result of a reaction against the urban vice with which he had come into contact in Johannesburg and Chicago. His parents' separation may also have played some indeterminate part in it. But more than any of these things, it was an extension of the innate conservatism which derived from his Chewa upbringing. This was a trait which showed itself most clearly in relation to the interaction between African and western culture. One of the few comments Banda made on Chief Mwase's visit was that chiChewa had become so anglicized in the years he had been away that sometimes he had difficulty in understanding it.[25] Such changes did not please him.

Banda discussed the problems of cultural intermingling at some length in the preface to *Our African Way of Life*, a volume of chiNyanja essays in whose translation and editing he collaborated in 1944 with Cullen Young:*

[The essayists] are conscious that much in their community thought and communal life has been judged unfitting and detrimental to progress [wrote Banda and Cullen Young]. Missions and Government alike have striven to expound and enlighten, yet there is so much in the new culture that seems, not merely no better but actually less good than what they know of the old, that they try – while yet there is time: while still the old they value is in being – to get through to the European mind some inkling of their African truth, their African scale of values, their African social ethic.

They went on to quote approvingly the opening sentences of the title essay of the book, by John Kambalame:

for dancing, it is not you my people. It will be the white men. . . .' By this time, however, Banda had himself danced with the wife of Malawi's Governor-General, Sir Glyn Jones, at a State ball to mark the country's independence.

* In this extract the words are Cullen Young's but the thought is clearly Banda's.

My purpose in offering this book is that our children should learn what is good among our ancient ways: those things which were understood long ago and belong to their own people. Thereafter they will combine them with the things that they are being taught today. Having done that, they will receive the thanks of both parties, as wise and worthy young people, because of their rightly using both old and new together.

It would be difficult to find a closer description of Banda's own thinking on this subject. For he, even more than Kambalame, belonged to 'the intervening generation' in Africa: those who were, as Cullen Young put it, 'sons of the old and fathers of the new. . . .'[26] The cultural tension which had first become apparent in the childhood conflict between mission teaching and Chewa tradition formed a constant if not always consciously felt backdrop to his life. In America and Britain, far away from Africa, its pressures diminished; but when Banda returned to Africa as a politician, it reasserted itself the more strongly for his absence.

If the puritanical conservatism of Banda's character can be traced back to the disparate beginnings of his upbringing, it is less easy to discover the origins of the obsessive prudery which complemented it. In this there was a strong element of Victorianism, but carried to such an extreme that even in straitlaced Edinburgh it seemed a little absurd. To Banda, a man who appeared in company without shoes and socks was literally 'exhibiting his nakedness'. On one occasion when this happened while Banda was present, he rushed out of the room and could talk of nothing for weeks afterwards but 'that revolting man'. In the same way he would never receive friends unless he was correctly attired.

To these traits Banda added an austere fastidiousness which combined with practicality and thoroughness. When he took meals in a restaurant, he carried with him a small hand-towel which he used in preference to that provided in its washroom. His choice of food would be determined not so much by his inclinations as by the nutritional values of the selection offered to him.[27]

Despite this pervasive asceticism, Banda was far from being a joyless figure. The severity of his personality was softened by a keen sense of humour, and he delighted, in an inoffensive way, in poking fun at those around him.[28] For all the oddity and extremism of some aspects of his character, Banda was in Edinburgh a well-balanced and on the whole self-consistent man, whose dominant trait was an unrelenting meticulousness. Thoroughness infused every facet of his being, manifesting itself in the correctness of his dress no less than in the diligence with which he applied himself to his studies. It was, above all, the characteristic of a doctor.

Medicine remained the overriding preoccupation in Banda's life. The Royal College had exempted him from attending lectures in virtue of his American qualifications,[29] and he was able to spend most of his time there reading and watching demonstrations by some of the great surgeons of the day. The techniques of men like Sir John Fraser electrified him,[30] and he grew fascinated with his subject in a way in which only a truly dedicated man can. He had, moreover, no financial worries, for Mrs Douglas Smith was still paying for the greater part of his education.*

Towards the end of his stay in Scotland, Banda began visiting sick people in some of the poorer districts of Edinburgh, partly as a means of gaining experience but also from a genuine desire to alleviate suffering.† He had, as one former patient put it, 'a

---

* Unattributable interview. Banda may also have received some assistance from John Moir, with whose nephew he stayed in Edinburgh while convalescing after an appendix operation (see Banda, Speech to nurses at Queen Elizabeth Central Hospital, Blantyre, 13 February 1970, privately held transcript; and Charles Jameson Matinga, interview with the author, Salisbury, 24 August 1969). Rotberg (*Rise of Nationalism*, p. 188) says that Banda also received financial support from three Scottish ladies. Allegations that Banda persuaded both the Church of Scotland and the Nyasaland Government, each in ignorance of the other, to grant him stipends of £300 a year appear to be untrue (see Munger, *Kamuzu Banda of Malawi*, p. 8; Sir Roy Welensky, *Welensky's 4000 Days: The Life and Death of the Federation of the Rhodesias and Nyasaland*, Collins, 1964, p. 48; and O. Ransford, *Livingstone's Lake*, John Murray, 1966, pp. 248–9).

† In these pre-National Health Service days, patients were either paying patients or 'panel' patients, so-called because they could be treated only by those doctors who had registered for the purpose on a 'panel', under the Insurance Act. 'Panel' patients often received inferior treatment.

gift for making illness seem bearable'. He took pains to explain, in simple but vivid terms, the causes of an illness, often using his hands to illustrate an anatomical point. It was a technique not far removed from acting, based on the twin premise that what was dramatic was consoling, and what was understood was tolerable.[31] Later, as a politician, Banda used a variant of this idea to put across to uneducated villagers in Malawi political and economic concepts.

Many of those Banda advised in this way attended the Rev. McPherson's church in a working-class district of the city, to which he also belonged, and it was these people who, in 1941, approved his ordination as an Elder of the Church of Scotland.[32] The attraction of this office lay in the status it conferred as a specially respected member of the community, for although Banda was genuinely religious, it was in an ecumenical* rather than a churchy sense. Banda's puritanism lacked the sectarian militance of a true Presbyterian; he was for all his extremism essentially gentle and pacifist in his beliefs. As he explained to a friend, he was a 'first-generation Christian', by which he meant that he believed in Christianity for itself and not merely as the inherited religion of his parents. The basis of his faith, Banda added, lay in Christ's injunction to the disciples: 'Love your enemies. . . .'[33]

Before many months had passed the strength of this faith was severely tested, for just as Banda was about to leave for Nyasaland, having been awarded the L.R.C.P. and L.R.C.S. (Edinburgh) and the L.R.F.P.S. (Glasgow),[34] his long-standing ambition to become a medical missionary had abruptly to be abandoned. This came about in a manner as simple as it was tragic. A group of nurses at Livingstonia wrote to the Church's headquarters in Edinburgh to say they would not be prepared to serve under an African doctor. Banda took this blow with remarkable calm. 'I'm glad they said it now,' he confided to friends. 'If I'd gone and found out there, how embarrassing it

---

*Witness, for instance, the ease with which Banda was able to switch his allegiance from the Church of Scotland to the A.M.E., and then back again. Later in life he became an ardent advocate of Church unity and a firm believer in the universality of God regardless of creed.

would have been.' But beneath his stoicism he was bitterly disappointed.[35]

Next he tried to enter the service of the Nyasaland Government, where his application evidently caused a great deal of heart-searching in the Secretariat at Zomba. There was argument over whether he should be paid as much as a European; over whether he was to be allowed to treat white patients; over whether he could use the newly built Zomba swimming pool; over where he should live, and a hundred other similar points.[36] Eventually he was offered a job as a medical officer at a starting salary of £650 a year, at the time the current rate for all races.[37] But soon afterwards a letter arrived from the Colonial Office, informing him that an extra condition was to be attached to his terms of service: he must undertake not to seek social contacts with white doctors.* 'Throughout my life,' Banda wrote afterwards, 'entering the employ of anyone under force of pressure of any description, whether directly or indirectly exerted, has been objectionable to me.'[38]

After one more unsuccessful attempt to return home, this time to work for the British Leprosy Relief Association,[39] Banda moved to Liverpool, where, late in 1941, he established a surgery in St James's Place.[40] He had not altogether given up the hope of an early return to Nyasaland, and enrolled for a course in tropical medicine at Liverpool University.[41] But, as the years passed, the idea gradually receded until it became a long-term rather than a short-term objective.

In Liverpool Banda became once more financially indepen-

---

* Unattributable interview. The letter was apparently addressed to Hastings Walter Kamuzu Banda, but whether this was a Colonial Office blunder or whether Banda had at one stage used the name Walter is not clear. This incident is usually dated – as it is here – after the Livingstonia affair, i.e. in mid-1941. According to Matinga, however, the Nyasaland Government first considered offering Banda employment in 1937 or 1938, and made him a firm offer shortly afterwards. Banda refused it, Matinga said, because he was offered only £300 a year, about half the European rate (Matinga, op. cit.). Phiri also gave this reason for Banda's declining to return to Nyasaland at this stage (Phiri, interview). Cullen Young's correspondence, on the other hand, appears to indicate that Banda was unknown to Nyasaland authorities until at least mid-1939 (Rotberg, op. cit., p. 189).

dent. His surgery flourished, and he registered on the 'panel' of the Liverpool Insurance Committee,[42] often waiving fees for patients too poor to pay. A number of wealthy patrons took note of his work and made periodic donations which he used for poor relief. During the winter of 1941 Banda personally paid the rents of many of his poorest patients, and kept some of them from actual starvation. It was his way of repaying Mrs Douglas Smith and all those others who had helped him during his own time of need.

Banda's stay in Liverpool was happy but brief, for in 1942 he was informed that he was to be conscripted as an army doctor. As a pacifist, Banda refused. While he was willing to work in Britain, he said, he would have no part in a war against which he was a conscientious objector.[43] In consequence he was forced, in March 1943, to move to Tyneside, where he worked first at a mission for coloured seamen, and later at a hospital near Newcastle.[44] While there he became aware of the relaxation in sexual morality wartime conditions had brought to Britain. Near the hospital was a W.A.A.F. camp, whose inmates would approach the doctors for help in dealing with unwanted pregnancies. Such experiences embarrassed Banda acutely, and he afterwards remembered his stay there with great loathing.[45] But it was not an entirely fruitless period, for it was during this time that Banda regained touch with events in Nyasaland, where, despite the war, political activity was now reviving.

The cessation of the settlers' efforts to promote closer association following the outbreak of war proved short-lived. In 1941, a permanent Inter-territorial Conference was set up, ostensibly to enable the governors of the three territories and their representatives to confer regularly on matters relating to the war. In practice it provided a forum for the surreptitious airing of amalgamationist sentiment, and its principal effect was to consolidate the bonds between the participating countries. The following year overt settler agitation began in Northern Rhodesia, and in 1943 Roy Welensky, the President of the Northern Rhodesian Labour Party, moved in the Legislative Council that the two Rhodesias be amalgamated 'under a constitution similar to that now enjoyed by Southern Rhodesia'. The motion was strongly supported by other unofficial members.[46]

The breakthrough for the settlers came in 1944, when the British Government, although still rejecting amalgamation as 'impracticable', decided to replace the Inter-territorial Conference with the Central African Council, an advisory body of the type envisaged by the Bledisloe Commission. Welensky and Huggins were not slow to appreciate the Council's potential. To the extent that it succeeded, they reasoned, it would demonstrate the usefulness of closer cooperation; and to the extent that it failed, it would show that closer cooperation was impossible without closer political association.[47]

The revival of amalgamationist agitation was watched with dismay by leaders of African opinion. As the Mlanje Native Association put it, meeting in April 1942, Nyasas were 'always alarmed to hear about the proposed amalgamation question.'[48] But now commingled with their concern was a new spirit of militancy. Nyasa soldiers returning on leave from combat overseas brought with them a heightened awareness of the outside world, which expressed itself as a determination to progress. Out of this combination of anxiety and aggressiveness was created Nyasaland's first national political movement, the Nyasaland African Congress.[49]

The acknowledged founder of Congress was James Frederick Sangala, a Mang'anja employed as an interpreter in the High Court at Blantyre, and a leading figure in the native associations. Sangala had first considered forming a territory-wide African association in 1939, following the visit of the Bledisloe Commission.[50] But it was not until 1943, when the threat of an Axis conquest of Africa had been effectively removed, that he felt able to proceed with his plans.[51] After obtaining official sanction and holding lengthy consultations with his colleagues, Sangala wrote on 1 October a 'Circular Letter to all Africans Resident in Nyasaland Protectorate', which was reproduced in the local press.[52] It proposed the establishment of a Nyasaland African Council, which would meet once or twice yearly to discuss 'matters affecting the Protectorate generally'. The 'chief reason' for its formation, Sangala explained, was 'because experience has taught that unity is strength'. The time had now come 'for the Africans in this country to fight for their freedom, progress and development of Nyasaland from one field'.[53]

The letter produced an unexpectedly strong response. Sangala received encouragement from a number of European sympathizers, and from Nyasas both within and without the country. Among the latter was Banda in Northumberland, who from this point on kept in close touch with the African intelligentsia in Blantyre, supplying at first advice and later financial support.[54]

Although Sangala carefully explained, in response to questioning from the provincial commissioner, that the phrase 'fight for their freedom' was not intended to convey armed conflict,[55] the circular letter remained a more determined statement of African political planning than any which had appeared before. Just how radical a departure from past practice Sangala was making became clear at the first meeting of the 'select committee' of what was now known as the Nyasaland African Association,* in Blantyre on 21 January 1944. In addition to restating long-standing demands for better education, equality of pay and opportunity in the civil service, and the restoration to Africans of undeveloped European-owned land, the committee demanded majority African membership of all advisory boards and direct representation in the Legislative Council.[56]

At an informal public meeting a week later with Bishop Thorne, who had been nominated to represent African interests in the Council, these points were reiterated yet more forcefully. Charles Matinga, a leading member of the Blantyre Native Association, read out a prepared statement in which Thorne was told bluntly: 'to suggest that missionaries can represent the interests of Africans is but to retard again their progress. . . .

*The name 'council' was discarded at the Government's request lest the organization be confused with the chiefs' councils. The Government may also have wished to reserve the term for the official African provincial councils, which it set up shortly afterwards. (ASS 4/13, vol. 2, Chief Secretary to Sangala, 20 October 1943, Zomba archives. See also Rotberg, op. cit., p. 189, and R. K. Tangri, 'The Rise of Nationalism in Colonial Africa: The Case of Colonial Malawi', in B. Pachai, G. W. Smith and R. K. Tangri, eds., *Malawi Past and Present: Studies in Local and Regional History,* mimeo., Blantyre, 1968, p. 105.)

There are many Africans . . . capable of representing us if you only give us [a] chance.' While Thorne was commended for advising against amalgamation, the committee warned that it could never consider any form of closer association 'until we have been given at least 99 per cent of the rights we are entitled to enjoy in the administration of our country'. This slight concession was followed by an attack on missionaries generally and a long discussion of African grievances. The statement ended bitterly:

Anything that makes a race progress has been denied to us and what has been done is to tell us to look for things that are in store in the next world while others so privileged because of their fair colour are making use of all and everything in this world. . . . If there are things that are good for Europeans, Indians or Half-Castes, we also want them.[57]

The impetus for this broadside came not so much from outside influences, as the Government of the day suspected, but from the changing mood of Nyasas themselves.[58] The dignified protests of the native associations had proved ineffectual. In the more vigorous climate of wartime, the Nyasaland African Congress, as Sangala's organization was soon afterwards renamed, sought to proclaim its grievances in more strident tones.

By October, when Congress held its first annual conference in Blantyre, the organization boasted seventeen native associations as affiliates and a newly formed branch in Johannesburg.[59] Levi Mumba, who had played a leading role in the formation of the North Nyasa Native Association in 1912, was elected its first President-General. Matinga became Vice President-General; Charles Wesley Mlanga, also from the Blantyre Native Association, Secretary-General; and Isaac Macdonald Lawrence, former subscriber to Garvey's *Negro World* and long-time friend of Clements Kadalie, Treasurer-General. Sangala, who was unable to be present because the Government had transferred him from Blantyre, became a committee member.

Banda's influence in the movement's affairs was by now considerable, and a number of the suggestions put forward at this conference may have originated from him.[60] One new idea,

which was later to occupy much of Congress's attention, was
that the Government should assume control of the mission
schools and introduce a system of free, compulsory education;
another was that members of the newly formed African provincial councils should be elected by the membership of Congress.[61]
Both requests were turned down, but Congress's efforts did not
go completely unrewarded. Two months later, on 20 December
1944, the Government accorded it official recognition as 'representing the various African associations in Nyasaland'.[62]

While these events were taking place in Central Africa, the
threat of Banda's conscription was lifted, and he was able to
leave the hospital at Newcastle and set up in private practice in
North Shields.[63] During his stay there he regained contact with
Hanock Phiri, with whom he had lost touch since the beginning
of the war, and wrote to him enthusiastically of Congress's
activities. The movement, Banda declared, would enable Nyasas
to achieve the objectives which Phiri's Livingstonia graduate
friends had been discussing during his boyhood at Kasungu.*
He stressed the dual religio-political nature of Phiri's responsibilities as the leader of an Ethiopian church, and urged him to
become a member of Congress. 'We must organize ourselves to
help ourselves and our country better . . . and the only way we
can organize ourselves effectively is through the Nyasaland
African Congress,' Banda wrote. Through Congress, he went on,
Nyasas could achieve direct representation in the Legislative
Council and on Government boards and commissions, and
hence a much greater measure of control over 'schools,
hospitals, internal trade and commerce and . . . many other
things.'[64]

As soon became apparent, Banda was being hopelessly over-
optimistic: initially Congress made little headway with its
demands. Discouraged by its lack of success, and saddened by
the deaths within three months of the first annual conference of
Mumba and Lawrence, its two most experienced members, its

---

*Banda was well aware of the role the Scots missionaries had played in
the development of political consciousness among Nyasas. He once said that
Livingstonia was the seed-bed from which grew the Nyasaland African
Congress (Shepperson and Price, *Independent African*, p. 414).

proposals grew more radical. At an executive committee meeting on 1 April 1946 under the Acting-Presidency of Matinga, it was decided that if the Government accepted the principle of African representation in the Legislative Council, 'Africans must be adequately represented in proportion to ... [their] population.' The committee also voted to seek a meeting with the Governor, Sir Edmund Richards, to put forward its proposals for the improvement of African education.[65] But for all its militancy, the committee recognized the need to keep on the right side of the authorities, and the same meeting approved a moderately worded constitution for Congress, drafted by Levi Mumba shortly before his death.[66]

The meeting with Richards, which took place seven weeks later, was only marginally more successful than Congress's earlier, epistolary submissions. The Governor indicated that he was planning to create a Protectorate Council to which the three provincial councils would send representatives, and from which in due course he might nominate a member to the Legislative Council. But he made clear that there could be no question of this last development taking place for some time. Similarly, while Richards agreed to make a few minor concessions in educational matters, he rejected on financial grounds Congress's carefully argued demands for fundamental changes in the educational system.[67]

Further discouraged by this setback and consternated by the formation of the Central African Council, Congress decided to strengthen its ties with the British Labour Party and the Fabian Colonial Bureau, and to seek affiliation to the Fifth Pan-African Congress, then about to open in Manchester. The commission of these tasks was entrusted to Dr Banda, who was soon afterwards appointed Congress's official representative in Britain.[68]

Banda was now established in practice as a National Health Service doctor in the London suburb of Harlesden, to which he had moved two months after the Armistice.[69] The transition from the relative obscurity of northern England to 'the very centre of the British Empire', as Banda described London, had affected him profoundly. In the lower-middle-class society of

Harlesden he found a degree of independence and security which had previously eluded him, and in the cosmopolitan life of the metropolis, an opportunity to air his political convictions. As his confidence grew, his reserve diminished and he became known as a man of great personal charm. But while this had the effect of moderating his fierce puritanism, it made his political pronouncements more authoritative, even dogmatic: 'The law must be changed,' he wrote peremptorily to Phiri, apropos of the system of nominating members of the protectorate and provincial councils, which he felt was biased in favour of traditional elements.[70] He became a member of the Willesden branch of the Labour Party, for which he voted in the post-war general election.[71] He joined the Fabian Bureau, becoming friendly with its founder, Arthur Creech Jones, and with Fenner Brockway, James Johnson and John Hatch. And he began to exchange ideas with other African expatriates then residing in Britain, some of whom later occupied high positions of power and influence in their own countries.[72]

The most outstanding of these men were Jomo Kenyatta and Kwame Nkrumah, both of whom played leading roles in the Manchester Pan-African Congress, which Banda also attended.[73] Although Kenyatta returned to Kenya soon afterwards, he and Banda formed a friendship during the few months of their acquaintance which held each in good stead when they met again in Africa, fifteen years later. Nkrumah, who remained in London until 1947, visited Banda frequently at his home, and the latter came to regard him as his protégé. After Nkrumah's return to the Gold Coast, Banda took a proprietorial interest in the progress made by his 'boy', as he described him to his Fabian friends.[74]

Towards the end of 1945 Banda met Sir Stewart Gore-Brown, then the nominated representative of African interests in the Northern Rhodesian Legislative Council, and through him was introduced to the man who was to become his bitterest political opponent: Roy Welensky. Banda's reaction has not been recorded, but Welensky recalled afterwards: 'He was quite amiable, though liable to become excited if anyone crossed him in an argument, and very insistent on the fact that he was a doctor.'[75] It was ironic that it should have been Welensky who recognized the one great difference which separated Banda from those around him. Banda *was* a doctor, and neither an actual nor an intending politician. In Scotland a friend had suggested that if he entered politics he might in time find himself Nyasaland's first Prime Minister. Banda had brushed the idea aside: a Prime Minister was the very last thing he wanted to become.[76] Although in London he began to play a more active role in politics, and particularly in the affairs of the Nyasaland African Congress, his medical vocation was not one he wished to change.

Closer association and educational reform still occupied the first place in Congress's attentions. At its second annual conference at Lilongwe in October 1945, delegates sought an assurance from the British Government that the Central African Council would not lead to the amalgamation of Nyasaland with any state 'without adequate consultation with the Africans themselves through ... the Congress'. They also requested, following Richards's rejection of Congress's educational programme, the setting-up of a commission to inquire into African education in the protectorate.[77]

In Britain, Banda composed a memorandum setting out at length the position Congress had taken, and submitted it to the Colonial Secretary, George Hall. With the help of his friends in the Fabian Bureau he also persuaded a number of M.P.s to ask questions on these and other matters in the House of Commons.[78]

These procedures, although protracted, gradually began to bear fruit. One early result was the announcement in the Commons that the Government hoped to seat African representatives in the Legislative Council 'as soon as practicable'.[79] But with its educational demands Congress made little headway. Early in 1946, Richards informed Matinga (who had now been confirmed as Congress's President-General) that there were insufficient grounds to justify the appointment of a commission of the type Congress had requested. Banda then tried unsuccessfully to raise the matter in London. Finally Congress decided, at its third annual conference at Salima in September, to seek permission to send a deputation to Britain for an interview with the Secretary of State.[80] In the apparent absence of any new threat from the settlers, this project dominated Congress's activities for the next two years.

In the meantime Banda had turned his attention to Congress's administration. Soon after the Lilongwe conference he wrote to Matinga suggesting that the movement be reorganized along sounder administrative lines, and that the collection and expenditure of Congress's funds be centralized.[81] As one who regularly contributed to its exchequer, Banda had every right to put forward this idea, but Matinga may have regarded it as unjustified interference. By this time he was beginning to see Banda as a possible rival,[82] and his suspicions of the latter's motives may well have been reinforced when, at the next executive committee meeting in Blantyre, on 20 April 1946, several delegates paid tribute to Banda for his assistance. B. R. K. Namboyah, the delegate of the Mlanje Foodstuff Growers' Association, expressed the feeling of the meeting: 'We have our cooperator in the person of Dr Banda in London, his service is like gold to us, it was best for us to give warning to Dr Banda to try his best to take great care of his life that he may live long for the good of our country.' In any event, Matinga saw to it that Banda's proposal was defeated (by 15 to 8), and the committee resolved that 'all branches will continue to keep their money as usual'.[83]

Banda had in fact appreciated one of Congress's great weaknesses: its lack of any adequate machinery to control its largely autonomous affiliates and branches.[84] A few months later he tried again to get the executive to rectify this situation by suggesting that Congress should employ a full-time organizing secretary, for whose salary he would make himself personally responsible. This proposal was well supported when it was first put forward at the Salima annual conference, and a subcommittee including Sangala and Congress's Vice-President, the Rev. Charles Chinula, recommended that a qualified secretary-general be employed at a minimum salary of £63 a year.[85] But Matinga disliked the idea, for he felt, as he explained later, that whoever was appointed would be loyal to Banda rather than to himself.[86] When the sub-committee's recommendation was put to the conference as a whole, it was defeated by 24 votes to 8. Banda was instead requested to buy a typewriter in lieu of the first year's salary, and to make available the sum of £18 a year to be paid out in honoraria to the present Secretary-General and his assistants.[87]

After this double rebuff, Banda made no immediate attempt to revive the question, and his enthusiasm for Congress seems temporarily to have waned. Although the movement remained at the confluence of the two main streams of his non-professional interest, politics and Nyasaland, he was now beginning to involve himself more in each distinct from the other.

He started meeting with Nkrumah, Kojo Botsio (later Ghana's Foreign Minister), George Padmore and a few other like-minded people in a basement in Soho, to discuss pan-Africanism and its relevance to African advancement.[88] Nkrumah and Padmore influenced Banda strongly in this respect, and he saw in their militant pan-African beliefs the logical successor to the Ethiopianism and Garveyism of his youth. But pan-Africanism was in any case to Banda an inherently sympathetic philosophy, for ever since he had left Africa he had been known not by his nationality but by his Africanism, and he had come to regard others from his continent in the same light. Much less sympathetic was the Marxism which Padmore in particular espoused. To Banda, with his mission schooling, his twelve years in America, and in particular his American degree in political science, communism was alien and totally unattractive.

Meanwhile Banda became interested in the aChewa Improvement Society, of which Chief Mwase was a leading member.[89] He also began discussing with Hanock Phiri an ambitious scheme to set up in Kasungu an experimental cooperative farm, to act as a model for similar African-run developments in other parts of the country.[90]

At about this time, too, Banda started to finance the education of needy African students. Many of these were Nyasas, but some were from other parts of the continent and at least one was from Northern Rhodesia, the child of a leper couple, whom Banda sent to Adams College in Natal. Although Banda was disciplinarian in their treatment, withdrawing his support immediately if any of them lapsed in their studies, he was also extremely generous. In the space of seven years some forty young people were educated wholly or partly at his expense. [91]

This concern with African advancement stemmed not only from the frustration of Banda's missionary ambitions, and from his continuing desire to repay the charity he had himself received, but also from his need to compensate for his failure to return to Nyasaland. For by this time Banda possessed sufficient funds to establish himself in private practice in any of the major centres in his country. Yet he chose to remain in London. His doing so did not alter the validity of his actions, but it did lend them added urgency.

Banda's reasons for remaining where he was were twofold. He did not wish to see his money dissipated aimlessly in supporting the numerous relations who would lay claim to him under the Chewa extended family system – and the importunities of Phiri and others of his close relatives must have convinced him that this was inevitably what would happen. [92] And he had grown accustomed to the British way of life and did not wish to change it. The second reason was the more important. As a politician in Malawi, Banda would later speak of having two homes, one in Kasungu and one in Britain. But during the years he spent in London, Banda had only one home – the one in which he lived.

Now aged fifty, Banda had become a typical British general practitioner, complete with all the accoutrements of a middle-class Englishman. He had bought himself a house in fashionable Brondesbury Park, where he lived in simple comfort (his surgery, however, remained in Harlesden); he drove a small car; he invested in a mild way on the stock market; he employed the wife of a local teacher, a Major French, as a secretary-cum-receptionist; he even became a freemason. To complete his doctor's image of urbane professionalism, he took to wearing a black homburg hat and carrying a rolled umbrella. [93]

By his 4,000-odd patients, almost all of whom were white, Banda was regarded with a respect bordering on reverence. When he entered the waiting-room of his surgery, everyone would stand up to greet him; Britons do not usually accord their doctors such courtesies. His benevolence became almost legendary. Years later former patients recalled how he had come to their houses in the early hours of the morning to care for a sick child, and left refusing to take a fee; or how he had 'added a year' to the life of an elderly relative.[94] If ever a man was esteemed within his community, it was Banda during the years he spent in Harlesden.

African friends who visited him at his home were impressed not only by the extent of his adjustment and the ease with which he had assimilated British attitudes, but by the efficiency with which he ran his practice and the high standard of living he had attained.[95] Few other black men, and perhaps no other African, had achieved such total integration into a white community. Banda could boast a white secretary and a standard of living higher than that enjoyed by many of his white neighbours, and yet have those neighbours accept that this was no more than was right and proper. In this respect alone, Banda must rank among the outstanding men of his time. What he achieved then would have seemed no less remarkable had it been achieved twenty-five years later.

Yet there was, at times, something incongruous in Banda's Englishness. Nowhere was this more apparent than in the region where politics overlapped with his domestic life. On Sunday afternoons he would invite his friends – members of African political groups, African students, Fabians, Labour M.P.s, left-wing journalists and sometimes an occasional missionary – to his comfortable house in Brondesbury Park. There he would preside while these men, some of whom like himself were destined to be branded as agitators and imprisoned in colonial gaols, debated the burning issues of the day over tea and cakes.[96]

Throughout 1947 Congress maintained pressure on the Nyasaland Government to allow the planned educational deputation to visit Britain, and by May of that year the 'Educational Deputation Fund', launched shortly after the Salima conference, had reached a sufficient sum to support the scheme. Banda had also been agitating for the visit and in July, Creech Jones, who was now Colonial Secretary in the Labour Government, indicated his willingness to receive the delegation. He suggested however, that 'Congress be made aware that [an] . . . interview with the Secretary of State is not granted lightly', and that their request be treated as 'an opportunity for political education'.[97]

Creech Jones's instructions were followed to the letter, and by September, when Congress held its fourth annual conference in Zomba – at which the opening address was delivered by no less a personage than Nyasaland's Governor – it had still not been informed whether the deputation might leave. Nonetheless, the subject was discussed at length, as was the perennial topic of Congress's organization. A letter was read out from Banda, 'wishing the conference a success and enlighten[ing] the conference . . . [on] good principles and proper organization . . . [and on] the selection of good leaders and [containing] a suggestion to centralize the Congress fund which accompanied a remittance of £10 and . . . [a promise] to send another sum of £11.' Congress, however, still felt that the time had 'not yet come to establish a central fund', and Banda was asked instead to become a member of the educational deputation if and when its visit was sanctioned. Six weeks later the executive committee was told that the Colonial Secretary had approved its request.[98]

The Nyasaland members of the deputation were to have been Charles Matinga, representing the southern branches of Congress, and the Rev. Charles Chinula, for the North. But before they could leave, Matinga engineered Chinula's displacement (amid bitter allegations of tribalism from Congress's northern branches) by Andrew J. Mponda, a close friend and fellow Yao tribesman who had recently succeeded Charles Mlanga as Congress's Secretary-General.[99] It was these two who arrived in London early in May 1948.

Although Banda took pains to make their stay pleasant, the visit was evidently a grave disappointment to him. On several occasions he quarrelled bitterly with Matinga, and later commented that he had seemed determined to take no advice but his own.[100] But their interview with Creech Jones did have some useful results, for it was announced soon afterwards that a new secondary school (Nyasaland's second) would be built at Dedza, and a teachers' training college at Domasi.[101] It may also conceivably have accelerated the Government's decision – which had been 'under consideration' for three years – to appoint the first African members to the Legislative Council.*

Barely a month after Matinga's return, it was alleged that he had embezzled £162 from Congress's funds. As a result of this accusation and the resentment engendered by the Mponda affair, he was stripped of office,[102] and Banda's old friend from the Livingstone Native Welfare Association, Sam K. K. Mwase, appointed provisional President-General in his place.[103] But Congress was in disarray and virtually insolvent.

Matinga's downfall, though it came ironically at the time of one of Congress's few successes, was symptomatic of a greater malaise for which peculation and administrative inefficiency were only partly to blame. Other more important weaknesses originated from the movement's nature and the circumstances of the time. The creation of the provincial and protectorate councils had provided alternative forums with which Congress had to compete. The threat of amalgamation, which had so assisted in its formation, had receded to such an extent that by 1947 it did not even merit a mention in the Zomba conference's agenda. Congress had remained an organization of the elite, without charismatic leadership and without mass support. Its membership consisted for the most part of civil servants, dependent for their livelihood – as successive Governors reminded them – on the Government's toleration of their activities. They had neither the means nor the capability to exert the degree of pressure required to achieve their ends, and so they failed. With failure came disillusionment, and with disillusionment, collapse.[104]

During the African winter months of 1948, Congress was at its weakest – so weak, indeed, that but for the efforts of Mwase, Sangala and a handful of others it might well have succumbed completely. It was then that the debate on closer association abruptly revived.

*These were E. A. Muwamba, who had been active in native associations in Northern Rhodesia, and K. E. Mposa, a close friend of Sangala. Banda met Muwamba when he and Clement Kumbikano visited London, shortly after Matinga, to attend the 1948 Colonial Conference as representatives of the African Protectorate Council.

Chapter 4

The Fight against Federation

After the Second World War pressure for closer association
had started building up anew, albeit gradually and, at first,
unobtrusively. Many in positions of power in Britain and
Central Africa had begun to favour the idea of an enlarged
territorial unit on economic, financial and strategic grounds.
The Central African Council had succeeded sufficiently
to demonstrate the immense practical advantages that closer
cooperation could bring. And the many small European
pressure groups in the two Rhodesias had kept the issue alive
politically.

The first public indication that the question was to be
reopened came from Sir Stewart Gore-Brown, who, perhaps
sensing that a new wave of amalgamationism was imminent,
resurrected a suggestion he had first put forward in 1936.
Federation, he told the Northern Rhodesian Legislative Council
in March 1948, 'would entail all the advantages of amalgamation without any of its disadvantages. Above all, it would
ensure the rights of Africans.' There the matter might have
rested, had not Welensky travelled to London in July and while
there been persuaded that the British Government might agree
to give federation a hearing.[1] Between these two events a third
took place: in May Dr Malan's Nationalist Party won an
unexpected victory in the South African general election. This
was to prove of crucial importance to the federalists' case. On
the one hand, it emphasized to British public opinion the cultural dissimilarities between South Africa and Southern
Rhodesia, and obscured the similarities in native policy. And on
the other it revived the Colonial Office's long-standing fear of
Afrikaner nationalism.

Welensky returned home and succeeded in convincing
Huggins that federation was an acceptable substitute for amal-
gamation. 'Under a federal system,' he told the Northern
Rhodesian Legislative Council in November, 'the chances of

the three territories getting dominion status must be immediately immensely improved.'[2] Soon afterwards the federalists adopted as their watchword 'partnership', a term which served to stress further the differences between Central and South Africa and which could cover a multitude of evils.

On 16 and 17 February 1949, a small group of settlers from the Rhodesias and Nyasaland met, at Huggins's suggestion, at Victoria Falls. Their deliberations took place amid a curious mixture of secrecy and publicity. No African or official representatives were invited; no formal demands were made, and no detailed arrangements formulated. All that emerged to public view was that the delegates had approved unanimously the creation of a Central African federation, and – via a series of inspired leaks to the press – a broad general picture of the federation they envisaged. This was a highly centralized grouping, in which the territorial governments would retain responsibility only for such matters as African administration, agriculture and education. As a further sop to Africans, they were to be allowed a token presence in the advisory upper house of the proposed bicameral federal legislature.

In private, Welensky made no bones about the fact that the attraction of federation to himself and his fellow Northern Rhodesian delegates was that through it they could rid themselves of Colonial Office rule.[3] To the Nyasaland delegates, who represented only a small proportion of their territory's Europeans, it was the prospect of accelerated economic development. To the Southern Rhodesians, it was the expectation of rapid progress to independence as a dominion, and a share in Northern Rhodesia's copper revenues.

Eleven days later, another small group of Central Africans met at Banda's house in Brondesbury Park, and 'decided, without a single dissent, that the proposed Federation of Central Africa would not be in the best interests of Africans of Nyasaland and Northern Rhodesia and must, therefore, be rejected.' Banda was asked to draw up a memorandum setting out a common policy 'on behalf of and on authority of Nyasaland and Northern Rhodesian Africans in the United Kingdom'.[4] It appeared on 1 May, and was distributed, over the

signatures of Banda and Harry Nkumbula,* then a student at
the London School of Economics, to the Nyasaland and
Northern Rhodesian Congresses† and other sympathetic
organizations in the protectorates and in Britain.

In common with many other Africans, Banda had hoped that
the interracial unity imposed by the war, when Africans and
Europeans had fought side by side in defence of the same liberty
and justice, might herald a new era of racial cooperation. In
Nyasaland something of this sort had indeed taken place, but
that it had not extended to the Rhodesias had been made clear
by the Victoria Falls conference. There, as Banda put it, Huggins
and Welensky had demonstrated beyond doubt that 'the proposed federation will not be a commonwealth, in which Europeans and Africans will be equal partners, but a slave state in
which the Europeans will be the privileged masters and the
Africans the unprivileged serfs.'

The basis of Banda's argument, which took the form of an
extended comparison of the policies pursued by the Colonial
Office, Southern Rhodesia and South Africa, was that a Central
African union would be dominated by the Government of
Southern Rhodesia – 'the accepted champion of the settlers'
interests and the recognized oracle of white supremacy in
Central Africa'. This would be bad from a political standpoint
alone, Banda reasoned, but in its effects on protectorate Africans it would be catastrophic. Whereas Britain regarded
Africans as 'human beings, with a right to a dignified and
refined existence', and had embarked upon a programme
of political and educational tutelage, Southern Rhodesia
rejected 'even the very idea of common and equal citizenship',
and discouraged Africans from studying overseas for fear
that 'when they return to Southern Rhodesia, they will . . .

* The meeting had requested Banda and Nkumbula to draw up the memorandum jointly, but the latter delegated the work to Banda. The quoted
excerpts which follow are taken from the typescript version of the document,
and the original punctuation has been retained (H. K. Banda, and H. M.
Nkumbula, *Federation in Central Africa*, 1 May 1949, photostat copy in
Salisbury archives).

† The latter was formed from the Federation of African Societies in July
1948 (Rotberg, *Rise of Nationalism*, pp. 211–12).

challenge . . . the notion that Europeans are intrinsically superior. . . .'

. . . of all the Europeans in Central Africa [wrote Banda], those in Southern Rhodesia have the worst antipathy towards Africans. They are against giving the Africans any rights whether civil, political, industrial, commercial or cultural. They look upon Africans as inferior beings, with no right to a dignified and refined existence and fit only as hewers of wood and drawers of water for Europeans. . . .

They do not even pretend that they are in Africa to help the Africans, but blatantly declare that they are in Africa to live and to rule. . . . Any African who is not demonstrably servile and obsequious is classified as cheeky or impertinent. And he can be kicked or beaten with no hope of receiving justice in the courts of law. Because all magistrates expect dutiful and good Africans to be servile and obsequious before all, and to all, Europeans.

It is these European settlers . . . who will rule and govern the federation. . . . From such Europeans and from such a Government, we . . . could never hope to receive the same treatment as we are now receiving under the Government provided for us by the United Kingdom. . . . Under the Government provided for us by the United Kingdom the relationship between us and the authorities is one of ward and warden, or trust and trustee. The cardinal principle in administration is guidance or guardianship. But under the government provided by Southern Rhodesia, the relationship between us and the authorities will be one of slaves and masters, and the cardinal principle in administration will be domination.

From this dual threat, of the turning back of the protectorates' 'political and cultural clock' and of Southern Rhodesian over-rule, Banda turned to the colour bar, which, he declared, had become 'the accepted political philosophy of the Colony . . . on [which], he [Sir Godfrey Huggins] has built his entire political career.'

Is it not, therefore, reasonable to suppose [he asked] that a man who has so vigorously and persistently pursued a policy of discrimination and segregation in Southern Rhodesia will extend this policy to Nyasaland and Northern Rhodesia?

Federation, Banda wrote, was 'the thin end of the wedge. . . .' It was 'amalgamation under the guise of federation. . . . the same old pill of amalgamation, coated with the sugar of federation to make it easier for the Africans and the Imperial Government to swallow.' Huggins and Welensky were still at heart amalgamationists, as they themselves had made clear, and 'only those who are politically blind' could fail to see that, once given the opportunity, they would transform federation into 'amalgamation in fact, if not in name'.

The settlers in Southern Rhodesia, like those in the protectorates, resented the restraints imposed on their native policies by the threat of the imperial veto, Banda declared. They resented even more the interest taken in their affairs by British M.P.s and pro-African pressure groups, and hence, indirectly, by the British people. 'British public opinion,' Banda wrote, was 'a thorn in [their] vulnerable and highly sensitive flesh.' But once dominion status was achieved, the settlers would have 'an imperium over the destiny of Africans of Central Africa' and the Colonial Office would no longer exert even residual control over the extent of their subjugation.

In a long concluding summary, Banda explained his own standpoint and that of the emergent intelligentsia for which he spoke:

We are not actuated by any unwillingness to enter upon a political union with our fellow Africans in Southern Rhodesia . . . [or] by any feeling of hostility towards Europeans of that colony. . . . [But] if we accept federation under present circumstances we will . . . jeopardize our political and social future. . . .

We are asked to believe, that if federation comes, none of the rights we now possess . . . will be tampered with. . . . Unfortunately we are unable to put our trust in any guarantees, given by any European community in Africa, in absolute political control over the Africans. . . .

With the bitter experience of our fellow Africans in the Union of South Africa before us, with the equally painful experience of our fellow Africans in Southern Rhodesia, what reasons have we for supposing that we . . . will fare any better? . . .

We are, therefore, unwilling to accept the proposed federation or even to discuss it, guarantees or no guarantees. . . .

In 1928, the Hilton Young Commission stated . . . that until the Africans were able to take part in a representative form of government, and until the Europeans were willing to accept them as full partners in such a system, the imperial government must retain the right to intervene in all business of government in East and Central Africa. We are in complete agreement. . . .

When that time comes, we . . . shall be willing to enter upon a federal union with Southern Rhodesia, providing the constitution of any such federal union guarantees . . . the Africans' universal suffrage, on the basis of common citizenship and common representation . . . [and] the right of secession by any of the federated territories. . . .

We reject the notion, and shall reject it . . . in the future, that because of the supposed backwardness and ignorance of our people, any group of self-appointed aristocrats, benevolent or malevolent,* has any right to deny us a voice in the affairs of the country we call our own and our home.

Promoters of the federation speak of partnership between Africans and Europeans. . . . We too desire partnership . . . but this partnership must be a real partnership, and not a façade, which conceals domination. . . . We, too, must be on the board of directors and in the inner councils of the affairs of the firm.

The memorandum was probably the most comprehensive statement ever to appear of the reasons for Africans' rejection of federation. Its 10,000 words added up to a closely argued, controlled exposure of settler hypocrisy. And while it was in its lack of personal abuse and vituperation a gentlemanly attack – prefiguring the idea which Banda would develop later that it was the system, not the individual, which was at fault – it reflected in him the beginnings of a new militancy and a retreat from pacifism.

In this he had been influenced as much by events in South Africa as by those in Southern Rhodesia. Throughout the postwar years Banda had watched with disgust the repeated failures of Smuts's Government to implement the democratic principles of which its leader spoke so often.[5] Now that Smuts had been displaced by Malan and apartheid had been introduced, he wrote of the servitude 'from which only a major war or a major revolution can ever free our brothers and sisters across the

*This reference is to an alleged statement by Huggins at Victoria Falls that 'he doubted if the Africans came from the same human family as other people and that, in his opinion, they . . . must be ruled by a benevolent aristocracy' (Banda and Nkumbula, op. cit.).

Limpopo'.[6] Such sentiments were far removed from the conscientious objection of his Liverpool days. But, as Banda
explained to a friend, he could no longer believe that pacifism
was practicable when the unarmed were utterly oppressed by
the very heavily armed.[7]

Banda's disillusionment with the white settlers also led him to
take up a more determinedly pan-African stance:

. . . if self-preservation is the first law of nature [Banda wrote],
solicitude for one's kinsman is the second. No responsible African in
Nyasaland or Northern Rhodesia would ever . . . be content with his
own political freedom while his brothers and sisters in Southern
Rhodesia suffer. . . .

The formation of an organic union between Nyasaland and
Northern Rhodesia was now 'overdue', he added.[8]

Just how little faith Banda had in the settlers of Central
Africa he demonstrated in a letter to Gore-Brown (who evidently now regretted ever having mentioned federation). 'All
talk of waiting for details,' he wrote, 'was simply falling into the
trap, which was being well set for us. And I for one was not
going to fall into that trap.'[9]

Others reasoned likewise. In Nyasaland Sam K. K. Mwase
called an emergency conference of Congress at Chilenje on 12
March, which declared, with less sophistication than Banda but
no less sincerity:

The pass law which we consider to be the Roman yoke, will be
introduced in Nyasaland and we shall not be a free people on our
own soil. . . . Our economic life will be crippled; family ties broken.
This is what we do not want to happen. Long live the Colonial
Office.[10]

In Northern Rhodesia, Congress, the African Representative
Council and the provincial councils all announced their opposition to any form of closer association. In the absence of official
representations from Salisbury or Lusaka, Creech Jones told
the House of Commons at the end of March that the Government saw no cause for calling a conference to discuss the Victoria Falls proposals. Six weeks later, when he visited Central
Africa to sound out local opinion, he assured Africans that there

would be no move towards federation without extensive consultation. 'We shall honour the responsibilities we have entered into and shall not transfer our responsibilities or abrogate them,' he told members of Nyasaland's Central Provincial Council.[11]

African fears then abated somewhat, if only because Creech Jones's performance had visibly exasperated the settlers. But Banda was not taken in. He wrote to Gore-Brown: 'As I can see it, the Europeans are angry with [Creech Jones] . . . not because he said anything that favoured Africans to any newer extent, but because he refused to reverse the British traditional policy in Central Africa.'[12] In the hiatus which followed Creech Jones's visit, white opinion steadily mounted in favour of federation and Banda strove to exert such influence as he could in the opposite direction. Banda now campaigned on two fronts. In Britain he agitated through the Fabian Bureau and sympathetic M.P.s. In Central Africa he concentrated his energies on his farming project at Kasungu. If Nyasas could show that left to themselves they could develop their country, Banda seems to have reasoned, they would have a strong argument against the much-vaunted economic advantages of federation. In any event, he spent a great deal of money on the venture, buying land and machinery, and was desperately keen that it should succeed.*

At some stage Banda also considered leaving London for Lusaka. This was apparently in the belief that if he could set up a determinedly multiracial practice in Central Africa, it might help to soften racial antagonisms and thus reduce federalist

* See Macdonald, *African Education*; and Banda to Phiri, 5 February, 14 June and 30 September 1950, privately held. Banda appointed Elias Mtepuka, a brilliant African journalist who had recently resigned from the settler-owned African Newspapers group, to manage the enterprise. He also launched, in 1951, a fish and foodstuffs transportation business under the name, 'The Malawi Trading and Transport Company'. Banda later claimed that he founded the latter concern to raise funds for Congress, but it seems more likely that it was designed to serve the same purpose as the farming venture, with which it was administratively interlinked. (Sanger, *Emergency*, p. 189; *Hansard*, Zomba, 13 December 1963, p. 1024, and 21 December 1966, p. 283.) Mtepuka was assisted by Phiri and Banda's two half-brothers, Rubben and Hanock (Banda to Phiri, ibid., and Sanger, ibid.; but *Sunday Mail*, 5 June 1960, conflicts).

momentum. Northern Rhodesia was the obvious choice for such a scheme, for in Southern Rhodesia segregatory legislation would have made it all but impossible, and in Nyasaland, where Europeans were for the most part still unconvinced of federation's advantages, it would have been unnecessary. However the Northern Rhodesian Government got wind of his intentions and informed him that if he proceeded with them he would be declared a prohibited immigrant.[13]

In December 1949, Huggins gave notice of Southern Rhodesia's intention to leave the Central African Council because its work was 'disappointing in relation to its cost, and ... further progress cannot be made without some form of closer political association.'[14] With the existing alternative to federation thus eliminated, the last obstacle in its way was removed. In Britain, financial and industrial circles were tending to the view that federation deserved closer examination; a group of senior officials in the Colonial Office regarded it as a possible counterweight to Afrikaner nationalism in the South; and another, less clearly defined pressure group was attracted to the grand design of a middle-of-the-road multiracial state in Central Africa in which Africans and Europeans would work together in 'partnership'. In Salisbury, Huggins sat tight to await the British general election.

Meanwhile in Nyasaland Congress's fortunes reached a new low point as a result of continued financial mismanagement. Sangala replaced Mwase as provisional President-General and entrusted Congress's administration to its Blantyre branch, pending the election of new office-holders. With advice and financial help from Banda, Sangala began the laborious business of trying to get the movement back on to its feet.[15]

The autumn of 1950 saw the Labour Party returned to power, but in place of the cautious and experienced Creech Jones a trade unionist with little experience of colonial problems, James Griffiths, became Colonial Secretary. In November, barely a fortnight after taking office, he announced in the House of Commons that a conference of officials from the Colonial and Commonwealth Relations Offices, the Central African Council and the three Central African governments would be held in

London to investigate the closer association issue afresh. Although he stressed that the conference would be 'purely exploratory', and that adequate opportunities would be afforded for the discussion of any proposals the officials might put forward, it was a victory for the federalists because it was a conference of officials – rather than of policy-makers. It is the task of civil servants to devise ways around problems, not to delineate them.[16]

Banda reacted sharply to this new challenge. While he did not question the British Government's good faith, he felt it would be 'political suicide' for Africans to rely entirely on its assurances. In February 1951, he had printed at his own expense several hundred copies of the 1949 memorandum, which he dispatched to the protectorates.[17] In a newly written preface Banda urged concerted action: the Congresses, he declared, must become truly mass movements and 'lead the fight against federation'.

Both in Nyasaland and Northern Rhodesia, Congress leaders must embark on an extensive and intensive campaign of organizing our people, politically. . . . In approaching chiefs, Congress leaders must show them their due respect. And they must explain to chiefs that . . . they are there to help them to understand the new way of life, and not to take away their power or influence. . . . Congress is not only for the educated people, but for all the people, educated and uneducated, chiefs and commoners.

In our fight against federation, we must expect strong opposition from European settlers. . . . They will call us agitators, extremists, troublemakers and even worse. We must not be daunted by all that. . . .

In the fight against federation we must all forget that we belong to this or that tribe, this or that district, this or that province. We must forget that we belong to Nyasaland or Northern Rhodesia. We must all unite . . . and . . . fight federation with one strong voice.[18]

The two Congresses, the African Representative Council in Northern Rhodesia and the Protectorate Council in Nyasaland all reaffirmed their irrevocable opposition to any form of closer association.[19] In Nyasaland Banda's exhortations had the additional effect of making Congress, under its new President-General, J. R. N. Chinyama, a Lilongwe farmer, redouble its efforts to recover from the Matinga crisis and its aftermath. But no matter how loudly the Africans protested, or how energetically Banda lobbied in London, it seemed that nothing could penetrate the studied calm of the officials' conference room. In June they pronounced, and found federation good.

Provided that some . . . form of closer association could be designed [their report stated] containing adequate provision for African representation and adequate protection for African interests, and provided that the services more intimately affecting the daily life of Africans were outside the scope of a Central African Government, Africans might well come to realize the very substantial advantages of closer association.[20]

The admittedly 'important difference' between the native policies of Southern Rhodesia and the protectorates, which had given the Hilton Young and the Bledisloe commissions so much trouble, presented the officials with little difficulty. 'It is essentially one of method and timing, the ultimate aim in both cases being the economic, social and political advancement of the African,' they declared, taking much on trust.[21] Federation being good on economic and ideological grounds, the officials preferred to think that African opposition was misguided. In these circumstances, 'adequate provision for African representation' entailed the indirect election of a few Africans to the proposed unicameral federal parliament; 'adequate protection of African interests' required the setting-up of an African Affairs[22] Board with powers to reserve legislation 'detrimental to African interests' for the decision of the British Government, and the appointment of a Minister of African Affairs.

The report of the officials took the federal case a long way very quickly. Griffiths decided that there was 'an increasing need for some form of closer association', and announced that a further conference would be held at Victoria Falls to discuss the officials' proposals after African opinion had been consulted.[23] In Nyasaland, Europeans, who only a year earlier had actually been relieved when Huggins had tried to excise the territory from the federal scheme,[24] began to appreciate the economic benefits they might receive. Although the majority still had reservations about allying themselves with Southern Rhodesia, a substantial minority supported federation enthusiastically. Humanitarian views were aired. The *Nyasaland Times* declared that the flow of Afrikaners into Southern Rhodesia 'underlined the urgent need for this Central African Federation, if on no other ground than on the ground of the future welfare of its African peoples, for the Afrikaners – whether Loyalist or Nationalist – share a common illiberal attitude to the Blacks.'[25] In the Rhodesias the settlers pressed home their advantage with a variety of propaganda.

Nyasas were not convinced by the Europeans' new-found solicitude for their welfare. Banda in London and Chinyama in Lilongwe both denounced the officials' proposals as a cynical plan to betray African interests.[26] District Commissioners seeking to consult African opinion, in fulfilment of Griffiths's promise, encountered suspicion and mistrust. When Griffiths himself and the Commonwealth Relations Secretary, Patrick Gordon-Walker, toured Central Africa, protectorate Africans told them they did not like Southern Rhodesia and feared that federation would lead to their absorption in it.[27] The Nyasaland Congress, whose views the *Nyasaland Times* no longer reported because they were so 'insulting and scurrilous',[28] presented the two Ministers with a long memorandum drawn up by Orton Chirwa, a Tonga from Nkhata Bay who had earlier completed a degree course at Fort Hare.* Two days later, at a meeting with the settlers' Convention of Associations, Griffiths was told: 'the Africans should be treated as children not quite old enough to decide for themselves and who had to be led'.[29]

The delegates who met at Victoria Falls on 18 September 1951 included, at Griffiths's insistence, three Africans from Nyasaland and two from Northern Rhodesia, all of whom refused even to contemplate closer association.[30] The conference ended abortively to make way for another British general election, but a communiqué was issued affirming – despite African objections – that it favoured federation in principle. The Nyasaland delegates, Chief Mwase, Clement Kumbikano and E. K. Gondwe,

---

* Chirwa had been in frequent correspondence with Banda for the previous four years (*Hansard*, Zomba, 8 March 1963, p. 659).

returned home to be accused of 'treachery' and of having compromised Nyasas' opposition by their very presence at the
talks.[31] Griffiths and Gordon-Walker returned to Britain,
where the following month a Conservative government took
power.

On 21 November, the new Colonial Secretary, Oliver
Lyttelton, announced in the House of Commons that 'His
Majesty's Government ... favour a scheme of federation
between the three territories on the general lines recommended
in the Officials' Report.' While recognizing the opposition of
Africans in the protectorates to the officials' proposals, the
Government trusted that, 'in the light of ... the economic and
other advantages of closer association, Africans will be prepared
to accept them'.[32] Thus it was decided that federation should
proceed regardless of what the majority of Central Africans
desired, and in spite of all assurances to the contrary.

Lyttelton's announcement confirmed Banda's worst fears. He
was forced to accept what until then he had refused to accept:
that Britain was indeed prepared to betray African trust. A few
months earlier an American professor had recorded his impression of a 'benign appearing physician ... [who] discussed
African countries ... with interest, but without much emotional
involvement'.[33] Overnight all this changed. Banda's earlier
motivations – the desire to help his countrymen, the need to
compensate for his failure to return home – were submerged in
a consuming, pathological hatred of federation and all its works.
For the first time in his life, politics held an equal place with
medicine.

With hopeless desperation, Banda sought to turn back the
federal tide. In February 1952 – after Lyttelton had held a preparatory meeting with Huggins and the two protectorate governors – Banda, the Rev. Kenneth Mackenzie, who had served as
a missionary in both Nyasaland and Northern Rhodesia, and
John Hatch, then a lecturer at Glasgow University, spoke at a
meeting called in Edinburgh by the World Church Group, an
inter-denominational body whose executive included Julius
Nyerere, then a student at Edinburgh University. 'Don't sell us

because you want copper,' Banda pleaded. Afterwards the meeting rejected federation 'without the free consent of the African peoples', and called for the acceleration of African political advancement in the protectorates. A few days later a similar meeting was held in Glasgow.[34] They were the first of many at which Banda spoke during the next fifteen months, some held under the auspices of the Scots clergy, others organized by Audrey Jupp's Union of Democratic Control, by the Anti-Slavery Society, in which Thomas S. L. Fox-Pitt, a recently retired Northern Rhodesian provincial commissioner, became the prime mover, and later by the Africa Bureau, founded by the Rev. Michael Scott.

In Nyasaland the realization that Banda's warnings were coming true imbued African protests with a new note of fearful urgency. Chiefs, commoners and the Congress intelligentsia did speak 'with one strong voice', but nobody would listen. The two African members of the Legislative Council, E. A. Muwamba and K. Ellerton Mposa, reminded Britain of its long-standing and oft-repeated promise not to transfer authority to anyone but the Africans.[35] In the villages and townships mass meetings were held at which Orton Chirwa, wearing academic robes, stirred up a ferment of anti-federal feeling the like of which Nyasaland had never seen before.[36] To the clamour were added the voices of the Scots missionaries. Northern Rhodesian Africans protested with equal vigour, and Nkumbula, now President of the Northern Rhodesian Congress, declared that there was 'a cold war between the British Government and the indigenous peoples of Africa'.[37]

In the House of Commons the Labour Party declared that, while it approved of federation, it disapproved of the Government's methods of imposing it. March saw the first of many protracted, exhausting and ultimately futile debates which resolved themselves into questions on the nature of trusteeship. If they achieved anything, it was to toughen Lyttelton's determination to hammer out some kind of federal scheme in the shortest possible time.

Six weeks afterwards – and three months earlier than originally planned – Lyttelton and Lord Salisbury, the Secretary for

Commonwealth Relations, chaired a conference at Lancaster House, at which the settlers' representatives won substantial modifications to the officials' scheme. The Minister for African Affairs was scrapped; the powers of the proposed African Affairs Board were eroded; and a number of subjects previously designated for territorial control were brought within the purview of the federal government, including the right to determine the federal franchise after the first federal election. One demand which Lyttelton did withstand was for the excision of Nyasaland from the federal scheme, though whether he did so on financial grounds or because it would necessitate too much rethinking is not clear. In any event, it was a doubtful benefit to the Nyasas.[38]

The conference was boycotted, with Banda's encouragement, by the eight Nyasa and Northern Rhodesian African delegates, who, after their experience at Victoria Falls, were wary of doing anything which might be construed as compromising their positions.[39] Before returning home they appealed, through the correspondence columns of *The Times*, 'to the electors of the United Kingdom, who are responsible for our welfare, to protect us from the machinations of the European minority among us, and not be deceived by their plots. . . .'[40] But this display of solidarity was marred by the two Southern Rhodesian African delegates, Joshua Nkomo and Jasper Savanhu (later a junior minister in the Federal Government), who, after agreeing at Banda's house on the conference eve to participate in the boycott, decided the following morning – at the behest of Edgar Whitehead, the Southern Rhodesian Finance Minister – that it was more prudent to attend after all.[41]

During this time a change was taking place, both in Central Africa and in Britain, in Europeans' appreciation of African opposition. As late as January 1952, the *Nyasaland Times* opined: 'They [Nyasaland Africans] are one hundred per cent against it – and that fact is well known to the Imperial Government and all the people of Southern Africa. . . . Nyasaland may have federation imposed upon it, but it will not be by the choice of any section of the Protectorate's Native population.' But the paper also noted that the African intelligentsia was 'receiving . . . directives from an ex-Nyasaland African now in London'.[42]

This cry was quickly taken up by others. Huggins spoke of 'professional agitators'.[43] Welensky referred to 'one of the most voluble African critics of federation . . . who has not set foot in Africa for about twenty years . . .'[44] and later began speaking of the 'Banda-Brockway-Pitt group'.[45] It was convenient to maintain that African opposition was not only misinformed, but deliberately exaggerated. And what was more, to those who had no first-hand knowledge of the situation, it was credible. It was a kind of nemesis that the greatest weakness in Banda's case was that he *had* stayed away from Africa for more than twenty years.

Two months after the publication of the Lancaster House Conference's 'Draft Federal Scheme',[46] the Minister of State for Colonial Affairs, Henry Hopkinson (later Lord Colyton), visited Nyasaland to discover the views of African leaders. He encountered a solid, unbroken barrier of outspoken rejection, and afterwards decided that 'most of the African people neither knew anything nor cared anything about federation'.[47] For British M.P.s representing provincial constituencies who uttered similar sentiments, there was the excuse of ignorance. But for Hopkinson, and others of his standing who followed his lead, there was no such exculpation. Before leaving the protectorate he further alienated Nyasas by informing them – by reference to the original treaties the Nyasa chiefs had made with Sir Harry Johnston – that there never had been any promise to devolve power to them. In London Banda succumbed to blank impotent fury.[48]

Meanwhile the advent of 'Gold Coast government' in West Africa, the advance of apartheid in South Africa and the beginning of the Mau Mau campaign in East Africa all helped the federalists' cause. In the protectorates administrators were instructed to abandon consultation and launch an energetic campaign to 'sell' federation. Huggins and Welensky reassured their supporters that the institution of a federal 'partnership' would entrench settler domination, not erode it. In Britain the delusion grew that African opposition was not what it seemed to be.

While the Nyasaland Congress looked about for a means of

injecting new vigour into its anti-federal campaign, Nkumbula
in Northern Rhodesia put forward a four-phase plan under
which the territory would progress to African self-government.[49]
Shortly afterwards the Nyasaland Council of Chiefs, formed by
Chief Mwase with Congress's backing, demanded an immediate
African majority in the Legislative Council. It further requested
the Government to cease its promotion of federation which, it
said, was 'a threat to [the] peace and good order of the country'.[50] But Nyasas soon realized that self-government, attractive
though the idea was, was too distant a prospect to generate the
momentum that Congress required. The only option left open
to them was a campaign of civil disobedience.

Such a step was too radical for the Congress leadership easily
to accept, and Chinyama, in particular, was afraid of the consequences non-cooperation might unleash. Banda, on the other
hand, who had made a careful study of India's progress to
independence and was an enthusiastic admirer of Ghandi, supported the plan.[51] It was from the disagreement between these
two that the first major split in Congress unfolded. The rift
came into the open in January 1953, when the leader of the militant faction in Blantyre, Mikeka Mkandawire, cabled Banda:
'If federation forced on us, non-violent resistance,' and Chinyama wrote to the *Nyasaland Times* to repudiate his action.[52]
The movement remained intact, but it had been weakened at a
crucial time.

In the same month the final inter-governmental conference
on federation opened at Carlton House Terrace in London.
Banda was joined by a delegation[53] of three chiefs, accompanied
by Orton Chirwa and B. W. Matthews Phiri, Congress's new
Secretary-General.* With Banda's help a memorandum was
presented to the Colonial Secretary, protesting against federation, demanding self-government, and proposing the replacement of the Governor and other senior officials.[54] Afterwards
the group set off on an extended speaking tour. But barely a
week later, the conference ended in agreement – at the price of
further concessions to the settlers.[55]

---

*Banda personally purchased winter clothing and paid hotel bills for the
entire group.

In a brief, bitter speech, Banda gave voice to the extent
of his disillusionment and, in so doing, the answer to his
critics. Britain, he said, was guilty of a 'cold, calculated,
callous and cynical betrayal of a trusting, loyal people'. He
went on:

> It is not I, the agitator in London, who is opposing federation. It is
> my people at home. You cannot bring to Central Africa partnership
> by force. Partnership between the Europeans and the Africans can
> only come from their hearts and minds. We, the Africans of Nyasa-
> land and Northern Rhodesia, are people. Some of the clauses of the
> Atlantic Charter which Mr Roosevelt and your Mr Churchill signed
> guaranteed territorial integrity and the right of any people to choose
> the form of government under which they would live. We, the
> Africans of Nyasaland and Northern Rhodesia, are people under the
> provisions of the charter and this clause that guarantees the rights of
> the people to choose their own form of government.[56]

Banda's retreat from pacifism was reluctant and incomplete.
Like those in Nyasaland, he had come to believe in non-violent
resistance, which in the context of Nyasaland would inevitably
become violent, because there was no other alternative.

In February the chiefs asked leave to present a petition to the
Queen. The Colonial Secretary advised against it, and permission
was refused.[57] In March the Council of Chiefs at Lilongwe discussed the rejection, and announced in a warning cable to the
Colonial Office: 'Imposition of Federation against Africans'
solid rejection will be resisted at all costs.'[58] Later that month
the House of Commons approved the Government's decision to
implement the Carlton House Terrace agreement.[59]

On 5 April the Rev. Michael Scott arrived in Blantyre bringing instructions from Banda on the carrying-out of the civil disobedience campaign.* That afternoon he spoke at an Emergency Conference of Congress in the Blantyre market, at which
– despite Chinyama's timorousness – some 3,000 Africans
resolved to meet the imposition of federation with 'the strongest

---

*It was perhaps at this stage that Banda intimated to Congress that he
might soon visit Nyasaland for a short holiday. In the event, however, it did
not materialize (Sanger, *Emergency*, p. 195).

non-violent resistance'. In response to a suggestion from Banda it was decided to set up a Supreme Action Council of Congress and the Council of Chiefs to direct the campaign. The conference further threatened a nation-wide strike, the non-payment of taxes, a boycott of European-owned stores, and, this time at Scott's suggestion, appeals to the United Nations and the International Court of Justice.[60] Scott, the *Nyasaland Times* concluded, had come to Nyasaland 'on a cranky mission'.[61]

On 9 April the Southern Rhodesian electorate, comprising some 50,000 people of whom 380 were black, voted in favour of federation.[62] Ten days later the Nyasaland and Northern Rhodesian Legislative Councils likewise voted their approval. In Zomba, before the vote was taken, Muwamba and Mposa 'rose and left the chamber' in dignified protest. As Mposa put it: 'It is for shame that a civilized and Christian Government should adopt such a scheme which is distasteful to the poor Africans.'[63]

One last attempt was made to find a constitutional remedy. Twenty-four chiefs, led by Chief Mwase, petitioned the Speaker to be allowed to appear before the bar of the House of Commons; alternatively, they suggested, parliament could follow the precedent of 1931 and appoint a select committee to ascertain the true feelings of the Nyasa people. On 4 May the petition was rejected.[64]

The Supreme Action Council ordered Africans to stay away from all official functions and to refrain from dancing, because 'it was a time of crying'.[65] Mwase refused an invitation to the Queen's coronation (but the Yao chief, Kawinga, was induced to accept in his stead).[66] In mid-May a number of prominent chiefs, including the Paramount of the Ncheu Angoni, Philip Gomani, instructed their people to disregard the much-hated agricultural regulations, known as *malimidwe,* and to refuse to pay taxes. Gomani was deposed by the Government and an attempt by the police to arrest him occasioned a minor riot. Subsequently he fled to Mozambique, accompanied by his two sons and the Rev. Michael Scott, whence all four were returned to Nyasaland by the Portuguese authorities. For Gomani the

incident brought banishment; for Scott, deportation. After
this show of strength the Government had little difficulty
in persuading the other chiefs to retract. The planned
boycott of the Coronation celebrations at the beginning of
June was only partially successful, and by July, when
Mckinley Q. Y. Chibambo and two others were charged
with sedition, the Government appeared to have the situation
well in hand.[67]

Although the pretence of non-cooperation was maintained
for some weeks longer, Congress became resigned to the
inevitability of federation. It was decided that Nyasas should
boycott all federal institutions, including the federal parliament.
But this was a controversial decision which gave rise to a further
split and the formation, by Charles Matinga, A. J. Mponda and
Orton Chirwa, of a new group, the Nyasaland African Progressive Association.[68] Congress, already labouring under internal
dissension, grew still weaker. The Supreme Action Council was
disbanded. And the mood of the Nyasa people settled into
sullen resentment.

On 1 August the Central African Federation came officially
into being. Many theories were later put forward to explain
why Africans resisted it. It was said that they had been prejudiced by the secrecy of the 1949 conference at Victoria Falls;
that consultation was a technique inappropriate to a colonial
autocracy; and that it was a fatal mistake, once having consulted African opinion, to reject it. All this was no doubt so.
But the truth of the matter was that the Africans of the protectorates had opposed any form of closer association with
Southern Rhodesia from the time they had first acquired a
political voice.

In the same month Banda left Britain for the Gold Coast.[69]
He had been bitterly disappointed by the collapse of the non-
cooperation campaign, and shocked by Attlee's announcement
that the Labour Party, recognizing that the Federation was an
accomplished fact, would henceforth do its best to see that it
succeeded.[70] Before he left he told friends that he did not wish
to remain in London where he would be obliged to continue in
opposition to the Federation, which he knew would in any case

at that stage be futile. And he vowed not to return to Nyasaland while it remained in force.*

But there was another and more important reason for Banda's sudden departure from London that August. Major French was about to sue his wife for divorce on the grounds of adultery. In that seemingly unrelated, unimportant event lay the seeds of the tragedy which was to be Banda's life for the next five years. It was he who had been named as co-respondent.[71]

* Unattributable interview. This was the substance of Banda's explanation to the Devlin Commission of his reasons for leaving London. Surprisingly he also told the commission that 'although his views about Federation were unaltered . . . he wanted to give it a chance' (Cmd 814).

Chapter 5
The Gold Coast Episode

A psychiatrist might argue that the extreme, obsessive quality of Banda's puritanism was such that a reaction against it was at some point bound to occur. But while there evidently was in his personality a conflict of some sort – otherwise it would be impossible to explain what later took place in the Gold Coast – it required a combination of exceptional strains and tensions to educe it.

At least three factors played a part in leading Banda to the anomalous situation in which he spent his last months in London. The first and most important was his acute sense of personal betrayal by the British Government, which clearly had a traumatic effect on him. The second was his failure to achieve the task he had set himself – the prevention of Federation. And the third was the collapse of his farming venture at Kasungu and of the Malawi Trading and Transport Company, as a result of the inexperience of those whom Banda had appointed to manage them.[1]

Thus it was in a world in which everything was turning sour that Banda looked to Margaret French for solace and companionship. But the nature of their relationship added a new tension to the earlier, causative pressures, for the puritanism he was repudiating was deeply ingrained. The shock of discovery and the humiliation of having his name paraded in the divorce courts (although Banda was fortunate in that very few of his friends and patients ever learnt what had happened) compounded the strain, and he reached Accra mentally exhausted and in a state of acute depression. It was then that the most crushing blow was delivered, from a different and quite unexpected source: the Nyasaland African Congress.

On the evening of 17 August, a small group of Europeans apprehended two Africans stealing oranges from the Tennent estate near Cholo. The commotion attracted other Africans and the Europeans, out-numbered, released their prisoners and fled, throwing into the boot of their car the sacks of stolen oranges. The Africans believed that the Europeans had killed the thieves and driven off with their bodies, and next morning a crowd numbering about a thousand attacked the Tennent estate office and near-by European dwellings. Shortly after midday an African was killed when a policeman accidentally discharged his rifle, and throughout the afternoon police and crowd inter-mittently exchanged tear-gas grenades and stones. The crowd eventually dispersed after police had arrested a village headman whom they described as a leading agitator.[2]

Although the Tennent incident, as it came to be called, was ostensibly non-political, it stemmed in large part from the polarization of racial attitudes which Federalism had induced. In the minds of Africans, Europeans had become so associated with the imposition of Federation that the distinction between the two had become blurred. The events of 17 and 18 August, while unimportant in themselves, completed this identification and set alight the smouldering discontent which had built up during the previous three months. Subsequent disturbances at Chiradzulu, Cholo, Domasi, Mlanje and Port Herald[3] were not the result of Congress intimidation, as the Nyasaland Govern-ment claimed,[4] but the unorganized, violent expression of Afri-cans' hatred of Federation and all they thought it stood for.

Congress was divided in its approach to these new develop-ments. While Chinyama vacillated, Mkandawire's faction encouraged the unrest by linking Federation with long-standing grievances, amongst them the shortage of land and the *thangata* system, under which estate owners were permitted to compel Africans living on their property to supply labour in lieu of rent.

At the end of August Nyasaland's Governor, now Geoffrey Colby, summoned Chinyama to the secretariat, where he is said to have reminded him of the summary execution of his father Filipo Chinyama, for his part in the Chilembwe rising.[5] The Congress Executive hastily issued a statement dissociating itself from the disturbances and terminating the non-cooperation campaign. A week later the Council of Chiefs followed suit, and by the end of September the disorders were at an end.[6] Eleven Africans had been killed and seventy-two injured.[7]

Soon afterwards Chinyama resigned the Congress Presidency and went temporarily into retirement. In his place the dominant figure in Congress was Wellington Manoah Chirwa, no relation to his namesake, Orton Chirwa, but like him a Tonga and recent graduate of Fort Hare. Chirwa was at his most effective when working in small groups, and it was he who reopened the debate on whether or not Congress should contest the Federal elections. Unless Congress put up candidates, he argued, the two Federal seats would go by default to the Nyasaland African Progressive Association, which would not defend Nyasa interests.[8] Eventually the Congress executive was won round to this view, and it was decided that Chirwa and Clement Kumbikano should stand, on the firm understanding that they would resign their seats once they had protested against Federation on Congress's behalf.

Chirwa – 'the master of intrigue', as fellow Congressmen called him – had little difficulty in ensuring that the African Protectorate Council elected himself and Kumbikano in preference to the N.A.P.A. candidates, Orton Chirwa and Matinga.[9]

To Banda, Chinyama's repudiation of 'direct action' and Chirwa's decision to become a Federal M.P. were the ultimate betrayal. Chinyama and the rest of the Congress Executive, he concluded, were cowards; Chirwa, by so compromising his position as to participate in a key Federal institution, was a stooge who would renege on his countrymen for an M.P.'s salary.[10] That Nyasas should so easily resign themselves to Federation Banda found inexplicable. Having no first-hand knowledge of the situation in Nyasaland, he underestimated the difficulties Congress faced, and began to wonder whether its opposition had ever been more than superficial.

In utter disgust, Banda issued a press statement condemning Chirwa's action and announcing his own withdrawal from politics.[11] Afterwards he paid courtesy calls on Kojo Botsio and Nkrumah, annoying the latter by his refusal to accept a medical post in the Gold Coast administration. Nkrumah evidently

wanted him to join George Padmore and the other old com-
rades with whom he liked to surround himself.[12] But Banda had
no desire to remain in the limelight, and settled instead in the
Ashanti capital of Kumasi, setting himself up in private practice.[13] There Mrs French joined him, and there they lived
together as man and wife.[14]

For the next three years Banda cut himself off completely
from his former life. He paid little attention to events either in
the Gold Coast or in the Federation, and refused to answer
letters from Congress. In their place, he devoted himself to his
practice[15] and his family.

Congress's failure to prevent the imposition of Federation discredited the movement in the eyes of most of its followers. The
300 branches it had boasted in 1953 were a year later reduced to
a mere fifteen of which only the Blantyre branch was effective.
The internal split between the Chinyama and Mkandawire factions, which lingered on long after Chinyama's resignation; the
external split with N.A.P.A.; Banda's withdrawal of support;
and above all the fiasco of the southern province disturbances
brought the movement to the brink of collapse. As in 1948, it
fell to Sangala, who had now assumed the Presidency, to keep
Congress ticking over under the watchful eye of a hostile and
suspicious government.[16]

For the next year Congress did little more than issue sporadic
public statements, demanding self-government and reiterating
the iniquity of Federation. Sangala wrote to sympathetic
British M.P.s of the unreality of 'partnership' and compared
the life led by African leaders to that in a concentration camp.
Congress resolved that Africans should not pay any income tax
the Federal Government might levy until they 'shall have
attained self-government ... and when there shall be no discrimination on the basis of colour'.[17] When the Colonial Secretary paid a brief visit to Nyasaland, a Congress delegation
voiced its grievances so volubly that 'Mr Lyttelton had a head-
ache and left unhappy'.[18] But Sangala made clear in a letter to
Congress branches that there was to be no question of unconstitutional action. Congressmen, he wrote, were 'required to

obey all the laws of the government and to refrain from doing things which will bring the Congress into disrepute or disgrace.'[19]

At the end of 1954, two events occurred which radically altered this situation. The first was the decision, after an informal meeting in Blantyre on 30 December, of a group of young graduates from Fort Hare and Makerere to ally themselves with Congress.[20] The second was the commencement of discussion within the Secretariat on the possibility of granting a larger measure of unofficial representation in the Legislative Council.[21] The one interacted with the other. The two leading members of the graduate group, Henry Blasius Masauko Chipembere, a plump, baby-faced Yao from Fort Johnston who had recently graduated from Fort Hare, and Murray William Kanyama Chiume, a small, restless Tonga from Usisya, lately of Makerere, injected into Congress a new vigour and enthusiasm. The Government, recognizing the need for a constitutional safety-valve, pushed ahead more quickly with its plans for reform.

Six months later it was announced that African representation in the Council was to be increased from three to five (a third African nominated member, counterbalanced by an extra European unofficial, had joined Muwamba and Mposa at the end of 1953), and the number of European unofficials from five to six. For the Government there would be eleven official members with the Governor presiding. Two of the European unofficials, who for the first time were to be elected directly, would sit on the Executive Council, while Asian representation and the seating of a missionary representing African interests would fall away. The African members were to be chosen by the provincial councils sitting as electoral colleges.[22]

Neither Congress, which had publicly campaigned for universal suffrage and an outright African majority, nor the settlers were satisfied with these arrangements, but each accepted them. In March 1956, both Chipembere and Chiume, who with help from Sangala and Manoah Chirwa had been chosen as Congress's candidates in the southern and northern provinces, were elected by a wide margin. Of its other nominees, N. D. Kwenje and Chinyama were successful in the southern and central provinces, but Richard Katengeza, Chinyama's running mate, was narrowly defeated by Dunstan Chijozi, a Congress sympathizer but not a member of the movement.[23]

Their success did much to restore Congress's self-respect, and it took on a more militant mien. In the Legislative Council, Chipembere and Chiume, and to a lesser extent the other African members, required answers to awkward questions, demanded an end to discrimination, vilified Federation, and generally made life difficult for the Government. Among educated Africans, *Hansard* quickly became a best-seller; no one before in Nyasaland had dared to question so openly the motives and methods of colonial autocracy.* Outside the Council, Congress's demand that Nyasaland be allowed to secede from the Federation, first put forward at the prompting of Chipembere and Chiume at its eleventh annual conference at Lilongwe in April 1955,[24] was pressed with such vigour that the British Government found it necessary to affirm in the House of Commons Nyasaland's continuing Federal membership. Shortly afterwards, Congress's new Secretary-General, T. D. T. Banda (no relation to Dr Banda), was convicted of sedition and fined.

Congress's achievement of territorial representation highlighted the anomaly of Manoah Chirwa's position in the Federal Assembly. When Congress had been at its weakest, Chirwa's and Kumbikano's presence in the Federal parliament had done much to keep the movement on its feet. But as it had grown stronger, demands had begun to be voiced for them to honour their pledges and resign their seats.[25] Chirwa was still the most influential man in Congress, despite his having no official status in the movement, and he had been able to argue successfully that his resignation would deprive it of a public platform which it could not replace.[26] Despite the protest resignation of T. D. T. Banda's predecessor, Kinross W. Kulujili,[27] and an

---

*The speeches Chipembere and Chiume made in the Legislative Council had the same effect on Nyasa youth as Banda's opposition in London to Federation had had on Chipembere, five years earlier. Chipembere later recalled how he had found it 'remarkable that an African could be so courageous or bold in attacking . . . the Colonial Office and the Nyasaland Government' (Chipembere, interview; see note 100, chapter 3).

attempt in December 1955 by Mikeka Mkandawire to force a confrontation on the issue,[28] his position had remained strong.

After the elections, however, Chirwa's usefulness in the Federal Assembly diminished, and Chipembere, Chiume and the other young militants began to feel that his presence there compromised their demands for secession. The controversy over Federal representation soon became the dominant issue in Congress and a rift appeared, similar to that of 1953, between the young radicals and the more conservative elements.[29] As the months went by, Chipembere and Chiume became increasingly dissatisfied with the timidity of their older colleagues, and towards the end of 1956 began to search for new methods of making the movement more effective.[30]

The next eighteen months saw the unfolding of a sequence of events which brought Banda to the nadir of his life, and in so doing provided the impetus for his return to Nyasaland. It began undramatically. In November 1956 he received a letter from Chipembere, who, perhaps remembering how three years earlier he had denounced Chirwa's election, now solicited his support for the campaign to bring about the Federal M.P.s' resignations. Banda evidently regarded this request with mixed feelings, for while he elected to reply he made plain that he was reluctant to involve himself anew in Congress's affairs. He counselled caution and recommended that Chirwa and Kumbikano be allowed to continue in office until the end of the Federal parliament's life, up to two years later.[31]

Chipembere and Chiume rejected this advice and on 31 December, at a Congress meeting in Ndirande, proposed a motion demanding that the two M.P.s step down. After a debate which is said to have lasted eleven hours, it was overwhelmingly defeated.[32]

This débâcle completed the young militants' disillusionment with the Congress leadership, but at the same time demonstrated to them that on their own they could not hope to win over the older Congressmen. Although they persuaded Sangala to step down in favour of T. D. T. Banda, they appreciated that this was only an interim solution.[33] T. D. T. Banda had 'great qualities', Chipembere later explained, but he lacked the stuff of true leadership. What was needed was a man of about fifty or sixty, who would command the respect of the moderates and yet be sympathetic to the aspirations of the younger men. The only possible candidate was Dr Banda in Kumasi.[34]

In March 1957, when T. D. T. Banda travelled to the Gold Coast to attend the Independence celebrations, he visited Banda and, at Chipembere's suggestion, asked him to come home to assist in Congress's leadership. But while Dr Banda may have found the idea attractive, he had no intention of returning to politics. He still shunned publicity of any kind, even to the extent of refusing, despite a personal invitation from Nkrumah, to attend the celebrations in Accra.* So when T. D. T. Banda announced, on his return to Nyasaland, that he had 'the inspiring news [that] our Dr Hastings K. Banda, Ph.B., M.D., L.R.C.P., L.R.C.S., L.R.F.P.S., will return to Nyasaland within a few years to come',[35] it was something of an exaggeration. Dr Banda had fobbed him off with the most noncommittal of answers.

A fortnight later, Chipembere again wrote to Kumasi, forcefully restating his reasons for wanting the Federal M.P.s to resign. He also discussed at length Congress's need for a leader. What was required, he explained, was a kind of saviour. While it was wrong to be led by a single man placed in a position of great power, 'human nature is such that it needs a kind of hero to be hero-worshipped if a political struggle is to succeed.' He and Chiume were too young to fill this role, and T. D. T. Banda lacked the necessary charisma and intellectual equipment. But Dr Banda had all the appropriate qualifications: he was the right age; he already enjoyed a high reputation among educated Nyasas;† he was an intellectual; and his character combined honesty, self-denial and a spirit of cooperativeness.[36]

* Sanger, *Emergency*, p. 197. Chiume, however, maintains that Nkrumah was still so irritated by Banda's withdrawal to Kumasi that he did not send him an invitation (Chiume, op. cit.).

† Banda was generally regarded as the first Nyasa doctor, for although Dr Daniel Malekebu had qualified before him, the latter had in later life taken little interest in politics and his name was not well known to those of Chipembere's generation. (Chipembere, op. cit.)

In the normal way Banda might have paid this fresh approac[
no more attention than earlier requests. But in April, an even[
took place which cast a new and sinister light on the future c[
the Federation. The Commonwealth and Colonial Secretarie[
now Lord Home and Alan Lennox-Boyd, attended a meeting i[
London with (now Sir) Roy Welensky, who had succeede[
Huggins as Federal Prime Minister, and Julian Greenfield, h[
Minister of Justice. From it emerged a 'Joint Declaration[
which announced *inter alia* that in 1960, the earliest possib[
date in terms of the Federal constitution, a conference would b[
convened to 'consider a programme for the attainment of suc[
a status as would enable the Federation to become eligible fc[
full membership in the Commonwealth'.[37] To Africans in th[
protectorates this meant amalgamation. To Banda, in Ghan[
it meant the realization of all that he had predicted in 1949; i[
spite of himself, he began to become involved.

In his reply Banda suggested that the time had come fc[
Nyasas to take up a more uncompromising attitude to Federa[
tion. But while he now approved Chipembere's plans to di[
lodge Chirwa and Kumbikano, he still gave no indication tha[
he was prepared to make an early return.

By June Chipembere had converted T. D. T. Banda to h[
way of thinking, and the latter wrote to Dr Banda asking him t[
submit a memorandum on Federal representation to Congress'[
forthcoming annual conference in August. A month late[
Chipembere informed him that he intended to ask the con[
ference to make a formal request that he return, and to appoin[
him in the meantime Congress's official representative in Ghan[
and a member *in absentia* of the executive committee. Thes[
proposals, he said, had already received strong backing fron[
Chiume and Dunduzu Chisiza, a slightly built, bespectacle[
young intellectual whom they had appointed Congress'[
organizing secretary.[38]

At about the same time, C. B. B. Kanchunjulu, who ha[
succeeded T. D. T. Banda as Secretary-General, sent writte[
notice to the two Federal M.P.s that they must either resig[
their seats or face ejection from Congress. Chirwa may still hav[
genuinely believed that Federation could best be attacked fron[

within; but he was also loath to resign what was a very lucrative post.[39] In any event, both he and Kumbikano refused to step down and when, on 3 August, Congress discussed their position, Banda's memorandum had a decisive effect in bringing about their expulsion. Chipembere's proposals met with strong support and a telegram was dispatched to Banda, urging him to return at the earliest possible date 'for the purpose of helping in the national leadership in the struggle for liberation'.[40] But at this point a new factor was introduced into the situation, for while Chipembere and Chiume were urging his return, Banda was undergoing difficulties in Ghana.

Since arriving in Ghana, Banda had been under constant strain as a result of the conflict between his avowed puritanism and his illicit relationship with Margaret French.[41] By the end of 1957 these pressures had been augmented by professional difficulties. On 7 December of that year, a notice appeared in the Ghana Gazette, signed by the Registrar of Medical Practitioners and Dentists in the Ghanaian Ministry of Health,[42] announcing that Banda had been suspended from practice.

The Gazette notice did not state any reasons and Banda himself has never spoken of this period of his life, although both Professor Edwin Munger[43] and Sir Roy Welensky[44] have referred to the suspension.

Shortly afterwards it was announced that the charges levelled against him which had led to his suspension were false; on 10 May 1958 a further notice appeared in the Ghana Gazette abrogating the earlier notice, and thus Banda was again free to practise in Ghana.[45] But five months had passed and by then he had already left his practice.

It is arguable whether Banda would have seriously considered returning to Nyasaland had these events not befallen him. But now that Ghana held no future for him he may have seen in the urgings of Chipembere and Chiume a chance to make a fresh start and return to respectability. Certainly he must have realized that in Nyasaland he was needed, whereas in Ghana it was patently apparent that he was not. Yet if Banda did look to Congress as a way out of the morass his life had become, it took him several months to reach a decision.* In doing so he was helped by a number of external influences.

The most important of these was the trend of political developments within the Federation. Towards the end of 1957, Welensky's demands for dominion status had become more strident, and, in response, Congress had begun to agitate for territorial constitutional advance. The urgency of its representations derived from the fact that internal reform was not due until 1960, by which time it might be too late to implement whatever changes were agreed before the Federal review conference. This in turn might mean that Congress would be unable to obtain adequate representation in Nyasaland's delegation, in which case its case at the conference would go by default. Nyasaland's new Governor, Sir Robert Armitage, held out little hope of an early start being made. He told Congress, moreover, that he felt its demands for an African majority in the Legislative Council, elected by universal suffrage, and a voice in the Executive Council, were impracticable and far too advanced.[46] In these circumstances, the Congress militants increased their pressure on Banda, augmenting the concern he himself felt at Welensky's pronouncements.

Meanwhile Banda had begun to receive letters of support from other, non-Congress sources. He had also been visited by Major Peter Moxon, a Nyasaland farmer whose brother worked in the Ghanaian Information Ministry, and the Rev. Andrew

* The 'official' version of Banda's recall from Ghana is as follows: Banda is said to have resolved on leaving London in 1953 that 'if at any time my people decided to fight and resist the Federation, and they wanted me to help them with it, then no matter what I was doing, where I was, how rich I was, what position I held, I would give up any and everything and return home.' The call came after Chipembere and Chiume, sitting under a banana tree discussing the state of the nation, 'jumped up . . . and shouted: "Hurray! Hurray! Kamuzu must come!"' The arrival of Congress's telegram in August 1957 was to Banda 'a dream', and he immediately made arrangements to return. (Banda, press-conference, 6 July 1964, privately held transcript; *Malawi News*, 30 March 1961 and 8 February 1963.)

Doig of the Blantyre synod of the Church of Scotland, the nominated representative of Nyasa African interests in the Federal Assembly. Both believed that he could exert a valuable steadying influence on the 'Young Turks', and encouraged him to return.[47] Understandably, Banda was still terribly reluctant to commit himself:[48] at the age of sixty, when most of his contemporaries were thinking of retirement, the career he was contemplating was dangerous, exacting and proverbially insecure.

When finally he intimated that he might be prepared to agree to Congress's request, Chipembere responded warmly, but warned him that it would be necessary to build up his image. He must not be frightened, Chipembere wrote, if he was 'heralded as a political messiah. Publicity of this sort could be used with advantage; it would cause great excitement and should precipitate almost a revolution in political thought.'[49] Banda's answer to that was to demand that he be guaranteed the Congress Presidency and given *carte blanche* to run the movement as he saw fit;[50] to this Chipembere agreed. In March T. D. T. Banda was suspended from office, and the Vice-President-General, B. W. Matthews Phiri, was installed in a caretaker capacity.[51]

After giving Congress a firm undertaking to return to Nyasaland within six months, Banda left Kumasi for Britain;[52] Mrs French remained in Ghana a year or so longer before she, too, returned home.[53]

In London, where he had spent his happiest and most successful years, Banda was returned to a close resemblance of his former self. He met old friends, and discussed with them the prospects for Nyasaland's secession. He spoke on television and gave interviews to the press. And he lectured public meetings on the evils of Federation, just as he had done five years before. But although his recovery was remarkable, Banda was not quite the man he had been then. The self-confidence which London had given him, Ghana had destroyed, and he would never regain it.

Meanwhile Congress mounted an intensive propaganda campaign against the day of his arrival. Chipembere later recalled preaching 'like John the Baptist' at mass meetings, extolling Banda's achievements and reeling off the long list of degrees after his name.[54] Others repeated the words John Chilembwe was said to have used shortly before he died:

There will arise in this country a greater man than myself over whom the forces of African treachery and colonial arms will not prevail. Some day this man will come. Be patient and of good cheer because Nyasaland's freedom is not lost.[55]

In June, Chipembere and Chisiza joined Banda for a meeting with Lennox-Boyd at which Congress's constitutional proposals were discussed.[56] The encounter confirmed the good reports Banda had heard of them, and he promised to leave for Blantyre as soon as he had settled his affairs. He was still uncertain of the rightness of his decision, and told friends before his departure: 'I shall soon be back, if I find that the people do not want me.'[57] But his hesitance concealed a desperate determination to succeed. In the final analysis, it was Banda's courage in adversity which returned him to Nyasaland, just as it had taken him from it, almost half a century before.

Chapter 6
Nyasaland Emergency

On Sunday, 6 July,* Banda arrived at Blantyre's tiny Chileka airport to be acclaimed as a saviour in his own land. To the three thousand Africans who gathered to greet him, it seemed like a second coming, and more than one mind turned back to the legend that John Chilembwe would one day rise again to lead Nyasas to freedom.[1] To Banda, it marked the end of a lifetime in self-imposed exile, and the beginning of a new life. He afterwards admitted that as he had stepped off the aircraft he had been close to tears.

Politics mixed incongruously with the general rejoicing. Small boys waved Union Jacks, hoarded since the visit of the Queen Mother a year before, and anti-Federal songs were sung to the tune of *John Brown's Body*;[2] Hanock Phiri gave his nephew a broom, with which to sweep away Federation;[3] and Chief Gomani's widow robed him in the skin of a civet cat, symbol of chieftainship, and garlanded him with a string of brightly coloured crackers.[4] But, beneath the gaiety, all those who welcomed him at the airport that day regarded Banda as much more than a chief. He had returned, as Chiume put it, as 'the symbol of Nyasa Independence'.[5]

At a press-conference shortly afterwards, Banda warned: 'Everyone expects that I have come with self-government in my handbag, but we will have to struggle for it.'[6] He declared that his campaign would be non-violent, and would aim at achieving universal suffrage, African majorities in the Legislative and

* Banda had been expected to arrive the previous weekend, and a rousing welcome had been prepared for him. When he had failed to appear, the crowd had become restive and refused to disperse until Chipembere had been allowed to search the aircraft. Afterwards it was discovered that his non-arrival was due to the miscarriage of a telegram, but the incident was sufficient to provoke demands by the Nyasaland members of Welensky's United Federal Party that the police force be strengthened, and that steps be taken to ensure that airways regulations were adhered to (Cmd 814, and *Hansard*, Zomba, 1 July 1958, pp. 33, 39, and 2 July 1958, pp. 71–2, 88).

Executive Councils, and secession from the Federation. But he stressed the importance of Nyasaland maintaining direct links with Britain, and spoke at length of his desire for racial harmony. His task, he said, was 'to bridge the gap of disunity' between the races.[7]

His statement was marked by the same note of caution which characterized all his actions in the first months after his return. In the novel situation in which he now found himself he felt his way carefully and often seemed worried lest Congress expected too much of him.

European reactions were on the whole favourable. The *Nyasaland Times* thought him 'a man willing to listen to argument, yet with firm views of his own', and hoped that, now he was in a position to study conditions at first hand, he would realize the advantages of Federation and withdraw his opposition to it.[8] Government officials on whom he called were impressed by the contrast between the quiet, middle-aged doctor and the young Congress militants with whom they had dealt before.

After Banda had paid brief visits to the central and northern provinces, Congress met on 1 August at Nkhata Bay for its annual conference, and he was elected President-General. He demanded, and was granted, the exclusive right to choose its office-bearers: as he later explained, he did not wish to preside over 'a fools' cabinet'.[9] Chipembere he appointed Treasurer-General; Chiume, Publicity Secretary; and Mrs Rose Chibambo, a relation by marriage of Mckinley Chibambo, to organize a Women's League. Dunduzu Chisiza, then studying economics at Fircroft College, Birmingham, was recalled to become Secretary-General, and two businessmen, Lali Lubani and Lawrence Mkata, were appointed committee members. The older men were ignored, not so much because they were old, although Banda said later that he preferred the excesses of youth to the failures of old age, but because they were discredited.[10] There was no room for ditherers.

Banda saw as his first task the building of the Party into a well-organized, disciplined and nationally based mass move-

ment, and much of the conference was given up to a discussion
of how to achieve this. Congress was heavily in debt, and for all
Chipembere's and Chiume's efforts it could claim a true
membership of not more than 15,000. To help right this situation Banda proposed the creation not only of the Women's
League, but also of a Youth League. These later proved highly
effective, both in their own right and as ginger groups.* Banda
also insisted, perhaps remembering his experiences at Wilberforce and Kokomo, that Afro-Asians and Anglo-Africans be
regarded simply as Africans.[11]

Organization, Banda maintained, was the *sine qua non* of
success: it was 'the one thing the British people fear'. Once
Congress was properly organized, 'nothing will stop us from
seceding from the Federation and getting self-government'.[12]
This was a phrase well calculated to instil in every delegate the
determination to succeed, and the conference ended on a note
of defiant optimism. The next day, a Sunday, Banda and other
members of the Executive Committee attended church: the
lesson, which he read himself, was taken from the parable of
the prodigal son.[13]

The Nkhata Bay conference marked the start of Banda's
active campaigning. Immediately afterwards he left for Mzuzu,
in the far North, to begin an extended speaking tour which
lasted until October and took him to almost every district in the
country. He later recalled having given himself six months to
set Nyasaland 'on fire';[14] one month was already up.

There is no reliable account of what Banda said, what he did,
or even of where he went, but it is clear that the tour was an
enormous success. According to the Devlin Commission, his
speeches were 'moderate in content – but highly emotional in
the way in which they were delivered', and Banda himself
remarked that he found he had an unexpected gift for mob oratory.[15] Their content was much the same wherever he spoke: he
preached the four virtues of Unity, Loyalty, Obedience and

---

* Traditionally Chewa women exhorted their menfolk in battle by singing:
'If you do not kill them, where are you going to sleep tonight?' In the modern
version members of the Congress Women's League withdrew their favours
f their husbands flagged in the nationalist struggle.

Discipline, condemned tribalism and other divisive influences, and attacked the injustice of *malimidwe* and *thangata*. Above all he vilified 'their stupid Federation', and that innocent adjective was laden with such venom that it soon became for Africans the most explosive of curses.

Banda always spoke in English with an interpreter in attendance,* but far from detracting from his popular appeal this served rather to heighten it by placing him on a par with the European ruling class. His European mannerisms reinforced this impression. Even on the hottest days he dressed as he would in England, in the familiar three-piece suit and black homburg hat, with a beige raincoat to keep off the dust and brown leather gloves. It was small wonder that Nyasas flocked to his meetings: his Englishness delighted them; his oratory stirred them. At the time of his return, Banda was already something of a legend in his own time, and thereafter Chiume worked indefatigably to create a personality cult of a kind unknown before in Central Africa. To the sophisticated minority, Banda was the supreme example of the African who had succeeded in the white man's world. To villagers, he was 'the Doctor' who would cleanse Nyasaland of the cancer of *Chitaganya* – Federation; the Moses, come to lead his people from bondage; the Messiah; the Christ-figure who would deliver Nyasas from oppression. It was a process which stopped not far short of deification.†

Banda viewed his overnight elevation to national leadership, and the massive adulation it entailed, with mixed feelings. On the one hand he regarded the messiah cult as a regrettable,

* The usual explanation for this, that during his long absence abroad he had forgotten how to speak chiNyanja, is only partly correct. In fact he could speak it, but haltingly and in phrases which were now archaic. But there were also other reasons for his preferring to use English: it was customary for a chief to converse through the agency of a go-between; and having everything translated gave him time to think what he would say next.

† The right-wing Rhodesian journalist, Harvey Ward, understated his case when he wrote (*Rhodesia Herald*, 28 November 1958): 'Probably no single man in Central Africa has exerted such a fanatical influence over the masses of a territory.'

tactical necessity: he disliked the sheep syndrome in mankind, and commented of his following: 'It makes one wonder about human nature, really.'[16] But on the other, he was grateful for the reassurance it provided at a time when he was chronically insecure. Banda's isolation and his seeming inability to adjust to his new environment showed through in a number of ways. He detested the discomforts he had to endure when touring; he sought an identity, while denouncing tribalism in others, in his own tribal affiliation, and frequently emphasized the fact of his being a Chewa;[17] and for all the sincerity of his non-racialism, he relished situations in which white people showed at a disadvantage. He later recalled how, after a meeting at Mzimba, crowds of singing women had pushed his car through the town, deliberately choosing a route past the European club, the golf course and the police station, 'to show the Europeans that at least on that Sunday they were in control of Mzimba'.[18] An old friend who visited Banda during this period described him as 'a very frightened man'.[19] It was a fair comment, for although to Nyasas Banda appeared as a hero, beneath his mask of public confidence he was racked by uncertainty and often took refuge in bluster and bombast. The differences between the public and the private man were summed up by Guy Clutton-Brock, then a member of the Executive Committee of the Southern Rhodesian African National Congress:

The leader at home, what is he like? A demagogue, self-important, intolerant, egotistical, vain? No, a humble man, rather shy, simple and meticulous of habit, of perfect courtesy, a man who can listen as well as speak, shrewd, with brain and intuition, a man of integrity and of culture, mature and with years of experience of the world. . . .

If Banda enjoyed the power he wielded, it was not merely for personal ends. Ever conscious of his image, he came to regard himself not so much as an individual but as, in Clutton-Brock's phrase, 'the embodiment of the will and spirit of the people'.[20]

Talks about Talks

On 24 October, at the invitation of the Secretary for African

Affairs, John Ingham, Banda held his first substantive discussions with the Government on Congress's demands for constitutional advance. Its prospects had not noticeably improved in the preceding three months. In June, when Banda had met Lennox-Boyd in London, he had been told that when the Governor returned to Nyasaland a statement would be made setting out the British and Nyasaland Governments' views.[21] But Sir Robert Armitage had returned on 15 August and ever since had remained obstinately silent. To add insult to injury, Sattar Sacranie, the Blantyre barrister who led the principal Indian association, the Asian Convention, left shortly afterwards for London to submit to Lennox-Boyd his own constitutional proposals. The Convention had until then appeared sympathetic to Congress, and Banda had come to think of it as a tacit ally. But the nature of the proposals, which envisaged parity of representation for Africans, Asians and Europeans (as did the then Tanganyika constitution), and above all the fact that Sacranie had left without consulting him, convinced him that the Asians were not to be trusted.[22] He delivered a blistering attack on Asian perfidy, and suggested that they would do well to keep out of politics.*

One word from me [he warned] and the Africans of this territory will boycott the Asian stores throughout Nyasaland. They know only too well what this will mean – bankruptcy – and they will have to clear out to Dar-es-Salaam or somewhere. . . .[23]

Despite these inauspicious beginnings, Banda's meeting with Ingham was on the whole encouraging. While they were poles apart politically, on a personal level they got on well. The scope of their discussions was limited to territorial matters, and Banda reiterated Congress's earlier demands for a Legislative Council of forty, comprising two officials, six elected non-Africans, and thirty-two African members elected by universal suffrage. He spoke at length of the injustice of the existing constitution, under which the white electorate of 2,500 had six seats in the Legislative Council and two in the Executive Council, while six

---

* As a result, most Asians voted for the U.F.P. in the Federal elections the next month.

hundred times that number of unenfranchised Africans*
merited only five representatives in the former. And he suggested that, much as Britain might aver that its aim was to bring
its colonial territories to self-government, colonial history had
proved that the vested interests of the Europeans and a fear of
precipitateness would prevail unless pressure was brought to
bear. He conceived his task as being, he reportedly told Ingham,
'that of organizing the people of Nyasaland behind him to bring
about the degree of pressure required to right the basic wrong
regarding political rights'.[24]

Banda then turned to other grievances, notably the practice
of requiring chiefs not to participate in Congress activities,
which, he complained, was isolating the people's natural rulers
from national feeling, and *malimidwe*. He said he recognized
the necessity for agricultural legislation, but contended that the
existing methods of enforcement often led to an offender being
punished twice for a single offence: first he was imprisoned, and
then his crops were uprooted so that, when he was released, he
and his family were without food until the next harvest, nine
months later.

Ingham reported afterwards that he thought it might be
possible eventually to reach a negotiated agreement on the constitutional question. Banda had emphasized that violence formed
no part of his programme, and had hinted that in private he
might be prepared to compromise, although in public he would
continue to restate Congress's original demands. Ingham, for his
part, had taken the line that the Government acknowledged
the possibility of giving Africans a further measure of political
power, but not to the extent demanded by Congress. It being
clear that there was a basis for further discussion, it was
arranged that Banda should meet Armitage on 30 October. In
the meantime a round-table conference was to be held to enable
him to discuss his other complaints with heads of department.†

* This assumes 1·5 million African adults out of a total African population
of about 3 million.

† Banda had initially asked for a round-table conference in preference to a
meeting with Ingham. On being pressed, however, he had agreed to this
taking place after their preliminary talks.

Before either meeting could take place, however, an incident occurred which exposed in dramatic fashion the tension building up between Congress and the Europeans, and cast a long shadow over the months that followed.

The Clocktower Incident

In September, Banda had established a small surgery in Limbe,* and thereafter found time to speak only once a week, on Sunday afternoons. It was after one of these Sunday meetings, in Blantyre on 26 October, that the so-called Clocktower Incident took place.

The meeting itself was orderly. After Banda had left, the crowd moved to a bus terminus near the Blantyre Clocktower to await transport home. The buses were few and the people many, and after a while the more impatient among them began to air their discontent by throwing stones at passing cars. Two European women were slightly injured; shop signs were torn down and dustbins overturned; and according to some reports, 'Asian children [were] chased'.[25] The disturbance lasted only ten minutes, and those who took part in it acted neither on Congress's instructions nor with its approval. Indeed, it was a Congress official who stopped them. As Chipembere later explained:

Dr Banda . . . had a way of speaking which would be quite extreme and radical [yet] without . . . racial overtones. . . . We would all go wild and crazy after his speech. People would think in terms of throwing stones at European-driven cars the minute they left his

* Banda seems to have had two reasons for returning to practice. The main one was financial, for he had left Ghana with little money and such funds as he did possess he expended on Congress (*Hansard*, Zomba, 8 April 1965, p. 577). But he may also have looked to medicine for support of another kind, seeing in it a reassuring link with his past. If so, he was frustrated in both intentions. He was not in Nyasaland the outstanding physician he had been in Britain, and his practice was only moderately successful; moreover, his financial difficulties persisted, and he ran up some substantial debts, a thing which to a man of his carefulness would have been unthinkable five years before. The effects of Banda's Ghanaian experiences had not completely worn off. (*Nyasaland Times*, 24 March 1959; Matinga, Chipembere and Chiume, interviews.)

political rally. But it would be a speech in which he had appealed for racial cooperation! He just emphasized the injustices. . . . [26]

The next day, however, under a banner headline, 'MOB VIOLENCE', the *Nyasaland Times* reported:

It was mob law at the Blantyre Clocktower yesterday afternoon, two hours of threatening violence when no European or Asian was safe to walk the streets or drive past in a car. . . . It was two hours of violent racialism, while the Police Mobile Force stood ready to move into action with batons and shields, fixed bayonets and riot guns. They could not do so until the Riot Act was read. It was not.

In a front-page editorial, the paper went on to accuse the Government of timidity and to demand that action be taken to reassure the (white) public:

Today the Government of Nyasaland must ask itself – and answer to the public – this question [it declared]: Will it continue to permit violence to be used as a political weapon? The rioting at the Blantyre Clocktower yesterday was [the] product of political enthusiasms whipped up earlier at the market place by the African Congress. It was a raw display of racial hatred without parallel in this country. . . . We must ask why the Riot Act was not read when there was every cause for it and why the Police Mobile Force was not allowed to break up the ugly mob. . . . The Government must let the people of Nyasaland know that it is indeed the Government of this country.

The settlers' leader, Michael Blackwood, suggested banning all future Congress meetings, and warned that if the Government was unable to protect the people it 'must expect the public to protect itself'. There was a rush of Europeans applying for pistol permits. The Asians deplored the incident, and the senior European unofficial in the Legislative Council, Arthur Dixon, blamed it on 'a few stupid extremists'. Banda said he was sorry, but denied that Congress was in any way responsible.

The Government then attempted to put the incident back into perspective, by issuing a statement which noted that little damage had actually been done and declared that 'at no time was the crowd riotously assembled'.[27] This made the settlers even angrier, and in its next editorial the *Nyasaland Times* accused the

Government of hiding its head in the sand. 'If women of any race cannot travel around Nyasaland without harm, then we will descend to savagery,' the paper declared. Blackwood reported: 'I have had grown men come to see me to tell me they were put in fear of their lives by the mob. If an average human being is put in fear by a crowd, that constitutes a riot.' Only those who had been there or who read the small print wondered if it had really been as bad as all that: whether, for instance, a news item which recorded, a few days later, that two small boys had hurled mud pies at a passing motorist (and missed), warranted the heading, 'Cars Stoned', on the front page.[28]

For all its pettiness, the Clocktower incident had a lasting effect on the attitudes of Europeans, particularly those in the civil service and the police. The settlers' disenchantment with Banda was not new: the *Nyasaland Times* had been complaining for weeks about 'rabid secession mongers'.[29] But the ferocity with which they had reacted to what was, in reality, a very minor disturbance was something which the authorities had not encountered before, and afterwards they were over-sensitive to Congress's doings.

The Tension Mounts

Banda's meeting with Armitage was cordial, but unproductive, and set the pattern for what proved to be a discouraging month for Congress. The Governor did not respond to his broad hints that Congress might be prepared to reconsider its demand for universal suffrage, and instead made plain that what he asked was far in excess of anything to which the Government could agree. The round-table conference promised by Ingham, which Banda attended with Chipembere and Chiume, was equally disappointing. He was heard politely, but it was clear that nothing would be done about his complaints.

On each of these occasions, large crowds gathered to watch Banda pass. Their intentions were peaceable, but they were held to constitute a threat to good order and were vigorously dispersed by the police, who made a number of arrests. The *Nyasaland Times* raised afresh an old question – the Federalizing of the police force – and the Government, in response to demands from the settlers, affirmed in a statement on 10 November its determination 'to maintain law and order throughout the Protectorate and to deal firmly and effectively with those who disturb the public tranquillity'.

As to the forces required to deal with such lawlessness [the statement continued], in addition to its own police force the Government has, as the Federal Prime Minister recently observed, the resources of the Federation behind it. It would make the fullest use of those forces should the need arise.[30]

The *Nyasaland Times* said the statement was welcome 'if a little late', and congratulated the police on their 'militant attitude' which, it asserted, would reassure the public.[31] The public, however, included a vast majority of Africans who could not have been more thoroughly unsettled than by the suggestion that Federal forces might be brought to Nyasaland. Only six weeks earlier, 500 men of the Royal Rhodesian Regiment had flown in for a week's exercises,* and the memory of their presence was enough to set on edge the most sober-minded of Nyasas.

These fears intensified after the Federal elections on 12 November, in which the United Federal Party won all but nine elected seats in the fifty-nine-member house, and returned all ten members in Nyasaland, seven of them unopposed. The Nyasaland and Northern Rhodesian Congresses boycotted the elections,† and Banda rested his hopes on the right-wing Dominion Party, led by Winston Field. If the Dominion Party could cut the U.F.P.'s majority, he reasoned, Welensky's bargaining power at the Federal review conference would be reduced. Although Banda strongly disapproved of the Dominion Party's racism, he found its honesty preferable to the hypocrisy of the

* This show of strength was apparently intended as a vote-catching device ahead of the Federal elections. Manoah Chirwa accused the Federal Government of trying to intimidate Nyasas, a charge which Welensky angrily rejected.

† So successful was the boycott that in Nyasaland only seventeen Africans registered as voters. The *Nyasaland Times* (28 October 1958) took this as an indication of 'sheer apathy, laziness or ignorance'.

U.F.P., and its failure to make much headway except in Southern Rhodesia was a considerable disappointment. As the *Nyasaland Times* pointed out, the U.F.P.'s clean sweep in Nyasaland was an 'additional guarantee' that the territory would not be permitted to secede.[32]

With the elections behind them, the settlers resurrected their long-standing demand for the Federalization of non-African agriculture, a possibility which Africans found no less disturbing than the threat to bring in Federal troops. The strong feelings which this issue aroused in both races derived from the belief that if non-African agriculture were Federalized, so too would be the control of non-African land matters. In fact it would not, but the misconception was widespread and difficult to erase, and the revival of land fears became a major factor in the build-up of tension towards the end of November. At about the same time an influential group of Europeans began speaking of 'having a showdown' with Congress in January or February, when the Africans would be tending their crops.[33]

Banda was keenly aware of the changing mood. At a meeting with the Acting Chief Secretary, Peter Youens, on 21 November, he referred for the first time to the eventuality of his going into *active* opposition, saying that, if he did so, it would be of a non-violent character.[34] A few days later, he told a Rhodesian journalist that he was unworried by the prospect of deportation or exile.[35] Like Chipembere, Chiume and Dunduzu Chisiza, Banda was beginning to realize that if Congress were to achieve its aims it would have to exert greater pressure than the constitution allowed or the Government could permit. But the time for a decision had not yet come, and in the meantime there was one pressing question which had still to be resolved: the position of the Congress old guard.

Exit the Moderates

On his arrival in Nyasaland, Banda had stated that, while he had no objection to the formation of other political parties, he did not think the time was right for it. Asked about existing splinter groups,* he had replied, 'I am hoping they will see the light and come back into Congress.'[36] But Manoah Chirwa, Kumbikano, Kwenje and the rest did not see the light, and by the end of October Banda felt that the time had come for their position to be clarified.

On 7 November he issued a statement in which he claimed that they were forming a new party. He welcomed it, he said, and told reporters, no doubt for the benefit of the Nyasaland Government: 'That's democracy.'[37] He hoped that people would get a chance to choose between Congress, which wanted secession, and the new grouping, which was working to achieve self-government within the Federation. Much of this was untrue, but it was a highly effective way of discrediting the supposed new party's leadership. Moreover, by making his statement when he did, Banda forced Chirwa to reply at a time when the Nyasaland and Rhodesian press had little space for news which did not relate directly to the Federal elections:

> Dr Banda's outburst [Chirwa declared] indicates clearly that he does not believe in stating the truth and shows that politically he has not yet grasped the rudiments of politics. . . . Such leadership is absolutely dangerous to the African people and the world at large. . . . In the end, when all the political emotions have rested in people's breasts, Dr Banda will learn that this country cannot be led by him.[38]

For all his denying that any new party had been formed, Chirwa's clumsily worded rebuttal did him more harm than good, by bringing into the open the extent of his disagreement with Banda. After this incident his popularity slowly declined, although he continued to receive some support from moderate elements.

A few days later, Banda made a last attempt to come to terms

---

*The reference was to the Congress Liberation Party, formed by T. D. T. Banda in May 1958, which drew its main support from the Tongas in its leader's home district of Nkhata Bay. It was clear by October that the C.L.P. would not pose much of a threat to Congress, of which it was a weaker and more moderate version (see its 'Statement of Aims', *Nyasaland Times*, 16 December 1958). The earlier breakaway party, N.A.P.A., was by now defunct.

with the Chijozi–Chinyama–Kwenje faction, but although on 30 November they met for four hours, their differences proved too great to admit of conciliation. Banda issued a statement saying he preferred 'open disagreement to phoney unity',[39] and the next day left for Ghana to attend the All African People's Conference.

Accra and After

In view of his recent experiences in Ghana, Banda had been understandably reluctant to take part in the Accra conference, and as late as 20 November had intended to send Chiume in his place.[40] Nkrumah, however, wanted the conference to be as representative as possible,[41] and in the end Kojo Botsio, now Ghana's Foreign Minister, succeeded in persuading him to attend in person.[42] Early on in his visit he made the headlines in the Ghanaian press, by declaring: 'The white man has nothing to fear from us. We do not want to dominate or be dominated. But the majority must rule and the majority in Africa is the African.'[43] But generally Banda shunned publicity, and refused a seat on the seventeen-man steering committee on the grounds that he had too much to do at home.[44] Although he dutifully attended Nkrumah's opening address, the conference routine bored him, and he played little part in it.*

Nevertheless, Banda's stay in Accra was in one respect invaluable, for it gave him an opportunity to evaluate dispassionately the progress which Congress had made and the tasks which lay ahead. At the time of his return, the party had been divided and largely ineffectual. But by early November, Banda had been able to write (in a letter to a Congress official), '. . . things are hot here. I have the whole of Blantyre and Zomba on fire. Very soon I hope to have the whole of Nyasaland on fire',[45] and by December that hope was all but accomplished.

---

*Banda's withdrawal may also have been due to the strain of being confronted with the scene of his unhappiest years. But that it was voluntary seems certain, although Munger (*Kamuzu Banda of Malawi*, p. 15) and T. P. Melady (*Profiles of African Leaders*, Macmillan, 1961, p. 169) both suggest that he was overshadowed by other delegates.

Nyasas were united as never before and watched with growing impatience the Government's inflexibility in the face of Congress's constitutional demands.

As early as May, Banda had said in a television interview in London: 'I don't believe in violence. I believe in negotiation. But if it does not get us what we want we will be forced to resolve the problem some other way.'[46] This question of 'other ways' had been much in his thoughts since the latter half of November, and at Accra he concluded that negotiation alone would not be sufficient to advance Congress's cause. He proposed, therefore, that Nyasas' opposition should take the form of a non-violent resistance campaign, similar to that mounted in 1953. Now, just as then, he realized that this must degrade into open confrontation. But now, too, just as then, there was no longer any alternative.

There were good reasons for not delaying the decision, for 1958 was coming to an end, leaving only one full year before the Federal review conference. At home the Congress militants, particularly Chipembere, Dunduzu Chisiza and his elder brother, Yatuta, and their supporters, were pressing for action. While Banda may not have seen in this any challenge to his leadership, he realized that, if Congress were to retain its cohesion, some outlet would have to be found for the frustrations of his followers. But there were also positive encouragements to action. The mere fact that he was in Ghana, which was already independent, made him reflect anew on the path Kwame Nkrumah had followed to achieve that goal. Then, too, he found that Kenneth Kaunda, the young leader of the breakaway Zambia African National Congress,* and Joshua Nkomo were also considering non-violent action. Indeed non-violence was much in vogue at Accra during Banda's stay, both within and out-

* Harry Nkumbula, from whose Northern Rhodesian African National Congress Kaunda's Z.A.N.C. had split away, was also in Accra, and Banda was one of a number of leaders who tried to heal the rift between them. Their efforts resulted in a loose agreement, which Nkumbula later repudiated, that the Congresses of the three Federal territories should in future work together. Subsequently the Southern Rhodesian Government cited this as evidence of a Federation-wide plot to overthrow white rule by violent means.

side the conference room. In the words of the P.A.F.M.E.C.A.*
delegate, Kenya's Dr Gikoyo Kiano, '. . . we are here particularly to seek answers to a very important question; and that
question is: by what methods, tactics and ideological approach
can we forever obliterate imperialism, colonialism and exploita-
tion of the African by foreign peoples?' The answer which the
conference agreed upon was, again in Kiano's words, 'the moral
and mighty principle of non-violence – but not the idea of
turning the other cheek'.[47]

After the conference ended, Banda travelled to Salisbury,
intending to fly to Blantyre the next day, a Sunday. But once
there he discovered that the Nyasaland Government had asked
the airline to withhold his onward booking until after the weekend, in the hope of avoiding a large crowd at Chileka. To compound his annoyance, the Federal Customs saw fit to detain
him for over an hour while his baggage and papers were
minutely inspected.[48] It was in marked contrast to his treatment
at Johannesburg, where he had stopped over on his outward
journey and had been 'pleasantly surprised'[49] by the cooperation extended to him. He emerged bristling.

The next day, when Banda addressed a mass meeting in the
African township of New Highfields, rage gave added impetus
to the defiance with which he had left Ghana. He urged Africans
to go to prison in their millions, 'singing Hallelujah', and
declared:

They can do what they like to me. They can send me to prison.
They can kill me. I will never give up my fight for freedom. We have
to be prepared to go to prison. We must fill the prisons, millions of
us. . . .

He had come, he told his audience, to break the 'stupid and
hellish' Federation:

* P.A.F.M.E.C.A. (the Pan-African Freedom Movement of East and
Central Africa) was inaugurated at Mwanza, Tanganyika, on 17 September
1958, with the aim of uniting member countries in the struggle for independence. The founder members were the Nyasaland African Congress (represented by Chiume) and nationalist parties from Kenya, Tanganyika, Uganda
and Zanzibar.

That is my job and I am going to do it. If they send me to prison I do not mind. They can put me on the Seychelles like Makarios, or on St Helena like Napoleon. I am prepared for anything, even death. I am not afraid of anything. I will fight Federation from prison. Even from the grave my ghost will return to fight Federation.

Partnership had turned out to be 'so much whitewash'. If Africans in the Federal territories wished to avoid the fate which had over-taken their 'brothers and sisters in South Africa',[50] they must be prepared for a struggle: the only salvation lay in extremism, because 'throughout the history of the world there is no incident where a so-called moderate has ever achieved anything'.*

On the Monday Banda was allowed to proceed to Nyasaland. A thousand or more Africans gathered in New Highfields to see him off amid scenes of unparalleled excitement. The Salis-bury *Evening Standard* reported: 'Men doffed their hats, youths fought to touch Dr Banda's car, and young women flung them-selves on the vehicle covering it with kisses.' At the airport he repeated his warning of the day before: 'Even when I am dead my bones will come and fight against Federation.'[51] It was language such as the Africans of Southern Rhodesia had not heard for sixty years or more, and when Banda claimed later: 'I got Salisbury rocking, rocking and got it awake out of its political sleep',[52] it was more than just an idle boast.

Southern Rhodesian Europeans were at first incredulous. The *Rhodesian Herald* said primly:

It is discouraging, it is unpalatable for us in the Federation to have to read the envenomed mouthings of Dr Hastings Banda, the leading African agitator in the country today. . . . It is also unpalatable to have to record and comment upon them, but it is essential that decent citizens of all races should know what is going on in their midst, what is likely to happen to this multiracial experiment of ours in an Africa in the ferment of rabid nationalism.[53]

* *Rhodesia Herald*, 22 December 1958. Six months earlier Chipembere had made the same point in strikingly similar, yet subtly different terms, when he told the Legislative Council: 'Anything like moderation will never get us anywhere. Whether we demand things in strong terms or whether we demand them in mild language we get nothing. . . . The only language which British Imperialism can understand is the language of extreme conflict . . .' (*Hansard*, Zomba, 4 July 1958, pp. 160–1).

A few days later the Southern and Northern Rhodesian Governments both declared Banda a prohibited immigrant. 'I have spoiled their natives for them' was his scornful comment.[54]

Passive Resistance

December saw a continuing deterioration in the relations between Congress and the European community. The Government introduced a bill extending police powers to deal with crowds, and an amendment to the Road Traffic Ordinance increasing the penalties for stoning motor vehicles. Both were enacted. But when Kwenje sought an assurance that there would be no further Federal erosion of territorial responsibilities until after the 1960 review, his motion was defeated. There was an upsurge of illegal meetings and arrests, and renewed trouble over the agricultural rules, notably in Fort Johnston where the situation grew serious enough to warrant the dispatch of two platoons of the Police Mobile Force. In two editorials in mid-December, the *Nyasaland Times* accused Congress of stirring up unrest and condemned its constitutional proposals as 'absurd'. From none of this could Africans derive much comfort.

Banda's speeches followed closely the pattern he had set in Salisbury. At Chileka he snapped at reporters: 'In Nyasaland we mean to be masters, and if that is treason make the most of it',[55] and thereafter made frequent allusions to the likelihood of his own imprisonment. In terms more inflexible than any he had used before he reiterated his implacable opposition to Federation. In an interview published in the *Evening Standard* on Christmas Eve, he went so far as to say: 'If Communism will take me out of the Federation, then I will have it.'[56] He meant that he would not have Federation at any price, but the Southern Rhodesians chose to see the remark in its most sinister light. 'How much longer must Southern Rhodesia put up with the caperings and vapourings of Dr Hastings Banda?' asked the Salisbury *Sunday Mail*.[57]

In public, Banda continued to demand African majorities in the Legislative and Executive Councils. But in private discussions with the Government he sought the compromise which he hoped might still be possible. As he wrote in a letter to the Labour Party's shadow Colonial Secretary, James Callaghan, on 9 January: 'We are not at the parting of the ways yet. As long as I can I shall do my best to let commonsense win.'[58] At a meeting with Youens, a week earlier, Banda had indicated that he would be prepared to reconsider his earlier insistence that there should not be more than three official members in the Legislative Council, provided that his basic demand for a clear African majority was met. He had stressed that this would not be equivalent to immediate self-government, since the Governor would retain the power of veto.[59] On 20 January, in talks with Armitage and Dixon, Banda enlarged on this idea. He would accept parity in the Executive Council – five Africans, two European unofficials, three officials and the Governor presiding – but in the Legislative Council there must be an African majority, whose size could be determined by further negotiation. Armitage rightly concluded that Banda would not budge from this last demand,* and negotiation on such a basis he regarded as 'a negation of negotiation'.[60] He felt it would be impracticable to rule without a majority in the Legislative Council, since the veto Banda suggested could only be used on the rarest occasions. The meeting lasted two hours before ending inconclusively.

That day Nyasaland had its first official riot. A group of women had gathered near the secretariat to watch Banda arrive and forty of them had been arrested for taking part in an illegal assembly. When afterwards Banda and Chipembere addressed a meeting in Zomba, both complained of the injustice of the arrests. As Banda put it, no one arrested women in the streets of London for waving to the Royal Family or Sir Winston Churchill. Chipembere went further, and in what the Devlin commissioners described as 'an intemperate and in parts extremely offensive speech',† called on his audience to 'see that

* In fact the scheme Banda suggested at this meeting was, as he had told Callaghan, 'the minimum I am prepared to accept personally, and to recommend to my people' (*Hansard*, House of Commons, 610/337, 26 July 1959).

† According to the commissioners, Banda later rebuked Chipembere for the offensive parts.

these women are released from police custody, today, this very instant'.[61] Thereupon a crowd numbering about 400 rushed to the police station, where it was held off with difficulty by a police cordon, which was liberally stoned. When it refused to withdraw, the Riot Act was read and the Police Mobile Force made a baton charge. Tear-gas grenades were fired, and after a second baton charge the crowd began to retreat, throwing a variety of missiles as it went. A European reported that an African had shouted at him: 'You b— European, go back to Britain or we'll shoot you tomorrow.'[62]

There were the usual protests from the press and the settlers, and it was again suggested that all African political meetings should be banned. But the time had passed when the *Nyasaland Times* and – with one significant exception – Blackwood and his settlers' Nyasaland Association had much influence on the pattern of events. The decisions which mattered would be taken in the secretariat in Zomba, in Whitehall and in Salisbury, and in the various meeting-places of the Congress Executive.

The Emergency Conference

Two days after Banda's meeting with the Governor, the Congress Executive met to prepare for an emergency conference proposed some weeks earlier by Dunduzu Chisiza. This conference, which was attended by some 200 delegates from ninety Congress branches within and outside Nyasaland, was ostensibly called to discuss the provision of new sources of finance in the event of Congress being banned in Southern Rhodesia and to give Banda a vote of confidence.* Its main purpose, however, was to plan the non-cooperation campaign on which Congress would shortly embark.

Banda played little part either in the preliminaries or in the conference itself, which took place on 24 and 25 January: he spoke only once, on the first day, when he received his vote of

---

*The Devlin Commission said a vote of confidence was needed to counter criticism from Manoah Chirwa (Cmd 814, para. 91). Banda himself was reported in the *Nyasaland Times* (30 January 1959) as saying it was required to approve the policies laid down during his first six months of leadership.

confidence, and afterwards, by his own account, took no further interest. The Devlin commissioners found his uninvolvement not unusual, and explained that he habitually left routine matters to the younger men. But while this was true, it was in this case no ordinary matter which was being discussed, and there can be no doubt that Banda's absence was pre-arranged.[63] It would have been acutely embarrassing for Congress if its leader had been the object of preventive action by the Government before the non-cooperation campaign could get off the ground.

On the second day the delegates met at an open place in the bush outside Blantyre. This in itself was not sinister – there was no hall available big enough to accommodate so large a gathering. But great secrecy was observed and no one was allowed to take notes. It was agreed first that Congress should maintain a list of African 'stooges' – by which were meant uncooperative chiefs and civil servants – who would be punished in some as yet undecided manner when self-government came. Suggestions apparently ranged from killing to deportation. It was also decided that Yatuta Chisiza, who had had wide experience as a senior police officer in Tanganyika, should be appointed Banda's personal bodyguard. Discussions on the more complicated question of non-cooperation took up most of the day, and there is some doubt as to whether a firm policy decision was ever reached at all. Some delegates insisted that if Congress were to move into active opposition, violence could not be excluded. According to the Devlin Commission, there was 'a great deal of talk about beating and killing',[64] and at least one faction is known to have advocated the elimination of the Governor, provincial and district commissioners, senior police and army officers and British officials. Running counter to the extremists, a strong body of opinion favoured a non-violent approach along Ghandian lines.

The understanding with which delegates left was in the nature of a compromise. Non-cooperation and civil disobedience were generally approved, as were acts of sabotage which did not directly endanger human life. The holding of illegal meetings was to be encouraged, and attempts to enforce the agricultural rules and other unpopular laws were to be resisted, if necessary with violence. But it was apparently agreed that violence should not be used except under provocation, and submission to arrest was a legitimate alternative. The eventual imprisonment of the Congress leadership was accepted as inevitable, and there was some discussion about engaging counsel from England to defend them.

To the Congress militants, the conference was a huge success. Chipembere wrote a few days later, 'for the first time Congress adopted "action" as the official policy – and "action" in the real sense of action'.[65]

Banda's reactions were much less straightforward. He told the Devlin Commission that no report on the proceedings was ever submitted to him since the members of the Central Executive who would have drawn it up were too busy to meet.[66] Nor, according to the commission, did Banda ever discuss what had passed at the conference with any individual delegate. In this it was mistaken, for Banda did receive verbal reports of what had taken place, although he may have been unaware of the extent to which some factions had advocated aggressive, as opposed to retaliatory, violence.

The dilemma in which Banda was placed with regard to the use of violence was reflected in the ambivalence of his public statements. Shortly after his return from Accra, when asked in a television interview what part violence played in his plans for fighting the Federation, he had replied: 'I mean not with violence, but one can't exclude that if we are not allowed to get out of it.'[67] Later he wrote to Callaghan: 'I am against violence whatever the newspapers say. But ... I will not betray the interests of my people just for the sake of being called a moderate or being popular with the Europeans.'[68] Despite these ambiguities, Banda was forced to countenance to a much greater extent than in 1953 the use of violence as a political weapon. If in the weeks after the emergency conference, he persevered in trying to lead Congress along the tightrope between retaliation and unprovoked aggression, it was with grave misgivings about his ability to succeed in it.[69]

Action or Anarchy

At the beginning of February, information began to reach the Government on the decisions adopted by the emergency conference. Much of it came from African Special Branch informers, who had not themselves been present, and was consequently of doubtful authenticity. But it was the only information available and had to be treated accordingly. The gist of it was as follows: Congress had decided on a protectorate-wide campaign of non-violent civil disobedience. If, as a result of it, Banda were arrested, the leadership would pass to a quadrumvirate of Chipembere, Dunduzu Chisiza, Chiume and Mrs Chibambo, who would decide on a day, to be known as 'R' day, when violence would begin. It would include the sabotage of communications and key installations; the mass slaughter of Europeans and Asians, including women and children; and the murders of key European officials, missionaries, African chiefs, and other uncooperative elements.

With the exception of a few small incidents in Blantyre, there was for some days no evidence to bear out these startling disclosures. Banda continued to hold his regular Sunday afternoon meetings, speaking at Dedza on 1 February and at Mlanje a week later. There was nothing seditious in the speeches, although the local administration was upset by his description of a district commissioner as 'a little boy of twenty-five years old direct from Oxford',[70] and European opinion was further jolted when he told crowds at Mlanje: 'If the God of the Christians does not look after us, then the spirits of our ancestors will.'[71]

But trouble was not long in coming. It began in the northern province, where Congress was most numerous and the police most vulnerable, with a series of illegal meetings and processions at Karonga. Two days later there were demonstrations at Visanza, and at Dowa, on 11 February, two European veterinary officers were injured in a fracas and twenty Africans arrested. At Nkhotakhota on 17 February, police used tear-gas and batons against rioters protesting the arrests of eleven

Africans at Visanza after disturbances there the previous day. On 16 February, Africans stoned the Karona police station and there were other incidents at Ncheu and Blantyre.

Nothing that happened during this period was in itself very serious. There was little damage to property and even less to persons. But the fact that disturbances and illegal demonstrations were taking place with increasing frequency in all three provinces accorded closely with the Special Branch information of a planned campaign by Congress to defy the Government. Intelligence having proved accurate in this particular, it was but a small step to accepting the murder plot *in toto*. When, on 18 February, the Police Commissioner received fresh information apparently confirming the earlier reports, he told the Governor that he thought the information about a Congress plan to massacre Europeans and Asians was correct. The Government, he felt, must act, or the country would be placed in a state of anarchy.

Two days later Armitage visited Salisbury for his regular monthly meeting with Welensky, Whitehead, and the Governor of Northern Rhodesia, Sir Arthur Benson. Although no firm decision was taken on the situation in Nyasaland, it was discussed at length and Welensky and Whitehead made it clear that they favoured preventive action. Welensky offered Federal support, which Armitage accepted, and Whitehead told him that a State of Emergency was imminent in Southern Rhodesia. That evening he returned to Zomba, where it had been announced that Lord Perth would visit Nyasaland at the end of the month for discussions on constitutional advance.

Armitage had grave doubts about the wisdom of this visit which, he thought, would provoke fresh disturbances. The deterioration in conditions over the next few days proved him right, and on 25 February he cabled the Colonial Office that an early declaration of a State of Emergency was inevitable. It was announced two days later in the House of Commons that Lord Perth's visit had been postponed. On 26 February Whitehead declared a State of Emergency in Southern Rhodesia and banned the three Congresses in the territory, and Nyasaland's Chief Secretary, C. W. F. Footman, flew to Salisbury to finalize arrangements for the dispatch of troops. That evening a newly created Operations Committee began to draw up plans for the State of Emergency which was to be declared in Nyasaland.

Conflict and Confrontation

While Armitage was in Salisbury conferring with Welensky, Banda attended a meeting with Footman in Zomba. The Chief Secretary spoke of the rapidly deteriorating situation, particularly in the northern province, where, at Karonga, the previous day, Congress supporters had freed prisoners and tried to immobilize the airstrip. He suggested that further disorders might make negotiation impossible, and hinted that the Colonial Office might already be reconsidering the proposed visit of Lord Perth. Banda reiterated his desire to proceed by negotiation, and Footman asked him to control his followers through the network of Congress branches. To this Banda gave no direct answer, but Footman went away with the impression that he had 'given him a good deal of matter for thought'.*

Banda was not alone in being evasive at this meeting. At one point Footman had mentioned that the Government had requested reinforcements from elsewhere in the Federation, but when Banda had asked for details he had declined to reply. Banda had expressed the hope that they would not be from Southern Rhodesia, since if they were it would 'really cause trouble'.[72]

That evening Banda heard on the radio that the troops sent into Karonga were indeed Southern Rhodesian. He gave up any

---

*Cmd 814, para. 142. Banda told the Devlin Commission that he had not entirely believed Footman's account of the Karonga disturbances, and had sent an aide to conduct an on-the-spot investigation. When this had confirmed the Chief Secretary's allegations, he had planned to call a meeting of the Congress Executive to see what could be done to prevent this type of disorder (ibid., para. 143). While this may have been true, other considerations were no less important. As Banda told a rally in September 1960: What did Mr Footman think of me? Chinyama? Manoah Chirwa? . . . my people were at war. And as Commander-in Chief, how could I go to stop battle when my people were in the heat of the battle?' (Malawi News, 15 October 1960).

thought of cooperating with the Government and, in an open letter to Armitage, accused 'someone in the secretariat of pandering to Welensky'.

> Karonga is a mere excuse [he declared] . . . It reveals clearly that the Government of this country is not a government in its own right – only a puppet in the hands of European settlers, particularly the European settlers in Southern Rhodesia.[73]

Law and order had not so broken down, said Banda, as to necessitate the calling in of Federal troops;[74] this was the show-down of which the Europeans had been speaking.

This last belief was strengthened when, on that same day, Friday, 20 February, the constitutional proposals drawn up by the Nyasaland Association were published in the *Nyasaland Times*. They were a great deal more complicated than any previously suggested, and were based on a dual roll system designed to ensure that only moderate Africans stood a chance of election. A sliding-scale method of advance was suggested which made it appear that it might take fifteen years or more before Africans were in a majority in the Legislative Council, while there was a possibility that in the meantime the majority might temporarily be held by the settlers. When Congress leaders remembered that six weeks earlier the European un-officials who led the Nyasaland Association had joined the U.F.P., they saw in the extreme stand the Association had taken the direct influence of the Federal government.

At Fort Hill, in the far North of Nyasaland, 20 February saw police open fire for the first time on demonstrators, wounding four. There were disturbances at Mzuzu, Mzimba, Ekwendeni, Loudon, Fort Manning and other places in the central and northern provinces. In Blantyre and Zomba there were also disorders, and cars and property were indiscriminately stoned. At Lilongwe, on 23 February, an African cyclist died after being struck on the head by a European special constable* who

---

* These were European 'volunteers' called up in support of the regular police force in times of unrest. Membership was obligatory for employees of statutory bodies and similar organizations, and there were cases of men being threatened with dismissal if they did not 'volunteer'.

thought he was cheeky. The following day two Africans were shot dead and one wounded when police opened fire on crowds in the Lilongwe market, and another African was killed when demonstrators at Balaka tried to release agricultural offenders. On 27 February, a fifth African died when soldiers of the King's African Rifles opened fire on rioters at Lirangwe.

It was a state of affairs which could not continue. Disorders were breaking out in almost every district and were becoming more and more difficult for the authorities to contain. In Mozambique, Northern Rhodesia and Tanganyika, troops were brought up to Nyasaland's borders, while in the protectorate itself a steady stream of reinforcements arrived from Salisbury. The announcement that Lord Perth was postponing his visit had signalled to Congress and the world at large that an Emergency was only a few days away, and there was a massive influx of overseas journalists. Scarcely a day passed without some new demand for action by the settlers. In utter exasperation, the *Nyasaland Times* inquired: 'How many more lives must be lost before Zomba decide, in their supreme red-carpeted wisdom, that an emergency has now arrived in name as well as fact?'*

To Africans, no less than to Europeans, the future appeared bleak. In a speech in Northern Rhodesia on 23 February Yatuta Chisiza warned: 'We mean to create disturbances from Port Herald to Karonga even if every person in the country dies.'[75] And in Blantyre, Chipembere declared: 'We are no longer playing. . . . We mean to die for this country or win liberation.'[76] Banda remained silent, knowing that there was now nothing he could do but wait.

Operation Sunrise

At a press-conference in Zomba on the afternoon of 2 March Sir Robert Armitage blandly declared that no State of Emergency was needed in Nyasaland.[77] It was a misleading statement and was intended as such, for at a few minutes past midnight on

---

*This issue (3 March 1959, but distributed the previous afternoon) was withdrawn a few hours after publication.

the morning of 3 March he signed the declaration which brought the Emergency into being.

Shortly before dawn two platoons of troops and the Police Mobile Force surrounded Banda's house in Limbe. A hand-picked commando group was assigned to the actual arrest and elaborate precautions were taken in case of armed resistance. But Banda was discovered sleeping peacefully in bed, whence he was peremptorily awakened and hustled in pyjamas and dressing-gown to a waiting Land Rover which took him to Chileka Airport. There he was joined by Chipembere and the Chisiza brothers and put aboard an aircraft bound for Southern Rhodesia. Operation Sunrise, as the exercise was known, had begun.

In the weeks that followed nearly 1,500 people were deprived of their liberty and forty-eight* lost their lives. All were Africans; no European was killed, and none was seriously injured.

* Not including the five who died before the Emergency was declared.

Chapter 7
Thirteen Uneasy Months

Once the Emergency had been declared, the Nyasaland Government was faced with two pressing tasks: it had to restore calm and good order quickly, and it had to justify the declaration to British public opinion and, more particularly, to the Labour Party. It was unlucky to fail conspicuously in both.

Armitage had hoped that Operation Sunrise would see the arrests of the hard-core Congress leaders completed by first light on 3 March, after which mopping-up operations could begin. Simultaneously a propaganda campaign would be launched to discredit Congress and restore African confidence in the protectorate Government. It soon became clear that this was wildly optimistic. The operation itself netted about half the wanted men, and as late as 7 March there were still a number of key Congress officials at large.* Moreover it proved necessary to detain large numbers of Congress supporters who were not on the wanted lists and for whom the Government had not bargained. This not only posed considerable logistical problems: it was also a disturbing portent for the future.

But most worrying to the administration was the loss of life which the Emergency provoked. Although, contrary to the Government's expectations, little violence was offered during the arrests of the principals, this was amply compensated by the intensity of popular reaction afterwards. The overnight proscription of the N.A.C. and the suddenness of the changes in the law which had made it possible seemed to Nyasas inexplicable, and the Government had neither the manpower nor the facilities to explain the actions it was taking. In a vain attempt to discover what was happening, many villagers made their way to

*The last prominent Congressman to be captured was 'General Flax' Musopole, who succeeded in hiding out in the wild Misuku hills, near the Tanganyikan border, until the beginning of August.

the *bomas** where they gave vent to their feelings of anger and
bewilderment in hostile demonstrations. All over the country,
groups of militant Congressmen erected road-blocks, and
sabotaged bridges and culverts; there was widespread damage
to property and a great deal of arson.

The security forces were caught off balance, and reacted by
treating every gathering as potentially dangerous: on several
occasions inexperienced reservists opened fire to disperse crowds
in circumstances where firearms need not have been used. By 7
March the death toll had reached forty-one and the disturbances,
while past their peak, were still far from over. The most tragic
incident was at Nkhata Bay, where twenty Africans were killed
and twenty-eight wounded only moments before the arrival of
reinforcements which would have made the action unnecessary.

Events such as this made the business of justification more
urgent than ever. Lennox-Boyd and his Under-Secretary, Julian
Amery, had been speaking in the House of Commons of the
likelihood of a bloodbath and plans to butcher Asians and
Europeans; clearly, dramatic evidence was needed if the shoot-
ing-down of unarmed Africans were to be convincingly explained. Thus it was perhaps natural for Armitage to decide to
present as the principal factor in his case the sensational, but
imperfectly documented, massacre plot, supposedly hatched at
the Congress Emergency Conference in January.

The Massacre Plot

Labour M.P.s were from the start highly sceptical of Lennox-
Boyd's statement on the night of 3 March that 'in fact a mass-
acre was being planned'. Speaker after speaker rose from the
Opposition benches to condemn the Government's explanations:
Fenner Brockway spoke angrily of 'the conspiracy of the
Prime Ministers of the Federation and of Southern Rhodesia
to have a show-down with the African population . . .' and
James Callaghan accused the Tories of provoking the situation
'by their own failure to take action in the last eighteen months,

---

* A chiNyanja word meaning 'government', or in this case, the administrative headquarters of a district.

and their cowardice in yielding to the Federal Government over a State of Emergency which was quite unnecessary'.[1] For all Lennox-Boyd's denials of Federal involvement, the Opposition made it plain that they did not believe him.

Scepticism extended beyond the confines of the Commons. The *News Chronicle* said the massacre plot was 'an excuse, not an explanation. It reveals the weakness of a bankrupt policy.'[2] Other British papers expressed similar views and, when news of the rising death toll in the Protectorate hit the headlines, British moderate opinion was strongly aroused. The *Daily Worker* spoke for much more than its usual readership when it said on 5 March: 'A massacre has taken place in Nyasaland . . . the massacre of Africans by the so-called security forces.'[3]

Both inside and outside Parliament, those who had known Dr Banda in England found it impossible to believe that he would have countenanced the sort of terror tactics the Government attributed to him.* Thus when Chiume, who had been in Mombasa when the Emergency was declared, arrived in London and denounced the massacre plot as 'a stupid fabrication'[4] a vocal section of the British Left was predisposed to believe him.

The Governor's dispatch, published as a White Paper on 23 March, did little to improve the Government's case. It was full of vague, unsubstantiated generalizations and contained none of the concrete evidence of a campaign of mass murder which M.P.s, and the public, had been led to expect. Only the *Nyasaland Times* was pleased and, hinting at darker revelations yet to come, told its readers: 'That noisy two-faced doctor . . . and his henchmen were dupes of larger powers, men skilled in the science of revolt.'[5] The *News Chronicle* came closer to the truth when it remarked: 'It is strange indeed that the "massacre plot" has not caused the death of a single non-African.'[6]

Even before the publication of the White Paper, the Govern-

---

* Banda's former patients in Harlesden presented a petition to Lennox-Boyd, demanding the release of their 'beloved doctor', and in North Shields people who had known him wrote angry letters to local newspapers. (*Drum*, East African edition, December 1959, and Rotberg, *Rise of Nationalism*, p. 186 n.)

ment had come to feel it had no choice but to agree to the insistent demands of the Labour Party for a Commission of Inquiry. Lord Perth made the announcement in the House of Lords during a long, bitter debate on the Governor's dispatch: it would be an independent Commission, headed by the judge Sir Patrick Devlin, and including a former colonial administrator and a scholarly one-time Intelligence Chief.* 'I do not doubt,' Lord Perth cheerfully remarked, 'that with such eminent men of such wide experience, we will get to the heart of things.'[7]

In Detention

Meanwhile, in detention camps and gaols in Nyasaland and Southern Rhodesia, Congressmen settled down to the monotonous routine of prison existence. Banda, Chipembere and the Chisiza brothers were housed in the European wing of Gwelo gaol, set apart from the other detainees. There they planned Nyasaland's political and economic future. They discussed the demands they would make at the constitutional conference which they hoped would take place after their release; they chose the cabinet Banda would lead after the achievement of self-government (from which Yatuta Chisiza, to his intense annoyance, was omitted);[8] and they pondered what strategy to use to break the Federation. Banda conceived the idea of moving Nyasaland's capital from Zomba to Lilongwe, and decided that a road should be built along the Lake Nyasa littoral to promote agricultural development. He also planned the establishment of a national university. And, from time to time, he lectured his companions on history, particularly the constitutional history of Britain and America.[9]

If Banda's sojourn in Gwelo allowed him to contemplate the political future, it likewise provided him with an opportunity to review his personal past. During the long periods he spent alone

* Its members were Sir John Ure Primrose; Sir Percy Wyn-Harris (formerly Governor of the Gambia); and Mr Edgar Williams, Warden of Rhodes House, Oxford, and wartime Chief of Intelligence to Field Marshal Montgomery.

in his cell, he wrote his autobiography, filling dozens of cheap exercise books bought at the prison canteen with big, uneven handwriting. How Banda treated his experiences in Ghana only he himself knows, for the manuscript has not been published. But whether he included an account of his breakdown, and in so doing came to terms with it, or whether he omitted it, and thus convinced himself that it had not happened, he succeeded in exorcizing almost completely its influence. Subsequently he visited both Kumasi and, on several occasions, Harlesden, without showing any strain. If afterwards Banda remained in his inner self an insecure figure, it was due much more to his situation and his own character than to any legacy from the immediate past.*

Elsewhere, at Kanjedza, in Blantyre, at Khami, near Bulawayo, and at Marendellas, the detainees set up schools where the better educated taught their less-favoured colleagues and presided over long political debates. Sometimes the two were combined. Orton Chirwa, for instance, who, after his unsuccessful association with Matinga, had qualified as a lawyer and returned to the Congress fold in the role of legal adviser, used Latin lessons as a cover for political conversations. But for all those in the camps it was a difficult time, for they knew that the future depended not on them, but on the villagers at home and on the politicians in London and Salisbury.

For Banda it was more difficult than for most, for he bore the brunt of the responsibility for their situation. He was also, at one stage, and quite unnecessarily as it turned out, subject to the additional strain of fearing that he might have cancer.[10] Nonetheless, Banda achieved a reputation as a model prisoner, who bore his detention cheerfully and got on well with his warders. Ten years later he invited one of them, a brawny Enkeldoorn farmer named Tony Barnard, to attend as his guest the fifth anniversary celebrations of Malawi's Independence.

---

*One respect, however, in which Banda did not succeed in returning to his old *persona* was medicine. The interest which had fired him in earlier years had left him for ever. (See also Munger, *Kamuzu Banda of Malawi*, pp. 17–18.)

Towards a Police State

In Nyasaland the Government had begun cordon and search operations to winkle out troublemakers who had evaded arrest and to pacify particularly difficult areas. The punitive aspects of these expeditions were stressed: six Africans were killed, some of them in questionable circumstances, and there was a great deal of rough treatment and brutality.

The most spectacular incident took place at Mlanje, where the district commissioner ordered the burning of twenty-eight houses belonging to Congress supporters. But all over the country, houses and property belonging to Congressmen were damaged, and agricultural implements were seized. Later collective fines totalling £30,000 were levied on districts where riot damage had to be made good. These were paid by innocent and guilty alike, and were designed, like other extra-judicial measures, to make Congress 'really unpopular' with the villagers.[11] Instead they succeeded in creating great hostility towards the Government: resentment was almost universal and became deeply ingrained, sometimes degenerating into sullen hatred.

While it was thus itself becoming utterly discredited, the Government's propaganda drive to discredit Congress began to gather momentum. It proceeded on the assumption that Congress supporters were in a small minority, and its efforts were consequently inept: 'Congress has been very wrong indeed, and has been both wicked and evil. Listen no more to the bad advice of Congress, but only to the wisdom of the Boma,'[12] villagers were told.

Sometimes Government handouts revealed something worse than mere ineptitude, as did this 'information' bulletin distributed on 6 May:

Do you know of any member of Congress living near you who has not been arrested? Do you know of any group of Congress members near you who are plotting to cause trouble? If you do, you must tell the Boma, so that these wicked people can be arrested and removed from your area. Tell your District Commissioner or your nearest Government Officer the names of any Congress member you know has not yet been arrested. You can either report personally to a Government Officer or, if you prefer to remain anonymous, send an unsigned letter to your District Commissioner or Police Officer, giving the name and address of any Congress member still at large. (There is no need to put a stamp on the letter.)[13]

Such tactics lent credence to the sensational verdict of the Devlin commissioners that 'Nyasaland is, no doubt only temporarily, a police state. . . .'

The Devlin Report

The report of the Devlin Commission, which Lennox-Boyd received on 16 July, was very nearly an outright disaster for the British Government. This was not because the commissioners had found the Emergency unjustified, or that Sir Roy Welensky had exerted undue pressure, as the Labour Party had charged. On the contrary they had concluded 'in the situation that existed on 3rd March . . . the Government had either to act or to abdicate'.[14] Rather it was the Commission's rejection of the 'massacre plot' and its rigorous condemnation of the techniques of autocracy which made the Conservatives and their supporters squirm. The report said unequivocally that, in numerous cases, unnecessary and therefore illegal force had been used, and that 'these illegalities were expressly or impliedly authorized from the top'.[15] Instances of brutality were set out systematically and in embarrassing detail.

It was this that led the Colonial Secretary urgently to summon Sir Robert Armitage to London for talks with himself, Macmillan and Lord Home. The result of their discussions was another dispatch from the Governor, published as a White Paper at the same time as the report, attempting to answer the commissioners' criticisms.

When the two documents were made public on 23 July there was a furore. In Parliament, party loyalty enabled the Government to push through a motion approving the favourable parts of the report while rejecting those sections which were critical – a measure which did more harm to its standing among Nyasas than ever it did good in the House of Commons. But outside parliament there was less unanimity. Conservative M.P.s, like their Labour colleagues, were getting thoroughly fed up with unpopular struggles to retain authority overseas.

The clue to how this responsibility should eventually be devolved, in the particular case of Nyasaland, was contained in the Devlin Report itself, though at the time it received scant attention. The commissioners had been much impressed by the character and abilities of Dr Banda, whom they had interviewed in Bulawayo. They had portrayed him as a sincere and dedicated man, and had effectively absolved him of personal responsibility for the violence which had taken place in Nyasaland. In their own words, 'He is the most distinguished of Nyasas and has had a remarkable career. . . . His origins are humble and he owes his success entirely to his own capabilities.'*

Of all the British press, only the *Observer* perceived the significance of these remarks, when it said, in its editorial of 2 August: 'Although Dr Hastings Banda and his colleagues are behind bars, it is really the Government which is the prisoner of Dr Banda. . . . The starting point for any fresh policy in Nyasaland must be the release of the African leaders. . . .'[16]

The Colonial Office was slowly coming round to a similar view. But the time was not right for any major change of policy such as Banda's release would entail. A general election was in

* Cmd 814, para. 20. That the commissioners should have underestimated the extent to which Banda was prepared to condone violence was one of the great ironies of their report, although by praising him too much they erred less than the Beadle Tribunal, set up by the Southern Rhodesian Government to inquire into the activities of the Southern Rhodesian African National Congress, which found him 'not a witness on whose word much reliance can be placed' (*Review Tribunal* (*Preventive Detention* (*Temporary Provisions*) *Act 1959*) *General Report*, CSR 27–59, Salisbury, 1959, p. 32). Even more ironic, however, was that the commissioners' rejection of the 'massacre plot', a rejection which provided the basis for Nyasaland's subsequent constitutional advance, may also have been overstated. New evidence suggests that there may indeed have been a plan bearing some resemblance to that claimed by the Nyasaland Government. But it was not discussed at the Emergency conference, and knowledge of it was confined to a few members of the Congress Executive. It was to be set in motion moreover, only in the extreme event of Banda being killed, and there is no evidence to suggest that Banda himself knew of its existence.

the offing in Britain and, until it was past, no one could do more than pick at the problem; only when the Government's policies had been vindicated at the polls could they decently be laid to rest and a more practical approach substituted.

In these circumstances Lennox-Boyd did the only thing possible, by announcing, on the eve of the publication of the Devlin Report, a manifestly unsatisfactory interim constitution to prolong the life of the Legislative Council beyond its expiry date of May 1960. Two Africans would be nominated to occupy the seats which had fallen vacant during the enforced absence of Chiume and Chipembere, and two others to give the Africans a majority over the European unofficials. Of these four, two would be appointed to sit on the Executive Council. The Government majority would be retained by the appointment of two more officials.

Armitage told the press he thought the new constitution would provide 'a two-year lull in the more spectacular forms of political activity', but he was almost alone in his enthusiasm. The *Guardian* commented dourly: 'One might as well ask for a two-year lull in the flow of the Zambezi.'[17]

The Revival of Congress

By the beginning of June Congress's organization had been smashed, and over a thousand of its members were in detention. But although there was a sharp decline in overt anti-Government activities, Nyasas continued to show, in a host of small, undramatic ways, their hatred of Federation and bewilderment with the British Government which now seemed to be abetting it. It was this unyielding persistence, more than anything else, which finally made the Nyasaland Government wonder whether its assessments might not have been wrong, and the Devlin commissioners right in their finding 'that the . . . membership of Congress . . . depended chiefly on popular support . . . [and] that the opposition to Federation was there, that it was deeply rooted and almost universally held.'[18]

Whether as a result of this new-found appreciation of African sentiment, or whether from the realization that as detainees were being released and filtering back to their villages, tension was again building up in the country, the Government decided that a substitute must be found to fill the vacuum Congress had left.

The answer it was seeking presented itself towards the end of August, when Orton Chirwa, recently released from Khami, requested permission to form a new political party. It was granted, and on 30 September, with Banda's approval, the Malawi Congress Party was launched.*

Whatever hopes the Government may have had that Chirwa would be a moderate in the tradition of Kwenje, Chinyama and the rest were quickly dashed, for the new party made plain that it regarded itself as a caretaker organization whose principal tasks were to agitate for the lifting of the State of Emergency and the release of the old Congress leadership from detention.

Under the administration of its Secretary-General, Aleke Banda, a young man of twenty with a flair for organization, who on the declaration of the Emergency had been arrested at his school desk at Bulawayo, detained and subsequently repatriated, the Malawi Congress Party flourished. Since the Emergency regulations forbade public meetings, Aleke Banda started a workers' broadsheet, *Ntendere pa Nchito*,† which became the Party's unofficial mouthpiece; in December it was replaced by an official organ, the fortnightly (later weekly) *Malawi News*. Party membership soared from 8,100 at the end of October to nearly 250,000 in March 1960:[19] here was the

---

* See also *Hansard*, Zomba, 8 March 1963, p. 660, and 13 December 1963, pp. 1024–5. The political use of the name 'Malawi', which is said to mean 'Flames', was prefigured in the Malawi Trading and Transport Company. It derives from *Maravi*, the ancient kingdom ruled by the Chewa chief, Karonga, in the sixteenth and seventeenth centuries. This was said to have extended from the Zambezi in the South to Mombasa in the North, and from the Indian Ocean as far inland as the Luangwa, including large tracts of Northern Mozambique, Northern Rhodesia and southern Tanganyika, as well as Nyasaland (Banda and Cullen Young, *African Way of Life*, p. 10, and G. Shepperson, 'The Fourth Melville J. Herskovits Memorial Lecture', North-Western University Press, Evanston, 1966, p. 24).

† chiNyanja for 'Happiness through Work'. Another journal sympathetic to Congress, *Tsopano* ('Now'), was launched at about the same time by two Europeans, Peter Mackay and James Skinner.

answer to those in Blantyre and Salisbury who still sought to maintain that opposition to Federation was not popularly held.

The Role of Macleod

In October the Conservatives were returned to power with a much increased majority and Macmillan started work on a new policy for Africa. Central to it was the Central African Federation, where the conflict between the 250,000 whites and five million blacks mirrored the larger dilemma posed for the Tories by black and white states in the continent as a whole.

In the early days of the retreat from Empire, immediately after Suez, Macmillan had believed that the simplest way of devolving responsibility in Central Africa would be for the Federation to become a (white-controlled) dominion in 1960: from this had followed the 1957 agreement between Welensky and Lennox-Boyd. But the Nyasaland Emergency, and the vehemence of the reactions to it by African statesmen, had shown this to be impossible if the goodwill of the new black states was to be retained. As Macmillan made clear in his 'Winds of Change' speech in Capetown, a few months later, in the new Tory scheme of things it was black Africa which counted most.

Macmillan's first moves were cautious and ambiguous. In July he announced the setting-up of a commission, under the chairmanship of Sir Walter Monckton, 'to advise . . . on the constitutional programme and framework best suited to the achievement of the objects contained in the Federal constitution of 1953, including the preamble'.[20] He told the House of Commons: 'When all the units of the Federation are in a position to agree, and are agreed, that British Government protection is no longer needed, then – and only then – can the whole Federation go forward to full independence and full Commonwealth membership.'[21]

At the time it was far from clear what Macmillan was getting at, but he was in fact preparing the groundwork for the advancement of the two northern territories until they were 'in a position' to agree (or to disagree). To the execution of this task he appointed Iain Macleod, a fellow Scot of great subtlety and determination.

Macleod was quickly made aware that there could be no meaningful talks about constitutional advance until Banda was released from Gwelo. The growth of the Malawi Congress Party was testimony enough to the strength of his following, and Orton Chirwa, at a meeting with the Colonial Secretary in London in November, had made clear that the party would not enter into negotiations except with Banda at its head. Pressure within Nyasaland was rapidly rising, and the need for constitutional change was patently apparent. One of the four newly appointed members of the Legislative Council, the Rev. A. D. Kayira, had resigned in October after the firing of his manse; there had been a rash of lesser arson incidents and stonings; and in November the M.C.P. had announced its intention of boycotting the Monckton Commission. Aleke Banda explained in *Ntendere pa Nchito*:

The main cause of the clash between the African people and the Government has been the deliberate delay by the British Government to introduce constitutional talks. . . . An interim constitution . . . will only help to fan the already irrepressible impatience of the Africans.[22]

In mid-December Macleod met Armitage in Dar-es-Salaam, and persuaded him to accelerate the release of detainees and to allow some of the more irritating of the Emergency regulations to lapse. But he found Armitage strongly opposed to the release of Banda and others of the hard core of the detainees. The Governor believed that a breakdown of law and order would almost certainly follow, and, as the man directly responsible for Banda's imprisonment, felt his own position would become untenable if Banda were set free. A compromise arrangement, under which Chipembere, the Chisizas and others would remain in detention but Banda would be released if he would undertake to abide by the Government's conditions, fell through because Banda refused to agree to it.[23]

Nevertheless, early in January, faced with mounting Nyasa unrest, Macleod and Macmillan decided that Banda would

have to be freed. While Macmillan went to Africa to propagan-
dize the new Tory view of the continent, Macleod laid the
groundwork for Banda's release. It was arranged that, once it
was accomplished, Armitage, who had expressed unwillingness
to remain Governor with Banda at large, should proceed on
leave. He was to be succeeded by Glyn Jones, then Secretary
for African Affairs in Northern Rhodesia, who in the meantime
would replace Footman as Chief Secretary.

Despite furious opposition from Welensky, who later claimed
he had been duped by the British Government, Macleod pushed
ahead with his plans and by the end of March the arrangements
were complete. This activity had not passed unnoticed, and
there were a number of false alarms that Banda was to be freed.
But it was not until Macleod arrived in Blantyre, 'to sound out
local opinion on constitutional advancement',[24] that the great
day arrived. It came none too soon, for Chiume, who had been
ceaselessly campaigning for Banda's release, had nearly
succeeded in persuading Iceland to arraign Britain before the
European Commission on Human Rights.

In the early hours of 1 April, Banda was awakened in his cell
at Gwelo and flown secretly to Zomba, where he was handed the
release order bringing his detention to an end.

Chapter 8
The Making of Malawi

'Congratulations Macleod! Good wishes Armitage!' said the *Malawi News* in its first editorial after Banda's return: 'The hour of happiness and jubilation has come like a thunderbolt from the blue. Our Messiah, our only beloved Kamuzu, has regained his freedom.' It was no exaggeration of African feelings. The tension which had steadily been building up for the best part of eight months suddenly melted away; as Aleke Banda wrote: 'The whole atmosphere changed. There was an air of friendship already for the first time after such a long time.'[1]

Banda's first concern after his release was for the preservation of this new-found and still rather precarious peace which had settled on Nyasaland. It had been easy to persuade Macleod that there was 'just enough common ground' for a constitutional conference in London in July, for if he had thought otherwise Banda would not have been released. The real problem was to persuade Nyasas to restrain their ebullience, for if there were disorders it would place a powerful weapon in the hands of the settlers, who would argue that Banda was unable to control his followers and that the Malawi Congress Party and its leaders had shown themselves unfitted for further responsibility.

He put across his 'GREAT MESSAGE OF PEACE', as the *Malawi News* called it, with characteristic bluntness:

I want you all to be peaceful. Everybody must be peaceful and quiet. . . . Do not trouble the Europeans. Do not trouble the Asians. Do not trouble the Police. As for the stooges – just ignore them. They do not matter. . . .

There must be peace in the country, from Port Herald to Karonga, so that you can help me to help Mr Macleod to help Nyasaland. Do not spoil my work. If you listen to me you will get your own Government. If you do not listen to me you will not get anything. Leave all the trouble-making to me. I will give them ample trouble . . . in

Zomba and . . . in London. But I will not do it by throwing stones. I will do it with my tongue and brains.[2]

The message sank in; the welcome he was accorded was enthusiastic but not boisterous.

On 5 April Orton Chirwa formally handed over to Banda the Presidency of the M.C.P.,* which now boasted, in sharp contrast to the old Nyasaland African Congress, a large staff, a Land Rover, and a bank balance of over £2,000, and the next day he left on a month-long tour of Britain and America.

There were several reasons for Banda's decision to go abroad before travelling within Nyasaland. He had been invited to speak on British television, and the House of Representatives Africa Committee had asked him to come to New York to attend African Freedom Day. It was thus a useful opportunity to put across his case for self-government and secession when his name was still fresh in the public mind and his impact would be greatest. Moreover, it would give him a chance to consult old friends like Dingle Foot and James Callaghan, and to sense the political climate in Britain. But perhaps the principal consideration was the possibility that a speaking tour within Nyasaland so soon after his release might spark off disturbances, especially since the State of Emergency was still in force. Like the Nyasaland Government, Banda thought a cooling-off period was advisable.

His first essay at propaganda was not very successful. He appeared on Independent Television a few hours after his arrival in Britain, to be confronted with a group of about thirty apparently hostile journalists: as the programme continued, he grew steadily angrier with the questions being put to him, and finally lost his temper, ranting incoherently about Welensky and the Federation.[3] It was not an auspicious beginning, but in the aftermath of Sharpeville, British public opinion was running too strongly in his favour to be upset by a single, faulty T.V. appearance. In individual discussions with Tory and Labour

---

*In other respects the Party's Executive remained unchanged. Chirwa continued in it as a Committee member, and a month later, Chiume, on his return from Britain, became its Publicity Secretary.

politicians, and in a lucid forty-five-minute television interview with John Freeman (later Britain's Ambassador in Washington) a few weeks later, he was able successfully to repair his image.

In the United States he was given from the start a more sympathetic reception. The Americans were charmed by his old-fashioned courtesy, and impressed by his readiness to pay tribute to the British – 'the only colonial people who send a man to prison today only to invite him to Westminster if not Buckingham Palace tomorrow'.[4] He quoted Patrick Henry to them, and praised their great men – Lincoln, Jefferson, Franklin and George Washington – and his demands for self-determination were by and large accepted. He returned to Nyasaland via East Africa in mid-May with firm assurances of support and his confidence restored.

There remained two months before the constitutional conference, and Banda made full use of the time to win support for his Party and to discredit the moderate African opposition groups. The M.C.P. held its first full-scale national conference in Blantyre on 14 and 15 May, and a fortnight later he was allowed to set out on a four weeks' tour of the protectorate's three provinces. The State of Emergency, already over in all but name, formally came to an end on 15 June.

The themes of the speeches at the meetings Banda addressed were always the same: peace and calm, self-government, secession and independence. But he injected into them a ferocious militancy, damning the 'stupid D.C.s' and threatening retribution to all African 'stooges'. He appealed, as ever, to the masses of ordinary Nyasas who made up the bulk of his following. At Nkhata Bay, he told them:

I have only one ambition in my life and that is that in my lifetime I must see that you, my people – men and women – are ladies and gentlemen in the land of your birth. . . . I want self-government for you now, and to Hell with their stupid Federation.

And at Karonga:

When we go to London we are going to demand self-government now and not tomorrow. If we do not get it then know that it is stooges like T. D. T. Banda, Matthews Phiri and others who . . . have blocked the way.[5]

The tour was an enormous success, and when Banda left for London on 13 July he took with him the knowledge that he had a formidable organization behind him.

At Lancaster House

The twenty-nine official delegates and advisers were with difficulty assembled in the cream and gold music room of Lancaster House on the afternoon of 25 July, and the Nyasaland Constitutional Conference began. Macleod himself had suggested the relative strengths of the delegations, and his arrangements were adhered to* – though not without protests from the M.C.P., which objected to being given parity with the U.F.P. and to the presence of the Congress Liberation Party.[6]

On one side was the M.C.P. delegation of four: Banda, Chirwa, Aleke Banda and Chiume, with three chiefs, including Willard Gomani, heir-apparent to the Angoni paramount chieftainship, and an Oxford don, Dr T. O. Elias, as advisers. With them were the two Asian delegates, Sattar Sacranie and A. J. P. Antao, whose Asian Convention had decided in June to back Banda's constitutional demands. On the other was the U.F.P., also with four official delegates, Blackwood, Dixon, Little and Matthews Phiri, and two pro-Federal chiefs as advisers. And in the middle were Armitage and the Nyasaland Government representatives; a delegation of five chiefs; Kwenje and Chinyama, representing the African M.L.C.s; and T. D. T. Banda, sole delegate for the C.L.P. Macleod had the unenviable position of Chairman.

Banda appeared at his most difficult, alternating between reasonableness and hard-line demands. On the eve of his departure for London, he had given a reception at his home in Blantyre at which the guests of honour were Peter Youens and two other senior Government officials (Blackwood and Dixon

*The Coloured community, however, which was offered one seat, did not attend because it could not agree on a representative.

were invited, but did not turn up). His speech then had been widely regarded as a hopeful sign. He had said:

I am going to take what I can take and give what I can give, and I am prepared to compromise if the other side is reasonable. . . . All we want is for the government of this country to be in the hands of the majority – whether those hands are 'civilized' or not.[7]

But once in London, Banda had revived the M.C.P. demand, first put forward in May, for an African majority in the Executive Council, and a Legislative Council of fifty-five members, of whom forty-six were to be Africans elected by universal suffrage. The remaining nine seats were to be taken by six elected non-Africans and three officials, and the scheme was to be implemented by September, in time for the Federal review conference.

The U.F.P. was equally unwilling to make concessions. Blackwood and Dixon were deeply suspicious of the new Tory policy and particularly of Macleod, its co-architect and director. The crisis in the Congo, which had erupted three weeks earlier, made them all the more determined to stand their ground. The warning had been spelt out by the *Nyasaland Times*: 'There, but for the Grace of God . . .'[8]

The only bright spot was the agreement of all parties that the question of secession should not be discussed. But even that, as *The Times* pointed out, was not really very helpful – for the future of Nyasaland could not be considered in isolation from the future of the larger entity of which it was part.[9] Federation remained the dominant hidden factor in the minds of both sides at Lancaster House.

Nevertheless, the conference opened in an atmosphere of optimism. In his formal address of welcome, Macleod said he saw the task ahead as 'to seek a pattern for the orderly evolution of Nyasaland's political institutions on a democratic basis, and in a form which will meet the aspirations and the apprehension of the peoples of Nyasaland, which will provide for the continuance of stable government and progressive administration, and which will enable H.M. Government effectively to discharge its protective responsibilities towards Nyasaland for so long as all its peoples so desire.'[10]

It was a typical piece of Macmillanish ambiguity, enough to give some comfort to both sides of the table, but which carefully obscured the basic dilemma with which the conference was concerned. It did not long remain hidden: in his speech of reply, Banda lauded the Colonial Secretary's intentions and reaffirmed his willingness to give and take. But he bluntly continued:

My people expect great things from this conference. If under the pretext of securing a stable government a scheme is hammered out here which does not satisfy my people I will not be a party to it.

Nyasaland is an African country. The time has come when Africans must govern. Our present type of Government is out of date and out of place. It is not drawn from the elected representatives of the people. I have great hopes because I know what the present Secretary of State has done for other territories, and I do not think he will fail with us. . . . We have had many dirty deals in the past. It is about time we had a fair deal.[11]

This problem – to arrive at a compromise which Banda could reasonably present to Nyasas as an acceptable substitute for the magic formula of 'self-government now' – was uppermost in the collective mind of the British Government throughout the conference. The alternative, as Banda succinctly pointed out, was 'another March 1959'.[12]

For the next three days, the three party delegations made submissions on their individual proposals. The Malawi Congress Party's demands, which had already been made public, were presented first, backed up by five detailed memoranda. The C.L.P. put forward a more moderate programme, aiming for full internal self-government and universal suffrage after a two-stage transitional period lasting five years, but demanding from the start African elected majorities in the Legislative and Executive Councils. The U.F.P. presented unmodified the same proposals which had so angered the N.A.C. when they were first unveiled, nearly eighteen months before. As expected, Blackwood and Dixon said the two African parties' demands were totally unacceptable. The talks met deadlock.

On 29 July, Macleod summed up and put forward the British Government's views in the form of four guiding principles.

They were phrased with great care, and Macleod made clear that they were not final conclusions but rather a basis for further discussion:

1. Nyasaland was destined to become an African state, and the time had now come for a clear African majority on the unofficial side of the Legislative Council. But non-African unofficial representation should be retained.

2. Unofficial M.L.C.s should be elected, but since the elections would be the first in which Africans took part on a country-wide basis, the franchise should be qualitative and broadly based, but not universal.

3. The Executive Council should be advisory to the Governor. It should neither be entirely responsible to the legislature (as the M.C.P. wanted) nor totally unconnected with it (as the U.F.P. wanted).

4. Some official representation would be retained on the Executive Council, but its unofficial members should be drawn mainly, and perhaps entirely, from those elected to the legislature. It might be appropriate to introduce some kind of ministerial system.[13]

After recessing for an uneasy week-end, during which there were fears that Banda might walk out[14] – groundless fears as it turned out, for he knew that to do so would be to play into the hands of the U.F.P. – the conference resumed on 1 August. Macleod's principles were in fact not too different from what Banda had expected. The real sacrifice was over the franchise, and this was acceptable so long as a reasonable substitute could be found. Moreover Macleod had given him what amounted to an assurance that after the first elections universal suffrage could be introduced.

The concrete proposals which underlay Macleod's four principles emerged during the three days of detailed discussion, in individual groups and in plenary session, which followed the conference's resumption. They entailed a dual-roll franchise, with twelve lower-roll seats, six higher-roll and five officials in the Legislative Council; and five officials and five unofficials, the latter drawn from the elected members of the Legislative Council, in the Executive Council. The Governor would retain control through a casting vote.[15]

Agreement on the broader aspects of the franchise was

reached surprisingly quickly. Both sides accepted the idea of a dual roll, and Macleod's proposal that about 100,000 people should be enfranchised on the lower roll was a reasonable compromise between the U.F.P. scheme (20,000 voters) and Malawi's (1 million). But there was enormous argument over how this should be achieved in terms of franchise qualifications, and what finally emerged was one of the most complicated systems ever devised for a colonial territory.

Representation in the legislature was from the start a more contentious problem. Macleod had shown his willingness to grant an absolute African majority in the Legislative Council, but there was a limit beyond which he could not go and still hope to retain the agreement of the U.F.P. For Banda, on the other hand, a substantial majority in the Legislative Council was essential if he were not to jeopardize his political position at home. The question of how large this majority should be took up much of the three days of bargaining, and agreement was only reached after Banda gave a firm assurance that the M.C.P. would do its best to make the new constitution work.

The last point at issue was the composition of the Executive Council, and here the agreed solution approximated to Macleod's original proposal, albeit with some concessions to the M.C.P. When Banda was granted a lower-roll majority in the legislature he was forced to retreat from his original demand for nine African members in an Executive Council of twelve. The compromise adopted fell neatly between his revised proposal, for five Africans out of ten, and the U.F.P. demand for nine non-Africans out of twelve.[16]

On Wednesday night, 3 August, the British press, which for days had been speculating on the likelihood of the talks failing, burst out in a rush of optimism. 'AGREEMENT SAID TO BE CLOSE', the headlines proclaimed – and indeed it was. The following day the conference ended with all delegates assenting to the final report.

The agreement which had been reached with such difficulty was as follows: In the Legislative Council there were to be five officials, eight higher-roll and twenty lower-roll seats. In the Executive Council there would be five officials and five appointees from the elected M.L.C.s, of whom three would come from the lower roll and two from the higher roll. Of the five Executive Council officials, three would be *ex-officio*, while two would be nominated members replaceable by M.L.C.s at the Governor's discretion. All appointments to the Executive Council would carry ministerial status, and provision would be made for the appointment of up to three parliamentary secretaries to understudy Executive Council posts. The detailed implementation of the constitutional proposals and certain contentious matters of minor importance were to be left to a Constitutional Working Party.[17]

Intimidation and the Smallpox Scandal

Banda returned home to a predictably tumultuous welcome, and found little difficulty in presenting the new constitution as the key to self-government and eventual independence. He laid great stress on Macleod's recognition that Nyasaland was an African, not a multiracial, state, and blamed the M.C.P.'s failure to obtain universal adult suffrage on the U.F.P., Matthews Phiri, the pro-Federal chiefs and the African M.L.C.s who, he said, had claimed that most Nyasas were too ignorant to be allowed the vote.

At the time this must have seemed a legitimate political ploy. But, in the excitement following the conference success, it had unforeseen and uncalled-for consequences. On 10 August Kwenje was mobbed in the Blantyre market, and a few days later Phiri was beaten unconscious in the town's main street by a rioting crowd which refused to disperse until tear gas was used. Reports of intimidation and politically inspired arson became more numerous. The *Nyasaland Times* urged the introduction of flogging and Dixon accused the M.C.P. of already having torn up the Lancaster House agreement.[18] At the end of August, Glyn Jones, who was again Acting Governor in the absence of Armitage, issued a statement, endorsed by Macleod, unequivocally condemning the 'hooligan actions' of certain sections of the community and warning that if they continued the constitutional agreement might be endangered. He also asked for, but did not get, an endorsement of his condemnation from Banda.[19] For a while it seemed as though there might yet be serious trouble ahead.

Banda was in fact in a difficult position, for the principal cause of most of the unrest was something which he and his party regarded as an act of bad faith on the part of the British Government: the continued detention, under public security laws introduced when the Emergency was brought to an end, of the last fourteen hard-core detainees, including Chipembere and the Chisiza brothers, and the restriction of some three hundred and fifty former officials of the old N.A.C. Both were matters of crucial importance to him, not least because his own position as a free man was invidious while his chief lieutenants were still in gaol.[20] While he was no less keen than Glyn Jones to see an end to the unrest, and repeatedly appealed for peace and calm, he felt he could go no further until the wrong which he believed was being done was righted.

The Governor, for his part, was under strong pressure from his advisers and from the settlers not to release the remaining detainees for fear that worse violence might follow. He was left in no doubt of the outcry which would be raised if that fear was realized, and it took a good deal of courage to put aside such considerations. But put them aside he did, and in so doing his friendship with Banda was cemented. On 27 September the restriction orders were revoked, and the fourteen 'camp finals' freed and flown to Nkhotakhota, where Banda ceremoniously presented them to the people at a mammoth rally. Chipembere was triumphantly reinstated as Treasurer-General; Dunduzu Chisiza became Secretary-General, and his brother, Administrative Secretary. Banda himself was elected Life President. The exercise was carefully staged to give the maximum effect to the achievement of their release, and Banda responded by denouncing outright the use of violence. Almost overnight the tension melted away.

The Federal propaganda effort, recently augmented by the employment of a British public relations firm, Voice and Vision, capitalized heavily on the unrest in Nyasaland. Part of what was written and said during this period was justified by fact, but much more was crudely and deliberately distorted. Some outrageous claims were made: in the Federal Parliament a Mr Wightwick suggested that perhaps Banda was not a Nyasa at all but a West African;[21] and in Nyasaland members of the territorial U.F.P. circulated a supposedly humorous lyric, purporting to have been written by a Malawi supporter:

> The sewage works will soon break down, the place will stink like
>   mad,
> But it doesn't really matter because it's what we always had.
> We'll all be top executives although we lack the brains
> Because it's frightfully infra-dig to clean the chims* and drains.
>
> *Chorus:*
> Freedom freedom freedom is just the thing for blacks
> Freedom freedom freedom will mean the end of tax.[22]

The low point of U.F.P. morality was reached in November, when accusations began to be heard that Banda and the M.C.P. leadership were impeding the work of Federal vaccination teams sent into the country to deal with an incipient smallpox epidemic. Photographs were circulated of hideously deformed children, and before long European emotions were inflamed to flashpoint. Banda was portrayed as a Moloch figure whose disregard for human suffering was matched only by limitless political ambition.

On 15 November, Chipembere and Chiume issued a joint statement in which they denied the U.F.P.'s allegations.[23] They said that while the Federal nature of the vaccination campaign precluded the M.C.P. as a Party from actively encouraging it, the Party was so far from being obstructive that in some areas, where the epidemic was reaching serious proportions, local party leaders had gone out of their way to make the work of the teams easier. By contrast they instanced cases of African U.F.P. supporters discouraging villagers from being vaccinated and then blaming the results on the M.C.P. – a claim which, sadly enough, was true, although it was ignored by the press.

Banda was in West Africa when the smallpox issue became

---

*Lavatories. The word is a corruption of the chiNyanja term *Chimbuzi*.

front-page news, and his first reaction was of disbelief. It was a dangerous mistake. Partly because of the frequency with which wild accusations had been levelled at him during the previous two years, and partly as a result of an innate reluctance to believe what he did not want to believe, Banda had developed a tendency to dismiss out of hand unfavourable criticism. So for nearly four weeks he maintained that the epidemic was a 'red herring' invented by the settlers to discredit him. Not until 8 December did he deny personal or party responsibility for the failure of the vaccination campaign, and even then his statement was weak and ambiguous.[24] He felt, presumably, that he could not risk spoiling party unity by issuing an outright denunciation. For some reason which has never been adequately explained, neither Banda nor anyone else ever publicly put forward the obvious explanation for the villagers' resistance to the immunization campaign – which was simply that mistrust of the Federal Government was intensifying.

By the time Banda returned to Nyasaland, a few days before Christmas, the smallpox scandal was wearing itself out. But a new problem was emerging: there was mounting unrest as a result of the delay in holding the territorial elections. This was largely Banda's own fault for persistently demanding that the elections take place before the end of 1960, ignoring the Government's view that it would be administratively impossible to hold them until several months later. At the beginning of December, M.C.P. supporters fired the house of Chester Katsonga, leader of the newly formed Catholic-backed Christian Democratic Party. Other incidents followed, some of them sparked off by a series of ill-conceived and inflammatory speeches by Chiume and Chipembere.

Having once been caught out in too much delay, Banda this time reacted quickly. Early in the New Year, delegates from all party branches were summoned to Blantyre to attend a massive 'Peace and Calm' conference, at which they were told bluntly that the disturbances must stop. In a long and passionate speech Banda said he accepted the delegates' explanations that trouble was being provoked by the U.F.P. (which, as he well knew, it was not), but went on:

I have called you here to beg you, to beseech you and to implore
you to maintain peace and calm at all costs. No amount of provocation must deflect you from the goal of peace and calm. Even if the
Police, Europeans and the District Commissioners provoke you, just
remember your Kamuzu wants you to keep peace and order. Even if
your heart is burning and you want to do something to him, just sing
a song. . . . Remember this: there is too much at stake. We must have
elections.[25]

The conference ended disastrously with a riot in which one
Congressman was killed. But it proved to be the last wriggle of
the dying python, and after it the unrest came to an end.

Shortly afterwards Chipembere was sentenced to three years'
imprisonment for sedition, as the result of a speech at Rumpi,
early in December, in which he had said, among other things:
'Give me the living body of Blackwood to tear to pieces. I'll do
the job in two minutes.'[26]

The Party steadfastly maintained that Chipembere was
innocent, and Banda was careful always to refer to him with
affection in his public speeches, realizing the need to retain the
support of his many personal followers. But he had more than
once warned Chipembere of the likely consequences if he spoke
in this vein, and there is no doubt that the trial took place with
Banda's approval. Banda never fulfilled a promise he made to
Chipembere to put pressure on Glyn Jones for his early release,
and seemed privately relieved that Chipembere was behind bars.
The absence of his most militant lieutenant made it that much
easier for him to maintain peace and calm; and the example of
Chipembere's imprisonment may well have deterred those who
might otherwise have favoured a more aggressive attitude.

Monckton and the Federal Review

While the arguments about intimidation and smallpox were at
their height, two events took place which were to have a decisive
effect on the future of the Federation. The first was the publication of the Monckton Report,[27] in October 1960; the second
was the Federal review conference convened in London six
weeks later.

The Monckton Commission had been the subject of controversy ever since it was thought up by Harold Macmillan in March 1959 as the solution to the dilemma raised by the Nyasaland disturbances. First there was argument over its composition, and then over its terms of reference. Welensky insisted that the question of secession be put outside the scope of the inquiry, and the Labour Party demanded that it should not. Macmillan was evasive, and neither side got the assurance it wanted. The Labour Party decided to boycott the commission, and Welensky several times asked that the idea be shelved.

But the British Government went ahead with its plans, and in February 1960 the twenty-six commissioners, including Manoah Chirwa and four other Africans, reached the Federation and set to work. Not surprisingly they were boycotted by the three main African nationalist parties, whose leaders believed, not entirely without reason, that they would turn in a report strongly favouring the continuance of Federation. The *Malawi News* described the Commission as 'the Wooden Horse of Central Africa', and warned its readers, in block capitals: 'REMEMBER WHAT HAPPENED TO THE PEOPLE OF TROY!!!'[28]

As it turned out, the decision to boycott the commission was right, though for the wrong reasons. The report which it produced was a far cry from the reassuring document which most Europeans in Central Africa had expected. It recommended, *inter alia*, parity of representation between Africans and non-Africans in the Federal Assembly, and an African majority in the Northern Rhodesian legislature. It was also highly critical of the Federal Government's failure to implement the ideal of partnership; of the retention of discriminatory legislation in Southern Rhodesia; and of the development imbalance between that country and the northern territories. But, worst of all, it did the one thing which, according to the Federal Government, it should not have done: it suggested that the British Government declare its intention to permit secession, if after a trial period any territory was still opposed to Federal membership. What made 'this terrible piece of high explosive',[29] as Welensky described it, so utterly damning was that it had been formulated by men who were widely reputed to have pro-Federal sympathies, and on evidence which omitted the views of all but the most moderate African groups.

In Kasungu, Banda pronounced himself indifferent to the report and its possible consequences. But beneath this feigned uninterest he was just as vitally concerned as everyone else with the effect that that crucially important recommendation on secession might have on the Federal review conference, due to open in December. Matters were made a little clearer by the British Government's announcement that the review conference would be 'free to discuss this and any other relevant issue'.[30] But still no one could foresee with certainty whether secession would be treated as a genuine possibility or merely as a tantalizing but empty word.

Whether or not to attend the Federal review conference was a question which had been troubling Banda for several months. The British Government wanted him there,* but most of his colleagues opposed the idea on the usual ground that attendance might be regarded as a concession to the Federal Government. While this decision hung fire, Banda contented himself with warning that if the M.C.P. sent delegates their brief would be contained in the single word: 'No'.[31] In the end, the Monckton Report and the British Government's statement on the conference's terms of reference decided him to go, and at the end of November, accompanied by Chirwa and Dunduzu Chisiza, he arrived in London.

The opening of the conference on 5 December ushered in the most difficult fortnight Banda had yet faced as a politician. His uncertainty of the outcome of the review discussion had to be weighed against the importance of appearing reasonable to the British Government. And against both had to be considered the need to reassure the Party in Nyasaland, where discontent over electoral delays was being augmented by anxiety over his presence at the talks. Over everything hung the shadow of the smallpox scandal.

* Macleod had considered appointing Banda to the Executive Council, so that he might attend the talks with ministerial status. He was dissuaded from this course by Sir Roy Welensky. (Welensky, *4000 Days*, p. 271.)

To meet these complex and often conflicting priorities, Banda adopted a policy of private charm and public intransigence. While the conference was in session he twice staged walk-outs, accompanied by Kaunda and Joshua Nkomo, during the speeches of Sir Edgar Whitehead, whom a few days earlier he had described as the leader of a government of 'fourth class artisans'.[32] Whitehead, Banda claimed, was trying to play at being 'Santa Claus'. In his own speech he pulled no punches:

I must state at once [he said] what I have already stated elsewhere – that it was not at all my intention to come here because, in my view, I am wasting my time here. We are meeting here, some say, to examine where the scheme has gone wrong and where the scheme has gone right. So far as I am concerned, I am not here for that. I am here to demand secession and secession now, not in five years time from now. . . . Everybody knows that the scheme can never work. . . . In fact, in my view it is a misuse, indeed a prostitution of the word Federation to use it as it applies to the relationship that exists between Nyasaland on the one hand and Southern and Northern Rhodesia on the other.[33]

A few days later, the opportunity came to assuage the British Government's ruffled feelings when, in the absence of progress at the talks, the principal delegates were invited to spend the weekend at the British Prime Minister's country house, Chequers.

Alone with Macmillan, Banda set out to be at his most engaging. The two men got on well, sharing a love of history and a peculiarly English sense of snobbery, and Macmillan showed little of the unease he usually felt in the company of Africans. Recalling the occasion, Banda said later, 'if my trip to London did nothing else, it allowed me to meet a great Prime Minister.'[34] The next day he returned to the conference for its final session.

When the delegates dispersed on 17 December, they were no closer to agreement than when they had first met. In theory the conference was to resume at a date to be fixed later. Banda returned to Blantyre where he announced that the Federation

was dead, and all that remained was to make the burial arrangements. His statement was greeted with jubilation by the party,
and poohpoohed by the European community. Not until much
later was it admitted that he was right. As Sir Roy Welensky
wrote: 'Though for two years longer they continued to deny it
most vehemently, those who had created the Federation of
Rhodesia and Nyasaland [had] . . . passed sentence of death on
it.'[35]

On to the Elections

For all Banda's complaints of unnecessary delays in the preparations for the elections, the Government had put in a great
deal of work since the end of the Lancaster House conference,
and such hold-ups as had occurred were not of its making. In
August, Glyn Jones had appointed the Constitutional Working
Party, whose report had been forwarded to Macleod two
months later. But the Colonial Secretary had been preoccupied
with other matters, and it was not until December that notice of
its approval, with some amendments, was received in Zomba.
The Order in Council giving effect to the Working Party's
recommendations was published, together with the regulations
made under it, on 3 January.[36] Immediately there was an outcry
from the U.F.P., which claimed that the regulations contained
fundamental departures from the agreement it had entered into
at Lancaster House. Dixon declared that the U.F.P. had been
'sold down the river',[37] and Welensky demanded an investigation by the British Government. The differences were not so
great as the U.F.P. tried to make out, and no one ever claimed
that they would affect the election outcome. Nonetheless, a
bitter dispute developed.

   Banda remained aloof from this issue and devoted his ener
gies to preparing the M.C.P. for the electoral registration cam
paign, which was to begin on 13 February; to fund-raising
mainly by *ad hoc* levies and the sale of party membership card
but also by the sale of cardboard badges on which was printe
'Kamuzu's Election Shilling' (later these were the source o
some confusion since many people thought that they conferre

on the wearer the right to vote);[38] and to repeatedly appealing for peace and calm.

When the registration campaign was under way, Banda made a lightning tour of the central and northern provinces to lend his support to the efforts of local party officials. Although most of those eligible to register did so in the first few days of the campaign, it proved a wise precaution, for in some areas, particularly in the northern province, registration was regarded as a Federal trick and people were loath to take part in it without Banda's personal authorization.[39]

By mid-March, when the registration period ended, 107,076 voters had been registered on the lower roll; 10,000 of these were chiefs, councillors and village headmen, who were not required to be literate, and an approximately equal number were women. On the higher roll there were 4,401 voters, 471 of whom were Africans. In view of the restrictive nature of the franchise, this was a gratifying achievement for the M.C.P., which had encouraged those of its supporters with the requisite qualifications to register on the higher roll. Banda registered in Blantyre on the lower roll, having been refused registration at Kasungu because he did not have the required residence qualifications.[40]

The next four weeks were taken up with the compilation of registers and the hearing of claims and objections to registrations. It was a useful respite not only for overworked party officials, but also for Banda, who took the opportunity of paying a month's visit to Britain and America, where he had been invited to take part in a colloquium at Yale University.

On 20 May the report of the Delimitation Commission was published, together with the electoral regulations, and a week later, Banda, following Nkrumah's example in the 1954 elections in Ghana, announced the names of his twenty* prospective candidates on the lower roll and two on the higher roll. Chipembere's prescriptive right to the Fort Johnston constitu-

*Two of these were later rejected on the grounds that they had an insufficient command of English to participate in parliamentary debates.

ency was recognized by the nomination of his father, an Anglican archdeacon.

Banda's higher-roll candidates were Ishmael Surtee, a coloured businessman from Balaka, standing for the Central Districts (comprising the central province except Lilongwe); and Mikeka Mkandawire, for the Northern Districts (the whole of the northern province). Later four others, including Major Moxon (Shire North, in southern Nyasaland) and a young lawyer, Colin Cameron (Soche, in Blantyre), announced that they would contest other higher-roll seats as Malawi-supported Independents. The U.F.P. likewise contested all the higher-roll seats, but the Christian Liberation Party – formed in March by a merger of the Congress Liberation and Christian Democratic parties – put forward no higher-role candidates.

On the lower roll, the M.C.P. was the only party to contest all twenty seats. Although both the U.F.P. and the C.L.P. had initially announced their intentions of doing the same, each had difficulty in finding candidates, and in some areas could not muster a sufficient number of supporters to obtain the ten names required to be endorsed on every candidate's nomination papers. In the end, the C.L.P. contested seven lower-roll seats and the U.F.P. twelve. Despite an agreement between these two to avoid three-cornered contests the parties overlapped in four constituencies, with the result that five M.C.P. candidates were returned unopposed on nomination day, 20 July. These included Banda (Kasungu-Fort Manning), Chiume (Rumpi), Dunduzu Chisiza (Karonga) and Mckinley Chibambo, now the Party's northern Provincial Chairman (Mzimba North).

The M.C.P. candidates were not chosen by the district committees of the Party in their constituencies, as is usual in a democracy, but by Banda in consultation with local party officials and chiefs. Party chairmen were repeatedly instructed through the *Malawi News* that there should be no electioneering until Banda gave the word, and the deciding of nominations had been one of the main purposes of his central and northern provinces tour in February. This was principally designed to ensure that those selected to represent the Party in the legislature were the best men available. But it was also, in a more general sense, a component of Banda's overall electoral strategy.

This was that the personalities of individual candidates should be kept in the background. They were there, in Banda's scheme of things, not so much in their own right but as 'representatives of Kamuzu'.[41] This was put across in a number of ways, mainly by the candidates themselves in their public speeches and group talks with constituents, but also through Party songs. In these the candidate's name would be coupled with Banda's; in the case of Chokani, in Chiradzulu, the song went:

> Whom shall we choose? Kamuzu Banda.
> Whom shall we choose? Chokani Banda.[42]

There were good reasons for such a policy. It ensured unity, and focused attention on the main question before the electorate which was, according to the M.C.P., did it want Banda or Welensky?

But it also marked a new phase in Banda's development as *the* political leader in Nyasaland. The personality cult which had been created so carefully by Chiume and Chipembere, nearly three years earlier, had been consolidated by Banda's acceptance of the Party's Life Presidency. Now was being added to it a steadily increasing measure of personal power.

The origins of this trend went back to the January 1959 Emergency conference. Whatever the extent of his knowledge at the time, Banda had realized afterwards that some things, at least, his lieutenants had kept from him. As a result, after his release in 1960, he took a much more active interest in the administration of the Malawi Congress Party than ever he had in the N.A.C. In some respects he took this to inordinate lengths, insisting that every Party cheque be signed by himself. While generally his position remained supervisory, he kept a watchful eye on all matters of detail. And it was clearly stated in the Party's revised constitution, drawn up after his release from detention, that 'the Supreme Executive power of the Party shall be vested in the PRESIDENT as advised by the Central Executive Committee.'[43]

The process was taken a step further after Chipembere's imprisonment in February, when an instruction was issued from Party headquarters that henceforward Party songs should praise only Banda and no other party leader.[44]

The announcement of the names of the M.C.P.'s candidates signalled the start of the election campaign proper, and on 29 May Banda set out on a countrywide tour which lasted until the eve of polling day,* 15 August.

The meetings followed a set pattern. The people would begin arriving, by bus, by taxi and on foot, hours before Banda was due to appear. While they waited, members of the local Women's League branch would perform traditional dances. Later, cheer-leaders would take over, exchanging slogans with the crowd until excitement reached fever pitch. Then Banda would make his entrance, and give out the Party rallying-cry: 'Kwacha! Kwacha! Freedom! Freedom! Ufulu! Ufulu! Ntendere!'†

He usually spoke for about an hour or more, contrasting the failures of the 'United Fools' Party' and its 'African Branch', the C.L.P., with the achievements of the Malawi Congress Party. He laid particular stress on his success in persuading the Government, a few months earlier, to bring to an end the prosecution of those who violated the agricultural rules, and on his efforts to obtain the vote for women. He thanked his audience for its support during the struggle for constitutional advance, whose details he recounted at length, and pledged that, when the M.C.P. came to power, the Government in Zomba would be 'your Government, the Government of the ordinary people in the villages'. It was a mixture of showmanship and shrewd politics which was everywhere immensely successful. And to Banda's credit, he constantly reminded his listeners that, after the election, they would have to work even harder than

* The tour ended officially at the beginning of July, but Banda continued speaking in his own constituency of Kasungu-Fort Manning, and at various other points in the southern and central provinces, throughout the following six weeks.

† Kwacha meaning 'Dawn', Ufulu meaning 'Freedom', Ntendere meaning 'Happiness'.

before. 'Money does not rain on anybody like manna from heaven. You have to work for it,' he would say.

But the dominant issue in all Banda's election speeches was not a domestic matter. 'The issue before our People in the coming General Election is simple,' he wrote in the *Malawi News*: 'SLAVERY WITHIN FEDERATION OR FREEDOM AND INDEPENDENCE OUTSIDE THE FEDERATION.'[45] It was clear-cut and readily identifiable, and the M.C.P.'s stand was publicized through every level of the Party machine; in a series of broadcasts on Radio Tanganyika (Malawi eschewed the Federal Broadcasting Corporation); and endlessly in the pages of the *Malawi News*. As the campaign reached its climax, no one doubted that the election would ultimately be decided as, in Banda's words, 'a referendum on Federation'.[46]

The U.F.P., with its pro-Federal stance, and the C.L.P., with a moderate policy but a pretence of being more anti-Federal than Malawi, ran into difficulties almost as soon as their campaigns began. This was not due to intimidation, as they claimed, but to the fact that those Africans who counted themselves their supporters were unwilling to demonstrate it publicly. In a situation where support of the M.C.P. was the moral norm, the subtler forms of social ostracism could be no less unpleasant than crude assault, especially in the tight-knit communal society of rural Nyasaland. After a few desultory attempts at public meetings, both parties elected to continue their campaigns, in so far as they were directed at African voters, at long range – through the press and by the distribution of circulars and pamphlets.

At the beginning of August, Sir Roy Welensky paid a brief and much-heralded visit to Nyasaland for what was described as a 'barnstorming' tour to whip up support for the U.F.P. In fact it was a very restrained affair, and did little to improve his Party's chances. But it gave Banda an opportunity for mischievous comment:

Since May 28 I have been fighting a rabble without a General [he said]. Now for at least three days, from August 2 to August 5, I will be fighting a rabble with its General. After August 15 I will be fighting a General in Salisbury without even a rabble in Nyasaland. Then the beauty of it to me is that the General will have shared the ignominious defeat of his rabble.[47]

Welensky's visit coincided with the last serious attempt the U.F.P. made to hold off their now inevitable election defeat. Between 26 and 28 July, nine houses were burned at Mbobo, near Nkhotakhota. One of them was being used by the U.F.P. candidate in that area, Gideon Makamo, and three others were owned by U.F.P. supporters. It was claimed that the burnings were politically motivated, and Blackwood demanded that the elections be postponed until law and order was restored. Welensky announced the setting-up of a distress fund, and said he would take the matter up with the British Government. Banda said he 'deeply regretted' all such incidents, and renewed his appeal for peace and calm.[48]

This time, however, the U.F.P. was isolated even from those who were usually its most ardent sympathizers. The *Nyasaland Times* editorialized with rare good sense:

Postponement of the elections, unless there was open insurrection in the country, would, at this stage, be the greatest blow that Nyasaland has yet suffered. It could, indeed, very well be the signal for such an insurrection.[49]

Macleod announced in the House of Commons that the elections would take place as planned, and Blackwood accused the Colonial Office of 'turning a blind eye to a state of affairs which bore no resemblance to a democratic election'. Much later Makamo and six other U.F.P. supporters were convicted of conspiring to defeat the course of justice by setting fire to their own homes and perjuring themselves to secure the wrongful imprisonment of others.

Polling began at 6.30 a.m. on 15 August and continued all day. In one place voters camped out the previous night to ensure themselves a place at the front of the queue, and everywhere people began assembling long before dawn. Multiple boxes were used inside the polling booths, each marked with the party's symbol (necessary since not all the voters were literate):

a cock for the M.C.P., a leopard for the U.F.P., and a cross and eagle for the C.L.P. Voting proceeded smoothly and with the solemnity appropriate to what many M.C.P. supporters regarded as a ritual demonstration of faith in Banda. At most stations all but a dozen or so voters had passed through by midmorning. The M.C.P. took all possible precautions to avoid incidents, and the League of Malawi Youth were instructed to stay away from the polling stations. Even Banda badges were left at home.

As the results came in, it became apparent that the M.C.P. had done better than even its most optimistic supporters had forecast. As expected, it won all the lower-roll seats; and on the higher roll, Surtee and Mkandawire were successful, as was Colin Cameron, who benefited from the Malawi-Asian entente in defeating his Asian U.F.P. opponent. The five remaining higher-roll seats went to the U.F.P., the three sitting members – Blackwood, Little and Peterkins – all being re-elected. But it was not so much this that was surprising as the fantastically high poll of 95·1 per cent on the lower roll. Of these votes more than 99 per cent were cast for the Malawi Congress Party. On the higher roll, where the poll was 85 per cent, 43 per cent of the votes cast were *against* the U.F.P.

In discussions with Sir Glyn Jones, who had succeeded Armitage as Governor in April, collecting a knighthood in the process, the U.F.P. maintained that it was entitled to two ministers and a parliamentary secretary by virtue of its majority on the higher roll. But the Government took the view that the M.C.P. had achieved an overall majority, and was only prepared to offer the U.F.P. one minister. This Blackwood would not accept, and on 2 September it was announced that the party would go into opposition. From the lower roll, Banda took the key Ministry of Natural Resources and Local Government; Chiume became Education Minister; and Augustine Bwanausi, a schoolmaster and fellow graduate of Chiume's from Makerere, who had been active in the Chiume-Chipembere group in the mid-1950s and was now the M.L.C. for Blantyre Urban, was appointed Minister of Labour. On the higher roll, Mikeka Mkandawire became Minister without Portfolio, and Colin

Cameron, Minister of Works and Transport. Orton Chirwa, who had been elected in his home constituency of Nkhata Bay, was appointed Parliamentary Secretary for Justice, and Dunduzu Chisiza for Finance.

One wonders if anyone remembered the words James Callaghan used during the Commons debate on the Nyasaland Emergency in March 1959: 'We shall use all the arguments we have used in the past and in the end we shall concede to force what we failed to concede to reason.'[50] Two years and eight months after Banda's last, fateful meeting with Sir Robert Armitage, he had achieved the terms which the Governor had then so confidently rejected.

In Office: 1961–3

The new Government set to work with enthusiasm. Energies which had previously been dissipated in electioneering were applied to more constructive tasks, and the five elected ministers soon confounded their critics by their ability and capacity for hard work. There was a campaign, on the Ghanaian model, to promote adult literacy; and a campaign to encourage the adoption of better methods of agriculture. And there was a spate of new legislation, much of it designed to give effect to election promises or to replace laws which were held to be discriminatory.

Banda, in his capacity as Minister of Natural Resources, introduced the Africans on Private Estates Ordinance, which abolished the 'evil, vicious and pernicious system known as *thangata*',[51] and the Land Use and Protection Ordinance, which finally did away with the coercive clauses of *malimidwe*. Orton Chirwa introduced the Local Courts Ordinance, which provided for the setting-up of courts, presided over by independently appointed chairmen, to try customary law cases. Previously these had been heard before chiefs or district commissioners, the duality of whose functions as administrators and adjudicators led to a certain amount of injustice and a great deal of illfeeling. Banda said later that the job of chiefs was not to rule but to reign, a nice distinction which may not have been understood but apparently placated them for their loss of real authority. He took a similar line in explaining the new laws, which, as Minister of Local Government, he initiated, providing for the election by universal suffrage of district councillors. In British Colonial territories this was the usual precursor of universal suffrage in general elections, but it had also the incidental effect of further weakening the position of the traditional authorities. To some extent this erosion of their powers was deliberate. But, like other African leaders, and indeed more than most, Banda was later to devote much attention to the problem of how to eliminate tribalism while retaining cultural continuity and traditional institutions.

For the moment, however, his preoccupation was with Nyasaland's economic difficulties and in particular with his personal responsibility, agriculture, the main foreign exchange earner, which after two years of political instability was in a parlous state. Banda had long dreamed of making Nyasaland 'a Denmark of Central Africa',[52] and now in power he sought to fulfil this ambition by an extended campaign to improve the standard of peasant farming and increase smallholder production. He worked tirelessly, explaining at meeting after meeting by simple metaphors and examples the improvements in farming practices he was trying to bring about. His efforts were rewarded, for within a year agricultural production rose by a third.

Banda's economic policies, which were founded in the belief that Nyasaland was, and would remain for many years, in essence an agricultural country, sought to combine elements of both socialism and capitalism. Initially communal effort and individual achievement were regarded as of equal importance. In this Banda was following the lead of Dunduzu Chisiza, who had proposed that Nyasaland should develop a 'mixed' economy, shaped to meet its particular requirements. In Chisiza's scheme of things, socialism was dominant. But later, under Banda, the bias was reversed, partly to retain the confidence of the European business community. After Chisiza's death in a car accident in September 1962, the capitalist tendency became more pronounced. The cooperative schemes, in which Banda, despite his own experience at Kasungu in the early 1950s, had placed much faith, were allowed to run down. Many of the policies Chisiza had advocated lost impetus or fell away. And such objectives as the 'reduction of inequalities in incomes, wealth and economic power'; 'the principle of equal pay for equal work'; and the 'provision of social security for those of the aged, infirm, and disabled who have no one to depend upon'[53] – all of which figured prominently in the Party's 1961 election manifesto – were largely lost sight of.

Chisiza's death, at thirty-two, was a tragedy for Nyasaland. The Malawi Congress Party lost its foremost intellectual, and the country an economic intelligence which, a decade later, it has not been able adequately to replace. Nonetheless, Chisiza's attempts to reconcile aspects of socialism and capitalism were fraught with difficulties, and it is doubtful to what extent he would have succeeded even had he lived. One key problem, which came to a head a few months before he died, concerned the trades union movement.

In 1961 the National Council of Labour, the left-wing pro-M.C.P. rival of the Nyasaland Trades Union Congress, had organized a number of strikes in support of wage claims. When Bwanausi became Minister of Labour, the use of the strike weapon was discouraged. For a few months there was an uneasy calm, but in June 1962, during Banda's absence in Europe, a bitter dispute developed between the Party and two of the most militant Council of Labour unions, the Transport and Allied Workers Union and the Commercial and General Workers Union. The union leaders, Suzgo Msiska and Chafuka Chihana, advocated nationalization and communal ownership, and both complained bitterly against what they regarded as the Party's betrayal of the workers' interests. On 16 June, Msiska said that the Transport and Allied Workers Union would not allow itself to become a puppet of the Government,[54] and shortly afterwards Chihana accused the M.C.P. of capitalistically exploiting Nyasa workers.[55] Both were promptly suspended from Party membership and denounced in the *Malawi News*.[56] This was the Party's ultimate sanction against dissidents, for the effect of these measures was to isolate those against whom they were applied from all other party members.* Thereafter the trades unions grew progressively weaker. Many of their leaders were absorbed into the civil service or the party hierarchy; the Council of Labour was absorbed into the Trades Union Congress; and the latter was made powerless by enforced subservience to the Party's wishes.

The crushing of all opposition and the proving of the new Government's maturity and ability were essential, though perhaps unrationalized, ingredients in Banda's preparations for the next round of constitutional talks with the British Government. The strategy which accompanied them was, however, quite deliberate: it consisted in winning the confidence of the European community.

This was the most adroit manoeuvre in all the long history of Banda's negotiations with Britain. Nyasaland sorely needed European skills and money if it were to progress quickly to economic viability, and its ability to retain them was a factor Britain could not ignore in deciding its rate of advance to self-government and beyond. This is not to impugn the sincerity of Banda's non-racialism; but it is to point out that, in its application to Nyasaland, non-racialism, like many others of Banda's policies, is based no less securely in realities than in idealism.

Throughout the 1961 election campaign, and indeed ever since his return to Nyasaland in 1958, Banda had stressed that his aim was to build a state 'in which colour, race or creed will mean nothing'.

Those Europeans who want to live in this country, to do business as traders, industrialists, farmers and any other occupations, and those Europeans who want to live in this country as our guests, friends and our citizens have nothing to fear from me or from any of my followers. We welcome such Europeans. Neither I nor any of my followers has any intention of driving this kind of European into the

---

* At the time of Msiska's and Chihana's suspensions, this was by convention rather than by virtue of any explicit instruction. Later, however, it was appended to the Party constitution: 'No member of the Party shall co-operate with or fraternize with a person who has been denounced, suspended or expelled from the Party.' (*Malawi Congress Party Constitution* (1969 Edition), Malawi Congress Party, Limbe. Appendix I, p. 19, regulation 8.)

Atlantic Ocean or this kind of Asian into the Indian Ocean. But let me be open and frank. Those Europeans who do not realize that this is not 1892 but 1960 and those Europeans who . . . want to come here to be our Lords and Masters . . . I say to them 'Pack up and go now!' For this kind of European, for this kind of Asian – there is no place for him here. This is our country, our home. The only home we know on the continent of Africa.[57]

It was the system, not the individual, that Nyasas must fight, Banda maintained. The point was vividly demonstrated when, in April 1961, he invited Sir Robert Armitage to a farewell dinner a few days before his retirement. He bore no grudge against the man who had gaoled him, he told guests at the function. He and Armitage had merely been carrying out their respective responsibilities, and the fact that these had conflicted was no ground for personal enmity.

At his first press-conference after his election victory, Banda took pains to emphasize that 'the future of Europeans in this country is more secure than ever it was before.'[58] Europeans, understandably, took some convincing of this. Many believed that Banda had been directly implicated in the 'massacre plot', and even those who did not were made wary by the nearness of events in the Congo. Nevertheless, he persevered, and gradually the barriers to understanding were lowered. The key to his eventual success was Michael Blackwood, who, shortly before the elections, had succeeded the inflexible Dixon as the U.F.P.'s territorial leader. Despite their differences on the Federation question, he and Banda built up a harmonious working relationship, and under his lead the five U.F.P. M.L.C.s played a constructive role as parliamentary representatives of minority interests. European fears were carefully assuaged. It was announced that European schools would not be integrated; farmers were told that steps would be taken to stop encroachment; businessmen were informed that the Labour Code of the International Labour Organization would be interpreted with flexibility; and civil servants were assured that there would be no premature localization. Some Europeans, unable to accept the idea of rule by a black Government, packed their bags and left; but the majority stayed.

The Banda–Butler Constitution

The transition to full internal self-government came quickly. After the M.C.P. had been in power for only three months, Sir Glyn Jones announced that he intended to exercise his discretionary powers to replace the two nominated officials on the Executive Council with elected M.L.C.s, so giving the party an absolute majority. In March 1962, John Msonthi, a schoolmaster and graduate of the University of Bombay, was sworn in as Minister of Trade and Industry; a few days later Chokani was appointed Minister of Labour, replacing Bwanausi, who took over the newly formed Ministry of Home Affairs.

In May, R. A. Butler, Minister in charge of Britain's new Central Africa Office, arrived in Nyasaland for talks with the Governor and the leaders of the two main political parties. After further discussions with Banda and Sir Glyn Jones in London six weeks later, he announced that a full-scale constitutional conference would be held in Britain in November.

The Marlborough House conference, which opened on 12 November, was a very different affair from the Lancaster House conference of two years before. Shortly before it began, Blackwood told a press-conference that he expected it to result in the introduction of cabinet government with Banda as Prime Minister. Banda, meanwhile, in his opening speech to the conference, paid tribute to Blackwood's 'responsible opposition' in the Legislative Council. He went on:

> When I came here in 1960 I said I came in a spirit of give and take. This time I have come in a spirit of take – to take what is mine by conquest at the ballot box and by successful and creditable performance in office.
>
> We face a great and hard task, but I am certain that we are old friends here and this will enable us to come through without any difficulty.[59]

And so it did. The negotiations proceeded with ritual formality for almost a fortnight, though there was not actually very much to argue about. One official said he could not recall having seen 'such harmony or so much willingness to cooperate'.[60]

The only real point at issue concerned the writing into the constitution of a Bill of Rights to safeguard minority interests. Banda maintained that it was not necessary; Blackwood maintained that it was. In the compromise which was reached, safeguards were entrenched although not quite as deeply as Blackwood would have liked. But as Banda pointed out, the only true safeguards lay not in paper guarantees but in 'the goodwill of the [African] people of this country'.[61]

On 23 November, the conference ended in unanimous agreement. Advance would take place by two stages, the first to become effective by an amendment to the present constitution not later than February 1963. Under it the Executive Council would be replaced by a ten-member cabinet, presided over by a Prime Minister, and including, at Banda's suggestion, the Financial Secretary, Henry Phillips, as *ex-officio* Minister of Finance. Ministers would be appointed by the Governor, on the Prime Minister's advice, from among the elected members of the legislature except that, as a transitional measure – again at Banda's suggestion – up to three ministers might be appointed from outside it. The cabinet would be responsible to the legislature, which was to be renamed the Legislative Assembly and would consist of the existing number of elected members, an elected Speaker, and such ministers as might be appointed from outside it. The second stage, which would entail the enacting of an entirely new constitution, would provide *inter alia* for an increase in the number of elected members of the legislature; the broadening of the franchise (in fact the introduction of universal suffrage, although this was not explicitly stated); and the seating in the legislature of representatives of minority groups. It would be introduced 'as soon as administratively possible'.[62]

By common consent, the question of Nyasaland's secession from the Federation was not discussed at Marlborough House, although inevitably it hung like a huge question mark over the proceedings. The British press took the view that, if Banda pursued his demands for his country's excision, it must eventually be allowed, but it was not suggested that any decision would be reached for several months. Then, at the beginning of December, a three-man Federal cabinet mission flew to London amid a sudden spate of rumours that secession was imminent. It began to look very much as if self-government was not all that had been decided on during Banda's stay in the British capital.

The Federal Break-Up

After the Federal review conference, the future of the Federation remained in abeyance for over a year. In January and February 1961 there were territorial conferences to decide on new constitutions for Southern and Northern Rhodesia, followed by a long and ultimately successful campaign by Welensky to get the agreed proposals for the latter territory modified.[63] The resultant 'solution' imposed by Macleod in June made it almost impossible for Northern Rhodesian Africans to obtain a majority in the legislature, but rather less difficult for the U.F.P. It did, however, ensure that the referendum in Southern Rhodesia on that territory's new constitution was successful. Kaunda, meanwhile, rejected the new Northern Rhodesian scheme and launched a passive resistance campaign, which by August was threatening to get out of hand. Macleod found himself in the impossible position of having to offer to reopen constitutional talks after twice having announced that they had been finally closed. Welensky was furious; Kaunda was intransigent; and Macleod was duly grateful when, in October, he was replaced as Colonial Secretary by Reginald Maudling. Under Macmillan's tutelage, Maudling continued Macleod's tactics, and four months later an unsatisfactory and barely acceptable compromise was achieved.

Meanwhile, in Nyasaland, Banda had been carefully preparing for his next assault on the Federal structure. His policy consisted of a deliberate polarization of what he called the 'reasonable' and the 'pig-headed' sides of his character.[64] In dealing with Nyasaland's territorial problems – constitutional advance, the protection of minority interests, the need to retain European expertise – he showed himself to be understanding and willing to come to terms with the British Government's wishes, even in some cases where they differed sharply from his own. But on the subject of Nyasaland's secession he was immovable.

Welensky took this as evidence that Banda had 'a split personality with a pathological hatred of Federation'.[65] But while Banda's facility for combining in his personality conflicting traits, of which this was an instance, did owe something to the strains of the previous decade, Welensky was wrong in ascribing what was a highly effective and quite deliberate political tactic to pathological prejudice. This same facility which Banda now used consciously, would later reappear undeliberately and unconsciously. But in the particular case of Federation, Banda was doing no more than to ensure, by his willingness to compromise on everything *except* this issue, that in this one respect the British Government would not lightly disregard his demands.

The Malawi Congress Party's refusal to accommodate in any respect to Federation or its agents was shown in a host of ways. M.C.P. ministers refused to open correspondence from the Federal Government.[66] The Party refused to recognize degrees awarded by the supposedly non-racial University College of Rhodesia and Nyasaland, in Salisbury, and when Chiume launched a 'Send the Student' fund, donors were expressly warned that the money would not be used to send students to that university, because, as Banda put it, 'it colonizes their minds'.[67] When the Governor-General of the Federation, Lord Dalhousie, paid a visit to Nyasaland in September 1961, the Party boycotted it.[68] And when the Federal Ministry of Health wanted to launch a vaccination campaign in schools, Chiume, as Minister of Education, forbade it.[69]

The most striking demonstration of Banda's intransigence concerned the much vaunted Nkula Falls hydro-electric scheme, on the Shire River in southern Nyasaland. The Federal Government had dithered for several years before deciding, at the end of 1961, for reasons of political expediency, to go ahead with it. The project was to cost about £3 million, and would be financed by the Federal Government. But Banda refused point-blank to agree, arguing that, if Welensky could raise the money to build it, so could he. Recalling, perhaps, Sir Edgar White-head's jibe that if Nyasaland seceded, its people would starve, he told a press-conference in Zomba:

> I will build the thing but it will not be with Welensky's help. I would rather see the whole of Nyasaland starve to death than accept charity from Welensky. I am not going to beat about the bush. If Welensky wants to build it he must build it with an army, but I don't think he is all that stupid.[70]

As it turned out, Banda's logic proved correct, and the project went ahead a few years later under the aegis of the Common-wealth Development Corporation. But it raised the much larger question of the economic relationship built up between Nyasa-land and the Federal Government during the eight years of the Federation's existence.

To Welensky this was the key consideration in any talk of secession. He could point to the Federal Government's expendi-ture in Nyasaland in the fields for which it was responsible (which on paper seemed quite substantial, though in fact it was only a fraction of what should have been spent), and to such development as it had initiated in the territory (which was pre-cious little, but Welensky argued *post hoc ergo propter hoc* that without Federation there would have been even less). He was able to argue convincingly, moreover, that at its present stage of development Nyasaland was not an economically viable entity on its own.

Banda, on the other hand, regarded the economic merits or demerits of Federation as largely irrelevant. What was import-ant, he maintained, was that Nyasas did not want it and would not have it. Like Nkrumah, he declared: 'Get political power first and then you can manipulate the economic situation.'[71] Few things enraged him so much as talk of the economic advantages Nyasaland was said to derive from membership of the Federation, and in 1958 and 1959 his irrational behaviour in the face of economic arguments alienated many who might otherwise have been more sympathetic to his cause, both in the

Federation itself and abroad.* This was doubly unfortunate since the Federalists' case was not as strong as most people believed.[72] Later, when Banda became a member of the Government with economics as one of his main concerns, he charged that since Nyasaland had been economically viable before Federation, its imposition had positively hindered development. Nyasaland's usefulness to the rest of the Federation was as a dumping ground for inferior merchandise, manufactured in Southern Rhodesia, and as a source of cheap labour, he declared. When Nyasaland seceded, he argued, investment would be stimulated by the ending of political uncertainty, and the popular enthusiasm generated by independence would result in vastly increased agricultural exports and a dramatic upsurge in commercial activity.

Like Welensky, Banda was not above distorting the facts to suit his purpose, and while there was a certain amount of truth in what he said, the fact remained that Nyasaland was a poor country. If it did secede, Britain would have to subsidize its budget to the tune of several million pounds a year.

When, in February 1962, with the Northern Rhodesian constitutional wrangle at its height, the Commonwealth Secretary, Duncan Sandys, flew to Salisbury to reopen discussions on the future of the Federation, Welensky sought to magnify the financial onus which would have to be borne and the economic catastrophe which he predicted would result, in the event of Nyasaland's withdrawal. None the less, he had realized by now that, in the light of Banda's election victory and subsequent pronouncements, Britain would almost certainly allow him to secede, and he told Sandys that, given certain assurances, the Federal Government would 'reluctantly' be prepared to agree to Nyasaland's excision.† The principal condition on which he insisted was that whatever was decided should be a composite

---

*In some other respects Banda also carried his obduracy too far: his refusal, for instance, to meet groups of British M.P.s, visiting the Federation at the invitation of Voice and Vision, on the grounds that they were prejudiced before they set out, lost him a number of potential supporters.

†By his own account, Welensky first reached this conclusion and communicated it to the British Government several months earlier (*Hansard*, Federal Assembly, Salisbury, 19 December 1962).

solution for all three territories. He went on to propose that the less productive parts of Northern Rhodesia should be allowed, like Nyasaland, to become black states, while the Copperbelt and the line of rail, together with Southern Rhodesia, 'the essence of the Federation',[73] as he called it, should go forward to full independence under a predominantly white government.* Welensky's readiness to sacrifice the 'inessential' parts of the Federation laid bare a great deal of Federalist hypocrisy.[74]

While in Central Africa, Sandys visited Zomba, where he had what appears to have been a rather formal, reserved meeting with Banda and Sir Glyn Jones, at which he invited the former to visit London in April for further talks on Nyasaland's relationship with the Federation. Shortly afterwards Banda announced that he was willing to visit Salisbury for discussions with Welensky, provided that the only item on the agenda was the method and implications of the Federal break-up.[75] Unsurprisingly, Welensky refused. Sandys returned to London, and soon afterwards Welensky followed for a series of unsatisfactory and inconclusive talks with Macmillan and Maudling, at which each side said it was the responsibility of the other to initiate proposals for the Federation's constitutional advance. Back in Salisbury at the beginning of March, Welensky dissolved the Federal parliament and announced a general election to seek, as he put, 'a mandate to prevent the break-up of the Federation'.[76] Banda's proposed visit to London was postponed. Although on 27 April the U.F.P. was returned to power with an increased majority, it was not a very convincing mandate, for the elections were boycotted by the three African nationalist parties and the majority of the European opposition groups.

---

*Lord Alport, then British High Commissioner in Salisbury, apparently raised this idea – which had first been put forward fifteen years earlier by Sir Stewart Gore-Brown – in conversation with Whitehead a few days before Sandys's arrival (Lord Alport, *The Sudden Assignment*, Hodder and Stoughton, 1965, pp. 165–9). It was introduced into the negotiations, however, as the fruit of the Federal cabinet's thinking, and Whitehead subsequently made it his own in the shape of the so-called 'Salisbury Plan'. Later Welensky lamented that these 'practical proposals for a readjusted and rebuilt Federation' had been 'ruthlessly disregarded' by the British Government (Welensky, *4000 Days*, p. 318).

In the third week of March, Macmillan announced that responsibility for Central Africa would be taken over by R. A. Butler, 'the most ingenious negotiator of all', as Anthony Sampson called him.[77] Butler tackled his new assignment with calm and evasiveness. In April, he told the Federal High Commissioner in London, Sir Albert Robinson: 'I intend to tell Banda that he won't get unilateral secession, and that whatever we do will have to be part of a general settlement. And I assure you that we shall do nothing without the most exhaustive inquiry.'[78] A month later, despite strenuous opposition from Welensky, he announced in the House of Commons the setting-up of a committee to carry out the 'exhaustive inquiry' in rather different terms:

It remains the view of Her Majesty's Government that there are great advantages for all the peoples of Central Africa in a continued association of the three territories. At the same time it is clear that there is widespread criticism of the present form of the Federation. Her Majesty's Government acknowledge that Dr Banda and the Malawi Party in Nyasaland, supported by a firm mandate at the last election, are not prepared for Nyasaland to remain with the present Federation. On the other hand Her Majesty's Government think it right that, before any firm conclusion is reached about Nyasaland's withdrawal from the present Federation, there should be a full examination both of the consequences of the withdrawal for Nyasaland and also of possible alternative forms of association with the other two territories.[79]

It is difficult to pinpoint exactly when Britain decided that Nyasaland must be given the right to secede. Banda's victory in the 1961 elections made it certain that if he persisted in demanding secession it would have to be granted; but it seems that no final decision was taken until after the failure of the 1962 London talks between Macmillan and Welensky. By mid-May of that year, when Butler and Dr Banda held their first talks in Zomba, it had become irrevocable. In October the committee appointed to examine the consequences of secession reported that the M.C.P. ministers were willing to take whatever measures were necessary to minimize its economic effects.[80] And on 5 November, Welensky was informed that Britain had decided

to permit Nyasaland to secede.[81] At his request, the announcement was delayed until after the Southern Rhodesian territorial
election on 14 December, in which, nevertheless, the U.F.P.
was trounced by the anti-Federal Rhodesian Front. In London,
Butler and Banda agreed that a statement would be made shortly before parliament went into its Christmas recess. And on
19 December it was announced in the House of Commons:
'Her Majesty's Government accept in principle that Nyasaland
shall be allowed to withdraw from the Federation.'[82]

In Salisbury, Welensky gave vent to his feelings in a bitter
tirade against British duplicity. 'The British Government have
ratted on us,' he told the Federal parliament. 'They have gone
back on the most solemn undertakings and intentions. . . . They
have been guilty of an act of treachery.'[83] It was an ill-conceived
speech, and much in it had been better left unsaid. But it was
perhaps excusable, for Welensky lived on to see his life's work
set at nought. The private tragedy inherent in his situation went
largely unremarked, but, years later, when Lady Welensky died,
Banda sent his old political opponent a long and sympathetic
message of condolence. In public, however, he continued to
portray him as the arch-fiend and perpetrator of Federation.

The Premiership

On 1 February 1963, at the start of a weekend of nationwide
celebration, Banda was sworn in as Nyasaland's first Prime
Minister. Chirwa came into the cabinet as Minister of Justice.
Bwanausi took over responsibility for Works and Housing. And
Chipembere, newly released from Zomba prison, was appointed
Minister of Local Government. It was the most able cabinet
Banda ever had. Henry Phillips and his Parliamentary Secretary,
John Tembo, a young graduate from Roma University in
Maseru, set about the complicated business of negotiating with
Britain an annual budgetary subsidy, while the wearisome dis-
entangling of Nyasaland's affairs from those of the Federal
Government was tackled with collective enthusiasm by a minis-
terial committee under the chairmanship of Chiume.

Chipembere's return was welcomed with all the enthusiasm

accorded a long lost son. Banda gave a cocktail party to cele-
brate his release and vigorously defended his earlier militancy.
Shortly afterwards, on his instructions, Archdeacon Chipembere
resigned his seat in the legislature to make way for his son.
Within the Party Chipembere was re-instated as Treasurer-
General, while Aleke Banda became Secretary General (following the demise of Dunduzu Chisiza) and Albert Muwalo, a
former administrative assistant in the Party, took over from
Yatuta Chisiza as Administrative Secretary.*

But despite this appearance of jubilation, Banda was at heart
far from happy at Chipembere's release. He had made no
attempt to cut short his sentence, as he easily could have done,
and although he kept his promise to have Chipembere freed
before he completed his term, it was only by ten days. Moreover, this was intended to forestall a massive demonstration of
support being planned by the Party. A month or so later, Banda
sent Chipembere with Chiume on a two months' study visit to
America, to allow the excitement at his return to die down.†

Banda's reaction to Chipembere's return reflected a new
trend in his accumulation of power. Whereas initially he had
concentrated on entrenching his own position, he was now also
seeking to increase his control over his colleagues. In his mani-

---

*Not all these appointments took effect at the same time. Aleke Banda
became Acting Secretary-General after Chisiza's death in September 1962,
while Chipembere was appointed in January 1963. Muwalo was not promoted until the beginning of April, following Yatuta Chisiza's appointment
as Parliamentary Secretary for Labour.

† Banda may also have feared that Chipembere's fiery oratory might spark
off disturbances. Nyasas were in a victorious mood following the achievement of self-government and secession, and in February and March there
was a certain amount of intimidation of former 'stooges'. That there was
not more was due to the fact that Banda was known to disapprove of it. As
he explained: 'I am doing my best, if I hadn't done what I have been doing,
they would have been torn to pieces by my people. . . . [They are] lucky to be
alive' (*Hansard*, Zomba, 8 March 1963, p. 673). Banda's fears were shown
to be partly justified, for after Chipembere's return from America there were
a number of minor incidents in the lower Shire valley. The Federal Government alleged that there had been a total breakdown in law and order in
Nyasaland. Banda turned a blind eye, and attempted with some success to
pretend that the incidents had never happened (ibid., 10 July 1963, pp.
707-61).

pulations of the Central Executive after Chipembere's release, he attempted to counterbalance the Chipembere-Chiume group with the new recruits, Muwalo and Aleke Banda. It was the familiar colonial technique of 'Divide and Rule'. The process was symbolized by Banda's assumption of the Premiership, but in fact it had begun several months earlier.

In July 1962, Banda had appointed a sub-committee of the Central Executive, under the chairmanship of Orton Chirwa, to inquire into party discipline with a view to improving the 'management of the Party as the sole ruler of this country'.[84] The intention was to set up suitable machinery for dealing with dissidents, notably the more militant trades unionists and members of the Convention African National Union, a left-wing party then being formed by Pemba Ndovi, a one-time M.C.P. National Organizing Secretary who had been dismissed in 1960. But when its report was published, five months later, it went very much further than its original, limited objectives had suggested. The preamble stated explicitly that 'in Malawi* the Party is supreme and ... no one is above the Party', and declared that its members must subordinate their personal interests to those of the Party 'because only then can the Party, like a disciplined army, carry out our promise ... and lead the Nation to prosperity'.[85]

The key recommendations were contained in the rules and regulations which made up the body of the report. Most of them dealt with the powers of the Life President. Rules 15 and 16 laid down that:

> The Life President, as the Supreme Leader and Symbol of the Supremacy of the Party, must be respected, honoured and revered by every member of the Party, high or low, and Party members, high or low, are expected to conduct themselves in a courteous and respectful manner in his presence.
>
> Any member of the Party guilty of disloyalty, rumour mongering, deliberate manufacture of destructive stories, invidious whisper campaigns, loose talk and character assassination against any member of the Party or the Party itself or who contravenes any of these rules

---

*The M.C.P. used the name to denote nation as well as party, and the distinction between the two frequently became blurred.

and regulations . . . shall be dealt with in such manner as the President in his absolute discretion may think fit.[86]

Thus Banda was given blanket powers to control not only the Party's rank and file, but also his most senior colleagues. The Discipline Regulations, as they came to be called, set out a list of slogans to be used exclusively in Banda's honour (including Ngwazi, Saviour, Messiah, and MOTO! [FIRE!]); forbade the use of Party machinery to organize demonstrations of popular acclaim for anyone except Banda (in practice exceptions were sometimes made in the case of visiting V.I.P.s, but only with Banda's express authorization); prohibited drunkenness, disorderly behaviour, the encouragement of tribalism, regionalism, sectionalism, parochialism, division or disunity, and the forming of personal cliques within the Party (on pain of 'severe punishment, not excluding expulsion from Party membership'); and deprived ministers of the right to make statements relating to Party policy without having first obtained Banda's approval. The committee's report was adopted unanimously on 15 February 1963, and was subsequently written into the Party constitution.

Meanwhile the dreary dismantling of the Federation continued. In March Welensky visited London for a forlorn meeting with Butler at which he was told that Northern Rhodesia, too, was to be allowed to secede. Three months later, at Victoria Falls, representatives of the four Governments decided that the dissolution should be completed by the end of December.

In September, Banda and Sir Glyn Jones travelled to London to negotiate the last stages of constitutional advance, and it was agreed that Nyasaland would become independent on 6 July 1964. Soon after returning home, Banda announced a general election to permit the enlargement of the Legislative Assembly. Under the Marlborough House constitution, which had been brought into effect in May 1963, fifty members would be elected on a general roll by universal suffrage, and, at Blackwood's insistence, five members on a special roll reserved for Europeans. Many Europeans, however, felt that this arrangement was racialist and refused to register. As a result of their representations, the number of reserved seats was reduced to three, and Europeans who did not wish to register on the special roll were allowed to do so on the general roll. The registers were compiled, the new constituencies delimited, and on nomination day, 6 April, all fifty M.C.P. candidates were elected unopposed, as were the three Europeans – Blackwood, Morgan and Peterkins.* The African opposition parties, C.A.N.U., the C.L.P. and a splinter group, Mbadwa, shortly afterwards disbanded.

The election campaign generated great excitement, and Banda's victory – 'a world record', as he called it – did no more than reflect his enormous popular support. But it was marred by a running conflict between the Youth League and Young Pioneers movement† and the Jehovah's Witnesses sect. The Witnesses, who eschewed all forms of temporal government, vigorously opposed the Party's campaign to persuade Nyasas to register as voters. As a result of this 'provocation', large numbers of violent clashes took place, some of them serious. All news of these incidents was carefully suppressed.

A month later, Banda announced the composition of the cabinet he would lead after independence. At sixty-six, he was by far its oldest member. Yatuta Chisiza, thirty-eight, came in as Minister of Home Affairs, and Mikeka Mkandawire went out, apparently at his own request, to further his education. Cameron took over the Ministry of Works, and John Msonthi, thirty-six, the Ministry of Transport and Communications, while Bwanausi, thirty-four, headed a new composite Ministry of Development and Housing. Chipembere, also thirty-four,

* All three were members of the Nyasaland Constitutional Party, as the territorial division of the U.F.P. had been renamed after the announcement that Nyasaland would secede. After independence its name was changed to the Constitutional Party.

† The Young Pioneers movement was founded in August 1963 as a means of directing the energies of militant elements in the Youth League, of which it remained an integral part, into constructive channels. Based initially on the Ghanaian movement of the same name, but later remodelled on Israeli lines, its members were taught modern methods of agriculture and then sent back to their villages to act as exemplars to the local people. The movement remained strongly political, however.

retained his newly acquired portfolio of Education but lost Local Government, which became part of Chisiza's responsibilities. Banda himself took over Trade and Industry, in addition to his other responsibilities as Prime Minister, Minister of Health, and Minister of Natural Resources, Surveys and Social Development. On Independence Day, John Tembo, thirty-one, would replace Henry Phillips as Minister of Finance, and Chiume, thirty-five, would become Minister of External Affairs, as well as Minister of Information. The three M.C.P. regional* chairmen, Chibambo, in the North, Richard Chidzanja, in the Centre, and Gomile Kumtumanji, in the South, all retained their appointments as parliamentary secretaries, as did Mrs Rose Chibambo.

At midnight on 5 July, the Union Jack was lowered for the last time, watched by Banda, Prince Philip and the representatives of some sixty other nations, and replaced by the red, green and black of Malawi. Bonfires blazed on the hills, and there were firework displays and traditional dancing: the old merged with the new, and everywhere there was joy, confusion and a hint of nostalgia. Banda delighted a radio audience by singing the old hymn, 'Bringing in the Sheaves', and the new state went forward to take its rightful place among the nations of the world.

Two days later the celebrations came to an end; the guests dispersed and the bunting was taken down. Banda set out to attend the Commonwealth Prime Ministers' meeting in London, and the summit conference of the Organization of African Unity in Cairo.

* Nyasaland's 'provinces' were renamed 'regions' in May 1963.

Chapter 9
Discretional Alignment and Co-existence

Banda never seriously attempted to play off East against West in the scramble for aid. In 1960, shortly after his release from Gwelo, he several times stated that if the West refused to help Nyasaland, then he might be forced to look to the East, but he always took pains to emphasize his reluctance in contemplating the alternative. 'Only if the West were to treat me like de Gaulle treated Sekou Toure would I be forced to look elsewhere,'[1] he told the American Committee on Africa when he visited New York in April of that year. And in the same month he declared that 'so far as we are concerned in Central Africa, there is no attraction to communism at all.'[2]

In practice the question of Nyasaland being forced to seek aid from the communist bloc did not arise, for the nations of the West proved willing donors. First America, in 1962, and then, a year later, Britain and Israel, followed by West Germany, Denmark and, to a lesser extent, Austria and France, came forward with loans and grants in cash and kind. It was with these countries that Malawi, on becoming independent, established diplomatic relations.*

Banda insisted, however, that he did not consider himself bound to any rigid alignment by virtue of aid or assistance. 'Our attitudes on particular issues will be dictated by the circumstances as we see them,' he told a correspondent of the Johannesburg *Star* in July 1963. 'We do not start with the hypothesis that the West is always right and the East is always wrong.'[3] This policy of 'discretional alignment', as Banda called it, was first put forward during his visit to Yale in April 1961, and two months later was proclaimed the M.C.P.'s official foreign policy in the Party's election manifesto. It was a somewhat

* Malawi sent permanent diplomatic representatives only to Britain, the United States and West Germany. In addition to these countries, France and Israel established embassies in Blantyre, while Denmark and Austria were represented on a non-resident basis.

unreal stance for a man to adopt who had never disguised his underlying sympathy with the West. But, as Banda made clear in a major speech on communism in April 1964, it connoted not so much distrust of Western intentions as a desire to safeguard his freedom of action when Malawi became independent.

The occasion of his remarks was a meeting of the Zomba Debating Society, a group of young intellectuals which included most of the cabinet and met regularly under the chairmanship of Chipembere. Banda began by recounting in great detail the historical processes which had created in Russia the 'special conditions' in which communism could flourish – 'conditions . . . so intolerable that they [the people] could see no salvation in anything else'. Communism, however, was not always the liberating influence it claimed to be, he said:

> Stalin and other Communists have told people that they did not believe in Imperialism, that they were out to liberate the people who were oppressed. . . . Those of us who know something about history are not convinced. . . . If they were out to liberate others why is it that they never left Rumania, Hungary, Poland and Eastern Germany after Hitler's armies had been smashed? . . . So far as I am concerned the only difference between Stalin and Peter the Great, Nicholas and other Russian Emperors is that the old Emperors from Peter's time down to 1917 did not beat about the bush. They . . . did exactly what they said. They were extending their Empire, but Stalin and other Communist leaders pretended to be spreading a form of social justice.

He went on to warn explicitly of the dangers of 'communist imperialism':

> After 6 July, we will have many many embassies here. Russians, Chinese maybe, Czechoslovaks, Yugoslavs and other countries. They will speak a very, very sweet language to you. They are all for you. They want to help you, and they will give big parties and . . . feed you until you are so full that after you have eaten you can't even think. But even more so, they will brain-wash you so that your minds will follow their ideas and you will say, 'Oh yes, this is it.'
> No, they are not for you. It is always for their own country.

Banda's deep-rooted prejudice against communism derived as much from his abhorrence of communist methods of rule as from his fears of communist foreign policy. The admittedly 'phenomenal' development of a country like Russia had been gained 'at the expense of human life and misery', he declared. 'To Communists the State is not only all powerful but has the absolute right to do anything with your goods, and even with your breath itself.'

Capitalism, by contrast, which Banda interpreted as 'total freedom for the individual to do what he likes with what he has', went too far to the other extreme. But while he tended to prefer socialism on the British or Scandinavian model, he made clear that his acceptance was by no means unconditional. In so doing he cast light on the thinking behind his 'mixed economy' approach.

I have to do what I think is in the best interests of my people, the people of this country [he said]. Not what some theoretical white-headed professor in a college says. Oh, no. Theory – yes. I know something, I've been to a university. I have attended all kinds of lectures, but to me, in my position now, I must not go by what people say either in America, Britain, Russia, or anywhere. . . . I have four million people to look after, four million. And to look after these four million I must not be swayed by theories either from the West or from the East because these theories, while they might work in Europe and Asia and other countries – or even in other countries on our own continent – they may not work in Malawi, and it is Malawi that counts.

It was this belief in Malawi's unique identity which, at first in an inarticulate and unrationalized form, and later consciously, provided the fundamental motivation for the policy of discretional alignment. It stemmed in part from Banda's strong sense of his own individuality, and in part from his awareness that neither the East nor the West had achieved the perfect solution to the problems of human society; that there was, in fact, no ready-made solution, and that Malawi would have to find its own answers to its own problems.

In terms of foreign policy, Banda's meaning was clear:

When the West is doing what I think is the right thing – what is good for Malawi – I will align with the West. When the East is doing the right thing – what I think is good for Malawi – I'll align with the East. But when either one or the other does something wrong, which is only in their own interests and not in the interests of Malawi, then we part company.[4]

Within the continent of Africa, Banda's sense of Malawi's uniqueness was initially obscured by his commitment to pan-Africanism. In 1958, he resurrected his old idea of a union of Nyasaland and Northern Rhodesia, which he now suggested should also include Kenya, Tanganyika, Uganda, Ruanda-Urundi, Zanzibar, and perhaps the Congo.*

Banda's first attempts at putting this plan across to other nationalist leaders were none too successful, and he received a sharp rebuff from Nkumbula (for all that he had been co-author of the 1949 memorandum in which the nucleus of the proposal had first been put forward), who told him to stop 'poking his nose into Northern Rhodesia's affairs'.[5] But eighteen months later, after his release from Gwelo, he found an enthusiastic supporter in Julius Nyerere, now President of the Tanganyika African National Union. At a rally in Dar-es-Salaam on 9 May 1960, Banda and Nyerere affirmed their support for a political union of Malawi and Tanganyika when their countries became independent. It would be, Banda said, the nucleus for a greater union of East and Central African territories. A joint communiqué, issued the following day, stated:

We publicly declare that the boundaries that exist between our two countries and indeed between any two African territories are the products of colonialism and are therefore artificial. We hope therefore that an early opportunity will be taken by our people and their neighbours, through their leaders, to consider how best our countries in East and Central Africa can forge ahead to greater unity and co-operation.[6]

* *Rhodesia Herald*, 7 August 1958. There is a marked resemblance between this grouping and the ancient *Maravi* kingdom, in which were said to have been included parts of all these territories except Uganda, Ruanda-Urundi and Zanzibar. Zanzibar, moreover, had strong ties with Nyasaland as a result of the slave trade. Whatever more conventional pan-Africanist motives helped to inspire Banda's suggestion of such a regional union, there is no doubt that one of the most important was his desire to restore the historical *Maravi* entity.

At a press-conference on his return to Blantyre, Banda said he looked forward to the day when Dar-es-Salaam would be the capital of a 'United States of Central Africa'.[7] To achieve that end he was prepared to 'play second fiddle to other African leaders'.[8] Shortly afterwards, the Malawi Congress Party's first national conference endorsed the Dar-es-Salaam communiqué and 'publicly declared [its] support' for the proposed union.[9] In June Nyerere suggested an East and Central African federation at the Conference of Independent African States in Addis Ababa.[10] Three months later the Malawi Congress Party again approved the union when it met at Nkhotakhota.[11] And in October, the plan was endorsed by P.A.F.M.E.C.A., meeting under the chairmanship of Tom Mboya at Mbale, Uganda.[12]

The *Malawi News* called on Nyasas to regard themselves 'first of all . . . as the PEOPLE OF MALAWI and then as THE AFRICAN PEOPLE'.[13] Congressmen were urged to learn a pan-African anthem. And Banda, visiting Nigeria in November, professed admiration for Azikiwe because he thought in pan-African, not parochial terms. He again expressed his willingness to surrender Nyasaland's sovereignty if it would further the cause of African unity,[14] and declared: 'To me there is no such thing as Nyasaland, Southern and Northern Rhodesia or the rest. There is just Africa.'[15]

Banda's ideas were never more closely aligned with those of other African leaders than during these nine months, from April to December 1960. Like them he condemned Tshombe, not only as a puppet of Southern Rhodesian and South African imperialism, but also as an enemy of African unity. Like them, too, he demanded the release of Jomo Kenyatta, restricted by the British for his alleged involvement in Mau Mau. And like them he declared his implacable opposition to the white minority governments of Southern Africa. Asked, in April 1960, what future he foresaw for South Africa, he declared:

Revolution! Revolution by the Black population. I see no hope for a peaceful solution. I do not necessarily mean that it will be a revolution with machine-guns – there are other ways, you know. The people could all go on strike and refuse to work for the white man. They could go on sit-down strike and exert moral pressure. . . . If there was a well-organized campaign of passive resistance you would see just what would happen.[16]

Unfortunate words, perhaps, a few days after Sharpeville, but conventional enough sentiment none the less. His reaction to that event, 'the brutal massacre of our brethren in South Africa', was equally orthodox. It was contained in the joint declaration with Nyerere: 'We pledge, therefore, on behalf of our people, our support of the boycott of South African goods.'[17]

If, at this stage, Banda's intra-African policies were in any way exceptional, it was in their dedication to the pan-African ideal. The Malawi Congress Party constitution declared that the Party's aim was 'to work with other nationalist, democratic and socialist movements in Africa and other continents with a view to promoting pan-Africanism',[18] and the 1961 election manifesto announced that this would be achieved by cooperation in the fields of culture, trade and defence, and by 'cultivating the habit of lending assistance to needy brethren, however meagre our resources may be'.[19] The Party played an active role at the sub-committee and plenary meetings of P.A.F.M.E.C.A., and its major conferences were attended by representatives of nationalist groups in Kenya, Tanganyika, and Northern and Southern Rhodesia. Banda travelled to Nairobi for talks with Tom Mboya and Dr Gikonyo Kiano, to Zanzibar to meet Abeid Karume,* and to Ghana for discussions with Nkrumah. And when, as often happened, he was too busy to travel, Chiume would go in his place. African solidarity was always high on the agenda, and friends and enemies alike declared that Banda was introducing 'Nkrumahism' to Central Africa.

The year 1961 was election year, and foreign affairs, not being a major electoral issue, were temporarily put aside. But with the elections over, and the Party for the first time in power, they resumed their former importance. This time, however, pan-Africanism was no longer the dominant issue. A new subject had come to prominence: Portugal.

* As a result of this visit, two of Karume's sons received their secondary education in Nyasaland. It was paid for jointly by Banda and the M.C.P.

By a quirk of colonial history, Nyasaland had been carved out of Africa by the Great Powers in such a fashion that its southern half protruded deep into Portugal's East African 'province' of Mozambique. The border between them, one thousand miles long, much of it passing through difficult, inaccessible country, held the key to their relationship. For Nyasaland, it meant dependence on Portugal's goodwill for its economic survival, since its principal trade route was the railway to the Mozambique port of Beira. For Mozambique, it meant a potentially grave security threat if a hostile administration were to come to power in Nyasaland. By the same token, it meant that any Nyasaland administration which determined to be hostile towards Mozambique would first have to assure itself of an independent supply route, passing through Tanganyika.

In the context of the Anglo-Portuguese entente, such considerations were irrelevant. Initially, at least, they also seemed so to Banda, for he believed that Mozambique, like other countries to its north, would by the mid-1960s achieve independence under an African government.[20] It would then, he hoped, become part of his proposed union of Central African states. Accordingly he made no bones about his dislike of the Portuguese administration, and openly declared: 'When Nyasaland is free I will not rest until the greater part of Mozambique is joined to it. We are all the same people.'[21] The *Malawi News* shared his distaste: Portugal, it said, was 'a country of 4Ps (Poverty, Prostitutes, Priests and Police)'.[22]

This animosity was reciprocated, and while the official relationship between Lisbon and the Nyasaland and Federal Governments continued tranquilly on, there was a progressive deterioration in the unofficial relationship between the Mozambique administration and the Malawi Congress Party. Nyasas were automatically regarded as agitators and many were beaten up for no other reason than that they were Nyasas. Others were imprisoned in wretched conditions without hope of trial. In April 1961, the *Malawi News* printed an account of the treatment of African prisoners in Mozambique:

The women ... were beaten on their palms and under [their] feet with *mbalamatorio** to ensure that they did not run away. They were forced to break stones. Two-foot-long irons with locks on both ends were locked between their legs to prevent their escape. These brutal tactics occur every day. There is no medical help offered to the women prisoners or their babies. Men in Quelimane are being tortured to madness. . . .

Just over the border [in Milanje] a woman prisoner chained like a slave and lashed sat up sobbing, pleading for mercy. To say Kwacha or Banda is an offence which has landed many P.E. Africans in trouble. . . .[23]

An editorial in the same issue, written by John Msonthi, warned that the Portuguese must learn 'to face facts before it is too late'; gunboat diplomacy had no chance of success in the face of the rising tide of African nationalism.[24] Other articles followed, and in May Banda reiterated his earlier statement that he would not stand for the oppression of 'his people' in Mozambique. He did not say what he planned to do about it but, echoing Nkrumah (and his own views as expressed in the 1949 memorandum), declared that Malawi's freedom would be meaningless unless the whole of Africa were free.[25]

December 1961 saw the expulsion of Portugal from Goa, to a background of criticism from many of the Western powers and plaudits from the independent African states. In a long, repetitive editorial on 4 January 1962, the *Malawi News* set out the Party's attitude to the Portuguese position:

Force is the only language the Portuguese know and understand. They have clearly shown this in all their colonies. Force is used ruthlessly and brutally to oppress, suppress and repress the African people in Angola and Portuguese East Africa. . . . Hundreds of thousands of Africans are beaten. Thousands of others are sent to prison. Several hundreds are killed. The only offence all these people commit is that they are critical of Portuguese rule.

Force is not only force when it is used against White people. If Salazar feels so free to use force, and brute force for that matter, against Africans in Portuguese East Africa and Angola, why should he scream when Nehru uses force to bring him back to his senses in Goa? There is a limit to what people can endure.

* A wooden stick, through which steel nails have been driven, used for the punishment of thieves and petty criminals.

. . . We would like to warn Salazar and all the Portuguese wherever they are that they are living in a fool's paradise. . . . And it will be too late when they discover that they have been cheating themselves.

The African in Portuguese East Africa and Angola . . . will one day rise up against the Portuguese, and the Portuguese will not be able to stand it. They will find things too hot for them. . . . They will have to give up.[26]

The editorial marked the climax of hostility between the M.C.P. and the Mozambique administration, for a month or so earlier Banda had received a visit which was to change the whole course of his policies towards Portugal. His caller was Jorge Jardim, a slightly built, dapper businessman, who had become one of the most influential figures in Mozambiquan politics. The meeting was secret, and even Banda's cabinet colleagues remained in ignorance of what was discussed. But its result was that he began to re-examine the position he had taken up in relation to the Portuguese authorities.

Banda had realized early on that his prediction that Mozambique would soon become an independent African state was unlikely to be fulfilled. Accordingly he had discussed informally with Nyerere the possibility of Nyasaland using a southern Tanganyikan port in the event of Portugal denying her sea access through Beira, and by the time of Jardim's visit a tentative agreement had been reached.* But although Banda had told a press-conference in September 1961, 'Dar-es-Salaam is open. I want Beira to be cut off tomorrow if you like,'[27] this was not a proposition he could maintain in the face of the economic realities. It would take, at the very least, four years to build up adequate communications links with Tanganyika, and in the meantime Britain would hardly be inclined to grant independence to a Nyasaland liable at any moment to economic strangulation.

Thus when Jardim arrived in Blantyre as the envoy of a

* *Nyasaland Times*, 5 September 1961. According to Dunduzu Chisiza, a railway would be built linking Blantyre with the northern shores of Lake Nyasa, whence a combination of lake and rail transport would be used to take goods to and from the port of Mtwara. (See also Munger, *Kamuzu Banda of Malawi*, p. 25.)

182   Banda

Portuguese Government which had suddenly been made aware
by the August elections that before long it would have to contend with another black state* on the borders of Mozambique,
Banda was moving towards a position from which he could
only extricate himself by an accommodation with the Mozambique administration. Early in 1962 it was agreed that he should
visit Lisbon for talks with the Portuguese Government.

The change in Banda's attitude towards Mozambique was not
immediately apparent. The ill-treatment of Nyasas by the Portuguese authorities continued as before, reaching such a pitch
that the Nyasaland Government felt constrained to make diplomatic representations to Lisbon.[28] The *Malawi News* continued
to feature anti-Portuguese material. And at a P.A.F.M.E.C.A.
conference in Addis Ababa, John Msonthi spoke of the 'bitter
sufferings and humiliations' Africans were enduring in Mozambique and Angola, and warned that: 'This struggle is going to be
bitter and most likely bloody. . . . No country ever became free
without some sort of violence.'[29] But there were rumours of an
impending meeting between Banda and Salazar, and talk of
extending to Nyasaland the railway then under construction
between the new Mozambique port of Nacala and Villa Cabral.
At the beginning of April the Portuguese Consul-General in
Salisbury, Dr Pereira Bastos, confirming that Banda was to
visit Portugal, declared that 'the harbours and railways of
Mozambique . . . are all at Dr Banda's disposal'.[30] In mid-
June, in the Portuguese capital, he was given firm assurances to
that effect by the Portuguese Foreign Minister, Dr Franco
Nogueira, and the Minister for Overseas Territories, Dr Adri-
ano Moreira.†

Banda's first public explanation of his new policy came in a
speech to the Portuguese Association in Blantyre on 30 March.
It was brief and to the point, and much of what he said would
have been familiar but for the fact that it had not before been

* Tanganyika, on Mozambique's northern border, became independent
in December 1961.

† According to the *Economist* (7 July 1962), the question of Banda's
relations with the Mozambiquan African nationalist groups was also discussed.

applied to foreign affairs. 'It is not individuals with whom African nationalism is at war. It is policy,' he declared, and went on:

You are quite welcome here. . . . I know I do not like the political system of Portugal and Salazar does not like my political system here. But that has nothing to do with you. Not as individuals, or business-men.

The British and the Russians do not like each other's system. But there are Russian businessmen in England, and there are certainly English businessmen in Russia. They do business. They trade . . . and I hope, between you and I, we can do some trading. I am interested in your port – not only Beira but Quelimane and Nacala. . . . I want you to build that railway from Nacala right up to Villa Cabral.

. . . I believe in co-existence. I believe in live and let live. Leave me alone and I leave you alone.

. . . If the Americans and the British on one side and the Russians on the other can co-exist, I do not see any reason why the Portuguese on that side of the border and Malawi on this side cannot co-exist.

In the middle of all this was a curious hint that the new policy of cooperation was motivated by something more complex than material considerations alone:

I do not agree with it [Portuguese policy in Africa], and I dare say there are many Portuguese in Lisbon now who do not agree with it – or even in Lourenço Marques or in Beira.[31]

This was an idea which could only have come from Jardim. Not until much later, however, was it apparent just how important an idea it was.

The detente with Portugal had at first little effect on Banda's pan-African initiatives. In October 1961, he attended a summit conference in Dar-es-Salaam with Kaunda, Jomo Kenyatta (newly released from restriction), Nkomo and Nyerere, at which they discussed the coordination of the activities of their respective nationalist movements. He returned home full of praise for Tanganyika and its Prime Minister. Of all the peoples of East and Central Africa, Banda declared, the Tanganyikans had most in common with Nyasas.[32] Two months later Nyerere sent a specially chartered aircraft to bring him to Dar-es-Salaam for

Tanganyika's Independence celebrations, a gesture which was made much of in the Malawi Congress Party's propaganda.

But by mid-1962, it became clear that Banda's enthusiasm for a union with Tanganyika was beginning to wane. He began to emphasize the proviso, which had at first seemed little more than a formality, that Nyasaland could not consider alternative forms of association until the present Federation was broken, and all the territories involved in the proposed new grouping were independent. Other conditions followed, and by mid-1963 the idea of a black federation of East and Central Africa had receded completely. In May of that year, Banda told an interviewer:

No one can tell what is going to happen. Maybe after we are fully independent . . . there may be other kinds of groups, even bringing in the Congo, Rwanda and Burundi. Nobody can tell – but that is for the future.[33]

In another interview in July, he put it even more plainly. The question of a new federation would be for himself and his people to decide 'when the time comes'. For the moment, he had enough to do recovering from the effects of the present Federation.[34] And there the matter rested.

This change of heart has never been adequately explained and Banda himself, in his subsequent pronouncements, has cast little light on the reasons for his rejection of his earlier ideas. The policy of co-existence with Portugal, in which he differed sharply from other nationalist leaders, may perhaps have played some part in it. A much more important factor was Tanganyika's interest in forming a tri-national East African federation with Kenya and Uganda, which made very much better economic (and political) sense than a union with Nyasaland, but which, in the first instance at least, appeared to exclude its former partner-to-be.* But the principal cause was that Banda's belief in

* Banda, interview with the Johannesburg *Star* (draft dated 12 July 1963, A.A.N.S. files, Salisbury). Banda implied that another reason for his reluctance to commit himself was the decision of the 1963 Addis Ababa Heads of State conference that regional associations should be entered into only if they were likely to advance, and not delay, the achievement of African unity.

his country's unique identity, which all along had underlain the wider aspects of his foreign policy, was now also asserting itself in the intra-African context. This in turn was mainly due to the imminence of independence, which had intensified his emotional involvement with Nyasaland.

By mid-1963, Banda was envisaging for the future Malawi a special role in African affairs as a 'mediator for peace', [35] which it could only fill if it were independent in every sense of the word. Its main task, he said, would be to try to minimize any tendency towards cleavage between groups of African states, such as that which then existed between the Casablanca, Monrovia and Afro-Malagasy groupings. This was a less orthodox pan-African approach than his earlier advocacy of a regional union, and betokened a marked change in his scale of priorities. In this, Nyasaland's self-government year, Banda was beginning to regard the achievement of African unity as a long-term objective. Of more immediate importance were issues closer to home, particularly the problem of Southern Rhodesia.

The key to Banda's policy towards Southern Rhodesia lay in his relationships with Winston Field and Sir Roy Welensky. To Banda, Field, like Malan, was a declared, open enemy, whereas he felt Welensky, like Smuts, was a hypocrite. As he later explained, 'With Malan . . . I knew where I was, but not with Smuts. With Winston Field I knew where I was, but not with [Welensky].'[36] It was systems which Banda opposed, not individuals.

Field had met Banda during a visit to Blantyre in 1958, and afterwards had tried to see him while he was detained at Gwelo. Later he had paid a number of visits to Zomba when Banda was in office, in the course of which, despite their differences in political beliefs, they had formed a firm friendship. Although this derived in part from their common opposition to Welensky's United Federal Party, and from Field's willingness to excise Nyasaland from the Federation, its rationale was in some respects analagous to Banda's Portuguese policy. He explained, again by reference to the Anglo-Russian example:

Harper and Winston Field do not shut their eyes or close their ears to facts and realities in Central Africa, as Welensky, Greenfield and John Roberts [the U.F.P. leader in Northern Rhodesia] do. . . . I have always maintained that these men, though much to the Right [in] their political ideas, are honest gentlemen. They do not say one thing and do another. And for this reason, were they in power in Southern Rhodesia, they and I would get on very well. After all, the Russians and the British get on somehow. And the political differences between William Harper and Winston Field on the one side and myself and Kaunda on the other are not exactly the same as those existing between the Russians and the British.[37]

When, in December 1962, Field and his new party, the Rhodesian Front, swept to power in the Southern Rhodesian elections, Banda was as good as his word. The icy hostility which had characterized his relationship with the U.F.P. Government of Sir Edgar Whitehead* gave way to a much friendlier atmosphere. In January and August 1963, Field, now Southern Rhodesia's Prime Minister, held talks with Banda in Zomba and shortly afterwards a trade agreement was signed under which the two countries would enjoy mutually preferential tariffs after the break-up of the Federation. Banda later commented that his entire Southern Rhodesian policy had been founded on his 'faith and confidence in Mr Winston Field'.[38] It was an oversimplification since, as in the case of Mozambique, economic factors, notably long-standing trading links, were a powerful incentive towards friendly cooperation. But it had a basis in truth.

Economics and personal friendship, however, were not the only determinants of Banda's policy towards Southern Rho-

* An exception to this was in the field of labour, since the presence of an estimated 200,000 Nyasa workers in Southern Rhodesia necessitated some form of contact between the two governments. In March 1962, the Southern Rhodesian Minister of Labour, Social Welfare and Housing, A. E. Abrahamson, held talks in Zomba with Banda and Bwanausi on the future of Nyasa migrant labour in the territory. At about the same time, it was decided that the Southern Rhodesian labour recruiting organization, Mthandizi, was to be allowed to continue its activities in Nyasaland (Nyasaland Information Department press release, 26 March 1962, and *Nyasaland Times*, 12 December 1961).

desia. Underlying his attitude was the belief that, in that territory as in Africa as a whole, the most useful role Nyasaland
could play was that of mediator.

Of all the three components of the Central African Federation, Southern Rhodesia, with its large, affluent and influential
white community, posed the hardest problem for African nationalists seeking majority rule. The crisis had come in February
1961, when Nkomo had first accepted and then repudiated the
new constitution, worked out under the chairmanship of Duncan Sandys, in which fifteen out of fifty seats in parliament were
reserved for Africans. The *Malawi News* had warned gloomily:

> Mr Macmillan and Mr Sandys may well be patting themselves on
> the back for their skill in unburdening themselves of a grave respon-
> sibility, but let them not delude themselves that the easy way out is the
> best way out. Sometime, in the not too distant future, Southern
> Rhodesia will pose Britain with one of its greatest problems, and
> Britain will rue its sloppy application of 1961.[39]

Banda never forgave Nkomo for his mishandling of this conference, and for the next two years their relations were strained.
In August 1963, a few days after the formation of the Zimbabwe
African National Union, under the leadership of the Rev. Nda-
baningi Sithole, he declared that Nkomo was 'spineless and
without guts'[40] and announced his support of the rival group.
Thereafter contacts ceased between Banda and the Zimbabwe
African People's Union, as Nkomo's National Democratic Party
was now called, and a new alliance was formed between Sithole
and the Malawi Congress Party.

Meanwhile – quietly and in his own way, as he put it – Banda
had been exerting pressure on Field to initiate a new series of
constitutional talks in Southern Rhodesia.[41] As he explained to
the Legislative Assembly in February 1963, 'There are times
when shouting does no good while working quietly brings good
results.'[42] In this kind of activity, Sithole was a much more
responsive partner than Nkomo, and, by April 1964, Banda
had succeeded in arranging for him to attend a meeting with
Field in Salisbury. It was to be the prelude, if all went well, to a
round-table conference in which Nkomo, representatives of the

British Government and other white Southern Rhodesian politicians would also take part. Field's removal from office, engineered by his fellow ministers only days later, was a bitter blow to Banda and he took the unusual step of calling a press-conference to explain what he had been trying to achieve:

> I am anxious, most anxious [he said], to find a peaceful and constitutional solution to the [Southern Rhodesian] problem. Therefore I made it my business ... to create an atmosphere of friendship between Southern Rhodesia and Nyasaland because I felt that that was the only way in which I would exercise influence on Winston Field and, through him, on the policy of his Government. Otherwise, if I kept aloof and said: 'Oh you, you Winston Field, you belong to the Rhodesian Front, I won't talk to you, I won't have anything to do with you' – I wouldn't achieve anything.

He went on to discuss his attempts to bring together the territory's European and African political leaders:

> I sincerely believe that the political problem of Southern Rhodesia cannot be solved by shouts and threats from anyone ... or [any] group of individuals or organization outside of Southern Rhodesia. ... It will have to be solved by the people of Southern Rhodesia – Europeans and Africans facing each other across a conference table. ... In my view, any African leader who wants or hopes to help Southern Rhodesia, or any European, whether he is in Southern Rhodesia or in Europe or anywhere else, who wants to help Southern Rhodesia, must not encourage the spirit of intransigence either among the Africans or among the Whites. He must try to make them see the wisdom of their at least talking, even if they do not agree. ... As long as Winston Field was there, there was hope that this kind of getting together of the African leaders with the British Government as umpire was possible. Now this is not possible.[43]

Banda's policy had 'for the time being ... been put out of action', and relations between Nyasaland and Southern Rhodesia could be expected to reduce to 'freezing point'. What happened next, he said, would depend on the attitude adopted by the new Prime Minister. While he had not met Field's successor, Ian Smith, he took little comfort from the mass arrests of Rhodesian African leaders or from Smith's statement that there would not be a majority government in the territory within his lifetime.* His one fear, he went on, was that Smith might unilaterally declare Southern Rhodesia independent. If that happened, he would be 'the first one to advise the Rev. Sithole and Mr Nkomo to sink their . . . present political differences and form a coalition government in exile either in Northern Rhodesia or in Nyasaland.'[44]

For the next few months, Banda's relationship with the Smith Government remained obscure. He told the press that he did not think he would be prepared to talk to Smith as he had to Winston Field.[45] But, even as he was speaking, one of Smith's senior ministers, Lord Graham, was visiting Blantyre at Banda's invitation. When the Southern Rhodesian problem was discussed at the Commonwealth Prime Ministers' conference in London, a week later, Banda was reported to have spoken like 'ten Nkrumahs'.[46] But, if this was true, it was also true that he laid great emphasis on the need to achieve a peaceful, constitutional solution.[47]

Southern Rhodesia, however, was not the only area of Banda's intra-African policy in which contradictory elements had begun to appear. In regard to Mozambique and Tanganyika, where ostensibly no changes had taken place, even more intriguing developments had occurred.

By the middle of 1962, Nyasaland's relationships with its northern and southern neighbours were inextricably linked with the transport dilemma. Since Banda was now on cordial terms with the administrations of both territories, two choices were open to

* At this point, Banda suggested that Field's resignation might mean that 'the Rhodesian Front will soon cease to exist, not only as a Government in Southern Rhodesia, but even more as a political party, and a new alignment of political forces might – in fact, I know or sincerely believe – will emerge which will make the whole thing a blessing in disguise.' By this he meant, presumably, that the right-wing policies of the Rhodesian Front would be unacceptable to the majority of Rhodesian Europeans and that a new, moderate grouping would accordingly come into being. In fact no moderate group appeared until 1969, when the Centre Party was formed. By then, however, the Rhodesian Front had itself moved much further to the right, and an even more extreme right-wing group, the Rhodesian National Party, had sprung up. Even under these circumstances, the Centre Party won little support.

him. Either he could orientate northwards, and build a railway
to Tanganyika. Or he could reinforce the present southwards
orientation, by building a railway to Nacala. For a year, he did
neither, and simply relied on the existing railway to Beira. But in
April 1963, there was a sudden spate of activity. Colin Cameron
and Msonthi were dispatched to Mozambique to sound out the
Portuguese on Nacala. And soon afterwards, Chiume, returning
from America, was diverted to Dar-es-Salaam to hold similar
talks with Nyerere.

Both missions were successful. The Portuguese reiterated
their willingness to extend the Nacala-Villa Cabral railway to
Nyasaland, and Nyerere offered to place Mtwara under a joint
Nyasa–Northern Rhodesian authority.

It was to this latter alternative that Banda at first inclined,
and by June, after Chiume had held talks with Kaunda, a firm
agreement had been reached that a railway would be built from
Broken Hill to Fort Manning and thence either round the
northern tip of Lake Nyasa or to its northern shores, as envisaged in the 1961 plan.

But then, as suddenly as it had begun, the idea of the Nyasaland–Tanganyika railway was dropped. A Portuguese mission
travelled to Zomba for further, unpublicized discussions, and in
May 1964, six weeks before Independence, Banda paid a one-day
'private' visit to northern Mozambique. On his return he gave
the first public indication that the Nacala railway would be built.[48]

Whether Banda had ever really had much choice in the matter
was open to question in view of the considerable economic
advantages of the Nacala link. Before the final decision was
taken, Banda had been told that the northwards link could not
be justified economically. The American transportation survey
team which had come to this conclusion had, however, cautiously approved the idea of a new eastward link.* Banda claimed

* Although the team's report was not published until June 1964, Banda
had been apprised of its preliminary findings several months earlier.

Banda's failure to proceed with the Tanganyika railway plan was later
contrasted unfavourably with Kaunda's determination to go ahead with the
Tan-Zam railway. However, it must be borne in mind that a large proportion of Malawi's exports are bulky, low-valued agricultural produce, relatively expensive to transport, which could not compete in world markets

afterwards he had also been independently advised that the planned Vipya plateau pulpwood scheme in northern Nyasaland would not be economic unless the Nacala link were built.[49]

While economic factors provided the public justification for the decision in favour of Nacala, Banda may also have been influenced by considerations of a different kind. In 1963 he had been given to believe, by sources he regarded as completely trustworthy, that within the next few years a situation might arise in which northern Mozambique might be ceded to the future Malawi. There have been a number of explanations, none of them wholly satisfactory, as to how this was to come about. The most usual is that the cession would be effected after a settler-led unilateral declaration of independence, probably to take place after the death of Salazar.* The intention would be to create a buffer zone between Tanganyika and the white-ruled southern part of Mozambique, so securing it from guerrilla attacks.

The attraction of this scheme to Nyasaland was that it would make possible the establishment of a wholly independent external trade route. There was even the possibility that such a trade route might be included ready-made in the ceded area – in the shaft of the Nacala railway. But there was a major obstacle to

---

unless exported by the cheapest possible means, whereas the greater part of Zambia's export revenue comes from copper, which is high-valued and relatively inexpensive to transport; and that Malawi, being a very much poorer country than Zambia, could not have met the loan repayments on the scheme (which would have cost almost as much as the £100 million Tan-Zam link) without the total dislocation of its economy.

* An alternative explanation is that the Portuguese Government itself was to make the cession. Both explanations became current early in 1964; both have been denied, either officially or unofficially; and both have reappeared at intervals ever since. The idea of a post-U.D.I. cession seems the less fantastic of the two. This was set out at length, amid a burst of Mozambiquan-U.D.I. speculation, in an article in *Le Monde* (13 November 1969), in which it was claimed that Jardim and the Portuguese financier, Champalimaud, were the prime movers behind the plan. Chiume, who, as Minister-designate of External Affairs, was most intimately concerned in the negotiations, also claimed that Jardim had been involved (Chiume, interview).

this plan. Even if the Portuguese wanted to cede their northern provinces, Banda might be prevented by his fellow African leaders, and by the Front for the Liberation of Mozambique, Frelimo, and its leader, Dr Eduardo Mondlane, from taking them over.

It was in seeking a way out of this difficulty that Banda returned to his old ambition, earlier apparent in his advocacy of a union of Central African states, to bring about at least a partial restoration of the *Maravi* kingdom. He believed that if he could demonstrate convincingly that Malawi had a well-established historical right to northern Mozambique, he would be able to persuade other African statesmen to support his claim. In this, however, he miscalculated. Nyerere, to whom he is said to have offered a strip of the ceded area adjacent to southern Tanganyika, rejected his overtures as outright imperialism. With the sole exception of Nkrumah, other African leaders with whom he, or, on his instructions, Chiume, broached the subject reacted in the same way.*

To all intents and purposes the plan then died a natural death. Banda's inability to bring about its acceptance was not the prime cause of its demise. Rather it failed because, in the event, the conditions in which northern Mozambique might have been ceded did not arise.†

Banda did not emerge unscathed from his first and last attempt at 'empire-building'. Although his prestige remained considerable, both as an elder statesman and as the man principally responsible for breaking the Central African Federation, his image had been tarnished. Moreover, his fellow leaders were uncertain about his relationship with Portugal, which, together

---

*Chiume, op. cit. Banda's approaches have been unattributably confirmed by one of the Heads of State concerned.

†None the less, speculation continues – cf. the *Le Monde* article – that if the Mozambique settlers were to declare themselves unilaterally independent of Portugal, a union of Malawi and northern Mozambique might yet take place. While this appears highly unlikely it is worth noting that a Mozambique African group called the União Nacional Africana da Rombézia, which supports the idea of such a union, has its headquarters in Blantyre and receives assistance from the Malawi Congress Party (see also E. Mondlane, *The Struggle for Mozambique*, Penguin Books, 1961, pp. 131–2).

with Egypt, Ethiopia and Ghana,* had been among the first
countries with which Malawi established diplomatic relations;
his attitude towards Southern Rhodesia; and his policy of
'discretional alignment', which, to some of them, seemed to be
in danger of becoming a rigid, pro-Western commitment.

In an atmosphere of puzzlement, not unmixed with suspicion,
Banda arrived in Cairo in July 1964 to attend the O.A.U. summit conference, delayed by two months to enable him to be
present as Prime Minister of an independent Malawi.

Banda's speech to the assembled Heads of State and Government was one of the most thoughtful and convincing he has ever
made. There was little of the repetitious woolliness which
marred many of his public statements, and each point was made
lucidly and forcefully, but without bombast. The mask of egotism, which had become so much a part of his public image that
it was now second nature, was for once absent.

He began by paying elaborate tribute to Haile Selassie, the
O.A.U.'s creator, and to Nasser, the host President, speaking
at length of Egypt's historic importance as the cradle of civilization, and of Ethiopia, the oldest of Africa's kingdoms. It was
Selassie and Nasser, he recalled, who, together with Bourgiba,
Nkrumah and Tubman, had come to the aid of Malawi's
nationalist movement at its time of greatest need.†

Banda went on to trace briefly the history of Malawi's struggle
for independence. He did so, he explained, 'so that no one
should be left in doubt as to where I stand in the struggle for
African freedom and independence, or on the question of
African unity.' He believed strongly in African unity, but it
must be 'real, true and genuine unity and not one which is a
unity only in name and disunity in fact'. If the O.A.U. were to

*These three countries, together with Kenya, Liberia, Nigeria and Tan-
ganyika, were Nyasaland's staunchest friends in Africa during the pre-
independence period. Banda visited each of them at least once (he travelled
to Liberia, Ethiopia and Egypt in 1962) and Ghana, which he described as
'the Malawi of West Africa', several times.

† In 1959 Nkrumah's Convention Peoples Party gave £10,000 to the Africa
Bureau to arrange for the legal representation of Banda and other Nyasaland detainees before the Devlin Commission. The nature of the assistance
rendered by the other Heads of State is not known.

succeed, he warned, there must be no sectionalism, no division into power blocs. Unless the dissolution of the former Casablanca, Monrovia and Afro-Malagasy groupings was complete the organization would not only fail to achieve unity, but 'worse than that', it would 'fail to be . . . the first step towards an all African Government'.[50]

Still on this theme, Banda spoke of the Commonwealth – 'the best club in the world',[51] as he once called it – and of the United Nations. The United Nations was not perfect, he declared, but it was 'necessary for world peace . . . [and] necessary for world progress and advancement in every field of human endeavour'.

Then followed the crux of what Banda had to say. He led into his subject by recalling Nkrumah's dictum on the meaning of Ghana's independence:

The independence of Malawi will be meaningless [he said] as long as there is an inch of African soil under colonialism and imperialism. I share the view already expressed at this conference and elsewhere that all independent African states and all African leaders must do everything possible in their power to help those countries which are still under the colonial yoke.

To help those countries and those of our brothers and sisters under the colonial yoke is sacred to all of us. But having said that it is necessary to point out that not all independent African states are in the same position to help . . . as much as they wish. . . . Some of the independent African states are almost helpless to help others by [virtue of their] geographical position. Malawi, my own state, is one of these countries. Zambia, when it becomes independent . . . will be one of them. And Basutoland . . . will be still another.

Malawi and Zambia have been denied ports of their own by colonial history and colonial geography. . . . They use . . . ports of . . . neighbouring . . . territories which . . . are under the control of a foreign power. They could not export a single product . . . without the goodwill or the tolerance or sufferance of the power . . . claiming to own and controlling the territory in which the ports are situated.

Therefore, while I feel strongly against imperialism and colonialism in any form, while I am just as anxious as anyone in this conference to help our brothers and sisters still under colonial rule in neighbouring territories, Malawi's power, my own power to help are limited and circumscribed by our geographical position.

I am quite certain ... that it is not the policy of the Organization of African Unity that in order for any country to be a good and loyal member of this organization that country must cut its own throat.

... I am saying all this because I want to make it quite clear here at this conference that the geographical position of Malawi makes it impossible for me and my country to sever all ties, diplomatic, economic and cultural, with a certain power still controlling great portions of our continent. I cannot promise here that I and my country will be in a position to carry out to the letter any resolution which demands total severance of all relations ... with that power.

This, not because I do not agree with any such resolution; not because I do not want to help my brothers and sisters still under colonial rule in that territory; but simply because it would be impossible for me and my country to carry out such [a] resolution to [the] letter without [the] economic strangulation of Malawi. And with economic strangulation would come political strangulation. The Government would fall and there would be chaos. ... Is that what anyone wants in this Assembly? I do not think so.

He concluded by explaining his belief in discretional alignment by reference to Suez and to the Congo crisis. In each case, he asserted, America and Russia had been right (in the one, by standing aloof from the Anglo-French invasion, and in the other, by affirming Congolese territorial integrity), while Britain and France had been wrong.

This is why [said Banda] ... no African state should ally itself permanently or automatically with one bloc or the other; because neither bloc, the Western bloc nor the other, the Eastern bloc, is always right or always wrong. Each bloc is sometimes wrong, sometimes right. And the only wise policy and wise course for any African statesman and any African independent state to take or follow is to judge each international issue strictly on its own merits at any given time. This means using discretion, it means using common sense, uninfluenced either by this ideology or that.[52]

Banda was afterwards fond of recollecting how, at this conference, he had defied 'single-handed' Ben Bella, Modibo Keita, Nkrumah, Sekou Toure and all the other great names in African politics.[53] In fact the question of defiance had not arisen, for his explanations had been accepted. No one disputed his courage in stating an unpopular view.* And no one protested when Malawi abstained from voting on a resolution calling for a boycott of white-ruled Southern Africa.

Certainly none of those who heard him would have suspected that the foreign policies which Banda set out would play a major part in a chain of events which, barely a month later, would bring his Government to the verge of collapse.

*Chiume claims otherwise, but no reliable evidence has been found to support him.

Chapter 10
The Cabinet Crisis

The years before independence had seen a gradual build-up of tension between Banda and his ministers which had made a confrontation between them ultimately almost inevitable. The circumstances and manner of his return in 1958 were in themselves a source of weakness in any Government he formed, for, by inviting him to assume the Congress Presidency, Chipembere and Chiume had surrendered their own claims to the leadership. It constituted, as they later admitted, a confession of failure.*
This in itself, however, was not enough to provoke real disaffection, for in the early days of Congress, in 1958 and 1959, hierarchical distinctions were largely avoided. In public Banda's attitude towards his lieutenants, his 'boys' as he called them, was unreservedly paternal – a tactic which enabled him to maintain his distance while yet not reducing them to the status of subordinates. And within the Party, at a time when the expansion of its machinery was of supreme importance, the administrative posts held by the younger men carried with them considerable power.

After Banda's release from Gwelo the emphases shifted. In the first place the closer watch Banda kept on the Party's affairs led to a reducion in the powers of its Executive. And secondly, the Party itself became less all-important. The real work was now being done not so much in the towns and villages of Nyasaland but in the conference rooms in London, where Banda's abilities far outstripped his colleagues'. Later, as his power accumulated and his personality cult grew, the disparity between their status increased still further.

* Banda himself was well aware of this. Speaking in April 1965, he asked: 'If Chipembere was a leader ... why did he and Chiume agree to my being sent for? Why didn't they say, "Oh, no. Chiume and I are here; we will fight Armitage and Welensky"?' (Banda, Speech to commemorate his release from Gwelo, 1 April 1965, Malawi Information Department transcript).

In the circumstances of emergent Malawi, much of this was necessary and indeed inevitable. But it is clear, in retrospect, that the extent to which adulation was lavished upon him was unwise. Any man, if compared often enough with Jesus Christ, Ghandi, Nkrumah and the like, and described in such glowing terms as 'the greatest Prime Minister Africa has produced', may come to accept such assertions as his due. As Chipembere, years later, ruefully admitted, by the time independence arrived they had made Banda a demi-god.[1]

Banda had not remained unaffected by his success as a political leader. Although his basic insecurity was still as strong as ever, there had been superimposed on it a veneer of confidence, which manifested itself in arrogance. His charisma increased, and he developed an awe-inspiring, intimidating 'presence'. His defensive egotism, which had appeared early on after his return to Nyasaland, was reinforced by latent vanity, now educed by the praises with which he was lavished.

In private, the effect of these changes was to strengthen the reserve which separated Banda from his ministers. Their relationships, never very close – even with Chipembere and the Chisiza brothers, with whom Banda had been incarcerated at Gwelo for thirteen months – became steadily more formal, and the small element of personal reciprocity which had at one time existed receded almost completely. They became, in fact, business relationships and nothing more. In public, Banda's paternalism became correspondingly more heavy-handed. It was not always liked. When, for instance, he told the Legislative Council in November 1961, 'I talk to them like children and they shut up!'[2] his audience was less than appreciative. 'They' included three members of the cabinet, Bwanausi, Chiume and Mikeka Mkandawire, and two parliamentary secretaries, Chirwa and Dunduzu Chisiza.

Until the beginning of 1964, Banda's occasional public dressings-down of his ministers were tolerated. They were in any case infrequent, and it was a time when unity was of paramount importance in the struggle against Federation and colonialism. But as independence neared, the climate altered. The Federation had been broken; self-government was a reality; and within a few months the Protectorate of Nyasaland would become the sovereign state of Malawi. The primary objectives had been achieved, and Chipembere, Chiume and the others began to regard themselves no longer as the leaders of a struggling nationalist movement in an obscure corner of the British Commonwealth, but as cabinet ministers-designate of a nation whose vote in international assemblies would equal that of the world's great powers.

Against this background, a number of areas emerged in which Banda and the ministers were in fundamental disagreement. Some were of recent origin, like the institution of a compulsory charge of a tickey (threepence) for hospital out-patients, and the decision to accept the Skinner Report,* which recommended economies in the pay and conditions offered to locally based civil servants. These measures, the ministers felt, were both unjust and politically unwise.

Other differences were of longer standing, but did not become important until independence was imminent. These included Africanization and foreign policy. Banda much admired the traditions of the British civil service and was wary of over-hastily promoting locally based officers, having witnessed in Ghana the corruption and inefficiency to which this could lead. He accordingly gave assurances to expatriate civil servants that they would not be prematurely retired, and declared that 'no African civil servant can expect promotion just because he has a black skin. Every African who gets promoted will do so on his own merit and efficiency.'[3] The ministers, by contrast, believed that Malawi's independence would be incomplete while its civil service remained dominated by expatriates. They recalled, moreover, that in its 1961 Election Manifesto the Malawi Congress Party had committed itself to 'immediate Africanization'.[4]

In the realm of foreign affairs the ministers favoured a more militant policy towards Southern Rhodesia and Mozambique,

---

* *The Report of the Commission to Examine the Salary Scales and Conditions of Service of Local Officers* (Nyasaland Government Establishment Circular, No. 148, 1 May 1964). The commission was chaired by T. M. Skinner.

and while recognizing the economic imperative to reach an accommodation with Portugal, were sceptical of the policy of peaceful co-existence. And, in the wider field of 'discretional alignment', they would have preferred to see discretion exercised towards the East, as well as the West.

By 1964, all these matters had been discussed by the cabinet, not once but many times, and Banda's policies had received its collective approval. The ministers' acquiescence was due mainly to weakness, the same weakness which had been responsible for their allowing, and indeed assisting, the uncontrolled growth of Banda's personality cult, and which had led Chiume to declare, a few weeks before Independence, that there was 'absolutely nothing wrong with dictatorship'.[5] But there were also other reasons for their failure to speak their minds, as Chipembere later explained:

There was the . . . temperament of Dr Banda to consider. Whenever you criticized him, he flared up so violently that you had to consider your own position. You didn't want to be dismissed from the Central Committee of the Party or from the cabinet. And secondly, you didn't want to risk a split at this stage. . . . Anyone who tried to pick a quarrel with Dr Banda on any grounds at all before independence would be hated by the people. You would be stoned. Everybody was saying, 'Let's unite. Let's work together. Let's get behind Dr Banda so that we can get our freedom. Nothing must be created which will provide the British with an excuse for delaying independence. . . .' And there was always Welensky to exploit whatever confusion there might be in the nationalist movement. So that although some of our reluctance to criticize Dr Banda was due to lack of courage and due to fear of his reactions, there was also this feeling that we must not risk a split before independence. You can quarrel after that but not before.*

*Chipembere, interview. See also *Hansard*, Zomba, 9 September 1964, p. 93. Banda's touchiness was most clearly apparent in his relationship with the press, which had steadily deteriorated since he had become Prime Minister. In 1963 the *Nyasaland Times* informed its readers in a front-page headline that Banda had called it 'stupid' thirty-four times in a single speech. After independence his animosity became even more pronounced. When, in 1968, Patrick Keatley, then Commonwealth Correspondent of the *Guardian*, criticized Banda's rule, he was denounced so violently at mass rallies that Malawian civil servants jokingly suggested the villagers believed 'Patrick Keatley' was an invading army.

Banda presented another side of the picture. He was, he said, 'very, very, very strict' with his ministers:

> I say a thing and when I say a thing nobody must say anything else and my ministers must do nothing before I approve of it otherwise there would be confusion.[6]

Although the ministers never voiced their grievances openly, Banda was well aware of the differences which existed. His response to them was contained in his speech to the Zomba Debating Society, in April 1964:

> Those of you who read books and newspapers from certain other countries [may] say: 'Why doesn't the Doctor do this? This is what they have done there!' My answer to that is 'Yes, that is what they have done over there. It may be good for them but it is not good for you here. . . .'
>
> Anything I do, everything I do, just remember this: that I think it is in the best interests of this country. To some of you some of the things I do now may not seem to you to be in the best interests of this country. But remember this: we are on trial. The eyes of the world are on us. We will be independent in July. Our economy is a frail one. We have to win the confidence of the outside world. People must come here confident that here there is a stable government and an efficient administration, and it is my job to see that this country has a stable government and an efficient administration, whatever anyone may do. I repeat, no one will divert me from that. I would rather die. . . .[7]

It was a remarkably comprehensive reply. But even more important than what Banda said was the way in which he said it. Had he always been as sensitive to his colleagues' feelings, he might well have avoided the crisis which was shortly to develop.

Independence was thus from all points of view a crucial factor in the build-up of discontent. Ironically, one of the most brilliant analyses of the consequences of independence in African states was written by Dunduzu Chisiza in Gwelo gaol in 1959. With uncanny accuracy he plotted, in general terms, the course his own country would follow in the years ahead:

> If a nationalist movement is to achieve the goal of independence [he wrote], it is vitally important that one of the leaders should be elevated

well above the others; that his former equals should look upon themselves as his juniors; that they should accept his decision as final; and that they should pledge loyalty to his leadership. But once independence has been achieved, the problem arises of reconciling submissiveness to the top leader and individual initiative on the part of second-level leaders. To a man who has been surrounded by submissive associates for a long time the exercise of initiative by his associates is easily construed as a sign of rivalry and disloyalty.[8]

In a later essay he expanded on these ideas:

The real problem is posed by those leaders who lapse into dictatorial tendencies because their countrymen trust them ... too much. ... When too much trust is reposed in a leader (sometimes) the thing goes to his head and makes him believe he is infallible. Such a man is not likely to brook criticism or to welcome alternative suggestions. It is his idea or nothing. ...

In framing policies and designing measures ... leaders must rely on public opinion and the opinions of colleagues. ... The task of leadership involves following as well as leading.[9]

Although he must have read Chisiza's writings, and may even have discussed them with him, Banda remained oblivious of the dangers of which they warned.* Certainly his own views on leadership were very different. He brought up the subject in a speech to a mass rally in Blantyre on 24 May, his last before independence.

So what does a leader do? [he asked] When I was negotiating a constitution, before my men knew what I was doing I had finished everything. I said: 'Well, boys, I've done this, that and that, finished.' Even when they were with me in London – Chirwa, Kanyama [Chiume], Aleke [Banda] and Chokani – they didn't know what I was doing. I had finished everything before they knew anything about it! Last October they didn't come with me to London. I didn't even take Chirwa, Kanyama [Chiume] and Chipembere – What's the use? I left them back home – I do the work myself. A waste of time, why take them? ... This kind of thing, where a leader says this, but somebody

---

* Some commentators have claimed that Chisiza's essays were intended as a direct warning to Banda of the likely course of events in Nyasaland. This seems improbable in view of the early date at which they were written.

else says that; now who is the leader? That is not the Malawi system. The Malawi system, the Malawi style is that Kamuzu says it's just *that*, and then it's finished. Whether anyone likes it or not, that is how it is going to be here. No nonsense, no nonsense. You can't have everybody deciding what to do.[10]

What prompted these remarks will probably never be known, nor is it particularly important. What was important was that while six months earlier they might have passed unnoticed,[11] in the changed circumstances of a Nyasaland barely six weeks from independence they provoked intense resentment. Earlier in the same speech Banda had replied to newspaper allegations that Nyasaland was a dictatorship by asking: 'If there is no opposition what do they expect me to do – manufacture one?' As it turned out, this was precisely what he was doing.

The Crisis is Born

Any of a number of factors might have been sufficient to explode the tacit disagreements which existed at independence into open discord. But in the event, it took a combination of two causes to precipitate a dispute.

The initial impetus derived from the disagreement over policy towards Mozambique. At the O.A.U. summit in Cairo, Chiume had tried to persuade Banda to make a more determined condemnation of Portuguese colonialism.[12] Banda had flown into a rage and had refused to speak to his minister for the rest of the conference. When he returned home, on 26 July, he gave vent to his displeasure in his address to the welcoming crowd at Chileka airport:

You, the common people, are the real Malawi Congress Party. Watch everybody! Even Ministers – and I tell you when they are present, right here. Watch them, everybody! If they do what you do not think is good for the Malawi Congress Party, whether they are Ministers or not, come and tell me. It is your job to see that nothing injures or destroys the Party. Ministers are human beings, you know. ... I am saying this because I know we have strange funny people here very soon, Ambassador for this country, Ambassador for that country, and they will be trying to corrupt people in the Party, and they will be starting with Ministers and Members of the National Assembly.

So I want you to be vigilant. One Party, one leader, one government, and no nonsense about it.[13]

This speech had a decisive effect in uniting the ministers against Banda. Until then he had succeeded in keeping his cabinet divided. Bwanausi, Chipembere and Chiume had formed one group; Chisiza, still nursing a grudge following his omission from the 'Gwelo cabinet', had opposed them; Chirwa had been a law unto himself; and Cameron, Chokani and Tembo had remained neutral. By openly displaying misgivings about their loyalty, Banda had undermined these carefully fostered hostilities.

A few days later six ministers* sought a meeting with him to ask him to clarify his remarks. It was the first time they had ever seriously questioned anything he had said, and he was plainly surprised. But he must have realized that he had gone too far for he reassured them that he did not doubt their loyalty and denied that he had meant to imply that he did. He apparently also accepted their carefully phrased request for a return to the system whereby allegations against Party officials were fully investigated before they were made public.† Emboldened by this success, the ministers resolved that in the event of any future disagreement they would stick together.

Thereafter events moved quickly. On 4 August Cameron resigned from the cabinet in protest against Banda's plans to reintroduce preventive detention.‡ His portfolio as Minister of

* Chiume, who was away in Dar-es-Salaam, and Cameron did not take part in this delegation. John Msonthi had been mysteriously dropped from the cabinet at the time of independence.

† Although a provision to this effect was entrenched in the Party constitution, Banda had developed a tendency to make public denunciations of Party officers whom he suspected of misdemeanours, without waiting for the Party's Disciplinary Committee to carry out an investigation, and often on flimsy evidence. A great deal of ill-feeling had resulted (see *Hansard*, Zomba, 9 September 1964, pp. 93–4).

‡ This may have been nothing more than a formal measure to increase Banda's reserve powers. Preventive detention had been permitted under the Preservation of Public Security Ordinance, enacted in 1960, but had been

Works was taken over by Bwanausi. A week later it was announced that Nyerere would pay a State visit to Malawi from 4 to 8 September to coincide with the first sitting of the new Malawi parliament. It was to be a red-carpet occasion, complete with nationwide tour, mass rallies to be jointly addressed by Nyerere and Banda, and a special issue of postage stamps. On 13 August, Chiume left for Chitipa to meet Oscar Kambona, the Tanzanian Minister of External Affairs. They were joined shortly afterwards by Bwanausi and Yatuta Chisiza for a week's tour of game parks in Zambia, Tanzania and Kenya.

At this point the Mozambique question again intervened. It was announced from Zomba that Malawi was negotiating a trade treaty with Portugal and that, pending the completion of the formal treaty, 'the Governments of Malawi and Portugal have agreed to develop trade relations in such a way as to encourage trade in goods locally produced or manufactured in the two countries'. To men like Kambona and Chiume this was heresy. Cooperation with Portugal in so far as it was dictated by geographical necessity was one thing. Voluntarily to encourage mutual trade, and thereby give sustenance to what they and most other African nationalists regarded as a particularly unpleasant colonial power, was quite another. The situation was not improved when, in another statement from Zomba, it was announced that Jardim had been appointed Malawi's Honorary Consul in Beira.

It was clear that if a stand were to be made it would have to be made quickly. Chiume, however, after his experience in Cairo, was loath to attempt again to make an issue of Portuguese policy, and the ministers' discussions on what strategy to adopt were inconclusive. But then Chiume had a meeting with the Chinese ambassador in Dar-es-Salaam, Ho Ying.

Early in 1964, Banda had stated that when Malawi became

---

endered unconstitutional by the Marlborough House constitution. Banda was now intending to introduce a constitutional amending act to unfreeze the 1960 legislation. An alternative explanation for Cameron's resignation, and one for which there is some evidence, is that he foresaw that a rift was imminent and had no wish to become involved in it.

independent it would recognize mainland China and press for its admission to the United Nations.[14] But he had also stressed that he did not intend to take part in any 'cold war' between China and Taiwan, and to this end had invited both countries to Malawi's Independence celebrations in July. Taiwan had accepted, but China had refused and, in a not unfriendly editorial in the Peking *People's Daily*, had chided Banda for inviting 'the Chiang Kai Shek bandit clique' and thus supporting 'the plot created by American imperialism to eternalize its occupation of Taiwan . . . and to commit further aggression against the Chinese mainland'.[15]

Meanwhile Ho Ying had approached Banda with an offer of £6 million in aid in return for recognition of the mainland regime and an end to the 'two-China' policy. Banda was wary, and two meetings later Ho had not elicited either a definite acceptance or a refusal. To the ministers, this hesitance was inexplicable. Malawi was desperately in need of development funds. Why, they wanted to know, was the aid not accepted? All that had been decided was that Malawi would send a ministerial mission to Peking, headed by Chiume, for further discussions on the proposal.[16]

It was to the finalization of this visit that Chiume's talks with Ho now related. In the course of their discussions, the Chinese ambassador increased the offer of aid to £18 million. This was the pretext for which Bwanausi, Chiume and Chisiza had been looking.

On 15 August, two days after their return home, Nyerere sent word to Banda that his projected State visit would have to be postponed indefinitely because of the deteriorating situation in the Congo.* To the ministers it seemed too good an opportunity to miss. Despite Chipembere's absence at an educational conference in Canada,† they decided to act the following day.

---

* It has been suggested that the true explanation of Nyerere's cancellation was that it had been engineered by Chiume through Oscar Kambona. While this is an attractive speculation, no factual evidence has come to light to support it.

† Chipembere had left for Ottawa on 19 August.

Confrontation

The next day, a Wednesday, the cabinet met,* as it did every Wednesday morning, to go through the business of the previous week. Banda himself opened the proceedings with the presentation of a paper on the establishment of the proposed University of Malawi. In the ensuing discussion, the subject came around to the latest Chinese aid offer. The exact sequence of events is not entirely clear, and Banda's description of the meeting is in this respect unhelpful, although it gives an accurate picture of his own reactions:

> They all attacked me. I was shocked. I was shocked ... because there was the Prime Minister isolated, deserted by every one of his Ministers. No one tried to support me. Not one of them tried to defend me. They all attacked and attacked viciously ... and most disrespectfully.[17]

Predictably he over-reacted. Not only did he fall into the trap of which Chisiza had written, of misconstruing individual initiative as disloyalty, but the whole issue was complicated by the generation gap between Banda and his colleagues. Most of the ministers were little more than half his age, and he had not lost his Chewa belief that youth should respect the views of its elders. Had the age differential been less, Banda's reactions might have been a good deal cooler. But as it was, when other causes of discontent (the tickey charges, Africanization, relations with Mozambique and Southern Rhodesia) made their entry into the discussions, he twice threatened to resign – an offer which the ministers hastily rejected. When the meeting broke up, at four in the afternoon, little headway had been made. It was to resume, at the suggestion of Orton Chirwa, the following evening.

In the interim Banda discussed the situation with Sir Glyn Jones, who prevailed upon him to reconsider the resignation threat, which, apparently, he had every intention of carrying out there and then. Jones advised him, for the meantime at least, to do his utmost to heal the rift.

* It is not clear whether Tembo was present at this meeting, but from the subsequent pattern of events it seems probable that he was not.

When Banda met his cabinet again, it was in a very different mood from that of the previous afternoon. As the discussions progressed, it became clear that the difficulties were not insuperable. The tickey charges, Banda said, could be reconsidered – they were not, after all, of great importance. The Skinner report, he admitted, was not perfect: again something could be worked out. On foreign policy there could be further discussions. On the question of Chinese aid, he said he appreciated the reasons for recognizing the mainland regime but wanted time to work out relations in his own way. The meeting ended amicably, with all present concluding that agreement was not far away. The ministers were to list the subjects on which they wished to have further talks, and Banda would consider them point by point.

The Rift Widens

It was in the compilation of this list that the ministers made a fatal mistake. Encouraged by their success at the Thursday meeting, they added to their original complaints two new ones. One of these, that Banda was treating the Government as his personal estate and refusing to allow adequate consultation within the cabinet, was in reality their basic grievance. The other was of a much more superficial nature. This was that, by appointing to high office such people as John Tembo (a relation of Banda's Private Secretary, Miss Cecilia Kadzamira) and Aleke Banda, he was guilty on the one hand of nepotism and on the other of favouritism.

The list was handed to Banda the following day, Friday, by Orton Chirwa. The cabinet did not meet again until its regular session on Wednesday, and in the intervening period Banda did two things which should have indicated to the ministers that all was not well. He recalled John Msonthi to take back his old portfolio of Transport and Communications; and he prorogued parliament for five weeks, until 6 October. In any open clash with the ministers, Msonthi could be relied upon to support him, while the postponement of parliament would give him time – or so he thought – to settle the dispute once and for all, whatever form it might eventually take. For by now Banda was convinced that something far deeper than mere policy differences was involved. Rumours of dissension within the cabinet had filtered out from Zomba, and he had begun to receive anonymous letters warning him that the ministers were inciting the people against him.* He started asking himself why the ministers, whom he knew had been divided only a few months before, should have acted in concert; whether, in fact, there might not be a conspiracy against him.

To the extent that the letter-writers influenced Banda's belief in a conspiracy, the ministers' complaint that he listened too willingly to anonymous allegations was shown to be justified. Yet in this case it was perhaps understandable that Banda should have given the warnings more credence than they deserved, for the circumstances were highly abnormal. The accusations of nepotism had cut him to the quick, and had turned his face from any thought of compromise with the ministers as surely as it had from the idea of resignation.

When Banda received his cabinet on 2 September, it was in a mood of defiance. He told them that he had not had time to consider their demands, and would not be forced into doing so before he was ready. The meeting was brief and stormy, and ended with Banda walking out.

Out of this rebuff grew the conspiracy which Banda believed had already been long in existence. The ministers decided that he must be forced to resign, and Chirwa should become Prime Minister in his place. Chipembere, perhaps at Chisiza's insistence, was to be excluded from the planned cabinet.† While the ministers canvassed support for their scheme, recruiting Rose Chibambo to agitate within the Women's League, the letter-writers became more persistent and the rumours of a split within the cabinet more widespread. By the weekend of 5 and 6 September, Banda felt compelled to act or face nationwide

---

* There is a certain amount of evidence to suggest that at least some of the letters were sent by M.P.s and Party officials who saw in the rift an opportunity for quick promotion. The charge that the ministers were mobilizing opinion against Banda was at that stage untrue.

† Chipembere did not learn of this betrayal until two years later.

unrest. He recalled parliament for an emergency sitting on Tuesday, 8 September.

On Monday, he announced the dismissal of the three ministers he regarded as the instigators of the cabinet split – Bwanausi, Chirwa and Chiume – and with them, of Rose Chibambo. A few hours later Chisiza and Chokani resigned in sympathy.

The Crisis Breaks

Banda was now in an extremely difficult situation. Of his former cabinet, the five ex-ministers opposed him; two ministers – Msonthi and Tembo – were for him; and Chipembere, now hastening home from Canada, was an unknown quantity.* The decision to recall parliament, and so bring out into the open matters which he would have preferred kept silent, had been forced on him rather than being of his own choosing. He might feel confident of carrying M.P.s with him, but he could not be certain. It was a calculated risk. But having taken the decision, he proceeded to act on it with ruthless determination. When parliament began sitting on Tuesday morning, he proposed a motion of confidence in himself and his policies on domestic and external affairs, and of support for the four cornerstones of the Malawi Congress Party – 'Unity, Loyalty, Discipline and Obedience'. He began rhetorically:

It is in deep sorrow and grief that I arise to speak this morning. . . . the four cornerstones on which . . . our State, the State of Malawi was built, have broken down; have broken down. Once these four cornerstones are broken away . . . there is no government . . . in this country, and there is no State. What do we get? Another Congo. Is that what anyone in this country wants?

I would rather see those [front] benches empty and myself in the bush, dead, than see these four cornerstones destroyed by anyone. Once there is no unity, no loyalty, no discipline, no obedience, we are finished; we are finished. Just as the Congo. It is finished.[18]

* Chipembere was not apprised of events at home until the day before parliament met, when he received a distraught telegram from Chiume urging his immediate return.

Turning to the ex-ministers' particular complaints, Banda asked a question which was later to figure prominently in his allegations of a conspiracy against him: why, he wanted to know, had the ex-ministers not spoken out against the tickey charges, the Skinner Report, etc., when they had first been discussed in cabinet?

On foreign policy he adopted a similar approach: why had the ex-ministers not objected to his policies towards Portugal and Southern Rhodesia when they were being initiated? Why had they waited until now? On China, one of the weaker points of his case – M.P.s might, after all, fail to understand why he was refusing £18 million in aid – he was more circumspect, admitting that 700 million people could not be ignored for ever. But he went on to accuse, 'This trouble that my ministers have been giving for the past ten days was set up by the Chinese Ambassador in Dar-es-Salaam.'[19]

Still on the attack, he claimed that the ministers had introduced their accusations of nepotism* in the hope that they would induce him to surrender to their demands for fear of a scandal. 'But, it so happens,' he told M.P.s, 'my conscience is absolutely clear. . . . I was ready to come here and let you judge me and them.'[20] It was a telling point, and one which was not lost on his audience. He did not deny that he ran the Government 'as if it were my own property'.[21] But the reason the ex-ministers had wanted greater cabinet responsibilities was to give them more power, and bigger opportunities for corruption.[22] To achieve this, they would have done anything – had they dared:

If they could have murdered me and got away with it and the people accepted them as leaders, they would have murdered me in cold blood without flinching, and if they knew they could have forced me to resign and got away with it by the people accepting them, they would have done it. But they knew very well that they could not get rid of me and get away with it; they could not murder me and get away with it; they could not force me to resign and get away with it, because the people want me in this country.

Prime Ministers differ, Mr Speaker, and this one happens to be

*The only charge he did not answer was that of favouritism.

different, very different indeed, very different. I will not surrender my powers to anyone . . . I will not. I won't. I would rather be shot dead as Olympio was shot dead in Togoland than surrender to blackmail.

I know I am a marked man. I have been for the past three or four years a marked man. They do not like me; I speak too bluntly, but that is my stuff.

Red China has to be reckoned with . . . but what changes are to be done in this country, either in domestic or foreign policy, are to be done in my own way, in my own time. . . .

I have said that I am a marked man; that we are marked people. Well, I am not afraid . . . because I am protected by you – my people.[23]

Hansard described the reaction to the speech by appending to it the italicized phrase: (*prolonged applause*) (*singing*) – no mean understatement for the standing ovation it received. It was a magnificent performance. To the ministers, if not yet to Banda himself, it was clear that the day had gone against them – a conviction which grew stronger as the hours passed and member after member rose to denounce them as 'traitors', 'conspirators' and 'power-hungry maniacs'. Had Chipembere been present to speak immediately after Banda, events might have turned out differently. But he was not; he was still *en route* from Canada; and this being the case, the ex-ministers had little choice but to attempt to minimize their differences with Banda, to re-affirm their loyalty to him, and to express hopes that a reconciliation might be possible.

Chisiza's speech, moderate, reasonable, and – in sharp contrast to Banda's – very much on the defensive, was typical of their attitude:

Is it really disobedience? Is it really being disloyal to the Prime Minister? Is it encouraging disunity if you go to him and say: 'We think, and sincerely so, that this and that. . . .' This and that is a pinprick in our country. Is that being disloyal? If it is . . . I accept the charge as a traitor. . . . Consider, even for one minute, brothers, that you could be mistaken; I may be mistaken. But who is the judge? Posterity.[24]

Chipembere Returns

Chipembere landed at Chileka as the afternoon debate in Zomba was drawing to a close. He was met by Gomile Kumtumanji, who handed him a letter from Banda asking him to remain in the cabinet. Not until he arrived in Zomba, however, a few minutes before the House adjourned, did he learn the full story of the past two weeks' events.

Having discussed the situation with the ex-ministers, Chipembere tried unsuccessfully to persuade Banda to allow Sir Glyn Jones to mediate in the dispute. That evening, and again the next morning, he tried to persuade the Governor to arrange a meeting between the two sides. But although, at his second attempt, Jones telephoned Banda to suggest this plan, Banda said that it was now too late and refused.

When parliament resumed sitting, later that morning, Chipembere took his place with his colleagues on the back benches. Events had moved too quickly to admit of any other choice for him. Apart from the pledge of mutual solidarity, which he had made with them five weeks earlier, he may have felt that by putting his voice with the others the balance would be partly restored, and compromise and eventual reconciliation made easier to achieve.

When he rose to speak, it was in much the same tone of moderation and reasonableness as had been used by Chisiza and the other ex-ministers the previous day. Unlike his colleagues, however, he aimed his remarks directly at Banda. It was a politician's speech; Chipembere, like Banda, had the knack of gauging his audience:

It gives me a heavy heart that Malawi, which was so proud of its unity, so famous for its stability, that Malawi, which people were regarding as a paragon of political organization and discipline and understanding, has now broken down. Broken down to the extent of the members of one party, the mighty Malawi Congress Party, attacking one another in public here, in the presence of . . . our former enemies, calling one another traitors. Wherever Welensky is today, he must be rejoicing. He must be celebrating. There must be a cocktail party somewhere in Salisbury as a result of what is taking place here. We are in utter disgrace.[25]

The unsaid question: 'Was it really necessary to parade our differences like this?' was not lost on Banda. And when Chipembere concluded by stating: 'I am perfectly convinced that one of these days the Prime Minister will evolve a solution to this problem, and that once more we shall be calling one another brothers and not attacking each other as monsters,' he accepted it as a suit for peace. Chipembere's speech set the tone for the remainder of the long day's debate, from which the violent, sometimes vicious, tirades of the previous day were strikingly absent.

When Banda wound up for the Government, it was in the same vein. The vote which was to follow, unanimously supporting the motion he had proposed, was a foregone conclusion, and with victory assured he could afford to be magnanimous:

Every one of these ex-Ministers has expressed his loyalty to me. ... I accept this in good faith. But I would rather resign than do anything under duress. ... nobody must be under any illusions. I am not afraid of death, and I am not afraid of going back to Kasungu to farm. I farmed as a boy of seven ... and I can do it again. I am not going to be forced into doing anything. ... China must ask me to recognize her. China must say to me: 'Kamuzu, you must recognize us. We are a great people. We are an ancient people. And there are 700 million of us.' That kind of language is easily understood by me. But the other kind of language, the kind of dangling bribes before my face and eyes, is not, Mr Speaker, easily understandable by an Elder of the Church of Scotland. This is not a cabinet crisis at all. It will be solved. This is a family affair, in which no outsider must try to meddle.

Let me say that if any outsider tries to intervene and make political capital out of this ... he will find that these very same men [the six ex-ministers] will be the very first ones to be on that man's neck. I know my boys. You must not try to say something against me in front of them, even now that they have resigned. Even now, you go and try.[26]

To Banda, it was a source of considerable comfort to know that the only member of his cabinet who could pose a real political threat was bent on healing the rift. It was this, more than anything, which lay behind the conciliatory nature of his closing speech. The opposition having been crushed, the question now was to discover what could be salvaged from the wreckage – or so Banda thought. But events were to take more than one strange turn before the crisis came to an end.

To Reconcile or Not?

The extent of Banda's parliamentary victory had convinced the five ex-ministers who had been party to the conspiracy that their plans to force his resignation would have to be abandoned. They still believed, however, that it would be possible, while negotiating the reconciliation which, following the smooth ending of the parliamentary debate, they expected to follow as a matter of course, to persuade Banda to agree to their original demands for greater cabinet consultation. In this, Chipembere concurred. So, instead of seeking an early meeting with Banda to hammer out an agreement, all the ex-ministers left Zomba for their constituencies to put their case to the people. Some of them may have felt it their duty to explain their actions to their electors. But there was also the feeling that their positions would be stronger with constituency support. In the event, however, the delay gave Banda time to make an announcement which radically altered the now delicate balance of conflicting loyalties.

It came at a press-conference in Zomba on Friday, 11 September. Five new cabinet ministers were to be appointed, he said, including McKinley Chibambo, to take over from Bwanausi as Minister of Works, Development and Housing, and Albert Muwalo, to become Minister of Information in succession to Chiume.* Chiume's other portfolio, External Affairs, he took over himself. The portfolios of Justice,† Education, Home

---

* Chibambo, the Party's Regional Chairman in the North, had been appointed a Regional Minister with non-cabinet rank shortly before the emergency debate, as had Chidzanja, in the Centre – who now also became Minister of Trade and Industry – and Kumtumanji, in the South. The other new cabinet ministers were Alec Nyasulu (Natural Resources) and Gwanda Chakuamba (Community and Social Development). All five were personally loyal to Banda.

† The post of Attorney-General, previously held by Chirwa, was taken over by a European, Bryan Roberts, who had until then been Solicitor-General.

Affairs, and Labour (formerly held by Chirwa, Chipembere, Chisiza and Chokani) were deliberately left vacant. He was sure, he said, that at least some of the ex-ministers would return.[27]

But Banda was reckoning without four things. He was still unaware of the extent of the conspiracy, and may even, at this stage, have begun to believe that the early reports he had heard were exaggerated. And he was in ignorance of the mutual solidarity pact the ex-ministers had entered into, and which was partly responsible, through the resignation of Chipembere, for the situation having grown as serious as it was. Moreover, he omitted to take account of the long-standing friendship between Chiume and Chipembere, and of the strong personal followings which some of the ex-ministers, and Chipembere in particular, had in their own areas.

It was a combination of these last three factors which led Chipembere, when he addressed a report-back meeting at Fort Johnston the following day, to take a much harder line than he had in parliament. To Chipembere, Banda's announcement that Bwanausi and Chiume would not be readmitted to the cabinet meant that a reconciliation would be much more difficult, and perhaps even impossible, to achieve. Although there is no reliable account of what he said, it appears that he attacked the Government over the tickey charges and Africanization. The *Times**
quoted him as saying:

The present Malawi Government is worse than Welensky's Federal Government. . . . When we were elected we promised the people that all jobs being done by Europeans would be done by Africans. But Europeans who shot our people, burning their houses and ill-treating them, are still holding high posts in Zomba, Blantyre, Lilongwe and elsewhere. . . .[28]

The same report also claimed that he was refusing to return to the cabinet.

While it seems unlikely that Chipembere would have gone quite this far – unfavourably to compare Banda with Welensky would have been tantamount to a declaration of war – the report appears to have been the only account of the meeting

*The *Nyasaland Times* was so renamed in 1963.

available to Banda, and as such, regardless of its accuracy, it proved an important factor in the developments that followed.

That Sunday, however, when he addressed a mass rally at Palombe, Banda appeared to be unaware of what Chipembere had said the previous day. It was his first public appearance since the cabinet crisis had broken and, as might have been expected from the nature of his audience, he spoke more harshly than at his Zomba press-conference. The ex-ministers, he said, had conspired against him 'like hyenas in the night'. He promised to introduce new blood into the Party's Central Executive – 'so that they can watch the hyenas'.[29] Although the appointment of new members to the Central Executive was a routine procedure after the appointments of the new ministers, it was none the less an indication that Banda was beginning to grow impatient with the way events were shaping.

There were a number of reasons for this. The emergency debate in parliament had not cleared the air as he had hoped it would. The discussions he had expected to hold with the ex-ministers immediately afterwards had failed to materialize and, up until that weekend, no date for a meeting had been set. When finally, through Sir Glyn Jones, a meeting was arranged, it was not to take place until 21 September, almost a fortnight after the House's adjournment. Furthermore the country was still restless, and reports were coming in of secret meetings in Blantyre and Zomba of African businessmen and civil servants, disenchanted with the Africanization policies and the Skinner Report.

In the midst of all this, the *Times* report of Chipembere's speech, published on 14 September, was a bomb-shell. The first reaction to it came from the *Malawi News*, which accused the ex-ministers of working against Banda in private, while publicly maintaining their support for him.[30] The next day, Wednesday, it was announced after a three-hour meeting of the Central Executive* that the six ex-ministers and Rose Chibambo were

*This was the meeting referred to by Banda in his Palombe speech. The four new ministers not already on the Executive (Nyasulu, Chakuamba, Chibambo and Chidzanja) were appointed members, as were Kumtumanji,

being suspended from the Party, 'pending an investigation into reports of their speeches at recent meetings, which seemed inconsistent with their affirmations of loyalty to the Prime Minister and Party in Parliament'.[31] It was the same technique as had been used so successfully in 1962 to break the trades union movement.

As the ex-ministers returned from their constituencies, the prospects for the planned meeting with Banda were already beginning to look doubtful. On Saturday, 19 September, Chipembere, Bwanausi, Chisiza and Chokani gave a cocktail party in Blantyre. They all four spoke, reiterating their loyalty to Banda and protesting their innocence of any design to oust him. They went on to restate the points of difference between themselves and the Government. In Chipembere's words, they felt that the Party, in some of its policies, had 'strayed from the true path of nationalism'. Banda, they said, was going further than was necessary in his relations with Portugal, which was leading to accusations from other African leaders that Malawi was 'playing stooge to the Portuguese imperialists'. At home, the pace of Africanization was too slow, and, as a result of this and of the tickey charges, there was genuine discontent among a substantial section of the people.*

Whatever the ex-ministers' intentions in their speeches that night, they proved to be the straw that broke the camel's back. To Banda it was now abundantly clear that there could be no reconciliation unless he was prepared to grant substantial concessions. He was not.

---

in his capacity of Regional Minister for the South, and two members of the League of Malawi Women, Mrs Margaret Mlanga and Miss T. D. Gondwe. Mrs Mlanga soon afterwards succeeded Rose Chibambo as the League's National Chairman.

* *Times*, 22 September 1964. In support of his claim, Chipembere quoted figures purporting to show that revenue from the sale of Malawi Congress Party membership cards had dropped from £50,000 in 1960 to £15,000 in 1964. Although this may have been an exaggeration, there is no doubt that Party morale slumped badly immediately after Independence (see *Hansard*, Zomba, 9 September 1964, pp. 93–4).

Not to Reconcile

The following day, addressing a mass rally at Chikwawa, Banda attacked the ex-ministers for 'criminal irresponsibility', and accused them of deliberately and maliciously inciting unrest against him.[32] He then asked Sir Glyn Jones to call off the meeting arranged for Monday. When Chipembere protested that he and the other ex-ministers had been willing to come to an understanding with the Prime Minister and to cooperate with him, but that the Prime Minister's attitude had made this impossible,[33] Banda retorted, in a nationwide radio broadcast, that if this was the case the ex-ministers had only themselves to blame. Instead of coming to discuss the dispute after the adjournment of parliament, they had gone to their constituencies and violently attacked him. 'They are saying that I must concede to their demands or else they are not coming back. To me that is not the language of men who desire reconciliation. Do they expect me to go down to them on my knees and beg them to come back?'[34]

In the meantime John Msonthi had been appointed Minister of Education in succession to Chipembere. The seals were fast setting.

Rebuilding the Party Image

Banda had acted, early on, to remove the principal source of popular disaffection – the tickey charges. At Palombe, he had promised that no one would be turned away from hospital because he could not afford treatment.[35] Indeed, he had gone further than this, claiming that there had been a standing instruction to this effect since the ruling had been introduced. If patients had been refused treatment, it was due to a misunderstanding, he said.

On Africanization, too, he took a more moderate line. At the Palombe meeting, he restated his refusal to Africanize 'simply for the sake of Africanization', but stressed that expatriates would be replaced by Africans as soon as they were equipped to do their work. A week later, at Chikwawa, he took this a step further. 'Very soon, those Africans who leave Mpemba,* and develop a sense of integrity, honesty and responsibility will be called to Zomba to be permanent secretaries and under secretaries,' he said.[36] At a meeting in Blantyre, he announced that civil servants who had resigned their posts in protest against Federation in 1959 would be taken back, and their salaries and seniority adjusted as though they had never left.

In the parliamentary Party, his first action after the emergency debate had been the appointment of the five new ministers. A sixth soon followed.† Nine M.P.s were promoted parliamentary secretaries, and three more were appointed before the year was out.‡

With these manoeuvrings behind him, Banda now felt, in the third week in September, that it was time to make a personal assessment of the situation in the central and northern regions, and on 26 September he set off for Lilongwe. Before leaving, however, he promulgated a decree banning all public meetings and processions in the southern region without police permission. As a precautionary measure, it backfired. On the night of his departure, one man was killed and sixteen injured in clashes in Blantyre between members of the Youth League and civil servants and Chipembere supporters. Incidents continued in Blantyre the following day, a Sunday, and by Monday had spread to Zomba, where the Malawi Congress Party District Office was burned down, and another man was killed. In Fort Johnston, Gomile Kumtumanji was menaced by an anti-Banda mob, and in Zomba itself a number of high Party officials, including Gwanda Chakuamba, were beaten up. By Wednesday the situation had deteriorated to such an extent that most shops remained closed and civil servants stayed at home to protect their families from violence.

After some hesitation troops were called in, whereupon order

* The Mpemba Institute of Public Administration near Blantyre.
† Alfred Chiwanda was appointed Minister of Labour in October.
‡ These included Musopole (the same 'General Flax' Musopole who had caused the colonial Government so much trouble in 1959), Kaphwiti Banda, Jeremy Kumbweza and Bundaunda Phiri. Phiri, who was related to Banda, was shortly afterwards killed in a car accident.

was speedily restored. The situation had been unpleasant, but never very serious. Yet it did have two important repercussions. On 30 September, when the disturbances in Zomba were at their height, new security regulations were introduced empowering Banda to restrict any person to a specified area, and to require him to report to the police at designated intervals.* The first person to be so affected was Chipembere, who was restricted to within a four-mile radius of his home at Malindi. Soon afterwards Banda cut short his tour of the northern region and returned to Kasungu, where he could keep in close touch with events in the South without actually returning to Zomba – which might have been interpreted as a sign of panic.

It was a bitter irony that, less than three months after Independence, Banda should have to resort to the same restrictive measures as had been so much hated when used by the colonial authorities against his own Nyasaland African Congress.

Despite the curtailment of his visit to the North, Banda could look back on his tour with a good deal of satisfaction. At the rallies he had addressed, explaining how a conspiracy† had been laid against him and denouncing the ex-ministers,

* Restriction orders were to be reviewed after six months, and thereafter, every three months.

† By this time the conspiracy theory had got completely out of hand. Banda now maintained that Chiume, whom he rightly regarded as the prime mover behind the split, had been plotting against him since the end of 1963. At that time it had been alleged that Chiume was seeking to enhance his popularity by having laudatory articles inserted in the Government newspaper, *Malawi Lero*, and that he was trying to form a personal power base in the newly created Young Pioneers movement. This was probably true, although Chiume claims that he was framed by Chidzanja. It was this which had led Banda to transfer to Chipembere the Education portfolio Chiume had held, and to appoint Aleke Banda Commander of the Young Pioneers, in place of the council, headed by Chiume, which had previously run the movement's affairs (see *Malawi News*, 6 October 1964).

Soon afterwards Banda took this a step further, claiming that he had been watching Chiume and Chipembere since April 1963 (i.e. since their joint visit to America). He had known all along that they had been planning to oust him, he said, but 'I gave them a long rope to hang themselves' (*Malawi News*, 20 November 1964).

particularly Murray William Chiume* – 'the evil genius', 'the snake', 'the Lucifer' – he had received massive demonstrations of support. In his own area, the central region, there was little discontent over the tickey charges and, with fewer civil servants than the other two regions, little resistance to his policies on Africanization. And in the northern region, where opposition might have been expected to be strongest,† he had found no evidence of widespread disaffection.

It was in Kasungu, on 5 October, that Banda finally dealt the deathblow to any last hopes of a reconciliation with the ex-ministers. He would 'not allow any of the sacked or resigned ex-ministers to return to Zomba', he said.[37] It appeared to be little more than a formality: Chipembere was in restriction; Chiume was in Dar-es-Salaam; and Chisiza, Chokani and Bwanausi were in Lusaka. Yet it was not entirely correct. There was one man who still stood a good chance of returning to office – Orton Chirwa.

The Timbiri Incident

After the emergency debate in parliament, Chirwa had vanished. When he reappeared, it was in Lusaka, where he made a brief

* On his return in 1958, Banda had required his colleagues to use their African fore-names. He himself had insisted on his second name, Kamuzu, being used, the first name, Hastings, being dropped except as an initial (Chipembere, interview). After the cabinet crisis, however, Banda frequently used the ex-ministers' English names – the implication being, apparently, that with European fore-names they were less good African nationalists than they made out. Thus M. W. K. (Kanyama) Chiume became Murray William Chiume; H. B. M. (Masauko) Chipembere, became Henry Blasius Chipembere, etc.

† This for two reasons: firstly, because four of the six ex-ministers were northerners; and secondly because the majority of senior civil servants came from the North. It is unhelpful to attempt to interpret the events following the cabinet crisis on purely regional lines (although it can fairly be pointed out that the two ministers who did not resign – Msonthi and Tembo – were both, like Banda, from the central region), since in the main it was personalities rather than regional or tribal feeling which were important. Nevertheless, regionalism and tribalism did play some part in the crisis, particularly in regard to Chewa support for Banda and Yao support for Chipembere. (See also J. McCracken, 'African Politics in Twentieth-Century Malawi', in T. O. Ranger, ed., *Aspects of Central African History*, Heinemann, 1968.)

statement to the press on 24 September. 'We like Dr Banda, we like him to lead us, and we wish him well. We realize the greatness of his achievements,' he was reported to have said.[38] Then, again, he vanished, this time turning up at Malindi, on a visit to Chipembere, at about the same time as Banda was making his 'no reconciliation' speech at Kasungu.

Nothing more was heard of him, by the general public at least, for about a fortnight. Then, on 23 October, it was reported in the *Malawi News* that Chirwa had been making attempts to see Banda to ask his 'mercy and forgiveness'.[39] This was, in fact, to have been the first step in a campaign to prepare public opinion for his eventual reinstatement. Chirwa had indeed approached Banda, who had been quick to realize the tactical advantage he would gain if he could take back even one of his ex-ministers. Chirwa, who had dissociated himself from his colleagues soon after the emergency debate and was as much a technocrat as a politician, was easily the most suitable candidate. Agreement had not proved hard to reach.

Yet, even before the ink on the front page of the *Malawi News* was dry, an event took place which threw a new and sinister light on the situation. In the early hours of the morning of 23 October, sub-Chief Timbiri, from Chirwa's constituency of Nkhata Bay, was murdered in Zomba. He had arrived in the capital the previous day to discuss with Banda disputes among the petty chiefs of his area – over whom Banda was considering making him a Native Authority. The appointment had political implications, and the police discovered what they believed to be conclusive evidence that Chirwa had been involved in the directive for his killing.

He disappeared for the last time, to join his colleagues in Dar-es-Salaam early in November.

The Party Purified

When Banda returned to Zomba on 14 October, he found the southern region much calmer than when he had left. The majority of the people were solidly behind him, and the civil servants, who provided the bulk of the ex-ministers' support, were, in his own words, 'afraid of their own shadows',[40] a state of mind which was encouraged by the rough treatment they received at the hands of the Youth Leaguers.

Banda's attitude to the violence which the crisis unleashed was much more straightforward than it had been in 1959, or, for that matter, in 1963 and the early part of 1964. There was now no dilemma between aggression and retaliation to confuse the issues at stake. There was not even the opportunity to turn a blind eye. The question before Banda was simply whether violence should be used as a political weapon or whether it should not. He decided without hesitation that it should.*

Meanwhile the purge of doubtful elements of the Party, which had been initiated early in September, was quietly continuing. By December about fifty people had been restricted, and a rather larger number suspended from party membership.† In the ex-ministers' constituencies, a number of chiefs were deposed and district councils were dissolved. Some of the ex-ministers' more determined supporters fled to join them in Tanzania.‡

At very short notice, a party conference was called for October. It was to be the final propaganda exercise before the resumption of parliament, three days later, and delegates were invited from all over Malawi, as well as from M.C.P. branches in Southern Rhodesia, Tanganyika, Zambia and Zanzibar. The conference deplored the 'despicable and high-handed' action of the ex-ministers, and passed a series of resolutions reaffirming its loyalty to Banda – 'the one and only true leader of the people

---

*See *Hansard*, Zomba, 30 October 1964, p. 253. Banda may have remained in ignorance of the worst excesses committed by his followers, although the same cannot be said of some of those who sat on the Party's Central Executive. Much of the severe physical intimidation which took place was authorized from a very high level.

†These included three M.P.s, Machuwira (Chiradzulu), Kanyanya (Karonga), and Ndomondo (Fort Johnston West), and one of the newly appointed junior ministers, Thengo Maloya (M.P. for Kasupe).

‡The purges were most severe in Karonga and Fort Johnston, reflecting the relative popularities of Chisiza and Chipembere.

of Malawi'. One resolution noted, 'as it has been proven in the past, Kamuzu knows best.'*

The main purpose of the conference, however, was to pave the way for Banda to present to parliament the constitutional amendment bill which would permit the reintroduction of preventive detention. It was partly to facilitate the acceptance of this measure and partly to rally public opinion still more closely behind himself and the Party that Banda now raised, for the first time, the possibility of the ex-ministers' attempting to regain control of the country by force of arms. 'I'll face Kanyama Chiume with his foreign allies . . . I know Kanyama is plotting. We must be ready for anything. Every man and woman will have to be taught how to use a gun – even a machine-gun,' he told delegates.[41]

In both intentions he was successful. But Banda was not yet to have things entirely his own way. On 28 October, he learnt that Chipembere had escaped from restriction. 'Henry Chipembere has run away from Malindi,' Banda told M.P.s. 'I have ordered a full search . . . I want him brought here, alive if possible, but if not alive then any other way.'[42] The constitutional amendment was enacted, and parliament adjourned with still no news of Chipembere's whereabouts. On 31 October, Banda announced that he was in Tanzania, plotting with Chiume, Chisiza, and 'a certain foreign power', but the air of uncertainty remained. For the next two weeks, official statements alternated between saying that Chipembere 'was' and that he 'was said to be' in Dar-es-Salaam.

The threat of invasion, which had originally been introduced more as a political tactic than as a genuine cause for alarm, began to be taken more seriously, and Banda announced that he was arming the Young Pioneers to act as a territorial reserve.

Within the Party the purges and realignments were now drawing to a close, and Banda decided to make another brief tour of the North, for a final check on some of the more doubtful areas – including Rumpi, Chiume's former constituency,

* M.I.D. press release, 25 October 1964. Resolutions of this kind were usually spontaneous, but went to Banda for vetting before they were published.

and Karonga, Chisiza's home area. Fort Johnston, where
supporters of Chipembere were still active,* would then be the
only district which he had not visited.

On 22 November, the Government stated categorically that
Chipembere had been located, staying with Oscar Kambona's
father in Tanzania.† Later that day Banda announced his intention of travelling to New York at the end of the month to
address the United Nations, as he had originally planned. There
was now, in fact, little to keep him at home. His visit to the
North had convinced him that he need expect little trouble from
that quarter, while the uncertainty occasioned by Chipembere's
disappearance seemed to have cleared. Even more important,
he had at last received reliable information on his ex-ministers'
activities in Tanzania.

Word had reached him, at about the same time as he had
learnt of Chipembere's supposed whereabouts, of a plot to
assassinate him at Dar-es-Salaam airport as he travelled to the
U.N. The information came from the Malawi Brotherhood
Society, a Congress party affiliate in Tanzania which had remained loyal. The plot being known, he was able to counter it
by changing his route to London. Moreover he could feel secure
in the belief that the ex-ministers were unlikely to be hatching
more than one scheme at a time, although the knowledge that
they were contemplating such drastic measures can hardly have
reassured him for the future.

It was a measure of Banda's confidence that, at the time of his
departure, no fewer than four of his key ministers were out of the
country – Tembo, Msonthi, Chidzanja and Nyasulu – and he
took with him Aleke Banda, the Commander of the Young
Pioneers and Secretary-General of the Party. As he left, he
made a last appeal for law and order;[43] and throughout his two

* Fort Johnston was the scene of the last disturbances of 1964, when, in
the second week in November, troops were called in 'to restore respect for
law and order' after a series of clashes between Youth Leaguers and
Chipembere supporters.

† In fact Chipembere was still in hiding in the border areas between south-
eastern Malawi and Mozambique. There is no doubt, however, that Banda
believed that he was safely in Tanzania (see also Banda, Speech at Fort
Johnston, 23 May 1965, M.I.D. transcript).

weeks' absence, there was not a single incident. But this was not the end of the crisis. Rather it was the calm before the storm.

Chipembere's Rebellion

The new year 1965 began with rumours and scares of invasions. It was claimed (quite baselessly) that Banda was planning to leave the country secretly to allow the ex-ministers to return; that arms had been captured on their way to the ex-ministers' supporters in Malawi (in fact arms were captured, but they were destined for Frelimo in Cabo Delgado); and that Banda had discovered a photograph of Chipembere in his breast pocket, and had replaced his African bodyguards with Europeans. Banda himself announced that Chiume had enlisted the services of John Okello, of Zanzibar revolutionary fame, to mount an invasion across the Tanzanian border, and groups of Young Pioneers were dispatched to the North. Units of the Women's League – the 'Amazon Army' – were reported to be standing by in reserve.

But when the invasion came it was from a different and quite unexpected quarter. At about 10 p.m. on the night of 12 February a band of 200 armed men under the leadership of Chipembere crossed from Malindi to Fort Johnston. They attacked the police station, killing the wife and child of an African police officer, and seized rifles and ammunition. One group was sent to the post office to destroy telecommunications links, while another fired houses belonging to Banda supporters in the nearby village of Chief Mponda. The party then re-formed and marched towards Zomba, reaching the ferry across the Shire river at Liwonde at about 2 a.m., only to find that the sole ferryboat was securely tied up on the far side. By this time, however, word of the attack had reached Zomba, and reinforcements had been dispatched. Shortly after Chipembere's men arrived at the river, the vanguard of the security forces appeared on the other side. With no hope of reaching the capital that night, the rebels retreated and crossed back to Malindi with the army, several hours behind them, in pursuit. They were followed to a camp in the forest reserve just east of Malindi where for weeks, unknown to the Government, they had been in training. There three were killed and seven captured. In the following week, fifty more were taken prisoner. And then began the long, tedious business, familiar from the dark days of 1959, of cordon and search.

In a strangely subdued broadcast on 18 February, Banda appealed for peace and calm and asked the public to cooperate with him in crushing the rebellion. Predictably, he accused Chipembere of running away and refusing to stand up and fight..He complimented the civil servants on their 'exemplary' conduct during the events of the past few days – none had stayed away from work as they had done in September – and praised the security forces, particularly the Army Commander, Colonel Lewis, and the Police Commissioner, Peter Long. But he was obviously a much saddened man, and his account of the incident itself was sombrely factual.[44]

The following day new public security regulations, made possible by the constitutional amendment of the previous October, were brought into effect, 'to make sure,' as Banda put it, 'that there is full cooperation between the security forces and the public.' They enabled him to detain without trial; to order the compulsory surrender of firearms by all persons other than members of the security forces; to empower the security forces to use any reasonable means, including firearms, to apprehend anyone suspected of being connected with the rebels, and to make it an offence, punishable by seven years' imprisonment, to consort with, harbour or give sustenance to a rebel.[45]

The arrests continued, punctuated by fresh disturbances. In Fort Johnston, Chipembere, who now had a price of £500 on his head, continued to elude the security forces. At Ntaja, at the end of February, there was an unsuccessful attack on a police post, and near Zomba, another attack, also unsuccessful, on an old chief who shot dead one of his attackers. In March, near Chitipa, there was an incursion led by Chisiza from across the border with Tanzania, in which two rebels were hacked to death by Young Pioneers and a Malawi Congress Party area chairman was killed. Elsewhere the country was tense but quiet.

On 1 April, in a speech to commemorate his release from Gwelo, Banda replied to growing overseas criticism of the rough treatment being handed out by the Young Pioneers and the Youth League. The initial shock of the rebellion had worn off, and he was very much on form again. The Pioneers, he explained, were 'not out to persecute anyone, but they are there to see for me, to hear for me, [and] to help the security forces ... wherever it's necessary'. He went on to cite the Chitipa incident as an example of 'how I want my Young Pioneers to behave'.

Anyone invading this country, deal with him! [he ordered] This is no play, no play. No football or tennis. [It is] war, war, war. And when you are at war anything is fair. I am not going to listen to any nonsense. Let the world criticize me and my Government. If I do not act there will be chaos in this country. ... Then the people sitting in the editorial chairs in London will say: 'Oh, we told you, Africans cannot govern themselves; there is another Congo; there is political chaos in Malawi.' That's what they will be saying. I want to make this quite clear. My first job as long as I am in Zomba is to maintain political stability in this country, and efficient, incorruptible administration.[46]

A few days later, parliament passed the Young Pioneers Act, which made the movement an integral and equal part of the security forces.* During the same sitting, an amendment to the penal code was enacted, redefining treason and providing for it a mandatory death penalty. The definition was extremely wide: as Banda put it, 'if [a person] even just thinks about it [the forcible overthrow of the Government] and speaks aloud and somebody hears about it, that's treason.'[47] He made clear, however, that the Government did not intend to be vengeful. The ringleaders would be 'made to feel it', but those who were merely misled must be forgiven. 'They are our people, we must not be hard on them, and my business is to lead all my people, guide them – and when they go astray, bring them back,' he declared.[48] At the same time he announced that, in view of Malawi's improving economic position, he hoped to make

---

*This process was taken a step further in November, when an amending act was passed, prohibiting the police from arresting a Young Pioneer without first consulting his district commander.

improvements in the conditions of service for civil servants laid down by the Skinner Report.

On 21 May, Banda announced in a nationwide broadcast that Chipembere was in America. Malawians, he said, would receive the news with mixed feelings, because they would have liked 'to see him hanging and his legs dangling and swinging from a pole somewhere in Zomba or ... Blantyre'. Chipembere's flight, Banda went on, proved that he now realized he had no support in the country.* He concluded:

Chipembere, Chiume, Chirwa, Chisiza, Bwanausi and Chokani have wasted our time and efforts since August 26. ... Now that Chipembere and all the others have run away, let us concentrate our minds, our thoughts, our efforts on nothing else but development, and not on bitterness, hatred or vengeance.[49]

Two days later he made the same point in a speech to a mass rally at Fort Johnston, which he visited for the first time since the cabinet crisis had broken, eight months before. Although disturbances continued in parts of the southern region for some months longer, to all intents and purposes Chipembere's rebellion was over.

*cf. Chipembere: '... the old man had the countryside behind him and we miscalculated' (Munger, *Kamuzu Banda of Malawi*, p. 22).

Chapter 11
Towards the West and the White South

The confusion which had been evident in some areas of Banda's foreign policy at the time of independence deepened in the latter half of 1964 in a way which belied his statement at the O.A.U. summit conference. There was no early clarification of his views on Southern Rhodesia and, far from there being a reconciliation of the political and economic components of his policy towards Portugal, the two further diverged. Although Banda clung tenaciously to the theory of 'discretional alignment', there was no move to establish relations with any of the communist countries. And in the field of intra-African affairs, Malawi's median alignment between its black- and white-ruled neighbours, which had formed the basis of Banda's O.A.U. statement, was disrupted by the rapid deterioration of its relationships with Tanzania and Zambia following the arrival of the ex-ministers in Dar-es-Salaam and Lusaka.

On 9 October the Tanganyika African National Union newspaper, the *Nationalist*, described Banda as a 'tin-pot Cromwell' and declared that recent events in Malawi had shown 'that he can now expect no real backing from the mass of Malawi citizens which has always been the basis of the political strength of Messrs Chiume, Chisiza and Chipembere.'[1] Shortly afterwards it published an unsigned article by Chiume comparing the 'indictment of fratricide, venality and corruption' outstanding against Banda with that against Tshombe. Banda was 'so swayed by superstition,' Chiume wrote, 'that he now walks with a limp because of a human molar tooth he has been advised to keep under his toe to counter witchcraft being used against him.'[2]

The day after this attack appeared, Nyerere announced that Tanzania would grant asylum to the ex-ministers, but that it 'would not countenance these or other refugees abusing our hospitality and undertaking any political or other campaign against the Malawi Government from our territory.' Whatever differences existed in the foreign policies of Malawi and Tanzania, Malawi's internal affairs were her own concern and Tanzania would not interfere in them.[3]

In Malawi these affirmations of neutrality were received with scepticism, and Banda questioned the contradiction between T.A.N.U. and Tanzanian Government policy. The *Malawi News* declared that unless Nyerere's words were supported by his actions, it would consider him two-faced.[4] But the attacks continued and intensified, and after the arrests, at the end of November, of the leadership of the Malawi Brotherhood Society, subsequent denials of Tanzanian support for the rebels were disbelieved.[5]

The deterioration in Malawi's relationship with Zambia was both less dramatic and less complete. When Zambia became independent on 24 October, a Malawian ministerial delegation travelled to Lusaka to participate in the celebrations, and the *Malawi News* published a cautious but none the less friendly editorial welcoming the new state.[6] Like Nyerere, Zambia's Home Affairs Minister, Mainza Chona, affirmed Zambian neutrality in Malawi's internal affairs. Malawians should not think that Zambia was hostile to her simply because some of the ex-ministers had friends in the Zambian cabinet, he said.[7] None the less, after a number of leading officials in Kaunda's ruling United National Independence Party had publicly attacked Banda, the *Malawi News* editorialized, in February 1965: 'We seek nothing but friendship with our neighbours ... [but] statements such as the ones that have come out of Zambia within the past few weeks are not conducive to the maintenance of ... good relations.'[8] A few days later Zambia deported three prominent M.C.P. officials from Fort Jameson for alleged 'anti-Zambian activities'.[9]

Parallel to this trend, Malawi's relationship with Portugal continued to improve, albeit somewhat erratically. After the announcements of the interim trade agreement and Jardim's appointment as Malawi's honorary consul came the inauguration of a Beira–Blantyre air service. But then, during the emergency debate in parliament on 8 September, Banda spoke of Mozambique being 'plagued by a power of Europe'.[10] Three weeks later, he took a very different line. Addressing members of the diplomatic corps at Lilongwe, he declared:

> There are people who think they are helping their fellow Africans by shouting. . . . This question of liberating Africa has two sides to it. We must fight if necessary, but I believe in keeping your powder dry, and at the same time negotiating if you can.
>
> It is all very well to shout, to make threats. True, we must fight if necessary. But find out what the other man is thinking. Have a talk with him. . . . I do not believe that every European is against us, that every Portuguese is against us, that every White man in Southern Rhodesia is against us. Not at all. There are some there you can talk with, and you discover that there is a great deal in common between him and you.[11]

It was the most comprehensive statement Banda had made of a political policy towards white-ruled Southern Africa, bringing together a number of previously disparate ideas. Yet, at the United Nations in December, in the middle of a violent attack on colonialism, he stated: 'She [Malawi] is condemned by force of circumstances beyond her control to have dealings with Mozambique or Portugal. No one regrets this more bitterly than I do.'[12] A month later he announced formally in parliament that the Nacala railway would be built.*

After the Chipembere rebellion and the Chitipa incident in March, the imbalance between Malawi's relationships with its black- and white-ruled neighbours crystallized. Banda no longer sought economic justifications for his dealing with Portugal, and it became clear that his earlier diffidence and tergiversation had reflected carefulness in suiting his statements to his audiences, rather than any inner uncertainty.† In September 1965 formal negotiations began in Lourenço Marques on the construction of the Nacala railway, and Banda initiated discussions with Japan

* Banda claimed later that he had been forced into building the Nacala railway because Kaunda and Nyerere had refused to cooperate in the pre-independence Malawi–Tanganyika railway plan (Munger, *Kamuzu Banda of Malawi*, p. 25).

† Banda himself likes to pretend that this was not so; cf. *Hansard*, Zomba, 20 May 1966, p. 615: 'What I say today, I say tomorrow, the day after that, the week after that, the month after that, the year after that – that's my nature.'

for the provision of finance for this scheme and a related project to exploit Malawi's bauxite reserves at Mlanje. Shortly afterwards the two countries concluded a visa abolition agreement. Although Frelimo was allowed to maintain a representative in Blantyre, the Front's activities were carefully controlled.*

Malawi's relationship with Tanzania, on the other hand, soon descended to the level of outright hostility. Supporters of the ex-ministers received training in guerrilla tactics from Chinese and Tanzanian instructors at camps near Kibaya and in southern Tanzania, and some were sent from Dar-es-Salaam to Algeria, China and Cuba for further instruction. Nyerere continued to profess neutrality, and when Banda confronted him with evidence of collusion between Chiume, Kambona and Job Lusinde, the Minister of Home Affairs,[13] he laughed it off. 'Ever since [the ex-ministers] ... came the good doctor has been saying we have been plotting against him. I have been telling him it is not true,' he said. 'I am just waiting to hear him make the same accusation against President Johnson because Chipembere is in the United States.'[14]

In July supporters of the ex-ministers infiltrating from Tanzania made unsuccessful attacks on houses belonging to M.P.s at Rumpi and Nkhata Bay. In September a third attack took place at Karonga, in which the Member of Parliament, Nelson Mwambungu, was severely injured and his two house-servants killed. Some of the weapons captured from the infiltrators proved to have been supplied by the Tanzanian Government. But when Banda wrote to Nyerere, demanding an explanation, the reply was 'not at all satisfactory', and subsequent letters went unanswered.[15]

---

* In 1965 large numbers of refugees from northern Mozambique began to arrive in Malawi following the launching of the Frelimo offensive in September 1964. They were at first housed in camps on Likoma Island and at Mlanje and Cholo, afterwards being integrated into the local population. Frelimo officials in Malawi were allowed to visit them to recruit supporters, but Banda insisted that they should not use Malawi as a base for raids into Mozambique. By tacit agreement with Mondlane, this arrangement has been generally adhered to, although Frelimo units often enter Malawi across the ill-defined border east of Fort Johnston to evade capture by Portuguese troops.

Faced with this continuing refusal to come to terms, Banda began to attack Nyerere personally. As the leader of the nationalist movement in a United Nations trusteeship territory, Nyerere had never had to fight for his independence, he told parliament in July. He had been given it 'on a silver platter':

> ... that man is simply suffering from a sense of inferiority, an inferiority complex, that makes him ... pose as a champion of Africa ... when he is no fighter at all but a coward.[16]

After Nyerere had again denied Tanzanian involvement in attempts to unseat Banda, the *Malawi News* commented: 'Either the President does not know what is going on in his own country ... in which case he is not fit to be President; or he is telling a deliberate lie.'[17] Later Banda also took up this theme in a speech at a mass rally to welcome back the leadership of the Malawi Brotherhood Society, who had recently been released from detention in Tanzania:

> The real ruler [in Tanzania] ... is not Nyerere, but Kambona. ... Kambona reduced Nyerere to a figurehead three years ago, two years ago. He is ruling Tanganyika now.
> That was what Chiume wanted to do to me. ... But I am not a jellyfish kind of Prime Minister. ... So Chiume could not do to me here what Kambona had done to Nyerere in Tanganyika. I refuse to be a puppet. If other people enjoy being puppets, Kamuzu does not, Kamuzu does not. I repeat, if others are jellyfish kinds of Prime Ministers or Presidents, this one is a Prime Minister with a spine.[18]

In October, when Nyerere relieved Kambona of the Foreign Affairs portolio and downgraded Job Lusinde in a post-electoral cabinet reshuffle, Malawi looked forward to 'a restoration of President Nyerere's powers'. But it quickly became apparent that Banda had been underestimating his man. Although Kambona and Lusinde were 'mainly responsible for ... there [being] ... now between Malawi and Tanzania a state of undeclared war', [19] as the *Malawi News* put it, the assumption that Nyerere was either unable to control or unaware of their activities was mistaken. At the O.A.U. summit conference at Accra in November, he threatened to withdraw Tanzania from the organization if Malawi were appointed a member of the African Liberation Committee.[20] And he reacted strongly against a suggestion that Nkrumah should mediate in his dispute with Malawi.[21]

The element of personal vendetta between Banda and Nyerere, which stemmed from their having been at one time on terms of close personal friendship, was absent from the dispute between Banda and Kaunda. Moreover, whereas Banda was convinced that Nyerere was responsible, whether by default or otherwise, for the Tanzanian Government's assistance to the ex-ministers, he distinguished between the views of Kaunda and those of U.N.I.P. Although some people in Zambia were sympathetic to the ex-ministers, 'Kaunda does not agree with any of this,' he explained.[22]

In May, a Malawian ministerial delegation led by Chidzanja visited Zambia, at Kaunda's invitation, to discuss common problems. On its return it reported that the Zambian Government had gone out of its way to be helpful.[23] But a month later U.N.I.P.'s official newspaper, the *Zambian Pilot*, asserted: 'When Banda goes ... the whole sycophantic set-up will perish like the bursting of a miasmatic bubble regurgitated from some subterranean sewer and Malawi will be born again.'[24] 'How can African unity develop from such words as these?' asked Albert Muwalo.[25] Although three weeks later, Banda was declaring, 'Zambia and we are friends – we are the same people,'[26] their underlying relationship remained tense and uneasy. Malawi's estrangement from Zambia was less complete than from Tanzania, but it was no less real.

The months after Chipembere's rebellion saw a clarification of the wider aspects of 'discretional alignment' comparable to that which occurred within the realm of intra-African affairs. In this the key role was played by China.

Despite Banda's suspicions of Chinese sympathy towards the ex-ministers – denied by Ho Ying as 'groundless fabrications and lies'[27] – he had favoured China's admission to the United Nations when he addressed the General Assembly in December 1964. Mao Tse Tung and Chiang Kai-Shek were both 'truly great and remarkable men', he declared. But in view of the disparity in the sizes of Formosa and of the Chinese mainland, 'Justice and fair play demand that the Government in Peking presided over by Mao Tse Tung be recognized as the legal and rightful Government of China ... and ... that it should be recognized by the United Nations ... now.'[28]

After Banda discovered that China was providing the ex-ministers with money and guerrilla-training facilities, these ideas changed abruptly.* 'What the Chinese want, I don't want,' he said simply. 'What the Chinese do not want, I want.'[29] He had no intention of 'playing a first or second fiddle in a Chinese propaganda orchestra of hate', or even of being part of its audience.[30] Mao Tse Tung, he declared, was developing delusions of grandeur; he was coming to regard himself as the re-creator of the Mongol Empire, the heir of Kublai Khan.[31]

In a message to the General Assembly in September 1965, Banda explained his new position:

The past record of the People's Republic of China is such in respect of her attitude to armed combat, her open interference in the affairs of other nations, and her outspoken antipathy to the United Nations organization itself that we feel that before any nation votes in favour of her admission to the United Nations there should be demanded of her some concrete evidence of a change of heart in these matters and a genuine willingness, if admitted, to respect and abide by the basic principles of the United Nations.

Malawi 'entirely disagreed' with the view that the expulsion of Formosa should automatically follow the admission of main-land China. To expel a nation which was one of the founder members of the U.N. would not only be 'utterly inequitable', but it would deprive Formosa's twelve million inhabitants of representation in the world body. Consequently Malawi would not favour a waiver of the rule that the admission of new members must be approved by a two-thirds majority of the Assembly.[32]

Two months later Banda signed a technical assistance

* Banda afterwards 'forgot' that he had supported China's admission to the United Nations in December 1964, and claimed that his opposition to the mainland regime dated back to the cabinet crisis, when he had 'exposed' to the rest of Africa China's attempts to 'bribe' him.

agreement with Formosa's Vice-Foreign Minister, Dr H. K. Yang, and in July 1966 it was announced that the two countries would establish diplomatic relations.

Banda's mistrust of China had been reinforced by events in Vietnam. At the Commonwealth Heads of State and Government meeting in London in June, he had supported the sending of a Commonwealth peace mission to Moscow, Hanoi and Peking. China's and North Vietnam's rejection of this proposal as an imperialist trap had demonstrated, he said later, that they were not interested in securing a peaceful, negotiated settlement:

It is not the presence of American troops that is . . . prolonging the Vietnam war. It is the desire of the Vietcong . . . to impose their will on the . . . loyal people of South Vietnam. It is the desire of North Vietnam . . . to extend its rule to South Vietnam. And above all . . . it is the desire of Peking to extend her influence . . . and rule that is preventing North Vietnam and South Vietnam from settling their differences. . . .

If American troops were removed from South Vietnam tomorrow, the Vietcong, the North Vietnamese troops, the Chinese and North Korean troops would overrun, not only South Vietnam but also Thailand, Malaysia, Philippine Islands and South Korea, and . . . that would not be the end.

Other countries in Asia would soon be similarly overrun because the North Vietnamese, Chinese, North Koreans are being backed up by another great country in Eastern Europe. They would not rest there, and we must not deceive ourselves: Africa and even Europe would not be safe. . . .

It is wrong . . . for anyone . . . to look at Washington as the lair of hawks in the Vietnam war, and Hanoi and Peking and the rest of the Communist capitals as the nest of the doves of peace and brotherly love on eggs.[33]

Despite Banda's support of the American cause in Vietnam, relations between Zomba and Washington grew strained towards the end of 1965. In October Banda learnt of the extent to which the C.I.A. had been involved, not only in procuring a visa for Chipembere, but also in physically extracting him from Fort Johnston and transporting him to California. What had begun as a jibe on the part of Nyerere ended as an international incident. Banda suggested that the Americans might be 'grooming' Chipembere as his successor in an attempt to forestall the Chinese, who were similarly 'grooming' Chiume.[34] 'Both the Chinese and the Yankees should be warned that the people of Malawi . . . will . . . not tolerate the Reds and the Yankees to interfere in our affairs,' commented the *Malawi News*,[35] and the following day the Party's annual convention 'condemn[ed], in no uncertain terms, Communist China and Imperialistic United States of America.' Meanwhile the American Ambassador to Malawi, Sam P. Gilstrap, was discreetly withdrawn.[36]

The altercation over Chipembere's presence in America was short-lived, and after it Banda's intensifying fear of communism meant the end of 'discretional alignment' as a practical policy. Apart from minimal trade links, Malawi never did establish contact with the communist bloc and when, in July 1966, a Russian delegation paid an exceptional 'goodwill visit', its stay was principally notable for the care with which its actions were overseen by the Malawi Special Branch.

Conversely, Malawi's Western orientation grew stronger. After a visit to Berlin in the middle of 1965, Banda pronounced himself in favour of the re-unification of Germany, and subsequently advocated it at the United Nations. West Germany showed its appreciation by increasing its aid and making available funds for the construction of the first stage of the lakeshore road, the 'Great Kamuzu Highway', as it came to be called. De Gaulle, whom Banda met at about the same time, proved altogether a wilier ally, and his request for finance for the Nacala railway was courteously refused. But France did make available limited technical assistance, and Banda afterwards paid a eulogistic tribute to the General's statesmanship. By 1966 Malawi's relations with the United States had normalized, and after Banda's declaration that he supported Johnson's Vietnam policy '150 per cent', aid and friendship flowed more strongly than ever. Denmark continued to provide development aid, and Israel technical assistance. And in 1968, after Banda had paid a State visit to Formosa, the Nationalist Chinese expanded their agricultural training schemes in Malawi. Britain, the United Nations Development Programme, the World Bank and the

African Development Bank all made available substantial development loans, and Britain also made annual grants-in-aid to cover Malawi's budgetary deficit. While Banda continued to deny that Malawi had adopted a pro-Western alignment, he did admit that '99 per cent of the time the West is in the right'.

Against this background of alienation from Tanzania and Zambia, cooperation with Portugal and commitment to the West, Banda's views on Rhodesia, the dominant issue of 1965, coalesced into a coherent policy.

The possibility of Southern Rhodesia declaring itself unilaterally independent, first mooted in the days of Sir Edgar Whitehead, had been much discussed since Ian Smith had become Rhodesia's Prime Minister. In October 1964 Britain's new Labour Prime Minister, Harold Wilson, had warned that such an act would be treasonable and would have dire consequences for Rhodesia's economy. Six months later, a Rhodesian White Paper discounted the use of economic sanctions on the grounds that the country was too valuable as a barrier against communism. If, however, Britain did act against Rhodesia's economy, it said, an 'inevitable first step' would be the repatriation of the estimated 240,000 Malawians living in the territory and a similar number of Zambians.[37]

The Rhodesian situation was discussed at length at the Commonwealth Heads of State and Government Conference in London in June. As in 1964, Banda advocated the holding of a constitutional conference at which Britain would mediate between the Rhodesian Front and the African nationalist parties. It was an orthodox view, and appeared as a unanimous proposal in the conference's final communiqué. But Banda differed from the majority of his fellow African leaders in his view of what should be done in the event of Rhodesia refusing such a conference. Whereas they urged Britain to suspend Rhodesia's constitution and appoint an interim government pending the holding of free elections, Banda declared:

It is not realistic on the part of any of the African leaders to ask the British Government to send an army to Rhodesia, suspend the

Constitution of Rhodesia and impose a new one by force, by killing the European settlers. . . .

Who are these settlers in Rhodesia? Britons, people of British blood, British birth, British descent. Some came directly from Britain . . . at the end of the last war. No British Government would give any British Prime Minister power to [send an army] . . . to Southern Rhodesia to shoot Englishmen, Scotsmen, Irishmen there.

Even if the Prime Minister was given power by Parliament, the majority of people in Rhodesia have brothers, and friends in Britain, in the British Army, the British Air Force and the British Navy. If any British Prime Minister sent an army, there would be a mutiny in that army. They wouldn't fight their own cousins. . . .[38]

Later he expanded on these ideas by reference to the racial situation in America:

We have in the United States now a population of about 150 or 200 million [he said]. Of these about 30 million are negroes, and supposing by a freak, a mere freak of fortune, these negroes were in power and the 130-odd million Whites were under those negroes, could we, Kwame, Kenyatta, I, Balewa, send an army? Would our own parliament allow us to send an army to America and kill our own brothers in order to put a White man in power, just because White men were in the majority? So how do you expect Britain to send an army to kill their own people in Rhodesia . . . in order to make Nkomo or Sithole Prime Minister?*

Rhodesia, Banda maintained, was a political problem, and 'war as a solution to a political problem is bankrupt statesmanship'.[39] The only lasting solution would be found in a negotiated constitutional settlement.

By October, when African Heads of State and Government met in Accra for a summit conference of the Organization of African Unity, it was a question of when rather than whether

* *Hansard*, Zomba, 9 November 1965, p. 216. Banda did not mention the differences which made his analogy inexact. Britain had stated that it would not permit the Smith regime to seize and retain power and, since the Southern Rhodesian Government owed allegiance to the Crown, such a seizure would constitute an act of treason. Neither factor obtained in his hypothetical American example, nor was there in it any colonial relationship between the United States and Africa like that which existed between Britain and Southern Rhodesia.

U.D.I. would be declared. Nkrumah opened the plenary session with a call for the use of force to topple the Rhodesian Government, and the first draft resolution before the conference urged Britain to suspend Rhodesia's constitution by whatever means proved effective. If Britain refused to do so, the resolution suggested, member states who were also members of the Commonwealth should resign from its membership and freeze their currency reserves in London. The O.A.U. itself should then undertake military action to overthrow the Smith government.

Supported by Kaunda and Sierra Leone's Prime Minister, Sir Albert Margai, Banda demanded that the resolution be given a full debate before a vote was taken. Rhodesia was not only too grave a problem to dismiss hurriedly, he said, but there was also a danger that the militant language in which the resolution was couched would drive Smith into U.D.I. as an act of defiance. Moreover, the passing of a resolution in such terms might jeopardize whatever residual chance still existed of Smith and Wilson reaching agreement.[40]

In the ensuing discussion, Banda's views conflicted with those of his colleagues more sharply than ever. As he explained to the Malawi parliament, two weeks later, he had noticed a tendency among the majority of the delegates 'to take the line of least resistance, the popular line'. He had refused to 'join the bandwagon', he said, because 'at no time have I ever courted, c-o-u-r-t-e-d, cheap popularity. ... Whatever I say, I say because I think it is the right thing to say ... not because I want to be popular.'[41]

The idea of African states threatening to leave the Commonwealth was risible, he said:

Withdraw from the Commonwealth? Who do you think would suffer? Britain? No! Freeze bank accounts? Which bank accounts? Overdrafts! Many countries who were talking in that way have an overdraft in London now. Childish nonsense![42]

Banda went on to repeat the arguments he had used at the Commonwealth conference, four months earlier. Economic sanctions were 'no use unless major powers apply them, and just now no major power is willing to apply them,' he said.[43] In modern history there had not been a single occasion on which sanctions had proved effective. The suggestion that the O.A.U. should mount a military offensive was similarly impracticable:

> Military force? African military force? O.A.U. military force? Let me really laugh again. What single country in Africa today ... from north to south, east to west, has an army that can take on and beat the Rhodesian Army? Not one!
> The Rhodesian Army, next to the Army of the Union of South Africa, is the strongest and the most efficient ... in the African continent, and I mean just that. Don't deceive yourselves. ... It is all right to have all these uniforms. ... It is one thing to impress, but it is quite another on the battlefield. ...
> Mr Smith knows the quality of this so-called army that some of my colleagues praise. ... Ten mercenaries will fix five thousand so-called army, you know. Do you think Mr Smith is afraid of that sort of thing? He is not a fool, you know. ...
> Let me be blunt. ... The Rhodesian Army, if Smith pushed, would conquer the whole of East and Central Africa in a week. ... The Rhodesian Air Force would reduce to ashes and dust all the capitals of East and Central Africa – Zomba, Lusaka, Dar-es-Salaam, Nairobi, Leopoldville, Brazzaville – within 24 hours. Within 24 hours I mean, and neither the Ghana nor [the] Nigeria Air Force, neither the Ghana nor the Nigerian Army, could do anything to rescue us. ...
> We must not beat about the bush. Even our friends in North Africa, the United Arab Republic, Libya, Tunisia, Algeria, Morocco, all of them couldn't help us. ... They wouldn't even get here.[44]

Two days later Smith announced that Rhodesia was unilaterally severing its ties with Britain.

Malawi's position was set out in a broadcast Banda made shortly afterwards. He stressed that Malawi was just as vitally concerned as any other country with the future welfare of the Rhodesian people, despite his different approach to the problems this posed. Yet his rhetorical comment on the declaration itself served to emphasize this difference, rather than the objective of majority African rule, which he still claimed to hold in common with other African leaders:

> Who is right and who is wrong in this tragic affair? Who is to blame for this sad and tragic affair? We do not know and we may never

know. But whoever or whichever of the two men is to blame for this great tragedy that has taken place – for a great tragedy it is that has taken place in Rhodesia through the action of a unilateral declaration of Independence – on his shoulders lies a great responsibility for the consequences that are likely to follow in the wake of this tragedy. On his head will be heaped the curses of generations for the suffering of millions of innocent people that will inevitably follow in the wake of this tragedy.

It was up to Britain to decide what action to take to bring the rebellion to an end, said Banda. The only course Malawi or any other Commonwealth country could take was to follow Britain's lead. And for Malawi, which had close economic links with Rhodesia as a result of their long historical association, the only way to follow Britain's lead was 'morally'.

Apart from currency control . . . there is nothing much we can do [he said]. We are not in a position physically, economically or otherwise, to do anything else.[45]

None the less, when Britain announced the imposition of sanctions and appealed to other nations to follow suit, Malawi abrogated the 1964 Trade Agreement. But Banda made clear that, while he would encourage businessmen to find alternative sources of supply, there could be no question of Malawi cutting overnight all its existing trade ties with Rhodesia.[46] He dissociated himself from the supposedly unanimous resolution of the O.A.U. Council of Ministers, meeting in Addis Ababa from 3 to 5 December, which required O.A.U. members to sever diplomatic relations with Britain if the Smith regime had not been dislodged by 15 December, and chided the nine states who complied with it for their haste:

It is unreasonable for anyone, no matter who he is and where he is, to expect sanctions to work miracles overnight. Sanctions must take time to have an effect in Rhodesia. But there can be no doubt at all in the mind of anyone who is reasonable and realistic that sanctions will be effective in quelling the rebellion and bringing about the fall of the Government in Rhodesia, or at least bringing about a situation where discussion is possible to a successful conclusion.[47]

Banda, like almost everyone else, was misled by the apparent co-operation Britain was getting from the major powers. It was small consolation afterwards that he realized more quickly than most that such optimism was unfounded.

In January 1966, Commonwealth leaders met in Lagos for inconclusive talks with a disconsolate Harold Wilson. Banda warned of the danger of a conflict arising between 'White Imperialism to the West . . . and Yellow Imperialism to the East' with Rhodesia as their battleground,[48] and spoke with increasing sarcasm of the military impotence of his fellow African statesmen and of their unfitness to give advice. 'I will not be guided,' he told the Malawi parliament, 'by people thousands of miles away from Rhodesia . . . people whose ignorance of conditions and the situation in Rhodesia is greater than their ignorance of the situation and conditions in the planets Mars and Venus.'[49] While Banda quietly but persistently championed the cause of the 'silent' black Rhodesians, the supporters of the African opposition in the Rhodesian parliament, Rhodesian Whites travelled the long, dreary road of their rebellious independence.

Until the autumn of 1965, Malawi had remained on cordial terms with the majority of independent African states. Although it was not 'the most popular country in this Africa',[50] as Banda claimed, the ex-ministers' attempts to isolate him had succeeded to any extent only in Tanzania and Zambia. Elsewhere Banda's personal reputation had ensured the continuance of relations not markedly different from those which had obtained before the crisis occurred.

In July, Malawi's first Independence anniversary celebrations had been attended by Kenya's Minister of Development and Planning, Tom Mboya, and the Minister of Agriculture, Bruce Mackenzie, and it had been announced that the two countries would establish diplomatic relations. The following month Emperor Haile Selassie of Ethiopia had become Malawi's first State visitor, and in September Banda had paid an official visit to Malagasy. Delegations had come and gone from Egypt, Ghana, Guinea and a group of the francophone West African states.

By September, however, the friendship which had formerly characterized Malawi's relationship with the rest of black Africa was beginning to wane. At the end of that month, when Alec Nyasulu read out Banda's message to the U.N. General Assembly, he was given a frosty reception by the Afro-Asian bloc.

There were a number of reasons for this deterioration. One was Nyerere's increasing influence in intra-African affairs. Another was the more critical view many African leaders were taking of Banda's association with Portugal. But the most important was Malawi's stand on Rhodesia. Banda's views on the Rhodesian situation were disliked not so much because they detracted from the general unanimity, nor even because what he said was uncomfortably close to the truth, but because of the domineering way in which he expressed them. The speech which finally tipped the balance of African opinion against him was his statement to parliament after his return from the Accra summit. No statesman could feel aught else but insulted after being told that his considered opinions were 'childish nonsense' and that his arguments derived from the standpoint of ignorance.

Banda's abrasiveness on this occasion was due mainly to his awareness that his policies *were* disliked and, to a lesser extent, to his irritation with Nyerere. But there were also other reasons. The impracticability of the policies advocated by the majority of African leaders for the solution of the Rhodesian problem exasperated him. The tabling of resolutions incapable of implementation was not only useless but dangerous, he declared:

It is not to our credit as independent African states to keep on passing resolutions which we know cannot be implemented. ... It only makes us look ridiculous and a laughing stock to the rest of the world, in my view.

There are those who argue that it is better to pass resolutions, even if we know that those resolutions cannot be implemented, just in order to put pressure on certain powers. ... My answer is that pressurization, as they call it, can be overdone. People are not fools. Pressurization overdone will rebound on us. ... It will have a boomerang effect on us as African leaders and African independent states, and as a result we will lose credit. ...

The rest of the world will become disenchanted, not only with us as

African leaders and independent African states, but also and even more with the very idea of African independence.[51]

Over and above this disagreement on tactics, Banda felt a profound disquiet over the future of African unity itself. It seemed to him that the fears he had expressed at the Cairo O.A.U. summit were being realized, and that the cleavage between the old Casablanca, Monrovia and Afro-Malagasy groups was widening, rather than narrowing. Interference by members of one group in the internal affairs of members of another had increased to such an extent that it was one of the major topics of discussion at the Accra summit, which itself was put in jeopardy by the claims of a number of O.A.U. member governments that Ghana was aiding their political opponents.

In the second half of 1965, Banda spoke frequently of the futility of discussing an All-African Government in these circumstances. As he put it on his return from the Ghanaian capital in November:

How can you talk about continental government when Malawi and Tanganyika are not on friendly terms, Somalia and Ethiopia are not on friendly terms, the United Arab Republic and Tunisia ... Morocco and Mauretania ... Ghana and Ivory Coast ... Ghana and Upper Volta. ...

These are our practical problems, practical difficulties, to which we must not close our eyes ... or put down our heads in sand like ostriches. We must face them realistically. Yes, continental government definitely, I believe in it. .... But let's face facts. The day hasn't arrived yet.[52]

The only thing any realistic pan-Africanist could do, Banda maintained, was to work for closer international cooperation within a regional framework.[53]

In the next four months, *coups d'état* took place in six African states: the Central African Republic, Congo (Kinshasa), Dahomey, Ghana, Nigeria and Upper Volta. January saw the assassination of one old friend, Sir Abubakar Tafawa Balewa, and February the fall of another, Kwame Nkrumah. A few weeks earlier, Banda had decided to close Malawi's High Commission in Accra and to request the withdrawal of Ghana's mission from

Blantyre. Shortly afterwards Malawi broke off diplomatic relations with Egypt, whose President Nasser was a third former friend.

In a major speech to parliament in March, Banda announced that Malawi would recognize the new military governments of both Ghana and Nigeria. It would do so, he said, because they had been welcomed by the majority of the inhabitants of the countries concerned and because to do otherwise would be tantamount to interfering in their internal affairs. He went on to discuss in general terms the problem of interference and its relevance to African unity:

Whatever anyone may say . . . the truth is that there is no genuine unity among independent African states. There is no genuine unity within the Organization of African Unity, and a number of African leaders in the Organization of African Unity are dishonest and devoid of integrity.

This disunity among African states is ideological in origin. . . .

Since the three groups [Casablanca, Monrovia and Afro-Malagasy] joined to form the Organization of African Unity, there has been a tendency on the part of the former Casablanca Group to . . . try to capture the Organization. . . . It has dominated the Organization out of all proportion to its actual numerical strength. . . .

But this group . . . has not been satisfied with its domination of the O.A.U. In keeping with its revolutionary nature, it has left no stone unturned to spread its own revolutionary ideas to those other African states in which the leadership is deliberate, patient, realistic and evolutionary in outlook. And this it has done by every means, fair or foul. . . .

This ideological division within the Organization of African Unity has bred dishonesty and lack of integrity. . . . Because they believe strongly that they know what is best for Africa . . . some of the African leaders are actively encouraging and even organizing subversive activities in those countries where leaders hold different views from those of their own. While calling other leaders at the O.A.U. meetings or in letters as brothers and colleagues . . . they are actively working for the overthrow of the Governments led by those very leaders. . . .

That was why the radio and press in Ghana gloated over the fall of the Balewa government, even . . . after it was announced from Lagos that Sir Abubakar had been assassinated. . . .

At that time in Ghana, in the opinion of some of the people there the Balewa government was a reactionary government, a tool of imperialism. It had to be overthrown by any means, fair or foul.

In my view this is sad, tragic for Africa. To talk of African unity when there is disunity among African states and African leaders, to talk of brotherhood and friendship when there is enmity, dishonesty and lack of integrity among African leaders, is very sad indeed and tragic for Africa.

It is the very negation of African unity and it makes nonsense of the Organization of African Unity. . . .[54]

Had Banda spoken less abrasively, his criticisms of the O.A.U.'s weaknesses might have been turned to constructive ends. But it was not in his nature to do so. He once told Party officials, 'I do not mince words. . . . If you want me you will have to put up with my bluntness.'[55] The Party was prepared to put up with it, but Banda's fellow African leaders were not.

After the overthrow of Balewa, the rifts with Nkrumah and Nasser – the result of their both being prominent in the Casablanca group – and Nkrumah's subsequent deposition, of all Banda's old friends only Bourguiba, Haile Selassie, Kenyatta and Tubman remained friendly and in power. Yet for all the unpopularity of Banda's plain speaking, and of his policies towards the white South of Africa, Malawi's gradual move into isolation at the end of 1965 and beginning of 1966 was not entirely involuntary. No less important was Banda's own disenchantment with the unrealism and discord which seemed to him to be becoming endemic, not only in African affairs and at the O.A.U., but also at the United Nations. He told parliament, two months before the second anniversary of Malawi's Independence:

I am not going just to listen to some fools of the O.A.U. who do not know what they are talking about. No! No! I am not. And even at the United Nations itself, some of the things, resolutions, passed there are just childish. Childish!

Some of the men who shout the loudest there, calling the tune, are not even in a position to pay the piper. . . .

Other Africans, other Prime Ministers or even other Presidents follow whatever is said by their friends without thinking for themselves simply because they are ignorant. It is true!

... That is the trouble in Africa today – too many ignorant people who do not know anything about history and if they do know anything about it, they do not know how to interpret and apply it. That is why Africa is in a mess. ... That is the tragedy of Africa: too many ignorant people are in a position of power and responsibility.[56]

If this was African politics, Banda seemed to be saying, he wanted no part of it. Although Malawi did maintain residual contacts with the rest of black Africa, Banda never again attended an intra-African conference. His days as an elder statesman in Africa were over.

Chapter 12
Despotism or Democracy

A few weeks after Chipembere's flight to America, Banda told Malawians that theirs was 'the only country in Africa where six ministers. . . . [can be] either sacked or resigned and the government goes on smoothly and even better'.[1] It was a pardonable exaggeration, for his achievement in steering Malawi through the cabinet crisis and the troubled months that had followed had been nothing short of remarkable.

Banda's success in uniting Malawians behind him in those first crucial, dangerous months of independence had derived mainly from his personal charismatic appeal and from his absolute control over the Party machine. Until the cabinet crisis Banda's authority had been unchallenged, and to the majority of Malawians it was unthinkable that it should be. The Party's discipline regulations, as enforced by the Young Pioneers and the Youth League, had sufficed to deal with the minority who disagreed.

From this position of pre-eminence, Banda had skilfully built up in the popular mind a picture of the ex-ministers as enemies of the State. He had spoken of the Chinese Ambassador in Tanzania 'setting up' the crisis; of 'Kanyama Chiume and his foreign allies' striving to overthrow him; and of Chipembere and the other ex-ministers plotting with 'a certain foreign power' in Dar-es-Salaam. By so doing, he had succeeded not only in branding them as traitors, but also in alienating them and characterizing them as un-Malawian.

After November 1964 the external threat which Banda had been positing was realized in the deterioration of Malawi's relations with Tanzania and Zambia; Chipembere's rebellion, the incursions in the North and the disturbances in the South; Chiume's alliance with China and Chipembere's, briefly, with America; and, finally, in Malawi's drift into isolation. Of all these, only the rebellion itself constituted a serious security problem, and after it was over Banda turned his attention to the consolidation of his strength at home.

In July 1965, a fortnight after Malawi had celebrated the first anniversary of its nationhood, he announced that it would embark on the final stage of its constitutional advance and become a Republic on 6 July 1966. It showed a masterly sense of timing. The newness of independence had worn off, and Chipembere's escape had left a feeling of anticlimax; Malawians wanted something to which they could look forward. It was this need that the transition to republican status was designed to fulfil. Meetings were held, opinions canvassed, proposals drafted and discussed. In sum, immense political excitement was generated.

But while the build-up to the Republic succeeded, as perhaps nothing else could have done, in strengthening Banda's position, it was not intended as an end in itself. Much more important were the changes to be introduced in the new republican constitution, whereby Malawi would become a one-party state with special emphasis on discipline and obedience. It was in this and allied processes of domestic reform that the disparity between the African and Western components of Banda's heritage became most clearly apparent. And it was out of the conflict between them that was evolved the system of government which Malawi would carry forward as an independent Republic.

Until February 1961, Banda had maintained publicly strict adherence to the Westminster ideal of democracy, emphasizing the right of his political opponents to 'freedom of speech and freedom of association', and declaring more than once that he would 'welcome' the formation of rival political groups.[2] In that month, however, came the first concrete indication that he planned to deviate from this formula. Banda's selection of the Malawi Congress Party's candidates for the 1961 elections may have been made, as he claimed, with due regard to the wishes of their prospective constituents, and the fact of his making it personally did not justify the U.F.P.'s accusation that he was 'making a mockery' of democracy. But it was, nevertheless, a radical departure from British electoral practice.

After the elections this trend grew more pronounced. In July 1962, in response to overseas criticism of the M.C.P.'s dominance in Nyasaland politics, Banda attempted to define what he termed 'Malawi democracy':

> To me the criterion of democracy does not necessarily lie in the two-party system or two-man leadership. It lies in the right of the people to choose whom they want to follow. They can join any party they want to join. . . .[3]

Later he enlarged on this theme, explaining in a letter to expatriate civil servants in February 1963:

> The fact is that the African people have indicated, through the ballot box, an overwhelming support for my party in preference to any other.
> I am not opposed to the existence of opposition parties; at the same time I do not myself propose to take the initiative in building up an effective opposition to my party. Moreover, if opposition parties should appeal, then, on the political level, my party will, like other parties elsewhere . . . seek to minimize their influence. . . . The basic fact is that, should the people as a whole tire of me and my party, then they will remove and replace us. Until that time comes we propose to govern.[4]

The concept of a 'Malawi democracy', different from all others, occupied Banda's attention a great deal in the immediate pre- and post-independence years. It complemented his sense of Malawi's unique role in foreign affairs, and central to it was the idea of what Dunduzu Chisiza termed 'a strong-man government'. Chisiza had defined this as 'a dictatorship which the citizens choose to put up with'.[5] Banda's version was slightly different. 'I am a dictator of the people. I dictate by permission, by consent,' he told visiting State Department officials.[6]

Banda's increasingly dictatorial attitude within the cabinet and the Party was reflected in the growing hostility of the right-wing British press. The *Sunday Express* described him as 'a ludicrous despot who requires even his ministers to adopt the postures of slaves'. But more often than not it was what Banda said rather than what he did which aroused editorial ire, as for instance when he told the directors of Lonrho, 'Anything I say is law. Literally law. It is a fact in this country.'[7]

Malawi could not be 'a carbon copy of any other country', Banda explained.[8] Nyasaland was and Malawi would be 'a guided democracy':[9]

> Democracy in Europe cannot be democracy in Africa. Any politician, any statesman who interprets democracy in Africa in terms of the British Constitution, the American Constitution, the Swiss Constitution . . . does not know what he is doing. Because we are not here living under the British conditions, the American conditions. . . .
> What is politics? You say that politics is the art of the possible. Possible where? Possible here, not in Europe or America . . . possible here, here in Malawi. . . . Here we have our own way of doing things, we are copying from nobody. We will adopt from outside what suits and fits the conditions of this country.[10]

By this stage, early in 1964, Banda was beginning consciously to consider the possibility of achieving a fusion of the African and Western political traditions. At the same time, he was moving further away from his former acceptance of the multi-party ideal. In December 1963 he had warned that any non-African who financed parties like Mbadwa and the C.L.P. 'must expect deportation' after independence (a threat which, in the event, was never carried out).[11] Five months later he announced that all clerks of district councils must be M.C.P. members. Non-Party men would 'sabotage' the councils' work 'just to prove that the Malawi Congress Party cannot run [them]'.[12]

In his approach to the concept of one-party democracy, Banda was more circumspect than the majority of his colleagues. As early as 1959, Dunduzu Chisiza had concluded that the criticism of opposition parties was a dubious advantage in a young African state. By 1962, Orton Chirwa and David Rubadiri, the young poet who later became Malawi's first Ambassador in Washington, were both openly advocating a totalitarian scheme of rule. And soon afterwards Chiume had looked forward to the day when the Party would be sole and supreme. But before Banda's ideas could develop to their conclusion, the cabinet crisis intervened.

The introduction of legislation permitting detention without trial, in October 1964, did not of itself indicate any major change in Malawi's system of government. In parliament Banda emphasized that he was merely reintroducing legislation which had been enacted by the former colonial regime, and afterwards he tried to disclaim even this responsibility by speaking of the powers he used as though they had been inherited without any reactivation having been necessary.

But if the fact of preventive detention was unrelated to the trend away from Westminster democracy, the way in which it was used was not. In January 1965, Banda announced the setting up of a detention camp at Dzeleka, near Dowa. Any of the fifty or so Malawians in restriction[13] who were found to have been wrongfully restrained, or who showed by their behaviour that while they had been restricted rightly they had 'repented sincerely', would be released, he promised. But for those others who showed no sign of repentance, restriction would be converted into detention – 'and the world can howl about dictatorship'.

Let Chipembere take them out of [the] . . . Detention Camp [said Banda]. . . . Let them wait for him in [the]. . . . Prison Camp. I will keep them there and they will rot . . . they will rot. And I am going to make sure that in addition to the regular prison officers we have additional . . . warders [Youth Leaguers] who . . . will know what to do with these fools . . . they will knock sense into their head[s], because then they won't be talking about Chipembere coming to-morrow. . . . I mean business.*

To justify pronouncements of this kind, Banda reverted to the thesis that the nature of democracy depended on its environment:

There was a time in Britain when they did worse things than we are going to do to these people now. . . . Britain is tolerant today because the Government has been established for centuries. . . . The people in

* *Hansard*, Zomba, 26 January 1965, p. 459. In the first months after the camp was set up detainees were systematically brutalized. Later however, at the insistence of Sir Glyn Jones, who made it his business to pay periodic visits to the camp for the duration of his Governor-Generalship, the Youth Leaguers were withdrawn and the treatment of the inmates became more humane.

Britain today take everything for granted – trade unionism, free assembly, and freedom of the press – but I can quote instances after instances to prove that it was not so in Britain at one time. . . . Therefore we have to do things here which in Britain and America, [at] the stage they have arrived at in their own history, [are] repugnant to their idea of freedom and justice, but [to us], [at] our stage of development, are the normal thing to do. This Government and the public must be protected from ambitious politicians like Chipembere, Chirwa, Chisiza, Bwanausi, Chokani and their dupes. . . . We are new; our Government, our constitution, our independence have to be protected by drastic measures. . . .[14]

Banda made much use of this idea, that democracy 'did not come to Britain on the platter from the Angel Gabriel in Heaven', to soften the harshness of his more extreme statements. In a speech on 1 April to commemorate his own release from detention, he introduced it to preface the warning:

If, to maintain political stability and efficient administration, I have to detain 10,000, 100,000, I will do it. I want nobody to misunderstand me. I will detain anyone who is interfering with the political stability of this country. . . .

When a country is building its political institutions it's likely to do many, many nasty things. Well, we are building our political institutions here now. . . .*

Later that month, however, the situation grew calmer and Banda adopted a more moderate approach. He again spoke of the Government's desire to free repentant detainees, and called on the people to forgive those who were released. But he warned that if any of them were detained a second time, 'never out will they come again'. Nor could subversive elements expect anything but rough justice if they showed their faces in Malawi:

These people are wild animals now [he told M.C.P. members]. They must be destroyed. No beating about the bush. Arrest them. but if they resist arrest, well, anything you do is alright so far as I am concerned. So remember that.[15]

* Banda, Speech to commemorate his release from Gwelo, 1 April 1965, Malawi Information Department transcript. In practice periodic amnesties have kept the number of detainees at any one time from rising above about 400. No official statistics have ever been issued.

Warnings of this kind, and the reminder that 'Chipembere's gang are now rotting at Dzeleka and they will rot at Dzeleka until Doomsday',[16] were reissued whenever afterwards there was a threat of renewed rebel activity.

The use of violence as a political technique, which constituted the other major departure from British democratic practice – as Banda pointed out, by reference to Spain and Portugal, not all Western countries interpreted democracy in the same way[17] – was less straightforward than preventive detention. Violence, as he soon discovered, had a tendency to spread into areas for which it was not intended.

Some District Chairmen of the Malawi Congress Party are misusing the Youth League [Banda declared, in a speech in October]. They tell them to beat people, send them to do this and that. No, that's wrong. And Youth Leaguers, Young Pioneers, if any Chairman tells you to beat people, unless you know that person is subversive, refuse, refuse. For example, that kind of thing ... happened at Mchinji, where some fool ordered Youth Leaguers to beat the Chairman of the Malawi Congress Party, to the point where he is now paralysed. That's not the way to use Youth Leaguers. . . .[18]

In many subsequent speeches Banda condemned the use of Party violence to settle personal disputes, but the corollary, that it *was* all right for Youth Leaguers to beat 'subversive' elements to the point of paralysis, remained in force. 'Subversive', in this context, denoted primarily rebels, but also, to a lesser extent, other dissidents.*

*See Banda, Speech to the M.C.P. Annual Convention, Lilongwe, 14 October 1965, Malawi Information Department transcript. In 1967 the latter category was enlarged to include the Jehovah's Witnesses, who, by their efforts to dissuade people from paying tax and from renewing Party membership cards, and by their persistence in preaching to those who did not want to hear them, were again inviting conflict with the Party. In April of that year Banda warned that, while every 'law-abiding citizen' would be protected from molestation, 'Jehovah's Witnesses must stop provoking ... people. And if they do not stop . . . then they must not complain if and when they are beaten up' (Banda, broadcast, 23 April 1967, M.I.D. transcript). In October, the banning of the sect as 'dangerous to the good government of the State' (*Government Gazette*, 20 October 1967) unleashed further violence. Although the Government described reports of brutality as 'gross distortion[s]', one group of Youth Leaguers was subsequently convicted of man-

By focusing attention on extra-judicial techniques of rule, the cabinet crisis had relegated to the background the theoretical argument over whether or not Malawi should become a one-party state. Yet at the same time it had focused attention on the existence of dissent, and in so doing, almost without anyone noticing, had transformed Malawi into something which, to all extents and purposes, was a one-party state. An attitudinal change had taken place. As A. W. Chipungu, the Parliamentary Secretary for Health, put it:

> There is no opposition in heaven. God himself does not want opposition – that is why he chased Satan away. Why should Kamuzu have opposition?[19]

The sentiment was not new; Chiume had used the same analogy a few months before his fall.[20] What was different was that whereas, before the crisis, the undesirability of opposition had been but dully appreciated, afterwards it was fiercely proclaimed, either openly, by the back-benchers, or implicitly, by Banda himself and the new ministers. Before the crisis it would have been possible – theoretically, at least – for a new African party to have come into being; afterwards it would not.*

---

slaughter. Many other cases of rape, arson and assault did not reach the courts. None the less it was officially maintained that such few violent incidents as had occurred were the result of 'extreme provocation'. Not until 20 November did Banda appeal for an end to 'trouble with the stooges' (Speech at Mlanje), by which time more than a thousand Witnesses had fled into Mozambique.

*See Banda, press-conference, Chileka, 8 July 1964, M.I.D. transcript. Related to this change in attitude was the admission into the Party, after elaborate rituals of forgiveness, of former members of the N.A.C., like Chinyama, Katsonga and Kwenje, who had at one time opposed Banda's leadership (see *Malawi News*, 9 March and 26 November 1965, and Banda, Speech at Chileka, 13 September 1965, M.I.D. transcript). Not all these old opponents were able to repent, however. T.D.T. Banda, Charles Matinga and B. W. Matthews Phiri remained in Southern Rhodesia, either because they would not return or because the people in their home areas refused to have them back. Manoah Chirwa, who was refused readmission in 1965, returned three years later but spent only a week in his home district of Nkhata Bay before being ordered to leave the country. It was claimed that his plea for forgiveness had been insincere.

The fact that the M.C.P. had been the only political party in existence at Independence (besides the Constitutional Party) made the nature of the change more difficult to perceive. But the transition to totalitarianism was no less real for being obscured. It was manifest in the use of violence, restriction and preventive detention against dissidents other than rebels. And it was apparent in the use of Youth Leaguers to picket market entrances and bus stops, forcing anyone who could not produce a Party membership card to buy one. In the circumstances of a Malawi which was, as Banda put it, 'at war' with the rebels, these changes were accepted by the vast majority of the population. Indeed, except to the extent that they had to remember to carry with them their Party cards, and to the extent that the Youth League wittingly or unwittingly victimized the innocent along with the 'guilty', few Malawians were affected by them.

The introduction of a one-party system through the constitution thus involved little more than the formalization of a situation which by mid-1965 was already in existence. None the less, Banda prepared for it with care. Just as, earlier, he had deflected accusations of dictatorship by claiming to dictate 'by consent', so now he began to stress that the Malawi Government was, in Abraham Lincoln's phrase, 'a government of the people, by the people, for the people'. He emphasized that the M.C.P. was already 'for all practical purposes the Government of this country'. And he repeated, over and over again, that the form the constitution would take and the nomination of the Party's candidate for the Presidency would be decided by 'the ordinary people in the villages', through the Party's annual convention. In his first major public statement after he had announced that Malawi would become a Republic, he contrived to make this point no less than nine times in the space of 250 words.[21]

In making ready for the convention, which was to debate a set of constitutional proposals drawn up by a ministerial Constitutional Drafting Committee, Banda began once more to discuss the nature of democracy. The ideas which had been forming just prior to the cabinet crisis had now crystallized. The economic, political and social institutions of a country were directly determined by (rather than merely dependent on) its 'surroundings and circumstances', he told Malawians.

> [There are] varieties of cow, varieties of sheep and goat, varieties of chicken – so why should there not be a variety of democracy? We have to have our own kind of democracy based on the old African institutions.[22]

Only such facets of non-African democracy as were compatible with traditional African ideas could be mixed with them, he added.

The transition from the pre-crisis stage, in which the Western idea of democracy had been dominant, to the post-crisis period, in which the reverse was true, had taken place with deceptive ease. But it had brought with it, for Banda, difficulties in the definition of the 'Malawi democracy' which was now nearing achievement. At his first attempt he suggested that a state was democratic as long as it was not a police state. Shortly afterwards, he produced a more interesting idea. Its substance was that if the people elected to choose a form of government which was inherently dictatorial, then the fact that the Government ruled in the way desired by the people made it democratic, notwithstanding its dictatorial nature. Banda put it much less openly than this, partly because to have done otherwise would have been politically unwise, and partly because the idea was not yet fully formed in his mind.* Political considerations likewise prevented him from completing the explanation by pointing out that Malawians were accustomed to a dictatorial system of rule, not only in colonial times, under a series of governors ranging, as he once described them, from the 'autocratic to the benevolently despotic',[23] but also in the pre-colonial era, under no less despotic tribal chiefs.†

Theoretical arguments, however, were of secondary import-

---

* Banda said: 'A Government chosen by the people themselves – whether it is a dictatorship or not, as long as it is the people who choose the dictator, it is not a dictatorship. That's all. That is what democracy is.' (Speech to annual convention, Lilongwe, 17 October 1965, M.I.D. transcript.)

† Later Banda did make this point but on its own. See *Hansard*, Zomba, 17 May 1966, p. 560.

ance to the practicalities of the constitution itself, and it was with this that the annual convention, meeting in Lilongwe from 13 to 17 October, was principally concerned.

The proposals put forward by the Constitutional Drafting Committee[24] recommended that Malawi should become a one-party state to avoid 'the wasteful disunity . . . and wasteful attrition engendered by small opposition groups'. It would have an elected executive President, this being conducive to 'maximum political and domestic unity and stability', but no Vice-President. It was felt that the existence of such an office, whose holder would be 'forever awaiting the opportunity to step into the President's place at some unknown and unforeseeable occasion in the future', was undemocratic and encouraged division. Instead it was proposed that the President be empowered to appoint a commission of three ministers to rule during his temporary absence or illness. In the event of his death a similar commission, comprising the Party's Secretary-General and two ministers, would fulfil the functions of the Presidency for the duration of the interregnum.

A Presidential election was to take place whenever a general election was held, normally every five years. In the event of the President dissolving the proposed uni-cameral parliament, either because of a majority vote of no confidence in him, or as a result of his having twice refused to assent to a bill parliament had passed, he would remain in office until an election had given him a new mandate or installed a successor.

Except for the first Presidential election, which would be effected by parliament, sitting as an electoral college, a two-stage electoral procedure was suggested. The names of prospective Presidential candidates were to be submitted to a National Electoral College, whose membership would be the same as that of the M.C.P.'s annual convention. It would comprise the Party's Central Executive and Regional Committees, the National Committees of the Youth and Women's Leagues, the Chairmen, Secretaries and Treasurers of the District Committees of the Party, the Women's League and the Youth League, and Native Authorities, M.P.s (unless parliament was dissolved at the time of the Presidential nomination), and

Chairmen of District Councils. The College would select, by secret ballot, a Presidential candidate, whose name would then be submitted to a referendum of the whole electorate. If the majority of those who voted approved his candidature, he would be declared elected; if not, the College would be asked to make a fresh selection. An additional qualification for a Presidential candidate was that he must be at least forty-five years of age.[25]

In the simultaneous parliamentary elections, only members of the Malawi Congress Party would be allowed to stand as candidates. They would be required to state in writing beforehand their approval or disapproval of the Presidential candidate, so that 'the electorate would . . . have a clear issue before it' in both polls. Similarly, in the event of an M.P. voting against the President on a motion of confidence, he would have to resign his seat. Moreover, if an M.P. was suspended from the Party, he automatically lost his seat* (and any other positions he might have held by virtue of his Party membership). The President himself would be able to participate in parliament either as Head of State or as Head of Government and, 'as a general rule', his cabinet was to be selected from among its elected members. To meet exceptional needs, he would be allowed to nominate up to three ministers from outside the House.† European representation in the legislature was to be retained, but by Presidential nomination rather than by direct election. Euro-

---

* Malawi (Constitution) Act, 1966, No. 23 of 1966. This provision had been introduced, as a result of the cabinet crisis, by a constitutional amending act, in October 1964 (see *Hansard*, Zomba, 29 October 1964, pp. 228–9).

† This had also been permitted under the Marlborough House constitution. It was retained to enable Dr Banda to appoint Aleke Banda Minister of Development and Planning, which he did six months before the new constitution came into force. Subsequently other ministers resigned their constituencies, claiming pressure of work, and returned to the national assembly as Presidential nominees. In 1968 the constitution was amended, by a two-thirds majority of parliament, to remove the limitation on the number of nominees, and by March 1970 only six ministers out of a cabinet of thirteen were still M.P.s. From Banda's point of view this was doubly advantageous in that it permitted him to retain the services of ministers who had become unpopular in their constituencies, and to deprive ministers who were becoming too popular of constituency support.

pean members, however, would have the right to vote in parliament, whereas nominated ministers would not, although they would be permitted to take part in debates.

After a brief debate* the Committee's proposals were approved, unanimously and unamended, on 16 October,[26] and Banda was adopted, amid scenes of great excitement, as the Party's candidate for the Presidency. Subsequently they were endorsed by parliament, and the necessary legislation was drafted and enacted. On 20 May 1966, Banda was elected President-designate of the future Republic of Malawi. He signified his acceptance 'in humility and fear, because the job is too big for any one of us, and the responsibility too heavy and too great'.[27]

As Banda had expected, the constitutional proposals were much criticized overseas. Objections centred not so much on the form the constitution had taken as on the powers with which the President was to be entrusted under it. He would be authorized to make or revoke all public service appointments, either directly or through the public service commission; to make statutory regulations governing the civil service; to appoint the Chief Justice; and, in consultation with the Judicial Service Commission, which was to be retained in an advisory capacity, to make or terminate other judicial appointments, except those of judges. To ensure the independence and impartiality of the High Court, a judge could only be removed from office if parliament petitioned for his removal, on the grounds of incompetence or misconduct, by a majority vote on a substantive motion debated in the national assembly. The President would also be Commander-in-Chief of the armed forces, and would have emergency powers allowing him to rule by proclamations reviewable within seven days if parliament were sitting or thirty days if it were not.

It had been partly to disarm censure on these grounds that Banda had been stressing that it was the people, not himself,

---

*Although the convention met for four days, only four hours were allotted to the discussion of the proposals themselves (*Programme of the Malawi Congress Party Annual Convention to be held at Lilongwe from Wednesday 13th October, to Sunday 17th, 1965*, duplicated, M.C.P., Blantyre).

who had decided what powers he should have. But while it was true that the proposals had been accorded an enthusiastic reception by Malawians, it was a falsification of the facts to maintain, as Tembo did, that Banda had played no part in their formulation and that it was the people who were 'going to impose this constitution on the Prime Minister'.[28] Banda himself was a little more truthful when he said, some months later:

I do not want all the powers of the Czar of Russia, Peter the Great or Ivan the Terrible, no, I do not want those powers. No, no. I just want enough powers to guide this country in the right way and in the right direction.[29]

In practice Banda's powers of guidance derived as much from the constitution of the Party, which had also been reviewed when the convention met at Lilongwe, as from that of the State. In his speeches to the convention he had repeatedly exhorted delegates to greater unity, and had complained of the tendency among party officials to establish personal power-bases 'by making [themselves] . . . secretly popular with a section of the population'.[30] Subsequently new clauses on Party discipline had been ratified, the most important being the injunction: 'Unity, loyalty, obedience and discipline . . . shall at all times be maintained and enforced within the Party.'[31]

The Party and republican constitutions were in several respects complementary, the one explaining what the other omitted. The Drafting Committee had stated, for instance, that 'the nomination of [parliamentary] candidates would be a matter to be provided for in the Malawi Congress Party procedure.' It had left unsaid that this procedure was that Banda had the sole right of selection, and that this, in conjunction with the Party's discipline regulations, precluded more than one candidate from standing.* The Party's constitution similarly limited the powers of M.P.s once they were elected. In theory, under the republican constitution, members were free to criticize the Government and to vote against it on any question except a motion of confidence. In fact the Party's discipline regulations prevented this. 'The

---

*In every African-contested election and by-election after the Malawi Congress Party came to power, its candidate was nominated unopposed.

minute you vote against the Government here, you yourself are out,' Banda warned.[32] The result was that no elected M.P. ever voiced, either in parliament or outside it, any direct or implied criticism of the Government's policies and none ever voted against them.

Banda was aware of the dangers of so completely removing the element of choice from the electorate and, partly to provide a safety-valve, and partly to compensate for the extension of the life of parliament until 1971 to make it concur with the Presidential term, introduced a mechanism whereby M.P.s could be unseated if their constituents petitioned the Speaker for their removal. None the less, the fact remained that parliament had been muzzled, as had the local press and other vehicles for public debate. But in fact it was not any of these institutions which ultimately determined the quality of Malawi's despotism or democracy; rather it was the nature of the Malawi Congress Party.

This had been recognized by the Constitutional Drafting Committee, when it had stated that in introducing a one-party state the Government did not intend to depart from the principle that every person should have 'a reasonable right of freedom of association and of self-expression':

Provided the Malawi Congress Party retains its essential democratic character [it had said] . . . there is no reason why persons holding conflicting opinions should not be free to express them within the Party framework if they wish to do so.*

The degree to which the expression of unorthodox opinions was permitted was in practice dependent on the subject under discussion. External Affairs, for instance, were considered to be Banda's exclusive domain, and deviations from the official line

* *Proposals for the Republican Constitution of Malawi*, duplicated, M.C.P., Blantyre, 1965. The Committee had suggested that the democratic character of the Party might be judged by the fact that 'officers of the Party at every level owe their position to the popular choice'. This was deliberately misleading, for the Party's Central Executive and Regional Committees were appointed by Banda in his sole discretion; moreover Banda himself, as a result of his being Life President, could not claim to owe his position to contemporary popular choice.

were forbidden within the Party no less than outside it. But internal affairs were not, and at the closed meetings of the annual convention delegates were allowed to criticize and put forward suggestions within 'reasonable' limits. On occasion this licence brought to the surface discontents which, had they remained hidden, might have led to unrest; more usually it had a cathartic effect, enabling frustrations to be discharged over relatively harmless issues like polygamy and beer-drinking. Despite the rigorous, pervasive control he exercised, Banda realized that to the extent that Malawi was a democracy, 'the authority of the Government depend[ed] on the consent of the people who [were] . . . governed'.[33] To the extent that it was a despotism it was in the main benevolent, not tyrannous.

In its qualified allowance of private debate and its complete prohibition of public criticism, in its totalitarianism and its ruthless suppression of dissenting minorities, Malawi's system of government paralleled the scheme of rule in a pre-colonial (Chewa) chieftainship. The effect of the transition to republican status had been to transform the Malawi Congress Party into a national tribe, to which every Malawian was expected, if not required, to belong. 'My tribe is the whole nation, the tribe of Malawi,'[34] Banda explained:

There will always be tribes in this country . . . [and] there will always be regions. . . . But these tribal designations, these regional designations, must exist, and we must recognize them, only as a means of identifying ourselves as true Malawians. . . .
I value my being a Chewa from Kasungu in the Central Region, only because and only as much as . . . [it] stamps on my forehead the sign that I am a true Malawian. . . . We have no longer a collection of tribes in this country now. We are a nation. Therefore we must think more of ourselves as Malawians and less, much less, as Nkondes, Tongas, Tumbukas, Ngonis, Chewa, Yaos, Nyanjas, Senas.[35]

In this quasi-tribal polity, the constitution had defined the roles of the executive, the administration and the legislature, but the justiciary and socio-cultural elements had remained virtually unchanged. It was to these, in the years after the Republic had come into being, that Banda's attention was mainly directed.

Before Independence, Banda had become concerned in the affairs of the judiciary because he wished to achieve its separation from the district and native administrations. To this end the Local Courts had been set up, replacing the colonial Native Authority's courts with the type of system which had been in force before the introduction of indirect rule. Their creation, Banda told parliament, was 'the beginning, the first chapter of a judicial Magna Carta ... for the Africans of this country'.[36] Initially the jurisdiction of the new courts was very limited, but as they assumed the functions previously exercised by the district administrators, sitting as junior magistrates, it was slowly increased. In July 1963, the penalties for contempt of Local Courts were raised, and they were empowered to remand prisoners for trial in higher courts.[37] In the same year a law school was set up at Mpemba, charged with the instruction of Local Courts' Chairmen and the preliminary training of intending Malawian lawyers.

Despite the vast difference between African and British law, the Local Courts system was founded on principles not entirely dissimilar to those operating in Britain.

... according to the British law and usage, judicial usage and practice [Banda explained], a person must be tried by his own peers, by his own people, people who know him, who know his habits. .... Why can't we do the same?[38]

In one important respect, however, the analogy broke down: Africans tried in the Local Courts were debarred from employing defence counsel. When the courts were made non-racial, Europeans were automatically excluded from this prohibition, but later the law was amended to vest the power of allowing legal representation in the Minister of Justice. Lawyers, said Banda, had 'not so much a sense of justice as a sense of technicalities':

Under the British law ... a man can be actually acquitted even when he is guilty if only the lawyers know how to twist it around. I wanted that to be prevented from happening in the Local Courts.[39]

The differing extents to which African and European minds attached importance to 'technicalities' formed one of the key areas in which their juridical approaches diverged.* While Banda promised that there would be no interference 'with the Courts in their everyday work, in their interpretation of the law', he warned that 'the people of this country are watching them'.[40]

The answer to these problems, in Banda's view, was to speed up the training of Malawians, who would 'administer our judicial system in accordance with the feelings of the people'.[41] As with democracy, so too 'the judiciary in any country must reflect the aspirations, the desires, and the actual social, political and economic life of the people. Otherwise it is no use at all. . . . We here are just a little different, we do things in our own way.'[42] There was a gulf, Banda declared, 'between the idea of justice and injustice, right and wrong, of my people and that of the European . . . which must be bridged.'[43]

The disparity between African and British jurisprudence was manifest not only in the uses to which violence and preventive detention were put in the aftermath of the cabinet crisis, but also in their differing requirements of evidence, particularly in capital cases. In August 1965, commenting on the Timbiri killing, Banda explained:

> According to the English or British law, you cannot accuse anyone of murder unless you have clear evidence. . . . But here . . . [under African] law, you don't always need to have clear evidence to accuse anyone. A man who kills another man does not have witnesses around him to tell that 'I am killing.' Under Chewa law, if you threaten a man [by saying], 'If you don't do so and so you are going to be killed,' and that man is killed the next day, you are guilty. . . .[44]

A few months later, Banda hinted that he might empower the Local Courts to try capital cases – because, 'Under English law, I may kill a man but if nobody saw me I am not guilty because

*If the Devlin Commission, for instance, had dispensed with 'technicalities' and admitted evidence which it suspected of having been obtained by force, it might have concluded very differently on the extent of Congress's preparedness to use violence.

nobody saw me.'* But in the event this was not done, and it was instead on the upper courts that, in the immediate post-independence period, the influence of African jurisprudence was brought to bear.

The cabinet crisis had educed the tendency to pre-judgement which had been implicit in Banda's complaints of 'unfair' verdicts being recorded by European judges. In July 1965 he had stated, 'I'm going to have them [Silombela and other leading rebels] captured, and once they are captured I'm going to have them hanged.'[45] When, four months later, Silombela was brought to trial, he told a mass meeting:

> I know he is going to be found guilty. What kind of a judge can acquit Silombela? No. . . . He will be found guilty. And after that, you come and watch him swing. That's all.[46]

In fact Silombela did get a fair trial, despite the bizarre publicity which attended the hearing. And although an act was passed to permit public hangings, his execution took place not in public but in Zomba prison, watched by some 400 Party officials and relatives of those he had killed.†

Banda's political outbursts during Silombela's trial were, from the viewpoint of Western jurisprudence, prejudicial to its outcome, and hence tended to alienate the Western and the African justiciary systems. In the main, however, Banda's

---

* *Hansard*, Zomba, 7 October 1965, p. 190. In this Banda was wrong, for British courts have convicted in murder cases on circumstantial evidence alone. But compare Banda to Phiri, 11 August 1932 (privately held), writing of Bishop Vernon's peculation of church funds: 'According to the laws of this country, I cannot say that because I did not see him actually using the money. There was no evidence to show, therefore, I cannot say anything about it.'

† The point of holding the execution in public was that it would prove that the Government had been 'doing its duty', as Banda put it (*Hansard*, Zomba, 10 November 1965, p. 251). It would also act as a deterrent to any other rebels still at large. There was precedent for this not only in colonial Nyasaland, where the British administration had publicly executed many of Chilembwe's followers and had afterwards displayed their bodies to the populace, but also in more recent times in Sierra Leone and in Kenya during the Mau Mau emergency. In Britain itself public hangings had been permitted until 1875.

energies were still directed towards bringing them together. It
was decided, for instance, that in cases of theft by a public servant, the onus of proof should be borne by the defence. There
had been instances, said Banda, of a man being acquitted when
'everybody knew that [he] . . . had stolen the money', simply
because the police had presented their evidence incorrectly.[47]
Later, trial by jury was introduced, replacing the assessor system at criminal trials in the High Court. A new Criminal Procedure and Evidence Code was enacted, requiring the courts to
administer 'substantial justice without undue regard to technicalities'. And as Malawian lawyers gained experience, so expatriates were phased out; the first senior post to be held by a
Malawian was that of Director of Public Prosecutions, localized
in 1968.

At the same time extra-judicial measures were introduced to
buttress the juridical reforms Banda had undertaken. The Forfeiture Act, enacted in 1966, empowered him to declare forfeit
the property of any person who, in his opinion, had acted 'in a
manner prejudicial to the safety or the economy of the State or
subversive to the authority of the lawfully established Government'.[48] Later the law was amended to permit its application to
a public servant who was alleged to have committed a theft, or
to have occasioned one by negligence, whether or not a conviction had been obtained in the courts. The purpose of this
new measure, Banda explained, was to relate 'the Malawi idea
of justice' to this kind of offence.[49]

None the less, the conflict between African and Western ideas
persisted, and in 1969 came to a head in the shape of a judicial
crisis. In September of that year a British judge, Justice D. D.
Bolt, acquitted five men being tried for murder before a jury in
the High Court, on the ground that the prosecution had failed to
make a case against them. The case had explosive political
implications, and a few days later Banda announced that he was
over-ruling the judge's verdict:

No. . . . They are not going to be let loose, I can tell you that. . . . No
matter what anyone in Blantyre or Zomba may say, those people
will never come out of there. Never, never, never. No matter what

anyone says or does. . . . Those people are not going to be let loose.
Not let loose. I am in charge, and I am not from England either.[50]
When parliament next met, six weeks after this incident, a bill
was passed which radically altered the status of the Local Courts
(or Traditional Courts, as they were afterwards called). The
Local Courts (Amendment) Act empowered Banda to permit
specified Traditional Courts to try all types of criminal case, and
to pass the death sentence; it further authorized him to direct
that no appeal should be allowed from such a court to the
High Court, so removing a right previously guaranteed by the
constitution. With Banda, moreover, lay the right to determine
the class of court in which a particular case should be tried, as
well as to permit or disallow legal representation.

Introducing the bill, Aleke Banda said its sole purpose was to
permit cases 'in which a predominant factor is the manifestation
of some local belief in witchcraft or superstition, or the existence
of some element of African custom which for obvious reasons is
not readily understood by judges and magistrates who are expatriates' to be tried by the type of court 'most appropriately
constituted to understand and decide the issues involved'.
Witchcraft trials had taken place, he said, in which the accused
had been acquitted 'on mere technicalities' because the judges
were unfamiliar with the issues at stake.[51] In the ensuing debate
many examples of this were cited. Demands were made for re-
trials where wrongful acquittals were alleged, and for the abolition *in toto* of legal aid. And in the process it was made clear
that the limitation of the Traditional Courts' enlarged powers to
witchcraft or customary cases would not be adhered to.

When Dr Banda addressed the House, four days later, he was
no longer thinking of 'bridging the gulf' between Africa and the
West. Malawian jurisprudence, as it had existed in pre-colonial
times, was 'far superior' to that which had been imported from
Europe, he said.[52] In those days it would have been unthinkable
for anyone to conceal or defend a man suspected of having committed a crime; a wife would not protect her husband, nor a
father his son. British justice suited Britain; Malawian justice
had 'no relation' to it:

Who was it – Kipling, who said, 'East is East and West is West . . .

and never the twain shall meet'. . . . He was of course exaggerating . . . but it is true that in certain aspects of ordinary human activity . . . the European cannot understand the African mind, no matter how hard he tries.[53]

The following day Malawi's four High Court judges, all of them British, announced in a joint statement their intention of resigning. They explained, 'Without wishing to question the sincerity of those who hold an opposite view, we cannot believe that justice will be adequately safeguarded in these circumstances.'[54]

The argument employed officially to counter such objections was that, 'In introducing the new law, the Government is simply restoring the powers that our traditional judiciary has had for centuries.'[55] In theory this was true, but in practice there were important differences between the pre-colonial chief's courts and the Traditional Courts. The chief had enjoyed such a status in his community that he was both independent and practically incorruptible. Yet only two years before the Local Courts (Amendment) Act became law, Banda had complained in a nationwide broadcast that Local Courts Chairmen were abusing their powers to settle old scores. Moreover the independence of the Chairmen's appointments had been eroded by the introduction of the one-party state. In the same broadcast Banda had found it necessary to remind them that they 'must not forget that they are there because of the local branch of the Malawi Congress Party'.[56]

What had really happened was that the judiciary in Malawi was now open to direct political control. It was a rather different situation from that envisaged by the Constitutional Drafting Committee, when it had stated, in opposing the insertion of a Bill of Rights into the republican constitution:

In a democratic State laws depend for their ultimate authority upon the desire of the people to see them enforced. . . . It is the duty of a responsible Government to guide and tutor the people in the appreciation of the benefits of fair and impartial laws. . . .[57]

In the development of a Malawian 'national conscience',*

* Hansard, Zomba, 12 November 1969, pp. 2–3. Banda apparently used the word 'conscience' to mean 'consciousness' in its general rather than in its moral sense.

within which its jurisprudence and its form of government would find their context, Banda pursued the aim of creating a 'composite culture – the Western culture and the African, the Malawi culture'.[58] The predominance of the former decreed that, in the first place, African culture should be encouraged, and this Banda tried to do, by recognizing such institutions as chieftainship, by reviving traditional dances, and by restoring to respectability customs like *vinyau*. But since these were tribal manifestations, rather than a national heritage, their preservation detracted from instead of promoting national unity. Whether by ratiocination or by unconscious perception, Banda realized this and accordingly set out to weld Malawi's tribal cultures into a national one. The technique he employed was the imposition of a common language.

The elevation of chiNyanja to a national language, co-equal with English, had first been suggested in 1963 by the Party's Regional Chairman in the non-chiNyanja-speaking North, Mckinley Chibambo. At that stage, however, Banda had rejected the idea because, he said, chiNyanja would first have to be standardized into 'a real chiNyanja, a real chiChewa', as it had been spoken in his youth and was still spoken in the villages of the central region. He did not want the anglicized 'chi-Mission or chi-Heaven or chi-Planter' which was current in the towns.[59] When, in March 1966, the suggestion was revived, again by a northerner, 'General Flax' Musopole, he raised similar objections.[60] But later that year plans were set in motion for the writing of a definitive chiNyanja dictionary, and in September 1968 the Party's annual convention, chaired, appropriately, by Chibambo, resolved that chiNyanja should become Malawi's second official language. It was no longer to be called chiNyanja, however; in future it would be known as chiChewa.

A number of factors may have induced Banda to make this change of name. It may have been due to the tribal consciousness which, in spite of himself, he had retained; to his close involvement with chiChewa since his stay at Chicago; or to his belief that the aNyanja and aMang'anja peoples, from whom chiNyanja took its name, were 'basically . . . all Chewa'.[61] But regardless of its motivation, it provoked intense resentment.

ChiTumbuka, the principal language spoken in the North, was
immediately discontinued on the radio and in the Party press;
the newly appointed Parliamentary Secretary for Education,
J. W. Gwengwe, announced that schoolchildren who failed
their examinations in chiChewa would be required to retake
their papers in all subjects (this was afterwards denied); and in
both the North and the South, there were fears of cultural subjugation by the Centre. Much of this might have been avoided
had Banda chosen a national rather than a tribal name. But as it
was the introduction of chiChewa proved a divisive rather than a
unifying influence. Although it was afterwards played down, it
was potentially a tragic mistake, leaving behind a residue of
discontent and removing, in the short term, the possibility of
making Malawi a cultural unity.

Two groups, the non-Africans* and the senior African civil
servants, were to a greater or lesser extent excluded from the
'Malawi tribe', the one by its race and the other by its position.
Each related to the other through the requirements of Africanization.

   During the campaign preparatory to the transition to republican status Banda had carefully wooed both these competing
factions. He had brought an end to the ostracism of African
civil servants, which had arisen as a result of the cabinet crisis,
by appealing to Party officials, M.P.s and ministers to cooperate
with them, and by denouncing Party elements who threatened
them with dismissal or violence. And he had emphasized the
Government's determination to Africanize, extolling its past
achievements and promising greater advances to come. At the
1965 convention he expressed hopes that the Africanization of
the public service and the army would be nearly complete by
the end of 1967. He was 'quite certain', he said, that by then

   *The Coloured community was supposed to be regarded as African, but
in reality many of its members were not, despite Banda's efforts to achieve
their integration. Both Africans and Coloured were to blame for this failure
to amalgamate which provoked, in April 1969, bitter complaints from
M.P.s during a parliamentary debate. This was the only occasion on which
there was even a slight element of public disagreement between ministers
and backbenchers. (See *Hansard*, Zomba, 21 April 1969, pp. 316–40.)

the Commander of the Malawi Army would be an African; there might even be a Malawian Commissioner of Police.[62] A few weeks later a Localization Committee was set up, and in January 1966 the first supernumerary appointments were announced of African senior assistant secretaries.

At the same time Banda assured non-African civil servants that they would not be Africanized out of their jobs; no African would be promoted until he could prove that he could work as well as, if not better than, the expatriate he was replacing, he said. The Government's policies on Africanization and towards non-Africans generally would remain unchanged:

> It is the right policy. There is no reason why we should change it after we become a Republic and we shall not change it because no one has any intention of changing it.[63]

The introduction of the republican constitution actually helped rather than hindered the continuance of harmonious race relations, for it completed the withdrawal of non-Africans from politics and so eliminated the possibility of inter-communal tensions arising from political causes. Although the Europeans lost the representation afforded them in parliament by the three Constitutional Party members, this was more than compensated by the nomination of five Presidential appointees in their stead. In other respects non-Africans felt that the one-party state promoted stability, which they welcomed.

Promises to the contrary notwithstanding, Africanization proceeded slowly, and by the end of 1967 expatriates still outnumbered Malawians in the higher grades of the public service,[64] although the year did see the appointments of the first three African permanent secretaries. To the extent that Africanization did take place, the African civil servants were appeased; to the extent that it did not, the Europeans (who predominated among expatriate civil servants) were reassured. In practice Malawi's 8,000-strong white community did enjoy a considerable degree of security, and Banda often stressed that non-Africans – except 'the crooks and the arrogant' – were welcome in Malawi. The only black spot was the ever-increasing use of forfeiture and arbitrary deportation, often on the flimsiest of pretexts.

Africanization, however, extended beyond the public service into the commercial and industrial sector, where it affected Asians as well as Europeans. Here it took two distinct but related forms: the direct Africanization of small-scale commerce, 90 per cent of which was Asian-owned; and the Africanization of the ownership of large-scale enterprises.

It was to the second of these that Banda had first directed his attention. An element of State participation in commerce had been carried over from the colonial administration in the shape of the Farmers Marketing Board and similar bodies, and in 1964 this had been extended by the setting-up of the Malawi Development Corporation, a statutory body whose function was to stimulate industrial and commercial development, either alone or in partnership with the private sector, in those areas where 'private enterprise alone was . . . unwilling, unprepared, hesitant or afraid to risk its capital'.[65] The M.D.C. would not be 'the thin end of the wedge' of State socialism or State capitalism, Banda had promised. In its economic policies, Malawi was 'not adopting any ideology of any kind at all, we are pragmatic'.[66]

The first major departure from this position came in 1966, when Banda nationalized the Malawi Railways, previously controlled by Lonrho. His declaration that 'we are not nationalizing the railways at all' marked the beginning of a lengthy and skilfully executed exercise in humbug.[67] In speech after speech throughout 1967 and 1968, Banda assured the business community that nationalization and State socialism were 'economic and political suicide' except in a sophisticated, affluent country or in an absolute dictatorship.[68] He derided the ideas of African socialism being discussed in Tanzania, and promised that nothing of that kind was contemplated in Malawi. In September 1968, the Party's annual convention, meeting at Lilongwe, resolved that Malawi's economic policy should be capitalism.* It omitted to state, and indeed Banda explicitly denied, that this

* A year later surtax was abolished, and income tax rates were sharply reduced for higher-income groups, while remaining unchanged for lower-paid workers. Similar reductions were made in estate duties. (See *Hansard*, Zomba, 12 November 1969, p. 13.)

would include State capitalism. Six weeks later, however, he announced that the M.D.C. and the Malawi Press, a company owned by himself and Aleke Banda, through which most of the Party's business activities were conducted, were jointly acquiring a majority interest in the Malawi subsidiary of the Booker Group, the country's biggest wholesaling, distribution and retailing organization. Other acquisitions followed,* but so convincingly did Banda deny that nationalization was taking place that he was widely believed, both within and without Malawi.

Measures of this kind were primarily intended to reduce the flow of profits remitted overseas, and to increase local control over the private sector.† In the case of the Booker Group subsidiary takeover, however, there was an additional reason. In January 1968, Banda had announced proposals to facilitate the entry of Africans into rural commerce. The domination by non-Africans of this aspect of the economy was 'inimical to the economic development and viability of the country,' he said.[69] Among his plans was the setting-up of a State-run wholesaling network which would supply goods to African traders at reasonable prices and on reasonable terms; it was this function that the National Trading Company, as Bookers (Malawi) Ltd was renamed, was intended to fulfil.

The means had now been created whereby Africans could enter business, but the opportunity was still lacking, and to provide it Banda would have to restrict small-scale trade in specified areas exclusively to Africans. This he was extremely reluctant to do, if only because it would seem that he was acting against a particular racial group, the Asians. Although non-African traders in the remote areas of Malawi were repeatedly warned that their activities would be curtailed, their removal from the villages to the trading centres and townships was not

---

* Among the concerns so affected was the Blantyre Printing and Publishing Company, proprietors of the *Times*, in which in April 1969 Banda personally purchased a 49·7 per cent holding. His interest in the company which controlled the one-time settlers' newspaper was not made public.

† At the same time legislation was passed extending the Government's powers of direct control over commerce and industry, particularly in licensing and import/export matters.

enforced until July 1970. Only then did the direct Africanization of Malawi's commerce begin.

Banda's assumption of the Presidency marked an epoch in his life; he could rise no higher. He possessed supreme power, and used it to secure an ever-increasing degree of control over every aspect of Malawian life. Only thus, he believed, could the Malawi nation be developed.

As President, Minister of External Affairs and, later, Minister of Works and Supplies, Banda held ministerial responsibility for more than a score of government departments. He oversaw the work of the ministries he did not control, and frequently undertook personally matters which another man in his place would have left to aides. Everything that came before him was submitted to meticulous, detailed examination, and no decision could be acted upon, if it was of the least importance, without his first having approved it. He devoted the same painstaking attention to the affairs of the Party. And he made frequent regional and national tours, tirelessly urging greater efforts in agriculture and economic development. The sheer volume of work Banda contrived to get through would have worn out a less dedicated man half his age.* His enemies spoke of Malawi as 'a one-man Banda'.

This thoroughgoing diligence was in part innate, but it had also an immediate cause in the cabinet crisis, which had cost Banda the majority of his ablest ministers. Their replacement by less independently minded men was not without advantages, however, for they were less likely to hold views which differed from his own. For all his dislike of sycophancy and his impatience of servility, Banda ensured that after the crisis his new associates remained submissive.

As Banda gained experience in the workings of the Government, he became increasingly contemptuous of advisers and experts. He accepted advice only 'when that advice agrees with what we think'; experts whose views conflicted with his own

* None the less, Banda's insistence on doing so much himself impaired the Government's efficiency, and there were often long delays in what should have been simple and straightforward procedures.

'do not know what they are talking about'.[70] This was the attitude of which Dunduzu Chisiza had written, 'It is his idea or nothing.'[71]

Banda's scepticism of 'so-called experts' was part of a larger aversion to intellectuals, which had been brought to prominence by the cabinet crisis. After it he began describing the more intelligent of the ex-ministers' supporters as 'yelping intellectual puppies'.[72] To press his point home, he extolled the virtues of the common man, 'the ordinary man and woman in the village'; it was for their benefit that he was in power; not for him a life 'up in the air with Socrates, Pericles and John Knox. No! You can have that.'[73] He grumbled about 'grey-haired lecturers and bald-headed men at universities',[74] and after Malawi's own university was opened, in October 1965, complained that it was 'destroying the character of our boys and girls'. The University, he said, was supposed to 'add to the training of character which the parents in the villages have inculcated in those boys and girls', and if this were beyond the capabilities of its lecturers they were 'absolutely useless' and should return to their own countries, failing which they would be deported. From this it was but a small step to declaring that politics, sociology and other sensitive subjects would be taught 'according to the conditions in Malawi'.[75]

In pronouncements of this kind, Banda was motivated less by the need to exert political control than by the desire to exert moral control, to preserve something of traditional attitudes and traditional ways of thought. He believed that, in the creation of its 'composite culture', Malawi must assimilate only those elements of Western morality which were compatible with its own moral code and ethics, and this combined with his puritanism to decide its 'spiritual development'.*

* Among the Western practices which Banda has found unacceptable is birth control, which he has actively discouraged; books on the subject have been banned and in 1968 a Dutch missionary, who had given marriage guidance talks, was deported. As a result of this policy nearly 400,000 babies are born in Malawi every year (between 30 and 50 per cent of whom die before the age of five), equivalent to a birth rate of 10 per cent. The true reasons for Banda's refusal to act in this situation are his belief that birth control is unnatural and the political difficulties which would be involved in

When Banda first began to lay down rules governing personal behaviour, at the 1965 convention, it appeared that he was merely extending the scope of the discipline regulations, for it was on drunkenness and similar vices that stress was mainly laid. In other respects the Party was so far from interfering in matters of morality that when the Women's League requested girls to refrain from wearing short skirts, Aleke Banda retorted that 'these things are too personal for anybody to issue rules or orders about'.[76] Yet in March 1968, Dr Banda banned the wearing of mini-dresses. Soon afterwards women were also forbidden to wear trousers. A year later he publicly lectured ministers and M.P.s, at a meeting of the Malawi branch of the Commonwealth Parliamentary Association, on various aspects of personal morality, including sex.

After 1968 Banda spoke frequently of the amorality which he felt was in the ascendant in the Western world. In Malawi, he said, 'We are not going to allow other people's idea of good conduct to override our own idea of good conduct':

> . . . in the West now there exists a permissive society [he told parliament]. Do you know what I call it? Depraved society – that's all it is. It is, it is. Women going unspeakably in public like that, and then in New York on the stage doing unspeakable things, and they call that art. . . . Call it art! You call that civilization? You call that Christianity? . . . No, to me, if that is civilization, if that is Christianity, then keep it in Europe, keep it in America.[77]

In another speech he amplified these ideas:

> At every stage of . . . civilization, there are certain institutions, certain traditions, certain laws and [a] certain code of behaviour that

---

introducing it. The official explanation is that Malawi has not yet attained its optimum population (variously estimated at between six and twelve million people), and that when it does so the position regarding birth control will be reviewed. (Banda's version of this is that birth control will not be considered until Malawi's population is sufficient to cultivate every acre of arable land, a proposition which ignores the possibility of mechanization.) The fact is that if birth control were introduced immediately Malawi would still be heavily overpopulated, even in terms of the most liberal optimum estimate, by the end of this century. The longer the delay, the more severe will be its consequences.

hold that particular civilization intact. Once you let these . . . go by the board, that civilization itself is gone to the dogs.

That happened among the Greeks, it happened among the Romans . . . [and] it is happening now. . . . This is a fact, once you talk about permissive societies . . . meaning promiscuity . . . [the] civilization under which you are living . . . is going to the dogs.[78]

The extent to which Banda was prepared to dictate on moral questions was determined by two factors. The first was the nature of traditional African jurisprudence, which considered matters amenable to the processes of civil law which in Western societies would be thought the prerogative of the individual.[79] The second was the change of status conferred on him by the Republic.

Within the 'Malawi tribe' the position Banda had come to hold was like that of one of the old *Maravi* kings, complete with divine right and absolute authority. So, at least, he saw himself, and so he wanted to be seen. At first, unlike a monarch, he was not Head of State for life. Nor, indeed, was this necessary, for Banda held the presidency of the Republic by being President of the Party, and he *was* President of the Party for life. For this reason the Constitutional Drafting Committee had rejected as undemocratic calls by party stalwarts at the 1965 convention, and at the many local meetings held beforehand, that he should be formally installed as Life President of Malawi.[80] If only for form's sake, the committee thought it desirable that the electorate should have the opportunity of renewing Banda's mandate. Otherwise, it argued, it would be difficult to rebut accusations that Banda's rule was despotic and divorced from his people's will.

In 1971, when the first presidential election was due to be held, such considerations were abruptly set aside. Parliament rubber-stamped a constitutional amendment which permitted him to become Life President of the Republic on 6 July, the seventh anniversary of Malawi's independence.

Banda seems to have taken this step, unprecedented except in Dr Duvalier's Haiti, for two reasons. On the one hand he feared that the national referendum which the election entailed would show that popular support for him was less than overwhelming (not by votes being cast against him, which was unlikely in the rigidly controlled state Malawi had become, but by a small turn-out for the poll). On the other, he felt the referendum would detract from the monarchic concept of the presidency he had cultivated, by underlining that the institution was in reality impermanent and that he was, in theory at least, removable by the collective expression of popular will.

In the special circumstances of Malawi in 1965, it would have been merely unwise for Banda to have accepted the Life Presidency of the Republic. At that time he could say, with some truth, 'the people in the villages are still living in the old days. To them the Chief must rule. So they wanted that kind of President.' That Banda should have become Life President six years later, when the situation in the villages had changed out of all recognition, showed how divorced he had indeed become from the popular will. The last vestige of democratic practice had been removed from Banda's rule. All outlets for dissent had been closed, and a formidable machine had been built up for its suppression by the Party, the Youth League and the Young Pioneers. After 1971, the only means Malawians had of changing their Government was to overthrow it by force.

As Malawi's President, and later, Life President, Banda no longer hid behind a public mask; rather he became the mask. Everywhere he went the Party and Government machines surrounded him with pomp and ceremony, and matters of status and protocol became increasingly important. In everything he did he was conscious of his dignity; it was pride, as much as self-interest, which led him to assign £1.5 million, which Malawi could ill afford, to the building of a luxurious Presidential Palace on a hilltop near Blantyre.* It became impossible to separate the man's substance from his image.

* When the project was first discussed, in 1966, it was estimated that it would cost £500,000. By 1971 the figure had more than trebled.

Chapter 13
Disarming Apartheid

Banda's alienation from his fellow African leaders and. his authority within Malawi formed the backdrop to the development of his policy towards South Africa. The constraints which contact with the mainstream of African thought would have imposed on him were absent; in his own country there was no one to contradict or question the schemes he set in motion. The adage remained in force, 'Kamuzu knows best.'

The transition from the militant, virulently anti-colonial stance Banda held in the 1940s to the pragmatic, yet pacifist, policy of two decades later took place very gradually. In 1960 he still believed that there could be 'no . . . peaceful solution' to South Africa's problems, and although he no longer spoke of 'a major war or a major revolution', in the sense of armed combat, as a prerequisite to its liberation, he retained the emotional approach which had led him, seven years earlier, to instruct his estate agents to accept no South Africans as tenants in his London house.[1] South Africa was 'a social and political cancer', he declared,[2] and when it was refused readmission to the Commonwealth, in 1961, he was jubilant. It should have happened 'years ago', he said.[3] Verwoerd – 'The Prime Minister of the White and bloody dictatorship of South Africa', as the *Malawi News* called him[4] – his Government and those who supported him were 'enemies of democracy', and their country's withdrawal would clear the way for Britain's African possessions 'to join the Commonwealth with a clear and easy conscience when they become independent'.[5]

To Banda, at that time, South Africa was the one country in which colonialism might linger on after Southern Rhodesia and the Portuguese territories achieved independence.[6] Two years later it was still 'the one country which comes to my mind very quickly' when white supremacy was discussed.[7] It was the exception to the rule, and accordingly remained outside Banda's initial movements towards a dialogue with Southern Africa.

While, in 1963, he was establishing links with Portugal and Southern Rhodesia, and dithering over whether it was because he would not or could not do otherwise, he maintained unequivocally that there could be 'no compromise whatsoever, none whatever' with South Africa and its apartheid policy:

As an African nationalist, I hate the present regime in South Africa and will have nothing to do with it when this country is independent. There will be no diplomatic or commercial dealings between the Union of South Africa and independent Malawi.*

Verwoerd and his supporters, said Banda, were 'bringing communism to Africa' by their policy of sustaining white supremacy by force.[8] South Africans and those who thought like them were not wanted in Malawi: 'I say to [them], pack up and go! Now! Now! Now! Now!'[9] Even South African Africans were viewed with suspicion, because some of them were 'quislings under the guise of political exile[s]'. Malawi would welcome genuine political refugees, Banda told the Legislative Assembly, but it would protect itself against South African spies.[10] In 1964 he took steps to reduce the volume of trade between Malawi and South Africa, instructing Government departments to purchase their requirements elsewhere.†

Only in one area, labour, did Banda make any concession. In 1960 he had promised to return to Nyasaland the 80,000 or so Nyasa migrants working in South Africa.[11] Later he recanted, partly for economic reasons (workers' remittances brought in on average about £1 million annually in foreign exchange) and partly, perhaps, because he felt that his having himself worked in South Africa invested labour migration with a certain propriety. He would not prohibit the Witwatersrand Native Labour Association from recruiting workers in Nyasaland,

---

*Banda, interview with the Johannesburg *Star* (draft dated 12 July 1963, A.A.N.S. files, Salisbury). Long after South Africa had become a Republic, Banda continued to refer to it as a Union.

†See *Hansard*, Zomba, 9 November 1965, p. 213. In this Banda was fulfilling not only recent pledges, but also the 1960 pact with Nyerere to boycott South African goods. Why this was not acted upon earlier is not clear.

he announced in 1961, 'because of my people's adventurous spirit'.[12] Two years later he confirmed that Nyasas were free 'to work where they wish and return when they want'.[13]

As in other areas of his foreign policy, independence introduced elements of confusion into Banda's views on South Africa. In a speech on Independence eve, he bitterly attacked Ian Smith for 'winning friends across the Limpopo'.

... it is a fool, a stupid fool, who thinks that the Limpopo can be a barrier against the rising tide of African nationalism [he said]. ... Smith is wasting his time. He can win Verwoerd's friendship, but that won't help him, we are not afraid of Verwoerd.[14]

Yet, when asked three days later how far he was prepared to go in opposition to Verwoerd, he was huffily evasive.[15] At the Cairo O.A.U. summit he refrained from making any reference to South Africa and, when Malawi abstained from voting on the resolution calling for a boycott of South Africa and Portugal, left it unclear whether it was because of its ties with the latter country or with both.

At the end of September, when he addressed the diplomatic corps at Lilongwe, Banda indicated that his uncertainty was bound up with the policies he was formulating in regard to Portugal and Southern Rhodesia. He explained:

The European [in Southern Africa] who dislikes [the] idea of African Government does so from fear, because they have never experienced African Government [over] ... a long [period of] time. Therefore, let we, the Africans who have the opportunity to be free, disarm their suspicion and fear by establishing a stable government – a government for all the people, regardless of race, white or black. ...

Once we have done that, even South Africa will learn a lesson from a black government.

If Southern African whites were allowed to 'get to know' blacks in the independent African states, Banda suggested, they might 'change their minds' about Africans.[16]

It was still very tentative and at the level of thinking aloud, but it was this idea, that the Southern African states could be influenced by interracial contact, which would later come to dominate Banda's policy towards South Africa. At the time, however, this was far from clear – even to Banda himself. For the next year he made no public statement on the subject apart from a few passing, disdainful references to 'Boers' as a category of person Malawi did not like and did not want.[17] And in the absence of any evidence to the contrary, it was tacitly assumed that his pre-independence attitude to the South African regime had remained unchanged, even if nothing had been done to implement a boycott.

At the end of 1964 and beginning of 1965, Banda still believed that the people of South Africa would one day throw off their foreign yoke, just as the peoples of Egypt, Portugal, Spain and innumerable other countries had done before them.[18] But he no longer knew how best to promote this end. He was growing increasingly sceptical of the effectiveness of boycotts, to which the Rhodesian situation had directed his attention. And, in the light of his relationship with Portugal, he doubted the wisdom of a policy of isolation. He was loath to discard his old belief that South Africa was a special situation and loath to accept his new belief that it was not.

The first hint of the new policy which emerged from this ponderation came in Banda's message to the United Nations in September 1965, a year to the day after his address at Lilongwe. He deprecated the practice among member states of using meetings of the Specialized Agencies for attempts to bring about the expulsion of 'some country or another' (South Africa was not mentioned by name) 'because of disagreement with the political policies of that country', and emphasized Malawi's belief in negotiation, not only in regard to Portugal and Southern Rhodesia, but also in regard to South Africa. It was his Government's view, he said, 'that colonialism must be got rid of from Rhodesia, from South Africa and from Mozambique . . . but . . . Malawi will fight for the eradication of colonialism . . . by peaceful means and not by the use of force, unless in the long run there should prove to be no other alternative.'[19] Six weeks later, in parliament, he derided the efforts of those who advocated an economic boycott of South Africa. The Rev. Michael Scott had been making 'his pilgrimages back and forth to the

United Nations' for ten years, he said, but South Africa was 'as strong as ever'.*

Statements of this kind did not go unnoticed in Pretoria, where Banda's moderate views on Rhodesia and his policy of cooperation with Portugal had already made a favourable impression. Cautiously the South African Government put out feelers. The Industrial Development Corporation made an unpublicized loan of £500,000 to one of the contractors on the Lonrho sugar scheme at Chikwawa.[20] Verwoerd sent an envoy to Zomba for a secret meeting with Banda.[21] And then, at the end of 1965, a seemingly quite unrelated event occurred which radically altered Banda's outlook towards South Africa. It concerned the building of Malawi's planned new capital city.

The idea of moving Malawi's capital from Zomba to some more congenial site, which Banda had conceived during his imprisonment at Gwelo, had remained in abeyance until 1963, when it was briefly discussed in parliament. Not until October 1964, however, did he disclose his plans in detail and reveal where the new capital was to be located.

He proposed that it should be built at a site twelve miles from Lilongwe along the Kasungu road. Lilongwe, Banda pointed out, was at Malawi's physical centre; it was in the richest agricultural area; it was topographically suitable for the building of an international airport; and it was close to the intersection of the main Central and East African air routes. There was, moreover, no shortage of land to impede the capital's expansion and, most important of all, its central disposition would help to right the economic imbalance between the South, where development had been concentrated during the colonial era, and the North, which had been neglected. Zomba, said Banda, possessed none of these advantages: it was uncentral

* *Hansard*, Zomba, 9 November 1965, pp. 216–17. At this point Banda began to 'rewrite' his Cairo O.A.U. speech: 'I refused last year in Cairo to revise my feeling about Portugal, South Africa and Rhodesia' (ibid., p. 218). Later he claimed that he had favoured a policy of cooperation with South Africa since 1963 (Speech at Banquet for South African Prime Minister, B. J. Vorster, Zomba, 20 May 1970, privately held transcript).

and mountainous and land was in short supply. He suggested that it should house Malawi's university after the new capital had been built.[22]

There were also other reasons, which Banda did not mention, for choosing Lilongwe as the site. Its centrality would facilitate political control as well as administration. By stimulating development in the relatively under-populated central and northern regions, the move would bring about a population shift, reducing the acute pressure on land in the South. And Lilongwe was, as Banda once described it, 'the Capital of the Chewa tribe'.[23]

After the scheme had been approved by parliament, Banda invited Britain to send an economic survey team to appraise it, preparatory to negotiations for its financing. He estimated that it would cost some £13 million.

The Hill mission, which arrived in June 1965 and spent six weeks in Malawi, comprised eight economists, including Arthur Hazlewood, one of the few men to have questioned the economic advantages of Federation. Its report, which Banda received a few months later, was from his point of view an unqualified disaster. Not only did it state that the building of a new capital was an insufficient priority to justify its likely cost, but it also rejected, as uneconomic, his other pet projects, the Nacala rail link and the lake-shore road. Later Banda was able to joke about this upset to his plans, averring that Noah's contemporaries had considered the ark 'uneconomic'. But at the time he fumed. 'It makes me really sick,' he told parliament bitterly. The Hill mission had been 'talking nonsense'; 'We are going ahead with the capital whether anyone agrees with us or not.'[24]

To go ahead with the capital, however, Banda needed money, and in the light of the Hill Report, Britain, whom he had expected to supply it, politely declined. The other countries which regularly gave aid to Malawi were similarly unprepared to embark on what many of them regarded as a controversial project, for whoever first contributed aid would run the risk of having to finance the capital in its entirety in the event of no other donor coming forward. A half-built city was of no use to anyone, least of all its financer. To Banda it seemed that the only country which might be willing to take a risk of this magnitude, if he could offer enough in return, was South Africa, which badly needed a breakthrough for its outward-looking policy.

The existence of a *quid pro quo* between Malawi and South Africa after the publication of the Hill Report stimulated and modified, but did not transform, the relationship which had been clandestinely under formation beforehand.

Addressing parliament in January 1966, Banda resurrected his thesis, unstated since September 1964, that 'the real cause' of Southern African Europeans' opposition to African rule was fear, and that this could only be removed by Africans in the independent African states showing that they could govern fairly, justly and non-racially.

If we [do this (said Banda)] . . . not only will we help our brothers in Rhodesia or even Angola, Mozambique, but we will cause the walls of Jericho, of apartheid, to crumble much more quickly. By this I do not mean that we must not raise our voices against injustices perpetrated against our brothers in South Africa, not at all. By all means let us raise our voices as high as we can. But . . . it is not enough for us [just] to shout.[25]

In the same speech he raised 'the very very tricky question' of the status of Europeans in Southern Africa. Those who said that white Rhodesians were interlopers, imperialists and colonialists should remember, he said, that for more than a thousand years large areas of Africa had been controlled by Arab colonists from the Arabian peninsular, who regarded the Africans as slaves and were regarded by them as bitter foes. Yet now Arabs and Africans treated each other as brothers.[26] He went on:

I contend that, just as . . . the Arabs . . . now look upon the Africans as their fellow citizens, fellow human beings . . . so too the time must come, and very soon, when the Europeans of Rhodesia must cease to think of themselves as White European people of superior race, and consider Africans their fellow human beings, their fellow citizens, if not brothers.[27]

Conversely, he declared, Africans would have to look on 'to-day's imperialists' as 'tomorrow's fellow Africans, tomorrow's fellow countrymen, tomorrow's fellow citizens'.[28]

A few days later Banda revived the idea he had got from Jardim, that many Southern African Europeans were in sympathy with the Africans. Among them, he said, were white South Africans.[29] At the same time he hinted that he might ask South Africa for assistance with the new capital. He didn't mind an 'alliance with the Devil', he said, if it was in the interest of Malawi's four million people.*

Throughout the next year Banda felt his way cautiously into the South African ambit. Further secret meetings took place and the possibility of ministerial exchanges was discussed. It was tentatively agreed that, at some unspecified date, Banda himself should visit South Africa.†

Shortly after his statement to parliament, the South African-born wife of the Minister of Local Government, Mrs R. B. Chidzanja, visited relatives in Natal. A South African Government car and police escort awaited her at Durban airport, and Banda reported afterwards that she was 'given the honour that is due to a Minister's wife'. South Africa, he told M.P.s, could not be 'all that bad. Whatever we may say against [their] . . . policy . . . at least they have good manners.'[30]

By May he had made clear privately that Malawi would welcome South African investment,[31] and in that month the two countries concluded an Extradition Agreement.[32] In July he began speaking of 'discretional alignment' as applying between North and South, as well as between East and West,[33] and in August he announced that the Government might seek South African expertise in the design of the new capital:

* *Hansard*, Zomba, 18 January 1966, pp. 413–14. Banda had spoken of having 'the Devil as my ally' two years earlier, referring to Portugal (Speech at Nasawa, 16 May 1964, Nyasaland Information Department transcript). Cf. Dunduzu Chisiza, speaking of Southern Rhodesia: 'We don't trade with devils' (*Malawi News*, 8 February 1962).

† Banda, press-conference, 8 July 1969, M.I.D. transcript. In August 1971, while this book was in preparation, Banda became the first African Head of State to visit South Africa.

... in matters of this kind ... we must not allow political or ideological consideration to cloud our judgement. We must ... accept a helping hand wherever we can find one ... whether on this side of the political and ideological barricade or on the other side, whether to the West of us or to the East of us, to the North of us or to the South of us.[34]

The following month, when Banda visited London for another desultory Commonwealth Heads of State and Government meeting, he had talks with Klaus Oppenheimer, head of the South African-based Imex Group. Oppenheimer agreed to establish a Malawian subsidiary to coordinate the planning of the capital, and to promote Malawian–South African trade.

A few days later, Verwoerd was assassinated. In his place Balthazar John Vorster, his granite-faced Minister of Justice, became Prime Minister. 'Judging by his background as the man who was in charge of police in South Africa,' Banda recalled afterwards, 'most people felt that when he took over the Government ... the gulf between black states and white states would be ... widened.'[35] He unburdened himself of his misgivings to Carel de Wet, then South Africa's Ambassador in London. But Vorster lost no time in announcing that he intended to pursue the outward-looking policy developed by his predecessor, and Malawi's relations with South Africa continued as before.

In his annual address to the United Nations in October, presented to the General Assembly by Alec Nyasulu, Banda dealt at length with South-West Africa and the decision of the International Court of Justice that Liberia and Ethiopia had an insufficient interest in its situation to petition for the revocation of South Africa's mandate. Malawi did not doubt, he said, that the enforcement of apartheid in the administration of the mandate was in breach of its terms, and that a 'radical change in the situation' was desirable. But he could not and would not support 'any proposals which are *prima facie* incapable of practical implementation'. Accordingly Malawi was abstaining from the resolution terminating the mandate and calling on South Africa to hand over the territory's administration to a United Nations Commission.[36]

Banda went on to discuss apartheid by reference to the idea of 'non-racial democracy' – elaborated earlier that year in relation to Rhodesia,[37] and deriving from his thesis that the European settlers in the white-ruled African states should be regarded co-equally with black Africans – under which people of all races would partake in the government. Malawi's beliefs in this respect were 'completely at variance' with the principles of apartheid, he declared:

> ... it is our earnest hope that one day the Government of South Africa will be moved to abandon their present policies ... not so much as a result of threats and disapproval voiced by other nations as by the example which Africa herself has set. ...
>
> May I express the hope that as better understanding between the peoples of Africa grows and fear and suspicion subside, that day may not be too far off.[38]

Addressing parliament two months later, Banda again discussed the South-West Africa issue. If what he had said at the U.N. had been for the benefit of world opinion, what he said now was for South African consumption. Malawi's belief that South Africa had breached its mandate, which Banda had loudly proclaimed at the U.N., went unmentioned. Far from wishing to see 'a radical change' in the situation in South-West Africa, he avoided any suggestion that the mandate should be terminated. On the question of whether the U.N. was (as it claimed) or was not (as South Africa maintained) the legal successor to the League of Nations, and hence jurisdictional over the mandate – and this, from the South African viewpoint, was the key issue – he refused to take sides (although his support for the U.N. position had been implicit in his message to the General Assembly). 'I am not saying they [the South Africans] are right. I am not saying the United Nations is right,' he told M.P.s.[39] What was of practical interest and importance was that South Africa was occupying and administering South-West Africa, that it had been doing so since 1914, and that it would continue to do so until evicted by force.

'Who in Africa, or in Asia for that matter, is in a position to

expel the Union of South Africa from South-West Africa?'
asked Banda. 'Not one state or group of states. . . .'[40] The
United Nations could not do so without the support of the
Great Powers, which would not be forthcoming. And if the
communist bloc decided to engage in such a conflict, it would
not be to liberate Southern Africa: 'They will conquer it for
themselves'.[41]

Even if the Great Powers had agreed to enforce South
Africa's withdrawal, Malawi would have opposed their doing so,
Banda said. For the war which would have followed would
have been 'long, unlimited, total and absolute';[42] it would have
been 'a disaster, indeed a catastrophe for Southern Africa':

The South African Army is the strongest, most efficient on our
continent. . . . If South Africa is attacked or is threatened to be
attacked over South-West Africa, she will not think she is being
attacked just to be expelled from South-West Africa. No! She will
think, feel and consider that she is being attacked in order to be wiped
out of existence as a Nation. And she will defend herself with all the
means and resources at her disposal – material and human. . . .

Nor is that all; this is one other point that many African leaders
never seem to realize. . . . The union of South Africa, Rhodesia,
Mozambique and Angola will become overnight, the minute South
Africa is attacked, one single, compact and solid laager. . . .

We can take it for granted that in any war against South Africa and
Rhodesia, the General Staffs of these two countries . . . would order
the occupation of strategic . . . centres in Malawi, Zambia and Congo
Kinshasa in order to deny anyone else from using these centres as
springboards against them. . . .

Germany has at least twice invaded Belgium in order to get at
France, and in that way at Britain. On the other hand . . . Britain has
always fought in the Low Countries – Belgium, Holland – in order to
prevent any other country from using [them] . . . as a springboard
against herself. As a result, Belgium has at least twice been the
major battlefield of Europe.

To me . . . it is most frightening – indeed horrifying – to think that
one day, as a result of the resolution passed by the United Nations,
Malawi might become part of a larger, bigger Belgium of Central
Africa. . . .

In such a war, Banda added, the 'innocent' Europeans, those

'who are on the side of the African', would suffer along with the guilty. And the Africans would suffer most of all. But the basic problem would still not have been solved, 'because the basic problem in South-West Africa is political . . . [and] political problems . . . can only be solved permanently by political means and political measures.'[43]

By the end of 1966, it was no longer a matter of merely preferring negotiation to force; force was ruled out entirely, even as a last resort. 'We believe that the use of force and the shedding of blood is both wrong in principle and impracticable,'[44] Banda had told the General Assembly. Whether from theoretical considerations of the immorality of war, 'the wrong of war itself',[45] as Banda called it, or from practical fears of a conflagration which might envelop all of Southern Africa, the retreat from the idea that 'a major war or a major revolution' must free South Africa was complete.

In the 1940s it had been the South African situation which had first eroded Banda's faith in pacifism. In the 1960s the process was reversed. He accepted the use of domestic violence to quell dissent, and supported America in the war in Vietnam. But in regard to South Africa and its white-ruled Southern African neighbours, he reverted to pacifism.

Until 1967, only Malawi's restrained attitude towards South Africa's policies, increased mutual trade and press speculation that South Africa might finance the building of the new capital – which Banda described as 'a malicious lie'[46] – signified the changed relationship between them. In March of that year, however, formal contacts began with a visit to South Africa by a Malawian ministerial delegation. A new trade agreement was signed and Aleke Banda afterwards reported enthusiastically to parliament that, 'Despite the fact that there is apartheid in South Africa, we were received on the basis of absolute equality.'[47]

The parliamentary debate on the delegation's visit provided Dr Banda with an opportunity to dilate upon his belief that the problems posed by South Africa could be solved only by discussion:

What . . . is the solution to the problem . . . of apartheid? I do not know. I have no answer. . . . But what I do know is this . . . that boycotts against South Africa, shouting threats every year against apartheid in Addis Ababa, London, New York, are no solutions. No solutions!

I know I will be criticized for saying this. . . . I know I will be accused of upsetting the African applecart. Yes – applecart, a-p-p-l-e-c-a-r-t. Those of you who do not know Shaw will remember that now. But . . . I am not afraid of criticism . . . I am used to it by now. . . .

The African applecart is already upset by African leaders themselves. Not by me. . . . It is upset . . . because they are . . . wasting time and energy and effort on the wrong things and neglecting the real things that matter. . . . They are wasting their energy and effort beating the dead horse of imperialism and colonialism. The problems in Africa today . . . are not really those of imperialism and colonialism. How many parts of Africa are still under imperial and colonial rule? How many?

The real problem . . . the problems that are crying to high heaven for solutions are economic inviability or dependence, political instability in or among African States and disunity among African leaders and African States. . . .

[Our] sending a mission to South Africa does not mean that we approve of apartheid, that we support apartheid, that we are converted to apartheid. No! No!

. . . did Mr Macmillan become tainted with Communism when he was in Russia? Did Mr Macmillan's going to Moscow mean that he approved of Communism? That he supported Communism? No! Not to my knowledge. . . .

[When] Mr Kosygin . . . was in London . . . he went to Buckingham Palace, where he had dinner with the Queen and the Duke of Edinburgh. . . . Does that mean that Mr Kosygin is now becoming a Monarchist? That they want to recruit a Windsor to put on the former throne of the Romanovs? Not to my knowledge. . . .

Mr Podgorny and His Holiness the Pope had discussions. Does that mean that Mr Podgorny is now becoming a Christian . . . [or] that His Holiness the Pope is becoming a Communist . . . an atheist? No! Not in the least. . . .

All it means is that Mr Podgorny realizes and accepts the fact that both Capitalism and the Church are here to stay . . . and he has to learn to live with them. . . .

In the same way . . . the African States on our continent have to learn to live with the Union of South Africa because . . . the Union of South Africa is here to stay. And the Union of South Africa has to learn to live with the African States, because the African States are here to stay.

. . . the politics of boycotts, shouting and shouts has failed. African leaders, African States have to think of other ways of solving the problem of Black and White on our continent.

When he had worked in South Africa as a young man, said Banda, he had believed that all whites were like those with whom he worked – 'not . . . educated, civilized, cultured' – only discovering that this was not so when he lived in America and Britain. In the same way whites in Southern Africa judged Africans by their 'kitchen boys, boss boys and mine boys', and must be shown that there were 'civilized, educated, refined, cultured African gentlemen and African ladies'.[48]

Two months after the signature of the trade agreement, a new Labour Agreement was signed in Zomba, regularizing the position of Malawian migrants, permitting them to pay tax to Malawi instead of South Africa, and enabling the Malawi Government to act as a recruiting agency, complementary to the Witwatersrand Native Labour Association. In the same month a team of broadcasters from the South African Broadcasting Corporation (which later introduced transmission in chiNyanja) had talks with Radio Malawi officials in Blantyre. Agricultural advisers came and went, and in July the Chairman of South Africa's Industrial Development Corporation, Dr H. J. van Eck, was an honoured guest at the Republic anniversary celebrations. Shortly afterwards the South African Prime Minister's Adviser on Economic Planning, Dr P. S. Rautenbach, headed an economic survey mission to study the planning and implications of the building of the new capital.

Malawi believed, said Banda, 'that it was essential in the interests of African nations that such matters as trade, commerce, technical cooperation and cultural contacts should be entirely freed from the ties of political ideology.'[49]

In June, after a visit to the United States, he declared that he was much encouraged in his attempts to 'preach the gospel of reconciliation' to blacks and whites in Southern Africa by the improvements which had taken place in race relations in America.*

> What is happening in the United States now proves me right . . . that force or violence is not the answer to the racial problem, either in America or in Africa [he said]. . . . Black people in America, white people in America must try to solve their problems by negotiation, co-operation, and not by . . . petrol bombs . . . [and so must] black [and white] people in Africa. . . .[50]

He also sought encouragement in the changes which had taken place in Mozambique. Before the M.C.P. had come to power, said Banda, the Mozambique administration had treated Nyasas very harshly. But afterwards, when the Portuguese had discovered that 'we were not wild animals', they had begun to treat Malawians less severely. At the same time their treatment of Mozambiquan Africans had improved.†

In another speech shortly after his return from America, he reverted to the analogy of the Arabs and the Africans:

> In my grandfather's time, the Arabs did not consider Africans brothers and yet today they consider Africans brothers. Is it impossible that 15, 20, 30 years' time from now, the white grandchildren of Verwoerd, Smith, Vorster, and your grandchildren, gentlemen, will be friends and brothers, just as we call those people friends and brothers now, even now?[51]

The obvious next step, to which all this was leading, was the formalization of the relationship between Malawi and South Africa. This had been discussed when the Malawian delegation visited South Africa in March, but Vorster, anxious not to exacerbate the split which was beginning to appear between the

---

*Banda evidently regarded the development of the black power movement as peripheral to the overall trend, which, in his view, was towards a racial situation vastly better than that he had known as a student in America (*Hansard*, Zomba, 27 June 1967, p. 439).

† Banda, Press-conference, Blantyre, 7 July 1967, partial text in Malawi News Agency Daily Bulletin of that date. There is an alternative explanation for the amelioration of the lot of Mozambiquan Africans which occurred after 1964. In that year the Frelimo offensive began, leaving the Portuguese with little choice but to improve conditions if they did not want the Frelimo movement to win countrywide support.

verligte ('enlightened' or outward-looking) and *verkrampte* ('narrow', traditionalist) elements of the Nationalist Party, had asked for time to prepare the ground. By August, however, *The Times* was speaking of an exchange of envoys as a *fait accompli*, and the following month, when the M.C.P. annual convention met at Mzuzu, this was officially confirmed. At the end of a three-hour speech, attended by members of the diplomatic corps and Malawi's envoys abroad, specially recalled for the occasion, Banda announced that Malawi would establish 'a direct, open and formal diplomatic relationship' with South Africa at legation level. It would be the first black state to do so.

As soon as 'possible and convenient', he said, the missions would be upgraded to embassies and a Malawian 'of African blood and origin' would be appointed Ambassador. Initially, however, Malawi's representative would be an expatriate. But the deputy head of mission would from the start be 'a full-blooded African', who would be accorded all diplomatic rights and privileges in exactly the same way as any other diplomat.*

Justifying this new development in Malawian–South African relations, Banda declared that it was 'not in the interest of my people or my country for ... the Government to boycott or isolate South Africa', because of the presence there of 80,000 Malawian migrants. He dwelt on the history of commerce between the two countries, from the time of David Livingstone's journey from Capetown to the Shire Highlands to the inter-Governmental exchanges of the past year, and concluded:

As a result of these contacts ... there has now developed between this country and the Republic of South Africa a feeling, if not exactly of friendship, shall we say ... of human fellowship and co-operation. I am putting it this way because one has to be careful and cautious in these matters.[52]

*It had been Verwoerd's refusal to admit of the possibility of a black diplomat serving in South Africa which had forced him in 1961 to withdraw South Africa's application for readmission to the Commonwealth, an event which, as we have seen, Banda had hailed with much rejoicing (A. Sampson *Macmillan: A Study in Ambiguity*, Penguin Books, 1967, p. 190). Three years later the same difficulty had proved insurmountable when Kaunda had suggested that Zambia should establish a mission in Pretoria.

Two weeks later, when Banda spoke of South Africa during an official visit to Kenya, he was even more 'careful and cautious', concentrating on the negative aspects of his policy. South Africa could not be 'boycotted or isolated into liberalism', he asserted. The policies of 'boycott, isolation, threats, bluff and bluster' were not merely unhelpful but actually harmful to the African cause by encouraging the development of a laager mentality among whites in South Africa, Rhodesia, Mozambique and Angola. He stressed that Malawi's relationship with South Africa did not imply approbation of apartheid and declared, 'I am just as strongly in disagreement with [it] . . . as any other African leader.'[53]

Despite the dilute form in which his policy was presented, Banda's courage in stating his views on South Africa during a visit to a black African state was widely hailed by the foreign press. Kenyans, although they disagreed with what he said, respected him for daring to say it. And Banda himself, when he returned home, said that he had felt that Kenya (*qua* black African state) was the one place where he should speak his mind. This tacit assumption of black Africa's hostility sombrely illustrated the extent of Malawi's isolation.

The tension which had become apparent in Malawi's relationships with the majority of black African states at the beginning of 1966 had gradually increased throughout that year. There had been no dramatic move towards deeper alienation, but Malawi's estrangement had persisted and had eventually come to be regarded as the norm. 'The odd man out in African politics' had become Banda's self-accepted description.

No sooner had this movement begun, however, than a counter-movement came into being, springing initially from the same source, the Rhodesian situation. U.D.I. brought about a *rapprochement* between Malawi and Zambia, through their sharing proximity to and dependence on their rebellious one-time partner in the Central African Federation. Zambia was offered the use of the Salima–Beira railway for transporting oil and other essential supplies, and it was agreed that the Zambian flue-cured tobacco crop should be packed at Limbe, instead of Salisbury. In

January 1966, shortly before the oil lift began, it was announced that the two countries were to establish diplomatic relations.

Two months later signs appeared of a detente with Tanzania. At the East and Central African Heads of State and Government meeting in Nairobi, in March, Nyerere approached the Malawian delegation with the suggestion that talks begin on the problem of Malawian refugees in Tanzania. Despite Banda's cock-a-hoop announcement, a few days later, that Nyerere had 'begged' for friendship,[54] contacts continued and in July Chidzanja and Kumtumanji travelled to Mwanza, on Lake Victoria, for two days of discussions with Tanzanian ministers. In the same month the ex-ministers' supporters in Tanzania were removed from the guerrilla training camps where they had been living since the end of 1964, and resettled at a non-military refugee camp at Pangale, administered by the United Nations.

The Mwanza meeting had resulted, according to Banda, in 'a large measure of agreement' on the majority of the points at issue,[55] and it was decided to hold further talks, this time in Malawi, during the first week of August. But then, in a speech to a mass rally at Chitipa, on 25 July, Banda claimed that the accord was due to Nyerere's realization that 'Chiume and other Malawi rebels could not do anything to Malawi and that he was just spending money on them for nothing'; the Tanzanians were fed up and wanted to get rid of them, he said.[56] This was in fact not far from the truth, for Nyerere had indeed concluded that if Banda could not be overthrown then he must be influenced. Banda's mistake was in saying it openly. Four days later Tanzania announced that it was breaking off the discussions. Three weeks afterwards, Chipembere returned to Dar-es-Salaam from America; there was a resurgence of hostility along the Malawian–Tanzanian border; and Banda warned that infiltrators would be 'meat for the crocodiles'.

The *rapprochement* with Zambia similarly failed to live up to expectations, although much less dramatically. For several months the superficial forms of friendship were maintained, but then Kaunda began to adopt a more militant approach to the Rhodesian question; nothing was done to implement the decision to exchange envoys; and after Chipembere's return, attention was once more directed to the presence of the Malawian refugees in Zambia.

In March 1967, after the signing of Malawi's trade agreement with South Africa, the rift became overt. Replying to criticism of his action in the Zambian press, Banda commented, not without justification:

> While they are criticizing me for trading with South Africa openly, they themselves are trading with South Africa secretly. While they are decrying South Africa, they are doing so on stomachs full of South African beef, South African butter, South African pork. Yes, they are doing so while their shops are full of South African consumer goods ... they are doing so while employing South African White miners to mine their minerals, they are doing so while allowing South African financiers, industrialists to invest heavily in their mines, their farms and their industry. . . .
>
> I treat them with utter contempt. . . . I say they are moral and physical cowards and hypocrites. . . .[57]

The oil lift and the export of Zambian copper through Malawi continued, because it was to the advantage of both countries that they should. But each viewed the other with antipathy and suspicion.

Zambia was not alone in deploring the trade agreement. In the weeks following its signature Banda was subject to almost universal opprobrium,* to which he responded by quoting Shakespeare:

> There is no terror Cassius in your threats [he declaimed in Parliament], for I am armed so strong in honesty that they pass me by like the idle wind, which I respect not.[58]

---

* It was not quite universal because Botswana, Lesotho and Malagasy likewise favoured the starting of a dialogue with South Africa; because Kenya, Nigeria and a number of other states refrained from public criticism, for reasons of old friendship or current political interest; and because a small minority of African intellectuals approved Banda's views. The *West African Pilot*, for instance, later commented: 'We agree in toto with Kamuzu Banda that the only way to bring down apartheid is for the Independent African States to fraternize with South Africa, and Rhodesia and Portugal. . . . Once the shrines of apartheid are desecrated by the free Independent African States, there will be freedom for all black men on the African continent.' (*West African Pilot*, 12 July 1967.)

None the less, two months later he admitted, not without a certain incorrigible relish, that he had become 'the most unpopular person in the continent of Africa' as far as his fellow African leaders were concerned.[59]

In June two events occurred which led to a further deterioration in Malawi's relations with Tanzania and with the Arab states.

In a speech at Iringa, Nyerere asserted that the north-eastern sector of Lake Malawi (which Tanzania maintained should still be known as Lake Nyasa) was outside Malawi's sovereignty and should be recognized as falling within Tanzania's boundaries.* That he should make such a claim, Banda commented afterwards, was 'adding insult to injury and rubbing salt in the wounds . . . Imperialism and Colonialism inflicted on the body of Malawi':

If . . . [anyone] has any just territorial claim on any of her neighbours [he told parliament], that country is Malawi. . . . If the people on the East of our Lake are being inconvenienced by the fact that the Lake belongs to us, then the best way is to cede Mbeya, Njombe, Songea [areas of Tanzania bordering the lakeshore] to us. In fact . . . it will not be ceding anything, it will be just giving us back what was taken away from us by the Germans by agreement with the British. That's all.[60]

While this local dispute was in progress, the Middle East exploded into the turmoil of the Six-Day War. Banda viewed the Arab defeat as a vindication of his contention that no group of African states could successfully attack Rhodesia, and gleefully declared that Israel had won because she had 'out-planned, out-generalled, out-manoeuvred and out-fought her adversaries'.[61] His subsequent allegations that the Arab Government in the Sudan was treating southern Sudanese Africans more harshly than ever white South Africans had treated

*In June 1962, Tanzania had formally renounced its claims to any part of the lake. Nyerere was now reviving the question because he wished to introduce a lake steamer service between the Tanzanian lake shore ports, replacing the Malawian service which had been discontinued after the cabinet crisis.

black;* his State visit to Israel, including parts of the Israeli-occupied Arab territories, in June 1968; and his suggestion that, if white colonialists were to be driven out of Southern Africa, then Arab colonialists should be driven out of North Africa first, all compounded Arab antagonism. When the 1968 O.A.U. summit conference took place in Algiers, Banda refused to send delegates because he feared for their safety (or so he said).

The announcement that Malawi was to exchange envoys with South Africa produced, in these circumstances, little of the 'hullaballoo, howling and snarling' which Banda had predicted.[62] Most of his fellow leaders took the view that whatever Banda did could no longer surprise them.

At this point, however, a fresh counter-movement began, similar to that which had started at the beginning of 1966. Once again it was Zambia and Tanzania which led the way. Its cause was an abortive *coup d'état* attempt by Yatuta Chisiza at the beginning of October. A small group of rebels under Chisiza's command entered the Mwanza–Neno district from Mozambique, intending to make their way to Blantyre, assassinate Banda and take over the Government. They evidently expected that their arrival would signal a popular insurrection. In the event, however, their presence was reported within forty-eight hours and before a fortnight had elapsed nine of the insurgents had been captured, five had fled and three, including Chisiza, had been killed.

A month or so later Kaunda sent a message to Banda denying allegations of Zambian complicity in the incursion. (The rebels had spent some weeks at a Z.A.P.U. training camp near Lusaka while on their way from Tanzania.) Nyerere followed suit by inviting him to attend the inauguration of the East African Economic Community at Arusha in December. Banda declined,

---

*Banda also used the Sudan situation as a club with which to beat Uganda's Milton Obote: 'Those very Africans who pose as champions of African liberty in Rhodesia, Mozambique, South-West Africa and all the rest ... are keeping quiet about the Sudan ... they are making State visits there to the Sudan, when the Sudanese Government is butchering Africans,' he said (*Hansard*, Zomba, 28 June 1968, p. 549).

but sent a ministerial delegation to represent him, and shortly afterwards told parliament that he was 'just a little hopeful' of an improvement in Malawi's relations with its black neighbours:

> To me it is a matter of bitter, sad regret [he said], that relations between Tanzania and Malawi, Zambia and Malawi, should be strained. . . . When we were under colonial rule . . . we, the Africans in these three territories, behaved like brothers. But since we became independent, oh, no! Oh, no! We have not behaved like the same people. . . . The way we are behaving now, as enemies, tends to prove – and I am putting it mildly – that we Africans in order to be united . . . need [to be under] someone else's thumb and someone else's heel. . . .
>
> I hope that very soon, Tanzania, Malawi and Zambia will prove to the world that those who think we need a thumb and a heel to reunite can be wrong sometimes.[63]

Despite an invasion scare shortly afterwards, contacts between Malawi and Tanzania continued. In February a Zambian ministerial delegation held talks in Blantyre, after which it was announced (now for the second time) that the two countries would establish diplomatic relations. Two months later a Malawian mission paid a return visit to Lusaka.

Encouraged by these developments, Banda resurrected the idea of Malawi playing a mediatory role in Africa. It was no longer, however, between the Casablanca and Monrovia groups, as he had first envisaged, but mediation in the form implicit in the unstated 'discretional alignment' which Malawi had tried to maintain between North and South in 1964. In an interview Banda recalled how, on his return to Nyasaland, he had said that he had come to 'bridge . . . the gulf of disunity between the Africans on the one side and Whites and Indians on the other':

> Now that I have done that in Malawi, I want to do it outside Malawi . . . between Rhodesia and South Africa on the one hand and the Africans [states] on the other. I am sincere about that.[64]

On 12 December 1967, the day on which Banda told parliament of his hopes for a *rapprochement* between Malawi and Zambia and Tanzania, a South African career diplomat, Jan François Wentzel, was accredited as his country's first Chargé d'Affaires in Malawi. A skilful diplomatist with a disarming smile, Wentzel quickly settled down to his pioneering role. Philip Richardson, a discreet former colonial servant, who had stayed on after independence to become Secretary for External Affairs, became Malawi's Chargé d'Affaires in South Africa, and Joe Kachingwe, an assured, unflappable 'full-blooded African', his First Secretary.

After this formal acknowledgement of their relationship, the dialogue between Malawi and South Africa became, for a while, primarily concerned with economic affairs, and in particular the new capital. In January 1968 Banda announced the results of the Rautenbach survey, which had concluded that the decision to transfer the capital to Lilongwe was 'the most important . . . taken thus far' in Malawi's development planning. This, he declared, was a 'realistic, practical and far-sighted' appraisal.[65] Two months later parliament empowered the Government to raise loans to finance the building of the new capital, and simultaneously it was announced in Capetown that South Africa was setting up a Loans Fund for the Promotion of Economic Cooperation, 'to grant direct assistance (for example, in the form of loans at low interest rates for sound development projects) to well-disposed developing countries – particularly in Africa'.

The first loan to be made from the Fund, it was announced on 4 May, would be of R8 million (£4.67 million), to Malawi, for the first phase of the construction of the new capital. Three days later a second announcement was made: South Africa's Industrial Development Corporation was to make a R11 million (£6.4 million) loan to the Malawi Railways to finance the Nacala rail link.*

A friend in need, n-e-e-d, is a friend indeed, i-n-d-e-e-d [commented Banda]. . . . To me personally, to the Government of this country and

---

*Although the previous September agreement had been reached with Japan for the financing of the railway, Banda preferred the South African loan offer, apparently because its terms were more favourable.

our people, the willingness of the Government of South Africa to give us financial assistance . . . makes that Government . . . in every sense of the word, truly a friend in need, who is a friend indeed.[66]

The friendship between Malawi and South Africa, no longer qualified by 'carefulness and caution', was cemented three months later by the visit to Malawi of South Africa's Foreign Minister, Dr Hilgard Muller, who spoke of his country's belief in 'co-prosperity' and warned, as South Africans are wont to do, of the dangers to Africa of communism.[67]

Trade boomed, doubling between 1967 and 1969, and South African private investment in Malawi increased. Several Malawian ministers visited South Africa, and a number of South African specialists and technicians, including medical workers, physical planners, telecommunications technicians and broadcasting and information personnel, were seconded to Malawi on short-term contracts. The South African Information Department made a grant of equipment, and the South African Broadcasting Corporation gave the M.B.C. a 20 kw. short-wave transmitter and equipped a studio in Zomba.

Aid of this kind was small-scale, undramatic and sometimes of doubtful value, but it consolidated the ties established by the major aid donations and normalized what had seemed previously an experimental relationship.

The improvement in Malawi's relationships with Zambia and Tanzania which had appeared at the beginning of 1968 continued unevenly until the autumn of that year. Then, in September, all that had been achieved was abruptly undermined by a speech Banda made at Chitipa. In the middle of a discussion of the agricultural prospects in the Songwe river area, he began talking about the Lake question, and declared:

We are not going to surrender a single inch of the Lake! What was stolen from us by colonialism must be given back now. Tukuyu, Njombe, Songeya, all those places must come to Malawi.

The true border between Malawi and Zambia, he added, was the Luangwa river.

Banda's intention in making these remarks was probably no

more than to excite feelings of chauvinism in his audience. But his speech was widely reported and drew angry reactions from both Dar-es-Salaam and Lusaka. Ten days later, opening the Party's annual convention in Lilongwe, he retorted that 'four districts in Zambia belong to Malawi, four districts in Tanzania belong to Malawi,' and announced that he was buying three British-built gunboats to carry out patrol work on the lake. 'Anybody who tries to do anything to these boats we will fight back. I want to make this quite plain. No nonsense,' he warned.[68]

Further protests from Nyerere and Zambia's Vice-President, Simon Kapwepwe, brought forth a furious tirade from Banda when he closed the convention the following weekend:

Now I hear someone in Dar-es-Salaam and someone in Lusaka are howling. . . . Dr Nyerere should be the last man to squeal and squeak. Why is he squealing and squeaking? Why is he howling? I did not begin it, he provoked me first, last year, by claiming part of our Lake. Did he expect me to remain silent? . . . What does he take me for? What does he think I am? A jellyfish like himself? . . .

As for Mr Kapwepwe, he did not know what he was talking about. Mr Kapwepwe said that I was campaigning for land in other African states, when I was silent about Portuguese territory next door. To begin with I was not campaigning. All I was doing was telling the truth. . . . And I have never confined myself to African states. I have said it more than once, that the present boundaries of Malawi to the North, South, East and West, all are artificial. . . . [But] the only place from where I have heard any howling is Dar-es-Salaam and Lusaka. The Portuguese have said nothing, maybe because the Portuguese are educated and not tanners and cobblers. . . .*

Banda himself, at such times, was not above the childishness of which he accused his fellow leaders.

During the build-up to the exchange of envoys with South Africa, Malawi's links with Portugal and Rhodesia had been strengthened. In March 1967, Msonthi and Tembo had visited

*This was an uncharitable reference to Kapwepwe. (Banda, Speech to M.C.P. annual convention, Lilongwe, 21 September 1968, M.I.D. transcript; in this text the word 'tanner' is wrongly transcribed as 'turner'.)

Lisbon to sign the formal agreement for the construction of the Nacala railway. Three months later, Tembo had returned for a second visit, to discuss the possibility of Malawi taking power from the Cabora Bassa hydroelectric scheme. The following month Portugal's Foreign Minister, Dr Franco Nogueira, had held talks with Banda in Zomba, and in September Malawi's High Commissioner in London, Timon S. Mangwazu, had been accredited as non-resident Ambassador in Lisbon.

The year 1968 saw the beginning of formal talks on the extension of the Nacala–Blantyre rail link westwards to Tete and Cabora Bassa. The following year Banda suggested that the completed rail system should be joined to the Rhodesian Railways at Shamva, so creating a continuous line of rail between Blantyre and Capetown. Although this idea remained in abeyance, it was agreed in 1970 that the Salisbury–Blantyre road through Mozambique should be tarred and realigned, for which purpose the Portuguese Government was to make available to Malawi a loan of £2.5 million, its first ever aid donation to a developing country.

While inter-Governmental cooperation increased, Portuguese investment in the private sector also rose. As early as 1967, Portuguese interests had subscribed 75 per cent of the capital of the Oil Company of Malawi. Two years later the Champalimaud Group backed the establishment of the Commercial Bank of Malawi. Champalimaud also held a substantial stake in the Aluminium Corporation of Malawi, formed, in the same year, jointly with Lonrho and the Malawi Development Corporation, to investigate the feasibility of extracting aluminium from the Mlanje bauxite deposits – a project which, if implemented, would transform Malawi's economy.*

The material benefits Malawi derived from its relationship with Portugal deterred Banda from protesting publicly at their concomitant, the periodic intrusions of Portuguese troops in search of Frelimo guerrillas. Although nothing more than discreet exchanges of diplomatic notes resulted from these

---

*It would call for an investment of around £84 million, and would produce exports worth £12 million annually. In 1968 Malawi's total revenue from domestic exports amounted to only £16·8 million.

incidents, in which a number of Malawians were killed, they were a constant threat to continued harmony.*

Just as the side-effects of the Frelimo war complicated Malawi's relations with Portugal, so, but to a much greater extent, U.D.I. affected its relationship with Rhodesia.

Throughout 1966 and 1967, Banda had maintained that the Rhodesian problem was 'Britain's baby'. He had encouraged moves towards a negotiated settlement, and had somehow managed to reconcile his partial support of U.N. mandatory sanctions – the volume of Malawi's trade with Rhodesia fell by 30 per cent between 1965 and 1967 – with his belief that a policy of boycott was in no circumstances a practical proposition. His policy of cooperation with the white-ruled regimes, in so far as it related to Rhodesia, was 'outside of U.D.I.', he had explained.

In 1968 the credibility gap widened between Banda's affirmations of support for sanctions and his disbelief in their effectiveness. For the first time since 1964, the level of Malawi's exports to Rhodesia rose (imports, however, continued slowly to decline). While the Rhodesian attitude towards Britain hardened, Banda continued to insist that a solution could only be achieved through negotiation. At the Commonwealth Heads of State and Government conference, in January 1969, he vigorously opposed the withdrawal of the *Fearless* proposals, and at the same time demanded the abandonment of NIBMAR (No Independence Before Majority Rule). NIBMAR, he declared, was 'an empty and idle slogan':

Let Mr Wilson and Mr Smith resume talks; come to an agreement of some kind. Out of that agreement, let some of the Africans enter the Government, then rule together. It won't be perfect overnight. No country is perfect. . . . No system of government is perfect.[69]

---

*The most serious known incursion occurred in October 1966, when six Malawians were shot dead and five others wounded by gunfire in the Fort Johnston district (*Annual Report of the Malawi Police Force*, 1966). Lesser incidents, many of which none the less resulted in death or injury to Malawians, continued, and early in 1970 Banda sent a private warning to Caetano that, unless the incursions stopped, the Malawi Government would have no choice but to regard armed Portuguese intruders as hostile and to repel them by force.

What Banda was in fact advocating, as he made clear in July 1969, shortly after Rhodesia elected to become a Republic, was a settlement at any price rather than a continuation of the existing stalemate. He advised the new Rhodesian African coalition party, the National People's Union, headed by Gordon Chavunduka (brother-in-law of Joe Kachingwe), to work within the Republican constitution and to concentrate on building up its strength in the rural areas (advice incapable of implementation because of the Rhodesian Government's prohibition on canvassing in the Tribal Trust Areas).[70] Some months later he announced that Malawi would cooperate with Rhodesia 'within certain limits'.[71] At the same time moves began in Salisbury to permit the allocation to Malawi of Rhodesian aid and technical assistance.

By the beginning of 1968 Banda's policy towards South Africa had been precisely determined. Thereafter he introduced no new theory to justify it,* nor any new analogy to vindicate it. But his interpretation of it became more forceful, and his criticisms of those who disagreed with it more intemperate: 'When are the Africans and the Asians going to grow up in the United Nations?' he asked, after the passage of a resolution demanding that member states sever all links with South Africa. 'When are the Africans and Asians going to . . . become statesmen, instead of high school debating boys? . . . Only a high school boy who doesn't know the realities of this world can even think of debating a resolution of that kind.'[72]

The emphases shifted. Banda spoke less of the economic imperatives for his policy, and more of his political motives. Even were Malawi not dependent on white-ruled Southern Africa, he declared, he would still favour cooperation with it 'from a purely political, sociological and humanitarian point of view'.[73] He rarely thought it necessary publicly to condemn

* Except that, in July 1969, Banda mentioned for the first time strategic considerations. He favoured a strong South African naval presence in the Indian Ocean, he said, to prevent the entry of Russia or China after Britain's withdrawal from East of Suez (Banda, press-conference, Blantyre, 8 July 1969, M.I.D. transcript).

apartheid and instead denounced the anti-apartheid movements, complaining that 'do-gooders do more harm than good'.[74] And when other leaders voiced fears of South African military aggression, Banda derided them: 'South Africa threatens no one. She is a peaceful country . . . [It is] . . . all [the] African states . . . [who] are shouting . . . threats against South Africa.' He deplored the arms embargo and wished South Africa 'very, very good luck' in building her own armaments.[75]

He claimed that 'already, because of our attitude here, the attitude of South Africans towards their own Africans is changing. They are becoming more liberal.' But he warned that 'they won't change totally overnight':[76]

People, over generations and generations, develop certain ideas, certain habits of thought, certain ways of doing things, and it's wrong to expect them to change those ideas, those habits of thought, overnight or within months or within a year. We just have to be patient. . . .

There are some who say, 'When are they going to do away with apartheid? When are they going to let Africans do this and that?' [But] . . . politics is the art of the possible, isn't it? Politicians cannot override the feelings of their followers. They have to bring their followers to their own way of thinking first. . . . And that is why I, for one, am prepared to be patient.[77]

Vorster, Banda suggested, favoured a strongly liberal approach, but was being held back by the reactionary elements in his party.

At the same time as he professed to see a change of attitude within South Africa, Banda claimed that many of his fellow African leaders were beginning to accept his ideas, although 'of course they cannot say so openly'.[78] He took hope from the announcement by Ghana's Prime Minister, Dr Kofi Busia, in 1969, that he would welcome a dialogue with South Africa. And he was encouraged by the Lusaka Manifesto, approved by the East and Central African Heads of State and Government meeting in Lusaka in April of that year. 'It begins to dawn now on quite a number of leaders that I am right and they are wrong,' he told parliament,[79] commenting on the Manifesto's acceptance of the right of whites in Southern Africa to consider themselves Africans, its moderate tone, and its stated preference 'to negotiate rather than destroy; to talk rather than kill'.[89]

The Lusaka summit saw the beginning of the last attempt of the 1960s to bring about a detente between Malawi and Zambia and Tanzania. While in the Zambian capital, the Malawian delegation had talks with Kaunda and with the Tanzanian delegates. Shortly afterwards Msonthi and Nyasulu flew to Mbeya for a meeting with Tanzania's Minister of State for Foreign Affairs, Stephen Mhando. Mhando later had a secret meeting with the Malawian ministers at Lilongwe at which it was agreed that further discussions should take place in Blantyre. Contacts with Zambia also continued, culminating in September in the exchange, at Kasungu airfield, of two Portuguese soldiers, captured by Zambia, for five Zambian civilians, arrested by the Portuguese for illegal entry into Mozambique.

The achievement of this exchange was a major diplomatic coup for Banda; it was the first success he had had in mediating between black and white Africa. But then, just as it seemed that there might be a real chance of a lasting improvement in the Malawian–Zambian relationship, the *rapprochement* lost momentum. It did so for the same reason that earlier attempts had come to grief: on neither side was there sufficient goodwill to sustain it.

In the same way the detente with Tanzania failed to materialize. Although two of the principal causes of the dispute were removed – in September Orton Chirwa left Dar-es-Salaam to settle in London, and three months later Chipembere returned to the United States (this time with Banda's approval) to study for a Ph.D. – the ministerial talks which were to have been held in Blantyre were twice called off by Nyerere at very short notice. After Vorster visited Malawi, a few months later, all hope of their resumption vanished.

It was claimed, falsely, that Banda had granted South Africa the use, for military purposes, of a new airport to be built at Lilongwe and that a defence agreement had been signed.*

---

* Rumours to this effect have been circulating since South Africa stationed a military attaché, Colonel J. W. van Niekerk, in Malawi in mid-1968. While no formal agreement exists, there is no doubt that South Africa would make available military assistance to Malawi if it were requested. There is, moreover, limited cooperation (on such matters as communist

There were renewed demands for Malawi's expulsion from the
O.A.U., and a torrent of denunciations from Dar-es-Salaam
and Lusaka. Malawi was once more isolated, not only from her
near neighbours, but from almost all the black African states to
her North.

Vorster's visit to Malawi, in May 1970, evoked Banda's clearest
statement of his commitment to pacifism. He explained his
position in a speech at an official dinner in honour of the South
African Prime Minister:

> You, in the Republic of South Africa, have your way of life. . . .
> We here have . . . our way of life. . . . Am I to be the judge that yours is
> bad and ours is good, or that ours is bad and yours is good? No. No
> one knows. . . . No one knows. . . .*
> What I do know is simply this: your way of life is your way of life.
> Our way of life is our way of life. There are certain things on which
> we agree, let's think more of those things, let's work more from the
> basis of those things on which we agree, on which we see eye to
> eye. . . . Those things on which we do not agree, on which we do not
> see eye to eye, will take care of themselves.[81]

His refusal to condemn or even to judge apartheid was explicit.
While Vorster enunciated the doctrines of separate development
and multi-nationalism (i.e. tribalism) and unequivocally rejected

---

activity) between the Malawian and the South African Special Branches,
and between the Malawian and Rhodesian Special Branches and the
Portuguese Security Police.

Malawi and Portugal have already cooperated militarily. During the
Chisiza incursion in 1967 they maintained close liaison, and when, in 1968,
Banda installed gunboats on Lake Malawi, Portuguese officers gave naval
training to the Young Pioneers who were to man them.

* Cf. Banda, speaking two months earlier on the subject of morality: 'It
seems to me . . . that there are some things you have to accept. If there is to be
order . . . there must be some standard, some guide, by which you can judge
people's behaviour. . . . If you say nothing is right, nothing is wrong,
nothing is good, nothing is bad, you are destroying the very foundations of
civilization. You are destroying it.' (Banda, Speech at Nasawa, 22 March
1970, privately held transcript.)

the very idea of multiracialism, Banda spoke only in conditional terms:

> If I do not agree . . . with your policy, if you do not agree with my policy . . . shouting at each other will not help. . . . We have to start talking, visiting one another's countries. . . . [82]

He extolled South Africa's beauty and the 'genuine down-to-earth kindness' of its people, and expressed 'the passionate belief and passionate desire' that Vorster's visit would be 'only the beginning' of a whole series of contacts between Malawi and South Africa 'at all levels':

> It is only contact [he told his guest] . . . that can reveal to your people that there are civilized people other than white people . . . that can [show] . . . our people that you are not the ogres that the newspapers make you out to be . . . that you [are not the sort of people who] do not want to sit next to Africans. . . . [83]

If it was an extraordinary speech (three weeks later Banda was agreeing with an interviewer in London that apartheid was 'wicked and evil'), so was the occasion of its delivery. Not only was it the first time for nine years that a South African Prime Minister had travelled outside his country, but it was the first time any had visited a black African state. As Banda walked from the banqueting hall, escorting Mrs Vorster, followed by her husband, escorting Miss Kadzamira, all of them must have reflected on the unlikelihood of this meeting, which even five years earlier would have been unthinkable. 'I am glad that God has preserved my life to this day,' Banda had told his guest that evening.[84] For Vorster, too, it had been a dramatic experience.

But while this visit of Vorster's to the black Africa which most South Africans still regarded as a hostile, savage place was momentous and even historic, its significance, in relation to the future of South African Africans, was open to question.

In January 1968, Banda had analysed the fear which he believed to be basic to apartheid. It consisted, he had suggested, of three distinct elements: irrational fear; fear of losing cultural identity by being overwhelmed by an inferior culture; and fear of losing an elite position held mainly on grounds of race.[85] But having reached this stage, Banda did not pursue his argument to its logical end, for the conclusions which followed from it invalidated the very premises on which his policy was built.

Contact between black and white Africans might, given time, eliminate irrational fear. In theory, it might also remove, partly, but not wholly, fear of loss of cultural identity, but in practice it would not, because of the 'drastic measures' – as Banda had described them – which the African states had to take to protect their independence: at the time of the Silombela trial, *Punch* had commented, 'We should like to congratulate Public Executioner Hastings Banda for his diligent work in furthering the cause of White Supremacy in Africa.'[86] The third element of white fear, however, is not amenable, either in theory or in practice, to influence through contact, for the natural desire of 'people to want to be at the top'[87] can only be countered by pressure – as Banda explicitly recognized in his own campaign to achieve independence.

It was this last factor which invalidated the comparison he drew between black and white Africans and Africans and Arabs. The change in the Arabs' attitude to the Africans, which occurred when the latter were on the verge of achieving political power, was not due to the inexorable march of history, but to the Arabs' recognition of the potential usefulness of the independent African states as diplomatic allies.*

Banda's acceptance of the existence of white cultural and elitist fears, and his refusal to accept the limitations they impose on his policies, leave unresolved a contradiction which can only be explained in terms of self-deception, for the sincerity of his belief in contact as the solution to the problems of black and white in Southern Africa is not in doubt. Allied to it are other, larger disparities, between his commitment to pacifism in Southern Africa and his permission of violence in Malawi; between his commitment to the West and his belief that the West is 'going to the dogs'; between his insistence on dealing

---

*On several occasions Banda referred to the relationship between Africans and Arabs as being one of convenience. But he refused to apply this thinking to his analogy with the situation in Southern Africa.

with the white-ruled African states and his refusal to deal with the communist bloc; and between his willingness to set aside the faults of the white regimes, in the hope of changing them, and his unwillingness to make the same allowances for his fellow black African leaders.

The contradictoriness of Banda's policies is in part the result of a pragmatism which is itself paradoxical in the context of his pacifism. 'I do things,' Banda once said, echoing Bismarck. 'Let others explain why.'[88] In part it is due to his facility for maintaining unintegrated an array of conflicting ideas. But above all it stems from the complexity of Banda's character, the product of a dual heritage of Africa and the West. In his own arrogant, slightly astonished self-judgement, 'I am not just another African. I am Kamuzu!'[89]

Bibliography

A. Articles, Books and Pamphlets

Alport, Lord, *The Sudden Assignment*, Hodder and Stoughton, 1965.

Banda, H. K., and Cullen Young, T., eds., *Our African Way of Life*, Lutterworth Press, 1946.

Banda, H. K., and Nkumbula, H. M., *Federation in Central Africa*, typescript, 1 May 1949.

    Federation in Central Africa, pamphlet, February 1951.

Banda, T. D. T., 'Nyasaland and Federation', *Africa South*, vol. 2, no. 2, Jan.-Mar. 1958.

Bruwer, J. P., 'The Composition of a Chewa Village (Mudzi)', *African Studies*, Johannesburg, December 1949.

Chisiza, D. K., *Africa – What Lies Ahead*, Indian Council for Africa, New Delhi, 1961.

    Realities of African Independence, Africa Bureau, 1961.

    'The Outlook for Contemporary Africa', in *Africa's Freedom*, Allen and Unwin, 1964.

Chiume, M. W. K., *Nyasaland Speaks – An Appeal to the British People*, Union of Democratic Control and the Movement for Colonial Freedom, 1959.

Clutton-Brock, G., *Dawn in Nyasaland*, Hodder and Stoughton, 1959.

Davis, J. A., and Praeger, J. K., eds., *Southern Africa in Transition*, New York, 1966.

Franck, T. M., *Race and Nationalism*, Allen and Unwin, 1960.

Franklin, H., *Unholy Wedlock*, Allen and Unwin, 1963.

Gray, R., *The Two Nations*, O.U.P., 1960.

Hall, R., *Zambia*, Pall Mall Press, 1965.

Hodgson, A. G. O., 'Notes on the Achewa and Angoni of the Dowa District of the Nyasaland Protectorate', *Journal of the Royal African Society*, vol. 63.

Jones, G. B., *Britain and Nyasaland*, Allen and Unwin, 1964.

Jones, P., *Kwame Nkrumah*, Hamish Hamilton, 1965.

Mair, L. P., *The Nyasaland Elections of 1961*, Athlone Press, 1962.

Mason, P., *Year of Decision*, O.U.P., 1960.

Matthews, D., *African Powder-keg*, Bodley Head, 1966.

Melady, T. P., *Profiles of African Leaders*, Macmillan, 1961.

318   Banda

Mondlane, E., *The Struggle for Mozambique*, Penguin Books, 1969.

Munger, E. S., *All African People's Conference*, American Universities' Field Staff, Hanover, N.H., 1959.

> *President Kamuzu Banda of Malawi*, American Universities' Field Staff, Hanover, N.H., October 1969.

Pike, J. G., *Malawi: A Political and Economic History*, Pall Mall Press, 1968.

Ransford, O., *Livingstone's Lake*, John Murray, 1966.

Rotberg, R. I., *The Rise of Nationalism in Central Africa*, O.U.P., 1965.

Sampson, A., *Macmillan: A Study in Ambiguity*, Penguin Books, 1967.

Sanger, C., *Central African Emergency*, Heinemann, 1960.

Segal, R., *African Profiles*, Penguin, 1962.

Shepperson, G., 'External Factors in the Development of African Nationalism, with Particular Reference to British Central Africa', *Historians in Tropical Africa*, mimeo., Salisbury, 1962.

> 'Nyasaland and the Millennium', in Thrupp, S. L., ed., *Millennial Dreams in Action*, Mouton, The Hague, 1962.

> 'The Fourth Melville J. Herskovits Memorial Lecture', North-Western University Press, Evanston, 1966.

Shepperson, G., and Price, T., *Independent African*, Edinburgh University Press, 1958.

Tangri, R. K., 'The Rise of Nationalism in Colonial Africa: The Case of Colonial Malawi', in Pachai, B., Smith, G. W., and Tangri, R. K., eds., *Malawi Past and Present: Studies in Local and Regional History*, mimeo., Blantyre, 1968.

Wallerstein, I., *Africa: The Politics of Unity*, Pall Mall Press.

Welensky, Sir Roy, *Welensky's 4000 Days: The Life and Death of the Federation of the Rhodesias and Nyasaland,* Collins, 1964.

B. Dissertations

Macdonald, R. J., *A History of African Education*, Ph.D. thesis, microfilm, Edinburgh University, 1969.

Watkins, M. H., 'A Grammar of Chichewa: A Bantu Language of British Central Africa', University of Chicago dissertation, published by the Linguistic Society of America as a supplement to its journal, *Language*, no. 24, April–June 1937 (Kraus Reprint Corporation edition, New York, 1966).

C. *Official Reports*

Report of the Commission on Closer Union (The Hilton Young Report), Cmd 3234, 1929.

Memorandum on Native Policy in East Africa (The Passfield Memorandum), Cmd 3573, 1930.

Rhodesia-Nyasaland Royal Commission Report (The Bledisloe Report), Cmd 5949, 1939.

Closer Association in Central Africa: Statement by His Majesty's Government in the United Kingdom, Cmd 8411, 1951.

Southern Rhodesia, Northern Rhodesia and Nyasaland: *Draft Federal Scheme*, Cmd 8573, 1952.

Southern Rhodesia, Northern Rhodesia and Nyasaland: *Report by the Conference on Federation Held in London, January 1953*, Cmd 8753, 1953.

The Federal Scheme for Southern Rhodesia, Northern Rhodesia and Nyasaland Prepared by a Conference Held in London, January 1953, Cmd 8754, 1953.

Report of the Nyasaland Commission of Inquiry (The Devlin Report), Cmd 814, 1958.

Beadle Tribunal (Review Tribunal (Preventive Detention Temporary Provisions) Act 1959) General Report, CSR 27–59, Salisbury, 1959.

Report of the Nyasaland Constitutional Conference (The Lancaster House Report), Zomba, 1960.

Report of the Advisory Commission on the Review of the Constitution of Rhodesia and Nyasaland (The Monckton Report), Cmd 1148, 1960.

Northern Rhodesia: Proposals for Constitutional Change, Cmd 1423, 1961.

Report of the Nyasaland Constitutional Conference (The Marlborough House Report), Cmd 1887, 1962.

D. *Periodicals and Newspapers*

The most important periodical and newspaper sources include:

Dissent, Salisbury, mimeo.

Evening Standard, Salisbury.

Malawi News, Limbe.

Ntendere pa Nchito, mimeo., Limbe.

Nyasaland Times (renamed the *Times* after 1963), Blantyre.

Rhodesia Herald, Salisbury.

Sunday Mail, Salisbury.

Tsopano, Salisbury.

Other cited periodicals and newspapers are:

Africa Today (New York), *Chicago American* (Chicago), *Chicago Tribune* (Chicago), *Christian Science Monitor* (Boston), *Congress Circular* (Blantyre), *Daily Mail, Daily Telegraph, Daily Worker, Drum* – East African edition, *East Africa and Rhodesia, Economist, Guardian, Le Monde* (Paris), *Liverpool Post, Nationalist* (Dar-es-Salaam), *New Commonwealth, News Chronicle, Observer, Other Lands* (Edinburgh), *People's Daily* (Peking), *Punch, Scotsman, Star* (Johannesburg), *Sunday Express, Sunday Tribune* (Durban), *The Times, West African Pilot* (Lagos), *Zambian Pilot* (Lusaka).

Where information has been derived from Government press releases or transcripts of speeches, *Hansards*, Malawi Congress Party documents, letters, interviews and other privately held materials, references have been given in the footnotes accompanying the text or in the notes at the end of this book.

Notes

Introduction

1. William E. Smith, notes dated January 1964, privately held. See also *Malawi News*, 27 December 1963 and 3 January 1964; and *Hansard*, Zomba, 7 January 1964, p. 1108.
2. ibid.
3. ibid.
4. *Rhodesia Herald*, 1 January 1964.
5. ibid.
6. Quoted in Nyasaland Information Department press release, 13 May 1964.
7. *Nationalist*, 26 May 1970 (picture caption).

1. The Child of Two Worlds

1. J. G. Pike, *Malawi: A Political and Economic History*, Pall Mall Press, 1968, p. 91.
2. Msulira, manuscript interview dated 31/2/68 (*sic*), privately held.
3. ibid.
4. Chewa oral tradition.
5. Rev. Hanock Msokera Phiri, interview with the author, Kasungu, 15 March 1969.
6. *Hansard*, 19 December 1968, Zomba, p. 162.
7. J. P. Bruwer, 'The Composition of a Chewa Village (Mudzi)', *African Studies*, Johannesburg, December 1949.
8. Unattributable interview.
9. Banda, Speech at Chimwankhunda, 7 September 1969, privately held transcript.
10. Msulira, op. cit.
11. Banda, Speech to Malawi Congress Party annual convention, 6 September 1969, privately held transcript.
12. R. J. Macdonald, *A History of African Education* (Ph.D. thesis), microfilm, Edinburgh University, 1969; Phiri, op. cit.; and *Hansard*, Zomba, 27 October 1964, p. 154.
13. Supposition from Bruwer, op. cit.
14. Unattributable interview.
15. Msulira, op. cit.

16. Banda, Speech at Chamama, 21 September 1969, privately held transcript.
17. E. S. Munger, *President Kamuzu Banda of Malawi*, American Universities Field Staff, Hanover, N.H., October 1969, p. 5.
18. Phiri, op. cit.
19. Macdonald, op. cit.
20. Phiri, op. cit.
21. ibid., and Banda to Phiri, 21 April 1946, privately held.
22. See G. Shepperson and T. Price, *Independent African,* Edinburgh University Press, Edinburgh, 1958, pp. 79, 120–1.
23. R. I. Rotberg, *The Rise of Nationalism in Central Africa*, O.U.P., 1965, pp. 116–17.
24. Phiri, op. cit.
25. Banda, Speech at Chamama, op. cit.
26. H. K. Banda, and T. Cullen Young, eds., *Our African Way of Life*, Lutterworth Press, 1946, p. 26.
27. ibid.
28. *Hansard*, Zomba, 29 March 1967, p. 297.
29. Phiri, op. cit., and R. Gray, *The Two Nations*, O.U.P., 1960, p. 122.

2. In Pursuit of an Education

1. Phiri, interview, and Malawi Information Department fact-sheet, *The President of Malawi, His Excellency Dr Kamuzu Banda*, undated.
2. Banda and Cullen Young, *African Way of Life*, p. 25.
3. Macdonald, *African Education*.
4. Phiri, op. cit.
5. ibid., and *Hansard*, Zomba, 25 February 1964, p. 1212.
6. Phiri, op. cit., and Rotberg, *Rise of Nationalism*, p. 187 n.
7. Phiri, op. cit.
8. ibid., and Banda to Phiri, 2 July 1946, privately held.
9. Phiri, op. cit., and Rotberg, op. cit., p. 187 n.
10. Phiri, op. cit.; Banda, Face to Face with John Freeman (television interview), B.B.C. transcript, 22 April 1960; and unattributable interview.
11. *Hansard*, 24 March 1970, Zomba, p. 481.
12. Unattributable interview.
13. Banda, interview with John Worrall, Malawi News Agency transscript, 18 January 1968; press-conference, Blantyre, 8 July 1969, M.I.D. transcript; and Speech at a banquet for Prime Minister John Vorster, Zomba, 20 May 1970, privately held transcript.

14. *Star*, Johannesburg, 2 December 1958.
15. Rev. Mother Emily Modikoane, interview with the author, Inyanga, Southern Rhodesia, 20 August 1969; Phiri, op. cit., conflicts.
16. G. Shepperson, 'External Factors in the Development of African Nationalism, with Particular Reference to British Central Africa', *Historians in Tropical Africa*, mimeo., Salisbury, 1962, p. 327.
17. Munger, *Kamuzu Banda of Malawi*, p. 6.
18. Modikoane, op. cit., and M.I.D., *President of Malawi*. Banda, Speech to English teachers, M.I.D., transcript, 10 December 1968, conflicts.
19. Modikoane, op. cit., and Banda, Face to Face.
20. Macdonald, op. cit.
21. ibid., and Phiri, op. cit.
22. Macdonald, op. cit.
23. Munger, op. cit., p. 6.
24. Phiri, op. cit. See also N N 1/20/3, Zomba archives.
25. Modikoane, op. cit., and Phiri, op. cit.
26. Phiri, op. cit.
27. Modikoane, op. cit.
28. Unattributable interview. See also *Observer*, 8 March 1959.
29. Rotberg, op. cit., pp. 187–8; Banda, Speech to English teachers, and *Hansard*, Zomba, 28 October 1964, p. 267.
30. Phiri, op. cit.
31. Unattributable interview.
32. *Africa Today*, New York, June 1960, and Banda, Face to Face.
33. Rotberg, op. cit., pp. 187–8.
34. ibid.; unattributable interview; and C. Sanger, *Central African Emergency*, Heinemann, 1960, p. 187.
35. Unattributable interview. Banda restated this reason in a number of speeches after his return to Malawi.
36. Macdonald, op. cit.
37. Unattributable interview.
38. *Christian Science Monitor*, 24 October 1963, and *Chicago Tribune*, 12 October 1963.
39. Rotberg, op. cit., p. 187.
40. Banda to Phiri, 11 August 1932, privately held.
41. ibid., and Banda to Phiri, 21 April 1946, privately held.
42. Banda to Phiri, 11 August 1932.
43. Quoted in Sanger, op. cit., p. 185.
44. *Africa Today*, op. cit.

324   Banda

45. Rotberg, op. cit., p. 188; *Christian Science Monitor*, 24 October 1963, and Banda to Phiri, 11 August 1932, differ in dating.
46. Banda to Phiri, 11 August 1932.
47. Rotberg, op. cit., p. 188.
48. *Chicago American*, 11 October 1963; Banda, interview with Albert Meyers, Zomba, Malawi News Agency limited circulation transcript, 18 March 1968; and Munger, op. cit., p. 7.
49. Banda to Phiri, 11 August 1932. See also *Christian Science Monitor*, 24 October 1963.
50. *Africa Today*, op. cit., and *Chicago Tribune*, 12 October 1963.
51. Unattributable interview.
52. ibid., and Rotberg, op. cit., p. 188 n.
53. cf. Munger, op. cit., p. 6.
54. But see R. Hall, *Zambia*, Pall Mall Press, 1965, p. 117.
55. Banda, Speech on Communism, Nyasaland Information Department transcript, 9 April 1964.
56. Banda to Phiri, 14 February 1937, privately held.
57. ibid.

3. General Practice

1. Hall, *Zambia*, p. 117, and letter to the author, 12 February 1970. See also ZA 1/9/45/1 vol. 1, Lusaka archives, and Banda to Phiri, 21 April 1946 and 2 July 1946, privately held. Philip Mason (*Year of Decision*, O.U.P., 1960, p. 137) and Rotberg (*Rise of Nationalism*, p. 188) give conflicting accounts.
2. Banda to the Secretary, the Anti-Slavery and Aborigines Society, 11 September 1938, British South Africa, Rhodesia G168–9, Rhodes House, Oxford.
3. Rotberg, op. cit., pp. 188–9; *Hansard*, Zomba, 8 March 1963, p. 659; and unattributable interviews.
4. The following account of the development of the closer association movement is based on: Rotberg, op. cit., R. Gray, *The Two Nations*, O.U.P., 1960, and G. B. Jones, *Britain and Nyasaland*, Allen and Unwin, 1964.
5. Cmd 3234.
6. Cmd 3573.
7. Cmd 5949.
8. Banda to the Anti-Slavery Society, op. cit.
9. Cmd 5949, p. 274.
10. Sanger, *Emergency*, p. 189.
11. Banda to Phiri, 21 April 1946, privately held.

12. Munger, *Kamuzu Banda of Malawi*, pp. 7–8.
13. Unattributable interview.
14. Sanger, op. cit., p. 191; Gray, op. cit., p. 192; and Rotberg, op. cit., p. 123.
15. Cmd 5949; Rotberg, op. cit., p. 112.
16. Rotberg, op. cit., p. 189; C. J. Matinga, interview with the author, Salisbury, 24 August 1969.
17. Quoted in Rotberg, op. cit., p. 189.
18. Banda and Cullen Young, *Way of Life*, p. 28.
19. Quoted in Rotberg, op. cit., p. 189.
20. *Other Lands*, Edinburgh, July 1940, p. 145; Banda to Phiri, 21 April 1946.
21. Unattributable interview.
22. Banda and Cullen Young, op. cit., p. 27.
23. Unattributable interview.
24. ibid.
25. Banda and Cullen Young, op. cit., p. 11.
26. ibid., pp. 6–7.
27. Unattributable interview.
28. ibid., and *Drum*, East African edition, December 1959.
29. Banda to the Anti-Slavery Society, op. cit.
30. Unattributable interview, and Banda, Speech to nurses at Queen Elizabeth Central Hospital, Blantyre, 13 February 1970, privately held transcript.
31. Unattributable interview.
32. ibid. and R. Segal, *African Profiles*, Penguin Books, 1962, p. 89.
33. Unattributable interview.
34. Rotberg, op. cit., p. 188.
35. Unattributable interview. Sanger (op. cit., p. 187), Munger (op. cit., p. 8) and Segal (op. cit., p. 89) are incorrect. Banda and Cullen Young (op. cit., p. 27) beg the question.
36. Matinga, op. cit.
37. Unattributable interview.
38. Quoted in Sanger, op. cit., p. 195.
39. Unattributable interview.
40. *Liverpool Post*, 21 June 1965.
41. Rotberg, op. cit., p. 188.
42. *Liverpool Post*, 21 June 1965.
43. Unattributable interview.
44. ibid. Rotberg (op. cit., p. 186n) and the *Liverpool Post* (21 June 1965) conflict on dating. See also Sanger, op. cit., p. 187.

45. Unattributable interview.
46. Rotberg, op. cit., pp. 214–15.
47. ibid., p. 216, and Jones, op. cit.
48. Gray, op. cit., p. 342.
49. For a fuller description of the events leading up to the formation of Congress see R. K. Tangri, 'The Rise of Nationalism in Colonial Africa: The Case of Colonial Malawi', in B. Pachai, G. W. Smith, and R. K. Tangri, eds., *Malawi Past and Present: Studies in Local and Regional History*, mimeo., Blantyre, 1968; Rotberg, op. cit., pp. 181–97; and Gray, op. cit., pp. 337–45.
50. Tangri, op. cit., p. 112.
51. ASS 4/13, vol. 2, Levi Mumba, presidential address to the first annual conference of Congress, 21 October 1944, Zomba archives. But see also Tangri, op. cit., p. 104.
52. Gray, op. cit., p. 337.
53. ASS 4/13, vol. 2.
54. Rotberg, op. cit., p. 186; Gray, op. cit., p. 340; *Nyasaland Times*, 16 January 1959; and *Hansard*, Zomba, 27 May 1964, p. 63.
55. Gray, op. cit., p. 337.
56. Rotberg, op. cit., pp. 189–90.
57. Gray, op. cit., and ASS 4/13, vol. 2.
58. Gray, op. cit.
59. 1a1424, Zomba archives.
60. Rotberg, op. cit., p. 194.
61. ASS 4/13, vol. 2.
62. 27A/111a, Zomba archives.
63. Unattributable interview.
64. Banda to Phiri, 21 April 1946, privately held.
65. 27a/111a.
66. ibid., and Matinga, op. cit.
67. Rotberg, op. cit., p. 196.
68. 1a1424.
69. Banda to Phiri, 21 April 1946.
70. Banda to Phiri, 2 July 1946, privately held.
71. Rotberg, op. cit., p. 197n, and H. K. Banda, and H. M. Nkumbula, *Federation in Central Africa*, typescript, 1 May 1949 (copy in Salisbury archives).
72. Welensky, Sir Roy, *Welensky's 4000 Days: The Life and Death of the Federation of the Rhodesias and Nyasaland*, Collins, 1964, pp. 48–9; *Drum*, East African edition, December 1959; and unattributable interviews.

73. P. Jones, *Kwame Nkrumah*, Hamish Hamilton, 1965, p. 30.

74. *Drum*, East African edition, December 1959; unattributable interviews; and *Malawi News*, 19 October 1961.

75. Welensky, op. cit., pp. 48–9.

76. Unattributable interview.

77. 1a1424.

78. Rotberg, op. cit., p. 198.

79. *Hansard*, House of Commons, 7 November 1945, written answers.

80. Rotberg, op. cit., pp. 198–9; 1a1424.

81. 1a1424.

82. Implied in Matinga, op. cit.

83. 1a1424.

84. See Rotberg, op. cit., pp. 197–8.

85. 1a1424.

86. Matinga, op. cit.

87. 1a1424.

88. Munger, op. cit., p. 28.

89. Banda to Phiri, 2 July 1946, privately held.

90. Macdonald, *African Education*.

91. Unattributable interview, and Sanger, op. cit.

92. See also Munger, op. cit., p. 8. Banda, *Face to Face*, conflicts.

93. Munger, op. cit., p. 9; Matinga, op. cit.; *Hansard*, Zomba, 15 July 1963, p. 871; and unattributable interviews.

94. *Sunday Mail*, 8 September 1963.

95. Munger, op. cit., p. 9.

96. *Drum*, East African edition, December 1959.

97. 1a1424.

98. ibid., and 27A/111a.

99. 27A/111a; also see Tangri, op. cit., p. 106, and Rotberg, op. cit., p. 213 n.

100. Interviews given by Henry Chipembere to David Martin in Dar-es-Salaam during 1969. I am indebted to Mr Martin for allowing me to read through this material, much of which will be incorporated in his forthcoming biography entitled *Henry Chipembere: 66 Days to Exile*.

101. ibid., and Banda, Speech to civil servants, Zomba, 17 December 1965, Malawi Information Department transcript.

102. Rotberg, op. cit., p. 213 n.

103. 27A/111a.

104. See Gray, op. cit., and Tangri, op. cit., pp. 106–7.

4. The Fight against Federation

1. Rotberg, *Rise of Nationalism*, p. 218.
2. ibid., p. 219.
3. ibid., pp. 220–3.
4. Banda and Nkumbula, *Federation*.
5. Banda, Speech at a banquet for Prime Minister John Vorster, Zomba, 20 May 1970, privately held transcript.
6. Banda and Nkumbula, op. cit.
7. Unattributable interview.
8. Banda and Nkumbula, op. cit.
9. Quoted in Rotberg, op. cit., p. 223.
10. 27A/111a, Zomba archives.
11. Rotberg, op. cit., p. 226, and Jones, *Britain and Nyasaland*.
12. Quoted in Rotberg, op. cit., p. 226.
13. Unattributable interview. See also Banda, *Face to Face*.
14. Jones, op. cit.
15. *Nyasaland Times*, 16 January and 1 May 1950.
16. Jones, op. cit.
17. *Daily Telegraph*, 25 June 1951, and Sanger, *Emergency*, p. 180. See also *Hansard*, Zomba, 8 April 1965, p. 589.
18. H. K. Banda, and H. M. Nkumbula, *Federation in Central Africa*, printed pamphlet, February 1951.
19. Rotberg, op. cit., p. 232.
20. ibid.
21. Jones, op. cit.
22. ibid., p. 144, and Rotberg, op. cit., p. 233.
23. *Nyasaland Times*, 14 June 1951.
24. ibid., 13 February 1950.
25. ibid., 2 August 1951.
26. Rotberg, op. cit., pp. 233–4.
27. *Nyasaland Times*, 30 August and 3 September 1951.
28. ibid., 13 August 1951.
29. ibid., 3 September and 10 September 1951; and T. D. T. Banda, 'Nyasaland and Federation', *Africa South*, vol. 2, no. 2, 1958.
30. *Nyasaland Times*, 30 August and 20 September 1951.
31. ibid., 27 September and 8 October 1951.
32. Cmd 8411. See also Jones, op. cit., pp. 139, 145.
33. Munger, *Kamuzu Banda of Malawi*, p. 1.
34. Hall, *Zambia*, p. 154; Welensky, *4,000 Days*, pp. 48–9; and *Observer*, 2 March 1952.
35. Rotberg, op. cit., p. 239.

36. Chipembere, interview (see note 100, chapter 3).
37. Rotberg, op. cit., p. 238.
38. ibid., pp. 240–1, and Jones, op. cit.
39. *Malawi News*, 9 August 1963; Rotberg, op. cit., p. 240.
40. Quoted in Hall, op. cit., pp. 154–5.
41. *Malawi News*, 9 August 1963.
42. *Nyasaland Times*, 31 January 1952.
43. ibid., 7 April 1952.
44. ibid., 28 April 1952.
45. ibid., 9 March 1953.
46. Cmd 8573.
47. *Nyasaland Times*, 21 August 1952.
48. Banda, Speech marking Republic anniversary celebrations, Blantyre, 7 July 1968, Malawi Information Department transcript.
49. Rotberg, op. cit., pp. 245–6.
50. *Hansard*, Zomba, 8 December 1952, pp. 63–4.
51. Chipembere, op. cit., and unattributable interview. See also *Drum*, East African edition, December 1959.
52. *Nyasaland Times*, 15 and 23 January 1953.
53. ibid., 26 January and 2 February 1953; *East Africa and Rhodesia*, 15 January 1953. T. D. T. Banda (op. cit.) conflicts.
54. *Nyasaland Times*, 16 April 1953.
55. Rotberg, op. cit., p. 247.
56. Quoted in ibid., p. 248.
57. Jones, op. cit.
58. *Hansard*, House of Commons, vol. 514, col. 11, written answers.
59. *Nyasaland Times*, 30 March 1953.
60. ibid., 9 April 1953; Rotberg, op. cit., p. 250; and T. D. T. Banda, op. cit.
61. *Nyasaland Times*, 16 April 1953.
62. ibid., 13 April 1953, and Rotberg, op. cit., p. 250.
63. *Hansard*, Zomba, 20 April 1953, pp. 18, 36.
64. Rotberg, op. cit., p. 251, and *Nyasaland Times*, 7 May 1953.
65. Rotberg, op. cit., p. 251, and *Nyasaland Times*, 18 May 1953.
66. *Nyasaland Times*, 21 May 1953.
67. ibid., 25 May, 1, 4, 11, 15 June, 6, 30 July 1953. See also Cmd 814.
68. Chipembere, op. cit., and Rotberg, op. cit., p. 262.
69. Sanger, op. cit., p. 194.
70. *Observer*, 8 March 1959; Chipembere, op. cit.
71. Certificate 4908, Divorce Registry of the High Court of Justice, London, 13 June 1955. See also D. Matthews, *African Powder-keg*, Bodley Head, 1966, p. 168, and Munger, op. cit., p. 9.

5. The Gold Coast Episode

1. *Hansard*, Zomba, 13 December 1964, p. 1024.
2. Rotberg, *Rise of Nationalism*, pp. 259–60.
3. ibid., pp. 260–2.
4. *Hansard*, Zomba, 30 November 1953, pp. 2–3.
5. Chipembere, interview.
6. Rotberg, op. cit., p. 262.
7. Cmd 814.
8. Chipembere, op. cit.
9. ibid.; Chiume, interview with the author, Dar-es-Salaam, 9 June 1970; Sanger, *Emergency*, pp. 194–5; and Cmd 814, para. 27. T. D. T. Banda ('Nyasaland and Federation', *Africa South*, vol. 2, no. 2, January–March 1958) wrongly supposed that Congress opposed their election.
10. Sanger, op. cit., pp. 194–5.
11. Chipembere, op. cit.
12. Chiume, op. cit.; Sanger, op. cit., p. 196; and *Hansard*, Zomba, 23 April 1969, p. 372.
13. Sanger, op. cit., p. 196.
14. Chiume, Matinga and unattributable interviews.
15. Sanger, op. cit., pp. 194–6.
16. Chipembere, op. cit.; Cmd 814; and 'Proceedings of the Tenth Annual Conference of the Nyasaland African Congress at Lilongwe, 12 January 1954', mimeo., Zomba archives.
17. Rotberg, op. cit., p. 267.
18. T. D. T. Banda, op. cit.
19. Rotberg, op. cit., p. 268.
20. Chiume, op. cit.
21. Rotberg, op. cit., p. 268.
22. ibid., p. 269; Cmd 814, para. 24; and *Hansard*, Zomba, 1 December 1953.
23. Rotberg, op. cit., pp. 268–70; Cmd 814, para. 24; and Chipembere, op. cit.
24. Rotberg, op. cit., p. 268.
25. Cmd 814, para. 25.
26. Chipembere, op. cit. See also *Nyasaland Times*, 10 February 1959.
27. T. D. T. Banda, op. cit.
28. Chipembere, op. cit.
29. ibid.; Rotberg, op. cit., p. 269; and Cmd 814, para. 27.
30. *Malawi News*, 30 March 1961.

31. Cmd 814, para. 27, and Chipembere, op. cit.
32. *Malawi News*, 30 March 1961.
33. *Congress Circular*, vol. 1, no. 1, January 1957, Zomba archives.
34. Cmd 814, para. 26; *Malawi News*, 30 March 1961; Chipembere, op. cit., and Chiume, op. cit.
35. *Congress Circular*, vol. 1, no. 2, March 1957, Zomba archives.
36. Cmd 814, para. 26.
37. Quoted in T. M. Franck, *Race and Nationalism*, Allen and Unwin, 1960, p. 302.
38. Cmd 814, para. 27.
39. Rotberg, op. cit., p. 284n, and Chipembere, op. cit., and Chiume, op. cit.
40. Cmd 814, para. 27.
41. Unattributable interviews.
42. Gazette Notice 2177, in Welensky, *4,000 Days*, p. 84.
43. Munger, *Kamuzu Banda of Malawi*, pp. 12–13.
44. Welensky, op. cit., p. 84.
45. Ghana Gazette, no. 42 of 1958, 10 May, Gazette Notice 942.
46. Cmd 814, para. 28.
47. ibid.; Sanger, op. cit., p. 199; and Rotberg, op. cit., p. 284n.
48. Sanger, op. cit., p. 201, and Chiume, op. cit., Chipembere, op. cit., and unattributable interviews.
49. As summarized in Cmd 814, para. 26.
50. Chiume, op. cit.
51. Rotberg, op. cit., p. 285.
52. Cmd 814, para. 28.
53. Chiume, op. cit., and unattributable interviews.
54. Chipembere, op. cit.
55. See *Hansard*, Zomba, 9 October 1968, p. 12.
56. Cmd 814, para. 29.
57. Sanger, op. cit., p. 201.

6. Nyasaland Emergency

1. G. Shepperson, 'The Fourth Melville J. Herskovits Memorial Lecture', North-Western University Press, Evanston, 1966, p. 14, and 'Nyasaland and the Millennium', in S. L. Thrupp, ed., *Millennial Dreams in Action*, Mouton, The Hague, 1962, p. 146.
2. Sanger, *Emergency*, pp. 7–8.
3. *Nyasaland Times*, 8 July 1958.
4. Sanger, op. cit., pp. 7–8.

5. *Nyasaland Times*, 8 July 1958.
6. Sanger, op. cit., p. 8.
7. *Nyasaland Times*, 8 July 1958.
8. ibid., 11 July 1958.
9. *Malawi News*, 8 February 1963.
10. Cmd 814, para. 48.
11. See *Hansard*, Zomba, 18 May 1966, pp. 588–9.
12. *Nyasaland Times*, 8 August 1958.
13. ibid., 5 August 1958.
14. *Malawi News*, 8 February 1963.
15. Cmd 814, para. 50.
16. Sanger, op. cit., p. 202.
17. Chipembere, Chiume and unattributable interviews.
18. Cmd 814, para. 62.
19. Unattributable interview.
20. G. Clutton-Brock, *Dawn in Nyasaland*, Hodder and Stoughton, 1959, pp. 55–6.
21. Sanger, op. cit., p. 227.
22. ibid., p. 231.
23. *Evening Standard*, Salisbury, 17 October 1958.
24. Cmd 814, para. 53.
25. *Nyasaland Times*, 28 October 1958.
26. Chipembere, op. cit.
27. *Nyasaland Times*, 28 October 1958.
28. ibid., 31 October 1958.
29. ibid., 19 August 1958.
30. ibid., 11 November 1958.
31. ibid., 11 and 14 November 1958.
32. ibid., 14 November 1958.
33. See Sanger, op. cit., pp. 21–5, 233–4.
34. Cmd 814, para. 60.
35. *Rhodesia Herald*, 28 November 1958.
36. ibid., 8 July 1958.
37. *Nyasaland Times*, 11 November 1958.
38. ibid., 14 November 1958.
39. ibid., 2 December 1958.
40. ibid., 21 November 1958.
41. E. S. Munger, *All African People's Conference*, American Universities' Field Staff, Hanover, 1959, pp. 8–9.
42. Sanger, op. cit., p. 243.
43. Munger, op. cit., p. 44.
44. Sanger, op. cit., p. 243.

45. Cmd 814, para. 69.
46. *Rhodesia Herald*, 3 May 1958.
47. Munger, op. cit., p. 41.
48. Sanger, op. cit., p. 243.
49. *Rhodesia Herald*, 3 December 1958.
50. ibid., 22 December 1958.
51. *Evening Standard*, 22 December 1958.
52. Cmd 814, para. 86.
53. *Rhodesia Herald*, 22 December 1958.
54. *Sunday Mail*, Salisbury, 4 January 1959.
55. *Nyasaland Times*, 23 December 1958.
56. *Evening Standard*, 24 December 1958.
57. *Sunday Mail*, 28 December 1958.
58. *Hansard*, House of Commons, 610/337, 26 July 1959.
59. Cmd 814, para. 85.
60. ibid., para. 88.
61. ibid., para. 89.
62. As bowdlerized in the *Nyasaland Times*, 23 January 1959.
63. See also Cmd 814, para. 102.
64. Cmd 814, para. 100.
65. ibid., Appendix I.
66. ibid., para. 102.
67. ibid., para. 84.
68. *Hansard*, House of Commons, 610/337, 26 July 1959.
69. See M. W. K. Chiume, *Nyasaland Speaks – an Appeal to the British People*, Union of Democratic Control and the Movement for Colonial Freedom, 1959, p. 10.
70. Cmd 814, para. 33.
71. *Nyasaland Times*, 10 February 1959.
72. Cmd 814, para. 142.
73. *Rhodesia Herald*, 24 February 1959.
74. Cmd 814, para. 143.
75. ibid., para. 139.
76. ibid., para. 138.
77. *Nyasaland Times*, 3 March 1959.

7. Thirteen Uneasy Months

1. *News Chronicle*, 4 March 1959.
2. ibid.
3. *Daily Worker*, 5 March 1959.
4. *News Chronicle*, 9 March 1959.

5. *Nyasaland Times*, 27 March 1959.
6. *News Chronicle*, 23 March 1959.
7. Sanger, *Emergency*, p. 276.
8. Chipembere, interview.
9. *Hansard*, Zomba, 8 January 1964, p. 1127, and 27 October 1964, p. 147.
10. Munger, *Kamuzu Banda of Malawi*, p. 17.
11. Cmd 814, para. 280.
12. Nyasaland Information bulletin no. 10, 13 April 1959, quoted in Clutton-Brock, *Dawn*, p. 147.
13. Nyasaland Information bulletin no. 13, 6 May 1959, quoted in ibid.
14. Cmd 814, para. 149.
15. ibid., para. 285.
16. *Observer*, 2 August 1959.
17. Sanger, op. cit., p. 286.
18. Cmd 814, para. 43.
19. *Malawi News*, 24 September 1960.
20. *Nyasaland Times*, 24 July 1959.
21. Nyasaland Information Department press release, 24 August 1959.
22. *Ntendere pa Nchito*, September 1959.
23. Banda, Face to Face.
24. *Nyasaland Times*, 29 March 1960.

8. The Making of Malawi

1. *Malawi News*, 2 April 1960.
2. ibid., 9 April 1960.
3. Banda, televised press-conference, 7 April 1960, privately held transcript.
4. *Africa Today*, New York, June 1960.
5. *Malawi News*, 14 June 1960.
6. ibid.
7. *Nyasaland Times*, 15 July 1960.
8. ibid.
9. *The Times*, 25 July 1960.
10. London Conference Dispatches: Nyasaland Government Official Coverage, 25 July 1960.
11. ibid.
12. *Guardian*, 26 July 1960.
13. *The Times*, and *Daily Telegraph*, 30 July 1960.

14. *Observer*, 31 July 1960.
15. Welensky, *4,000 Days*, pp. 200–1.
16. ibid., p. 205, and *Daily Mail*, 4 August 1960.
17. *Report of the Nyasaland Constitutional Conference*, Zomba, 1960.
18. *Nyasaland Times*, 19 August 1960.
19. ibid., 30 August 1960.
20. Banda, *Face to Face*.
21. *Malawi News*, 23 April 1960.
22. ibid., 10 September 1960.
23. ibid., 19 November 1960.
24. ibid., 10 December 1960.
25. ibid., 26 January 1961, and *Nyasaland Times*, 24 January 1961.
26. *Nyasaland Times*, 3 February 1961.
27. Cmd 1423.
28. *Malawi News*, 2 January 1960.
29. Welensky, op. cit., p. 270.
30. ibid., p. 283.
31. *Malawi News*, 15 October 1960.
32. ibid., 17 December 1960.
33. ibid., 24 December 1960.
34. *Nyasaland Times*, 20 December 1960.
35. Welensky, op. cit., p. 283.
36. The Nyasaland (Electoral Provisions) (Amendment) Order in Council, 1960, S.I., 1960, no. 2414; and The Legislative Council (Registration of Voters and Delimitation of Constituencies) Regulations, 1961.
37. *Nyasaland Times*, 20 January 1961.
38. L. P. Mair, *The Nyasaland Elections of 1961*, Athlone Press, 1962, p. 20.
39. ibid., p. 19.
40. ibid., pp. 45–6.
41. ibid., p. 67.
42. ibid., p. 69.
43. ibid., Appendix I, p. 85.
44. ibid., p. 38.
45. *Malawi News*, 11 May 1961.
46. ibid., 3 August 1961.
47. ibid., 31 July 1961.
48. ibid., 3 August 1961.
49. *Nyasaland Times*, 4 August 1961.
50. *News Chronicle*, 4 March 1959.
51. *Hansard*, Zomba, 1 June 1962, p. 266.

52. *New Commonwealth*, 31 March 1958.
53. *Malawi Congress Party Manifesto, General Election, 1961,* Malawi Congress Party, Limbe, pp. 13–14.
54. *Nyasaland Times*, 19 June 1962.
55. ibid., 3 July 1962.
56. *Malawi News*, 29 June 1962.
57. ibid., 15 October 1960.
58. *Nyasaland Times*, 18 August 1961.
59. Nyasaland Information Department press release, 14 November 1962.
60. *Nyasaland Times*, 23 November 1962.
61. *Malawi News*, 1 March 1963.
62. Cmd 1887.
63. H. Franklin, *Unholy Wedlock*, Allen and Unwin, 1963, pp. 207–10.
64. N.I.D. press release, 23 November 1962.
65. Welensky, op. cit., p. 344.
66. *Nyasaland Times*, 29 May 1962.
67. *Malawi News*, 22 March 1962.
68. ibid., 14 September 1961.
69. *Nyasaland Times*, 18 May 1962.
70. ibid., 28 November 1961, and *Malawi News*, 30 November 1961.
71. *Nyasaland Times*, 29 May 1962.
72. Franklin, op. cit., pp. 160–70.
73. Welensky, op. cit., p. 318.
74. See Alport, Lord, *The Sudden Assignment*, Hodder and Stoughton, 1965, p. 168.
75. Welensky, op. cit., pp. 318–19. See also *Malawi News*, 15 February 1962.
76. Welensky, op. cit., p. 327.
77. A. Sampson, *Macmillan: A Study in Ambiguity*, Penguin Books, 1967, p. 192.
78. Welensky, op. cit., p. 331.
79. *Hansard*, House of Commons, 8 May 1962.
80. ibid., 3 December 1962.
81. Welensky, op. cit., p. 349.
82. *Hansard*, House of Commons, 19 December 1962.
83. *Hansard*, Federal Assembly, Salisbury, 19 December 1962.
84. *Malawi News*, 28 December 1962.
85. ibid. See also *Malawi Congress Party Constitution* (1969 edition), Malawi Congress Party, Limbe.
86. *Malawi Congress Party Constitution* (1969 edition).

9. Discretional Alignment and Co-existence

1. *East Africa and Rhodesia*, 28 July 1960.
2. *Tsopano*, May 1960.
3. Banda, interview with the Johannesburg *Star* (draft dated 12 July 1963, A.A.N.S. files, Salisbury).
4. Banda, Speech to Zomba Debating Society, 29 April 1964, Nyasaland Information Department transcript.
5. *Rhodesia Herald*, 12 February 1959.
6. *Malawi News*, 21 May 1960.
7. J. A. Davis, and J. K. Praeger, eds., *Southern Africa in Transition*, New York, 1966, p. 397.
8. *Tsopano*, May 1960.
9. *Malawi News*, 21 May 1960.
10. I. Wallerstein, *Africa: The Politics of Unity*, Pall Mall Press, p. 47.
11. *Malawi News*, 8 October 1960.
12. Wallerstein, op. cit., p. 47.
13. *Malawi News*, 17 September 1960.
14. ibid., 26 November 1960.
15. ibid., 17 December 1960.
16. *Evening Standard*, Salisbury, 14 April 1960.
17. *Malawi News*, 21 May 1960.
18. *Dissent*, no. 12, 1959.
19. *Malawi Congress Party Election Manifesto, General Election, 1961*.
20. *Evening Standard*, 14 April 1960.
21. *Sunday Mail*, 8 May 1960.
22. *Malawi News*, 4 June 1960.
23. ibid., 20 April 1961.
24. ibid.
25. ibid., 11 May 1961.
26. ibid., 4 January 1962.
27. ibid., 7 September 1961.
28. *Hansard*, Zomba, 6 March 1962, p. 111.
29. *Malawi News*, 15 February 1962.
30. *Nyasaland Times*, 6 April 1962.
31. *Malawi News*, 5 April 1962.
32. ibid., 19 October 1961.
33. Banda, interview with Hamilton Fraser (broadcast by Radio Tanganyika on 22 May 1963), privately held transcript.
34. Banda, interview with the Johannesburg *Star*.

35. Banda, interview with Hamilton Fraser.
36. Banda, Speech at a banquet for Prime Minister John Vorster, Zomba, 20 May 1970, privately held transcript.
37. *Malawi News*, 15 March 1962.
38. Banda, press-conference, 20 April 1964, Nyasaland Information Department transcript.
39. *Malawi News*, 8 June 1961.
40. *Times* (as the *Nyasaland Times* was renamed in 1963), 13 August 1963.
41. Banda, press-conference, 20 April 1964.
42. *Malawi News*, 8 February 1963.
43. Banda, press-conference, 20 April 1964.
44. ibid.
45. Banda, press-conference, 6 July 1964, Malawi Information Department transcript.
46. Quoted in *Malawi News*, 31 July 1964. See also *Scotsman*, 11 July 1964.
47. Banda, press-conference, 26 July 1964, Malawi Information Department transcript.
48. Banda, Speech at Colby Community Centre, 25 May 1964, Nyasaland Information Department transcript.
49. *Hansard*, Zomba, 25 January 1965, p. 432.
50. *Malawi News*, 7 August 1964.
51. *Hansard*, Zomba, 2 January 1964, p. 1110.
52. *Malawi News*, 7 August 1964.
53. See, for instance, Banda, interview with John Worrall, Malawi News Agency transcript, 18 January 1968.

10. The Cabinet Crisis

1. *Daily Telegraph*, 2 April 1965.
2. *Hansard*, Zomba, 29 November 1961, p. 101.
3. *Nyasaland Times*, 29 May 1962.
4. *Malawi Congress Party Manifesto, General Election, 1961,* p. 8. See also *Hansard*, Zomba, 9 September 1964, p. 87.
5. *Hansard*, Zomba, 26 February 1964, p. 1272.
6. ibid., 29 May 1964, p. 93.
7. Banda, Speech to Zomba Debating Society, 29 April 1964, Nyasaland Information Department transcript.
8. D. K. Chisiza, 'The Outlook for Contemporary Africa', in *Africa's Freedom*, Allen and Unwin, 1964, p. 43.
9. D. K. Chisiza, *Realities of African Independence*, Africa Bureau,

1961, p. 11. See also D. K. Chisiza, *Africa – What Lies Ahead*, Indian Council for Africa, New Delhi, 1961, pp. 10–16.

10. Banda, Speech at Colby Community Centre, 24 May 1964, N.I.D. transcript.
11. See, for instance, *Malawi News*, 8 February 1963, and Banda, Speech at a dinner for Lonrho executives, 8 November 1963, N.I.D. press release.
12. Chiume, interview.
13. Banda, Speech at Chileka airport, 26 July 1964, Malawi Information Department transcript.
14. *Hansard*, Zomba, 11 January 1964, p. 1129.
15. *People's Daily*, Peking, 6 July 1964.
16. *Hansard*, Zomba, 9 September 1964, p. 53.
17. ibid., 8 September 1964, p. 10.
18. ibid.
19. ibid., p. 17.
20. ibid., p. 18.
21. ibid.
22. ibid., p. 17.
23. ibid., p. 19.
24. ibid., p. 40.
25. ibid., 9 September 1964, p. 89.
26. ibid., pp. 140–1.
27. Banda, press-conference, 11 September 1964, M.I.D. press release.
28. *Times*, 14 September 1964.
29. Banda, Speech at Palombe, 13 September 1964, M.I.D. press release.
30. *Malawi News*, 15 September 1964.
31. ibid., 18 September 1964.
32. Banda, Speech at Chikwawa, 20 September 1964, M.I.D. press release.
33. *Times*, 22 September 1964.
34. Banda, broadcast statement, 24 September 1964, M.I.D. transcript.
35. Banda, Speech at Palombe.
36. Banda, Speech at Chikwawa.
37. Banda, Speech at Kasungu, 5 October 1964, M.I.D. press release.
38. *Times*, 24 September 1964.
39. *Malawi News*, 23 October 1964.
40. Banda, Speech at Liwonde, 14 October 1964, M.I.D. press release.

41. Banda, Speech to the Malawi Congress Party Conference, 25 October 1964, M.I.D. press release.
42. *Hansard*, Zomba, 28 October 1964, p. 164.
43. Banda, Speech at Chileka airport, 29 November 1964, M.I.D. press release.
44. Banda, broadcast statement on the Chipembere rebellion, 18 February 1965, M.I.D. transcript.
45. ibid.
46. Banda, Speech to commemorate his release from Gwelo, 1 April 1965, M.I.D. transcript.
47. *Hansard*, Zomba, 12 April 1965, p. 641.
48. ibid., 13 April 1965, p. 714.
49. Banda, broadcast statement on Chipembere's arrival in America, 21 May 1965, M.I.D. transcript.

11. Towards the West and the White South

1. *Nationalist*, 9 October 1964.
2. ibid., 17 October 1964.
3. *Star*, 19 October 1964.
4. *Malawi News*, 20 and 27 October 1964.
5. See ibid., 4 and 25 December 1964.
6. ibid., 27 October 1964.
7. ibid., 4 December 1964.
8. ibid., 9 February 1965.
9. *Times*, 16 February 1965.
10. *Hansard*, Zomba, 8 September 1964, p. 15.
11. *Rhodesia Herald*, 29 September 1964.
12. Banda, Speech to the United Nations General Assembly, 2 December 1964, Malawi Information Department pamphlet.
13. *Daily Telegraph*, 15 June 1965. See also *Malawi News*, 7 September 1965.
14. *Scotsman*, 17 June 1965.
15. *Hansard*, Zomba, 10 November 1965, p. 273, and 19 January 1966, p. 442.
16. ibid., 14 July 1965, pp. 100–1.
17. *Malawi News*, 7 September 1965.
18. Banda, Speech marking the release of the leadership of the Malawi Brotherhood Society, 19 September 1965, M.I.D. transcript.
19. *Malawi News*, 5 October 1965.
20. Wallerstein, *Politics of Unity*, pp. 172–3.

21. *Hansard*, Zomba, 10 November 1965, pp. 274–5.
22. ibid., 5 October 1965, p. 442.
23. ibid., 14 July 1965, pp. 101–3. See also *Malawi News*, 11 May 1965.
24. *Zambian Pilot*, 12 June 1965.
25. *Sunday Mail*, 27 June 1965.
26. *Hansard*, Zomba, July 1965, p. 132.
27. *Times*, 16 September 1964.
28. Banda, Speech to the United Nations, 2 December 1964.
29. Banda, Speech at Chileka Airport, 19 October 1965, M.I.D. transcript.
30. Banda, Speech at Chileka Airport, 17 September 1965, M.I.D. transcript.
31. Banda, Speech at Chileka Airport, 19 October 1965, M.I.D. transcript.
32. Banda, Message to the United Nations, 27 September 1965, M.I.D. pamphlet.
33. *Hansard*, Zomba, 16 December 1966, pp. 74–6.
34. Banda, broadcast, 10 October 1965, M.I.D. transcript, and Speech to a mass rally at Lilongwe, 17 October 1965, M.I.D. transcript.
35. *Malawi News*, 15 October 1965.
36. ibid., 19 October 1965.
37. *Daily Telegraph*, 27 April 1965.
38. *Hansard*, Zomba, 12 July 1965, p. 11.
39. ibid. See also *Daily Telegraph*, 2 July 1965.
40. Banda, broadcast, 14 November 1965, M.I.D. transcript.
41. ibid., and *Hansard*, Zomba, 9 November 1965, p. 215.
42. *Hansard*, Zomba, 9 November 1965, pp. 215–16.
43. ibid., p. 216.
44. ibid., p. 217.
45. Banda, broadcast, 14 November 1965.
46. *Hansard*, Zomba, 18 January 1966, p. 412.
47. ibid., 11 January 1966, p. 283.
48. ibid., p. 284.
49. ibid., 8 March 1966, p. 457.
50. Banda, Speech to the Malawi Congress Party annual convention, Lilongwe, 14 October 1965, M.I.D. transcript.
51. *Hansard*, Zomba, 16 December 1966, p. 70. Banda had first spoken in these terms in an address to members of the Women's League nearly twelve months earlier (see Banda, Speech at State House, Zomba, 1 January 1966, M.I.D. transcript).

52. *Hansard*, Zomba, 9 November 1965, p. 219.
53. ibid., 5 October 1965, p. 162.
54. ibid., 8 March 1966, pp. 460–4.
55. Banda, Speech to the Malawi Congress Party annual convention, Lilongwe, 17 October 1965, M.I.D. transcript.
56. *Hansard*, Zomba, 17 May 1966, p. 564.

12. Despotism or Democracy

1. *Malawi News*, 1 June 1965.
2. *Nyasaland Times*, 30 September 1960.
3. ibid., 31 July 1962, and Banda, Speech to Economic Symposium experts, 27 July 1962, Nyasaland Information Department press release.
4. *Malawi News*, 1 March 1963.
5. Chisiza, *Outlook for Contemporary Africa*, pp. 43–4.
6. *Malawi News*, 22 February 1963.
7. Banda, Speech at dinner for Lonrho executives, 8 November 1963, N.I.D. press release.
8. *Malawi News*, 22 February 1963.
9. *Hansard*, Zomba, 13 December 1963, p. 1013.
10. ibid., 24 February 1964, p. 1213.
11. ibid., 12 December 1963, p. 1010.
12. Banda, Speech to Local Government conference, Lilongwe, 16 April 1964, N.I.D. transcript.
13. *Malawi News*, 22 December 1964.
14. *Hansard*, Zomba, 26 January 1965, pp. 463–4.
15. Banda, Speech at Chileka, 13 September 1965, Malawi Information Department transcript. See also *Hansard*, Zomba, 20 May 1966, pp. 620–1.
16. Banda, broadcast, 23 April 1967, M.I.D. transcript.
17. Banda, broadcast, 12 September 1965, M.I.D. transcript.
18. Banda, Speech to M.C.P. annual convention, Lilongwe, 13 October 1965, M.I.D. transcript. See also Banda, Speech to the M.C.P. Political Education Conference, Blantyre, 18 April 1966, M.I.D. transcript.
19. *Malawi News*, 20 December 1964.
20. *Hansard*, Zomba, 29 May 1964, pp. 92–3.
21. Banda, Speech at Lilongwe Airport, 15 August 1965, M.I.D. transcript.
22. Banda, broadcast, 12 September 1965, M.I.D. transcript.
23. *Malawi News*, 1 March 1963.

24. *Proposals for the Republican Constitution of Malawi*, duplicated, M.C.P., Blantyre, 1965.
25. See Malawi (Constitution) Act, 1966, no. 23 of 1966.
26. *Proposals for the Republican Constitution of Malawi*, White Paper W P. 002, Zomba, 1965.
27. *Hansard*, Zomba, 20 May 1966, p. 618.
28. ibid., 9 November 1965, p. 234. See also ibid., 17 May 1966, pp. 566–7.
29. ibid., 17 May 1966, p. 560.
30. Banda, Speech to the M.C.P. annual convention, Lilongwe, 17 October 1965, M.I.D. transcript. See also Speeches to the same, 13 and 14 October 1965, and Speech to mass rally, Lilongwe, 17 October 1965.
31. Malawi Congress Party Constitution, duplicated, M.C.P., Blantyre, 1965.
32. *Hansard*, Zomba, 17 May 1966, p. 550.
33. *Proposals for the Republican Constitution of Malawi*, duplicated, M.C.P., Blantyre, 1965.
34. *Hansard*, Zomba, 20 May 1966, p. 620.
35. ibid., p. 619. Cf. Chiume in ibid., 8 March 1963, p. 664.
36. ibid., 29 May 1962, p. 197.
37. ibid., 6 March 1963, pp. 581–3, and 15 July 1963, pp. 856–7.
38. ibid., 6 March 1963, pp. 588–9.
39. ibid., 15 July 1963, pp. 858–9.
40. ibid., 12 December 1963, p. 991.
41. *Malawi News*, 11 January 1963.
42. *Hansard*, Zomba, 12 December 1963, p. 990.
43. ibid., 15 July 1963, p. 859. (*Hansard* consistently mis-transcribes the word 'bridge' as 'breach'.)
47. *Hansard*, Zomba, 7 October 1965, pp. 183–6.
48. Forfeiture Act, 1966, No. 1 of 1966.
49. *Hansard*, Zomba, 14 October 1968, p. 115. See also ibid., 11 October 1968, pp. 98–9.
50. Banda, Speech at Mayani, 29 September 1969, privately held transcript.
51. *Hansard*, Zomba, 17 November 1969, pp. 56–7.
52. ibid., 21 November 1969, p. 220.
53. ibid., p. 222.

54. Joint Statement issued by the Chief Justice, Sir Peter Watkin-Williams, Justice D. D. Bolt, Justice P. V. H. Smith, and Justice Sir Philip Pike, typescript, 22 November 1969, privately held.
55. *Malawi News*, 28 November 1969.
56. Banda, broadcast, 23 April 1967, M.I.D. transcript.
57. *Proposals for the Republican Constitution of Malawi*, duplicated, M.C.P., Blantyre, 1965.
58. *Malawi News*, 15 March 1963.
59. *Hansard*, Zomba, 15 July 1963, p. 844. See also ibid., 12 July 1963, p. 810.
60. ibid., 10 March 1966, p. 541. See also ibid., 9 March 1966, pp. 494–5 and 499.
61. ibid., 5 October 1965, p. 161.
62. Banda, Speech to mass rally, Lilongwe, 17 October 1965, M.I.D. transcript. See also speeches to M.C.P. annual convention, Lilongwe, 13 and 14 October 1965, M.I.D. transcripts.
63. Banda, broadcast, 20 July 1965, M.I.D. transcript.
64. Banda, Speech to M.C.P. annual convention, Mzuzu, 10 September 1967, M.I.D. transcript.
65. *Hansard*, Zomba, 9 January 1964, p. 1180.
66. ibid., 29 May 1964, p. 131.
67. ibid., 19 January 1966, pp. 451–2. See also ibid., 23 August 1966, pp. 25–7.
68. See for instance Banda, Speech to Chamber of Commerce, Blantyre, 28 October 1967; Speech at Lilongwe Town Hall, 4 April 1968; and Speech at M.C.P. Political Education Conference, 15 May 1968, M.I.D. transcripts.
69. *Hansard*, Zomba, 29 January 1968, pp. 242–3.
70. Banda, Speech to M.C.P. annual convention, Mzuzu, 10 September 1967, M.I.D. transcript.
71. Chisiza, *Realities of African Independence*, p. 11.
72. Banda, Speech to mass rally, Lilongwe, 17 October 1965, M.I.D. transcript.
73. *Hansard*, Zomba, 14 December 1967, p. 201.
74. ibid., 17 May 1966, p. 563.
75. Banda, Speech at Malawi Distillery, 24 February 1967, M.I.D. transcript.
76. *Malawi News*, 1 June 1965. See also ibid., 16 April and 7 May 1965.
77. *Hansard*, Zomba, 24 March 1970, p. 489.
78. ibid., 31 July 1969, p. 430.
79. ibid., 29 May 1962, p. 198.

80. ibid., 9 November 1965, p. 234, and 17 May 1966; and *Proposals for the Republican Constitution of Malawi*, M.C.P., Blantyre.

13. Disarming Apartheid

1. *Evening Standard*, 5 March 1959, and *Sunday Mail*, 8 September 1963.
2. *Rhodesia Herald*, 14 April 1960.
3. *Malawi News*, 16 March 1961.
4. ibid., 3 August 1961.
5. ibid., 16 March 1961.
6. *Rhodesia Herald*, 14 April 1960.
7. Banda, interview with Hamilton Fraser (broadcast by Radio Tanganyika on 22 May 1963), privately held transcript.
8. *Malawi News*, 22 February 1963. See also ibid., 1 February 1963.
9. Banda, press-conference, Chileka, 8 July 1964, privately held transcript.
10. *Hansard*, Zomba, 16 December 1963, p. 1081, and 12 December 1963, pp. 1009–10.
11. *Rhodesia Herald*, 19 October 1960. See also *Nyasaland Times*, 30 December 1958. Cf. *Malawi News*, 15 October 1960.
12. *Nyasaland Times*, 9 May 1961.
13. Banda, interview with the Johannesburg *Star* (draft dated 12 July 1963, A.A.N.S. files, Salisbury).
14. Banda, Speech at unveiling of Independence Monument, 5 July 1964, Malawi Information Department transcript.
15. Banda, press-conference, Chileka, 8 July 1964, privately held transcript.
16. *Malawi News*, 29 September 1964.
17. See, for instance, Banda, Speech to M.C.P. annual convention, Lilongwe, 14 October 1965, M.I.D. transcript.
18. See Banda, interview with Hamilton Fraser.
19. Banda, Address to United Nations, 27 September 1965, M.I.D. pamphlet.
20. *Rhodesia Herald*, 30 August 1966.
21. Banda, press-conference, Blantyre, 8 July 1969, M.I.D. transcript.
22. *Hansard*, Zomba, 27 October 1964, pp. 149–56.
23. Banda, Speech at Lilongwe Airport, 15 August 1965, M.I.D. transcript.
24. *Hansard*, Zomba, 18 January 1966, pp. 413–14.
25. ibid., 11 January 1966, pp. 288–9.
26. ibid., pp. 285–7.
27. ibid., p. 288.

28. ibid., p. 286.
29. ibid., 19 January 1966, p. 451.
30. *Hansard*, Zomba, 18 May 1966, p. 589.
31. See ibid., p. 591.
32. Malawi Treaty Series, Edition III, 1966, Treaty Notice no. 84.
33. *Hansard*, Zomba, 7 July 1966, p. 7.
34. ibid., 23 August 1966, pp. 29–30.
35. Banda, interview, Zomba, 25 April 1969, privately held transcript.
36. Banda, Address to United Nations, 11 October 1966, M.I.D. pamphlet.
37. See Banda, Speech to the M.C.P. Political Education Conference, Blantyre, 18 April 1966, M.I.D. transcript.
38. Banda, Address to United Nations, 11 October 1966, M.I.D. pamphlet.
39. *Hansard*, Zomba, 16 December 1966, p. 63.
40. ibid., p. 64.
41. ibid., p. 66.
42 ibid., p. 67.
43. ibid., pp. 66–8.
44. Banda, Address to United Nations, 11 October 1966, M.I.D. pamphlet.
45. ibid.
46. Banda, Speech at the official opening of Development House, Blantyre, 25 November 1966.
47. *Hansard*, Zomba, 30 March 1967, p. 378.
48. ibid., 29 March 1967, pp. 304–6.
49. Communiqué issued at the end of the visit of Chief Leabua Jonathan, 12–17 May 1967, M.I.D.
50. *Hansard*, Zomba, 27 June 1967, pp. 439–40.
51. ibid., 30 June 1967, p. 535.
52. Banda, Speech to M.C.P. annual convention, Mzuzu, 10 September 1967, M.I.D. transcript.
53. Banda, Speech at Nairobi Agricultural Show, 27 September 1967, M.I.D. pamphlet.
54. Banda, Speech to the M.C.P. Political Education Conference, Blantyre, 18 April 1966, M.I.D. transcript.
55. Malawi News Agency Bulletin, 21 July 1966.
56. As summarized in M.A.N.A. bulletin, 26 July 1966.
57. *Hansard*, Zomba, 29 March 1967, p. 302.
58. ibid.
59. Banda, Speech at State Banquet for Chief Jonathan, Blantyre, 15 May 1967, M.I.D. transcript.

60. *Hansard*, Zomba, 30 June 1967, p. 538.
61. ibid., 27 June 1967, p. 438.
62. Banda, Speech to M.C.P. annual convention, Mzuzu, 10 September 1967, M.I.D. transcript.
63. *Hansard*, Zomba, 12 December 1967, p. 136.
64. Banda, interview with John Worrall, Blantyre, 18 January 1968, M.A.N.A. transcript.
65. *Hansard*, Zomba, 29 January 1968, pp. 233–5.
66. ibid., 25 June 1968, p. 466.
67. Speech by Dr Hilgard Muller at an official dinner, Blantyre, 27 August 1968, M.I.D. transcript.
68. Banda, Speech to M.C.P. annual convention, Lilongwe, 16 September 1968, M.I.D. transcript.
71. *Hansard*, Zomba, 12 November 1969, pp. 21–2.
72. ibid., 20 December 1968, p. 234.
73. Banda, interview with Albert Meyers, Zomba, 18 March 1968, M.A.N.A. transcript.
74. *Hansard*, Zomba, 23 April 1969, p. 375.
75. ibid., 19 December 1968, p. 163. See also Banda, interview with Hans Germani, Zomba, 16 March 1968, M.I.D. transcript.
76. Banda, interview with Albert Meyers, Zomba, 18 March 1968, M.A.N.A. transcript.
77. Banda, interview, Zomba, 25 April 1969, privately held transcript.
78. Banda, interview with Hans Germani, Zomba, 16 March 1968, M.I.D. transcript.
79. *Hansard*, Zomba, 23 April 1969, p. 374.
80. *The Times*, 22 May 1969.
81. Banda, Speech at a banquet for Prime Minister John Vorster, Zomba, 20 May 1970, privately held transcript.
82. ibid.
83. ibid.
84. ibid.
85. Banda, interview with John Worrall, Zomba, 18 January 1968, M.A.N.A. transcript.
86. *Punch*, 17 November 1965.
87. Banda, as summarized in interview with Worrall.
88. *Hansard*, Zomba, 29 April 1964, p. 131.
89. ibid., 17 May 1966, p. 564.

Index

Accra Conference (1958), 102–4
African Methodist Episcopal Church, 19–20, 23
African Representative Council, 64
Africanization: of public service, 199, 219–20, 274–6
Aggrey, J. E. Kwagyir, 18–19, 20
agriculture: demand for federalization, 100; Banda's policy as Minister, 155
Alport, C. J. M., Baron, 165n
amalgamation, see federation (of Central African territories)
America, see United States
Amery, Julian, 118
apartheid, see South Africa
Arab states, 297, 302–3, 315
Armitage, Sir Robert: and demands for constitutional advance, 86, 98; and Nyasaland Emergency, 107, 112, 117; Devlin Report, 123, 125; release of detainees, 128–9; dines with Banda on retirement, 158
Asian Convention, 94

Banda, Aleke, 126, 128, 168, 280, 294
Banda, Hastings Kamuzu, chronology: birth, 5; names, 5n, 6, 8, 40n, 222n; parents, 5–6; early childhood, 6–8;

baptism, 8; initiation, 9–10; in Hartley, 14; in South Africa, 15–20; in the United States, 20–7; in Scotland, 28–40; evidence to Bledisloe Commission, 31–2; discussions with Chief Mwase, 33–4; as a doctor in Edinburgh, 38–9; elder of the Church of Scotland, 39; fails to become medical missionary, 39–40; refuses medical post in Nyasaland, 40; in Liverpool, 40–1; conscientious objections to conscription, 41; in Tyneside, 41, 45; and Nyasaland African Congress, 45–6, 48–50, 53; in London, 46–52; joins Labour Party, 47; finances needy African students, 50–1; opposes federation, 56, 75; Kasungu farming project, 50, 62; in the Gold Coast, 76–88; and Mrs French, 76, 79; withdrawal from politics, 78–9; advice and support for Nyasaland sought, 82–7; regarded as first Nyasa doctor, 83n; return to London, 87–8; arrival in Nyasaland, 89–90; leads campaign for constitutional reform, 90–116; medical practice in Limbe, 96; and Accra

Kambona, Oscar, 205, 235
Kanchunjulu, C. B. B., 84
Karonga: disturbances at, 113–14
Kasungu, 5, 50, 62, 76
Katengeza, Richard, 80
Kaunda, Kenneth, 103, 161, 236
Kayira, A. D., 128
Kenyatta, Jomo, 47, 177
Kiano, Gikoyo, 104
Kulujili, Kinross, W., 81
Kumbikano, Clement, 66, 81, 85
Kumbweza, Jeremy, 220n
Kumtumanji, Gomile, 172, 215n, 220
Kwenje, N. D., 80, 138, 258n

Lancaster House Conference (1952), 69
Lancaster House Conference (1960), 133–8
Lawrence, Isaac Macdonald, 44, 45
leadership: Banda's attitude to, 202–3
legal system: Malawi, 263, 267–72
Lennox-Boyd, Alan, 84, 88, 94, 118, 125
Liverpool: Banda's life in, 40–1
Lubani, Lali, 90
Lyttelton, Oliver, 1st Viscount Chandos, 67, 69

Mackenzie, Kenneth, 67
Macleod, Iain, 128–9, 134, 136–7, 161
Macmillan, Harold, 127, 143, 145
Makamo, Gideon, 152
Malawi: origin of name, 126n; independence celebrations, 1–2, 172; cabinet crisis, 197–230; relations with Portugal, 205, 232–3, 307–9; relations with China, 205–6, 236–8; Chipembere rebellion, 227–30; relations with Tanzania, 231–2, 234–6, 300, 302, 303–4, 306–7, 312; relations with Zambia, 232, 236, 299, 300–1, 303–4, 306–7, 312; relations with U.S., 238–9; relations with W. European countries, 239–40; relations with S. Rhodesia, 240–5, 309–10; relations with other African states, 245–50; system of government, 250–82; proposals for new constitution, 261–4; judiciary, 263, 267–72; imposition of common language, 273–4; Africanization of public service, 274–6; nationalization, 276–7; relations with S. Africa, 283–316; new capital city, 287–9, 305; Chisiza's *coup d'état* attempt, 303; Vorster's visit, 313–14: see also Nyasaland
Malawi Congress Party: foundation, 125–7; Banda becomes President, 131; elections (1961), 146–54; Discipline Regulations, 169–70; relations with Mozambique, 179–83; constitution reviewed, 264–5; see also Nyasaland African Congress
Malawi Development Corporation, 276